Dispersion

GW00568944

Dispersion

Thoreau and Vegetal Thought

Edited by Branka Arsić
Assistant Editor, Vesna Kuiken

BLOOMSBURY ACADEMIC
NEW YORK · LONDON · OXFORD · NEW DELHI · SYDNEY

BLOOMSBURY ACADEMIC
Bloomsbury Publishing Inc
1385 Broadway, New York, NY 10018, USA
50 Bedford Square, London, WC1B 3DP, UK
29 Earlsfort Terrace, Dublin 2, Ireland

BLOOMSBURY, BLOOMSBURY ACADEMIC and the Diana logo are
trademarks of Bloomsbury Publishing Plc

First published in the United States of America 2021
This paperback edition published 2023

Copyright © Branka Arsić, 2021

Each chapter copyright © of the contributor, 2021

Cover design by Eleanor Rose and Namkwan Cho
Cover image: Thoreau's drawing of a tupelo in the journal entry from February 12, 1859,
in: Henry David Thoreau, *The Writings of Henry David Thoreau*, Vol. 17, Edited by Bradford
Torrey (Boston and New York: Houghton Mifflin and Company, 1906), p. 443. Image
reproduced by Butler Library, Columbia University in the City of New York.

All rights reserved. No part of this publication may be reproduced or transmitted
in any form or by any means, electronic or mechanical, including photocopying,
recording, or any information storage or retrieval system, without prior
permission in writing from the publishers.

Bloomsbury Publishing Inc does not have any control over, or responsibility for,
any third-party websites referred to or in this book. All internet addresses given
in this book were correct at the time of going to press. The author and publisher
regret any inconvenience caused if addresses have changed or sites have ceased
to exist, but can accept no responsibility for any such changes.

Whilst every effort has been made to locate copyright holders the publishers
would be grateful to hear from any person(s) not here acknowledged.

Library of Congress Control Number: 2021935695

ISBN: HB: 978-1-5013-7058-8
         PB: 978-1-5013-7062-5
         ePDF: 978-1-5013-7060-1
         eBook: 978-1-5013-7059-5

Typeset by Integra Software Services Pvt. Ltd.

To find out more about our authors and books visit www.bloomsbury.com
and sign up for our newsletters.

CONTENTS

Notes on Contributors   vii

Introduction: Thoreau's Vegetal Ontology—The Aerial, the Rootless, and the Analogous
Branka Arsić   1

1   Thoreau Experiments with Natural Influences
Jane Bennett   21

2   A Material Faith: Thoreau's Terrennial Turn
Laura Dassow Walls   37

3   Auto-Heteronomy: Thoreau's Circuitous Return to the Vegetal World
Michael Marder   59

4   Thoreau's Garden Politics
Antoine Traisnel   69

5   "Wild Thinking" and Vegetal Intelligence in Thoreau's Later Writings
Michael Jonik   85

6   Green Fire: Thoreau's Forest Figuration
Monique Allewaert   105

7   The Riddle of Forest Succession
Mark Noble   127

8   Low-Tech Thoreau; or, Remediations of the Human in *The Dispersion of Seeds*
Jason Gladstone   143

9   On Thoreau's Ecoerotics
Cristin Ellis   165

10 Chance Encounters: Thoreau's Pomontology
   Vesna Kuiken   189

11 "Wild Only Like Myself": Thoreau at Home with Plants
   Mary Kuhn   205

12 Plant Life and Poetics of Transtemporality
   Gillian Osborne   217

Notes   235
Bibliography   283
Index   294

CONTRIBUTORS

Monique Allewaert is Associate Professor of American Literature at the University of Wisconsin, Madison. She is the author of *Ariel's Ecology: Personhood and Colonialism in the American Tropics, 1760–1820* (2013). She is currently working on a book provisionally titled *Luminescence: Insect Knowledge, Power, and the Literary: 1705–1814*, which explores an occluded colonial way of thinking the small and the partial.

Branka Arsić is Charles and Lynn Zhang Professor of American Literature in the Department of English and Comparative Literature at Columbia University. She is the author, most recently, of *Bird Relics: Grief and Vitalism in Thoreau* (2016), which was awarded the MLA James Russell Lowell prize for the outstanding book of 2016. She has also written *On Leaving: A Reading in Emerson* (2010), and a book on Melville entitled *Passive Constitutions or 7½ Times Bartleby* (2007). She co-edited (with Cary Wolfe) a collection of essays on Emerson, entitled *The Other Emerson: New Approaches, Divergent Paths* (2010) and (with Kim Evans) a collection of essays on Melville, entitled *Melville's Philosophies* (Bloomsbury, 2017).

Jane Bennett is Andrew W. Mellon Professor in Humanities at the Johns Hopkins University. She is the author of *Influx and Efflux: Writing Up with Walt Whitman* (2020), *Vibrant Matter: A Political Ecology of Things* (2010), *Thoreau's Nature: Ethics, Politics, and the Wild* (2002), *The Enchantment of Modern Life* (2001), and *Unthinking Faith and Enlightenment* (1987). Professor Bennett is one of the founders of the journal *Theory & Event*, and is currently the editor of *Political Theory: An International Journal of Political Philosophy*. She has been a Fellow at Oxford University (Keble College), Birkbeck Institute for the Humanities (University of London), and the Humanities Research Centre at the Australian National University.

Laura Dassow Walls is William P. and Hazel B. White Professor of English at Notre Dame University. She is the author of *Henry David Thoreau: A Life* (2017), *The Passage to Cosmos: Alexander von Humboldt and the Shaping of America* (2009), *Emerson's Life in Science: The Culture of Truth* (2003), and *Seeing New Worlds: Henry David Thoreau and Nineteenth-Century Natural Science* (1995).

Cristin Ellis is Associate Professor of English at the University of Mississippi. She is the author of *Antebellum Posthuman: Race and Materiality in the Mid-Nineteenth Century* (2018). Her work has appeared in *American Literature* and *Political Research Quarterly*, among other places.

Jason Gladstone teaches in the English Department at the University of Colorado Boulder. He is co-editor of *Postmodern/Postwar—And After* (2016), and special-issue co-editor of the volumes "Environmental Trajectories" (*English Language Notes*, 2017) and "Postmodernism, Then" (*Twentieth-Century Literature* 2011). His work has appeared or is forthcoming in *American Literature, Contemporary Literature, Criticism,* and *Twentieth-Century Literature*. He is currently completing a book manuscript entitled *Lines in the Dirt: American Postmodernism and the Failure of Technology*.

Michael Jonik teaches American literature and contemporary critical theory at the University of Sussex and is the author of *Herman Melville and the Politics of the Inhuman* (2018). He writes on pre-1900 American literature, continental philosophy, and the history of science, with essays on Berkeley, Emerson, Thoreau, Hawthorne, and James. He has been a Research Fellow at the Paris Institute of Advanced Study (2018–19), and is founding member of the British Association of Nineteenth-Century Americanists (BrANCA), and Reviews and Special Issues editor for *Textual Practice*.

Vesna Kuiken is Lecturer at the University at Albany, SUNY. She is currently completing a book manuscript on American women writers and islands. Her work has appeared in the collection *American Impersonal: Essays with Sharon Cameron* (Bloomsbury, 2014), *J19, Arizona Quarterly, Nineteenth-Century Prose,* and the *Henry James Review*. She is the recipient of the Leon Edel Prize for the best essay on Henry James in 2016.

Mary Kuhn is Assistant Professor of Environmental Humanities in the English Department at the University of Virginia. Her work has appeared in *American Literature, English Literary History,* and *Common-place*. Her current project examines the ways in which nineteenth-century US writers used novel ideas about plant life to address political questions.

Michael Marder is IKERBASQUE Research Professor of Philosophy at the University of the Basque Country (UPV/EHU), Vitoria-Gasteiz, Spain. He is the author of a dozen books and numerous articles in the fields of phenomenology, environmental philosophy, and political thought. His forthcoming monographs are *Philosophy for Passengers* and *Senses of Upheaval: Philosophical Snapshots of a Decade.*

Mark Noble is Associate Professor of English at Georgia State University. He is the author of *American Poetic Materialism from Whitman to Stevens* (2015). His essays have appeared in *American Literature, Nineteenth-Century Literature, LARB, J19,* and *American Impersonal: Essays with Sharon Cameron* (Bloomsbury, 2014). He is currently at work on a new book that explores unlikely intersections between ontology and politics in early American writing.

Gillian Osborne is research associate and Instructor for Poetry in America courses at the Harvard Extension School, which cover 400 years of American poetry. She is the co-editor of *Ecopoetics: Essays in the Field* (2018), and a former fellow at the Harvard University Center for the Environment. Her work on nineteenth-century American authors has been supported by fellowships from the American Antiquarian Society and the Emily Dickinson International Society, and appears in such collections as *The New Melville Studies* and *The New Dickinson Studies.* She is at work on a book about flowers in American poetry from the nineteenth century to the present, and a collection of poems.

Antoine Traisnel is Assistant Professor of English and Comparative Literature at the University of Michigan. He is the author of *Hawthorne: Blasted Allegories* (2015), coauthor with Thangam Ravindranathan of *Donner le change: L'impensé animal* (2016), and translator of Robert Montgomery Bird's gothic novel *Sheppard Lee.* His latest book, *Capture: Early American Pursuits and the Making of a New Animal Condition* (Minnesota, 2020), traces the prehistory of "capture" as a material and representational practice to account for the systemic disappearance and biopolitical management of animals in nineteenth-century America.

Introduction: Thoreau's Vegetal Ontology—The Aerial, the Rootless, and the Analogous

Branka Arsić

If Emerson argued that the relationship between man and vegetable is fundamental but occult—as *Nature* posited, there is "an occult relation between man and the vegetable"—Thoreau tried to get to the very center of this opaque occultism and to work out its nature.[1] This is not only to say that the vegetal rather than the animal came to embody for him a life that is most intimately related to the human and thus revealing what might be understood as human; and it is also not to state merely that Thoreau promoted the vegetal into a special obsession of his thought, as demonstrated by his *Journal* filled predominantly with long observations of various forms of plant life. It is also to say that plant life instructed him about what kind of relations exist among humans, animals, and plants, and so clued him into the logic of all life. The vegetal thus emerged in Thoreau's thought as both a primary ontological "entity"—without which no understanding of any being is possible—and the mode or manner in which all beings relate, which promised access to beings and phenomena as diverse as fish and clouds. Both an entity and the way to entities, the vegetal revealed itself to Thoreau in its counter-intuitiveness, simultaneously a relate and a relation, both the what and the how of life, thus grounding his ontology as well as his epistemology.

While Thoreau's attention to plant life can be traced to his very first recordings of nature, it was in May 1851 that he came to formulate a complex vegetal theory of all life and especially the "life of the human being ... both of [its] body & the mind."[2] Notes that capture the essence of this theory are spread over several pages in Thoreau's *Journal*, which suggests that what he had in mind was a broad claim about the plant nature of the human. If in the end he didn't develop the notes to connect them into a coherent whole—an essay, lecture, or even a letter—leaving them instead as traces of an attempt to theorize the vegetal that didn't succeed, that might be related not only to the fact that the notes are often contradictory and even mutually exclusive, but more importantly, to the fact that any explanation would involve fundamental claims that would have been impossible to formulate, since their eccentricity would verge on the fantastic. Yet, despite the fact that his notes are scientifically incredible, and often even depart from a commonsense experience of the vegetal, they are philosophically rich and thus worthy of salvaging. Their starting point was Asa Gray's observation according to which, as Thoreau recorded it, "the plant—develops from the first in two opposite directions, viz. upwards [to expand in the light & air] to produce & continue the stem (or *ascending axis*), and downwards [avoiding the light] to form the root (or *descending* axis. The former is ordinarily or in great part aerial, the latter subterranean" (*PJ* 3: 225)). Gray doesn't seem to be claiming that plants begin "from the first" to grow, really or botanically, in two opposite directions out of the stem. Instead his observation reads as a symbolic lesson in plant life, a lesson cautioning that, just as a plant lives partly in the darkness of matter and partly in the brightness of air, so all life is a admixture of the obscure and the bright, of heaven and the "underworld."

Thoreau's appropriation of Gray's ideas safely avoided theological or moralistic overtones. He takes his statement seriously, first in the botanical sense, as though it claimed that plants begin ("from the first") to grow from some middle, prior to sending down roots which they do only retroactively, as they grow. But he then takes this understanding of the plant life to be ontological, positing that, like Gray's plant, the human (life and mind) also "develops from the first in two opposite directions" (*PJ* 3: 225). If this claim about the plant as well as the human being is eccentric from this very first claim, as I suggested, it is because in countering reliance on common sense, it posits that plant and human never begin from but only arrive at their roots, being at "first" rootless, adrift in the air. They don't ascend into the air from a subterranean root but are somehow already in the air from which they root while simultaneously ascending higher into the air. If they "develop," then, as Thoreau's phrasing suggests, they don't do that in a linear or genealogical way. Neither form of life evolves teleologically or epigenetically, from roots to fruit, from embryo to predestined form, from what is early to what is late, from cause to consequence. Instead, both their "past" (roots, typically understood as the beginning and cause of growth) and future (flowers and fruit) emerge from their present. They "begin" from a "middle" that precedes any roots or fruit; they are mediums and milieus of growth and development, which makes them relations themselves. The examples from vegetal life that Thoreau summons here to index this life from the "middle" are the oak and white pine, for "the oak ... has not so much root as branch," slowly growing roots out of its branches, whereas white pines are so "slight and near the surface" that they verge almost on not having roots at all, being from the first life that grows in the light of the air (*PJ* 3: 225). Like the rootless pine, so the "mind develops from the first in two opposite directions—upwards to expand in the light & air; & downwards, avoiding the light to form the root" (*PJ* 3: 225). Lacking origin and finality like the plant, the mind also is "not well balanced & firmly planted" (*PJ* 3: 225). Rather, it generates its roots as well as its "flowers," from its middle, which constitutes it. Such a "middle" for the plant is the "stem," since Thoreau interprets Gray's remark—"the plant develops—upwards ... to produce & continue the stem and downwards to form the root"—as stating that the plant develops both upwards and downwards from the stem; hence, he can claim that "roots may spring from any part of the stem" (*PJ* 3: 226).[3] In the case of the human mind, such a middle is a succession of thoughts or the "shooting" of thoughts (*PJ* 3: 225), which are "rudimental," "unfolded" "unclear" and only "partially developed" (*PJ* 3: 225); or, in Thoreau's less clear gloss, thoughts are "like shoots grown in a cellar" (*PJ* 3: 225). The stem of the mind thus seems to be something like a flow of sensations and thoughts un-reflected upon, one dissolving into the other. And that such a stem is what precedes the human person can only mean that for Thoreau no essence of the mind precedes the production of thoughts, no body precedes sensations. In contrast to the whole tradition of Western thought, in this view no "pure mind" conditions thinking, for thinking is the only mind there is; alternatively, no human "essence" precedes human being to decide who is human; such beings only and always become so.

Understanding plant, human, and by extension all life as rootless is thus a radical reversal of the way the philosophical and scientific tradition of the West thought about life and its forms. Most obviously, in contradistinction to the long tradition of thinking about the vegetal as immobile because it is tied by roots to the earth, Thoreau posits it as initially rootless and thus mobile and aleatory. And in contrast to the same tradition that understood human essence or personal identity as something that conditions and "roots" thinking so that thoughts are the predicates of the subjectivity from which they "stem," Thoreau suggests that such predicates are the only subjectivity there is. Individuations such as selves, persons, or subjectivities are contingent and changeable clusters of attributes with no substantives. Inasmuch as it is rootless, the plant-mind is a drifter, and because it is "at first" neither solely in the moistness of the earth nor in the light of the air, because it is tied neither to a pre-fixed body nor to the form of the mind, it is a heterogeneous mix of the two—the middle out of which they develop and therefore also the site at which they meet—which then shoots its sensations and ideas, its roots and flowers, its causes and consequences up and down. Being in the middle the plant is a mix of two elements, composed of both heavy and airy material, just as the human is a mélange of the embodied sensations and thoughts belonging to no self, a case of sensations individuating a body and thoughts becoming clearer, a clustering into reflections that emerge only slowly out of the mix in which they are confused.

How this proliferation of roots and fruits, bodies and minds occurs is also counterintuitive. For Thoreau will claim that even if the plant stems down to a root and up into a flower its real root is the flower; analogously, the human will be well planted if it roots itself in the "most clear & etherial ideas (Antaeus like)" (*PJ* 3: 226) springing from the mix of sensations and thoughts, which function as the stem" (*PJ* 3: 226). The claim thus confusingly suggests that both plant and human root themselves in what is most unrooted (ethereal ideas, flowers), that they come to be well stabilized and balanced when they reach a realm so amorphous and delimited that it is hard to imagine how anything can be stabilized in it. Yet, even if that confounds common sense, Thoreau's claim is rigorous; for the emergence of the "most clear" idea out of the flux of unorganized and confused sensations and thoughts—out of the flux of sap in the stem that they are—is what he identifies as the appearance of the truth, which, on his definition is what "allies" itself or leads itself "to the primal womb of things," which is in turn the nexus of many truths. The emergence of a clear idea represents the emergence of a single truth that opens up the possibility of accessing other truths, for there is "no idea … so soaring but it will readily put forth roots—wherever there is an air & light" (*PJ* 3: 227).[4] Thus, what emerges as an "ethereally" clear, and therefore true, idea is called a root of the mind on the grounds of its truthfulness. For the truth is what stabilizes the drift of confused thoughts and sensations, directing them towards other truths, or as Thoreau has it, soiling the field of other truths (*PJ* 3: 226). Out of the truth of one clear idea-root there will emerge other truth-roots, making the air a humus of roots and making the clouds heavy with rhizomes.

The vegetal reveals the same logic whereby what is most aerial turns into a force of rooting. For, on Thoreau's understanding of Gray, it isn't the root but the flower—the most ethereal moment of the plant—that is its "truth," since being "strictly connected with the earth" (*PJ* 3: 227) the flower soils it with the root and thus roots the plant. According to this circular logic, then, flowers (analogous to the "most clear ideas") root the roots in which they are then also rooted; they enact the rooting of the roots in the soil, which functions analogously to the "dark womb of things" in the realm of ideas, explaining Thoreau's at first sight confusing claim that there is "no thought but is connected as strictly as a flower, with the earth" (*PJ* 3: 227).[5]

However, roots that grow from the ethereal and that spring from lightness are far from a version of Platonic idealism whereby what is purely disembodied and enlightened descends into the matter and the opaqueness of the body, which then confuses its clarity and dims its truth. That is because, on Thoreau's circular account, the flower-truth can generate other flowers only via the darkness of the soil in which the root is rooting; the flower is "strictly connected to the earth" (*PJ* 3: 227), despite being an aerial phenomenon, because it is in earth's "moist darkness" that the root sustaining the stem will root and so enable the emergence of other flowers. No flower makes a flower, no air regenerates its clarity, unless it goes through the soil and darkness. If the aery flower is "eager to be soiled," it is because the soil has the "moist" that feeds and safeguards the vegetal life imbedded in the flower. The opaque earth is the adequate ambiance for the vitality of the aery. The same needs what is heterogeneous to it in order to maintain itself. Far from putting in jeopardy the "truth" of the flower and dimming it, as would be the case in Platonism, the moist, heaviness, and humus-ness of the rooted are its constitutive moment.

That is similarly the case in the domain of the human, where a "clear" and aerial idea has to be rooted in the body and pass through it in order to prove its truthfulness. That is why "the most clear & etherial ideas ... readily ally themselves to the earth. ... They put forth roots as soon as branches. ... No thought but is connected as strictly as a flower, with the earth" (*PJ* 3: 226, 227). There is no truth at all unless it is earthed or embodied (for the body is the earth of the thought). Truth that does not affect the body does not have the status of truth. All truth must pass through the density and opaqueness of the body; it must become embodied, affecting the body, if it is not to remain abstract and thus not truthful at all. The opaqueness of the body doesn't dim the truth as in Plato, but enables it by living it. That is what Thoreau confirms when, in a rigorously anti-Platonic claim, he says that "No thought soars so high that it sunders these apron strings of its mother [earth] ... if our light & air seeking tendencies extend too widely for our ... root or stem we must send downward new roots to ally us to the earth" (*PJ* 3: 227). If it is going to be truthful, everything ideated—everything ethereal and bright—must be brought back to the darkness of earth and the body. An idea might appear as clear as daylight but without earth to give it a body it remains abstracted and thus false.

Not only is this rooting of the airy into the embodied not Platonic; neither does it entail for Thoreau fixing into immobility what "started" by drifting freely in the unobstructed medium of the ethereal. For something or someone to be rooted doesn't signify the a posteriori acquisition of firm identity because roots as Thoreau imagines them are not a semblance of any essence. On Thoreau's account every flower pushes for a new root (and is its potential) just as every truth pushes for a new idea so that "for each successive new idea or bud—[there is] a new rootlet in the earth" (*PJ* 3: 226).[6] The logic of the claim is clear: there is no one truth out of which many ideas would spring because if each clear idea roots a truth, then truth is always beholden to a particular thought; truths are always singular. Similarly, because the plant doesn't grow from a single root but out of multiple flowers that grow roots, then roots must be multiple also. The multiplicity of flowers grows a multiplicity of rootlets, thus turning "one" plant into multiplicity.

On Thoreau's understanding of vegetal life, plants do not move only circularly—ascending and descending—but live also by a different, "horizontal" mobility that spreads through the earth. That is to say: not only does what is in the "middle" spring up into an airy flower that then descends into the earth to root the root out of which the stem will proceed and ascend to produce another flower. For while each rootlet does move "vertically" toward the earth's surface and into the stem, it also pushes laterally into the darkness of the earth. Rootlets expand under the earth and into it, and via the earth they become materially connected to other rootlets. For "the branches & branches of the root are ... repetitions for the purpose of multiplying the absorbing points, which are chiefly the growing or newly formed extremities, sometimes termed *spongelets*" (*PJ* 3: 226). A root is not a completely unified or fused entity but something that pushes out of itself in multiple lateral directions, growing its "extremities" and spreading through the earth which in turn becomes the material connection for, or continuous network of these multiplying roots. On this account, each root is a rhizome or a network of "extremities" continuing into other roots, which also expand laterally, via the commons of the earth. The earth can itself thus be understood as a rhizome, one that changes as the rhizomes that it connects change, and one that is transformed by the arrival of new root-networks and the decaying of old ones. But this multidirectional continuity of a formally heterogeneous vegetal—the idea that the plant lives simultaneously in milieus as heterogeneous as humus and air; that it is a circular continuity of forms as diverse as flower and root; that it is also a lateral continuity of roots whose form pushes out of itself—also suggests that, however identifiable a vegetal form be, it is not completely closed off, for if that were so no "continuation" would be possible. For a formally differentiated flower to push for a rootlet and so expand into something formally different, it must be able to re-form; similarly, a rootlet isn't completely discrete to the extent that it continues into different "forms," namely into the earth and other rootlets.

Thoreau explicitly claims the same logic for humans: "As with the roots of the Plant so with the roots of the Mind," they "branch & branch" (*PJ* 3: 226). The circular movement analogous to plants would, in the case of humans, presumably be initiated in the flow of unclear sensations and thoughts out of which a clear idea or truth emerges, even though, as I maintained, that truth can be affirmed in its truthfulness only if rooted in the body (just as the flower roots a root in the soil). This novel situation of the body now differently affected by the newly felt truth would cause it to push "upwards," pressing for other unclear thoughts to be clarified. But if Thoreau's analogy is to be complete, then the "roots" of the mind—true ideas affecting the body—must also spread laterally, "multiplying ... extremities" through the body, which is the earth of the mind. And that is what he also suggests in saying that "the mind flashes not so far on one side—but its rootlets its spongelets find their way instantly on the other side into a moist darkness" of the body (*PJ* 3: 227). An embodied truth doesn't only spring up, again, into the air of the mind, but it also rhizomes through the earth of body, turning the body into a network of affects. According to the logic of vegetal life, then, human life—and by extension all animal life—is such a continuity of thoughts and bodies, a flow of the heterogeneous.

Only the plant could come to stand for a life understood as a continuity of what is heterogeneous and formally divergent, for the logic of animal life is its exact opposite. As Hegel explained to his Jena students at the beginning of the nineteenth century (1805–6), summing up the scientific stance of his day, the crucial point of the many differences between vegetal and animal life is that the latter form can't be reformed—either by extending itself out of its form, as can a root, or by continuing into what is heterogeneous to it—for it maintains its unity; or, as he put it, "animal growth is only an alteration of size but at the same time remains one shape, because the totality of the members is taken up into the subjectivity."[7] The "unity" of animal form thus means for Hegel that an individual maintains its shape throughout its life, establishing a relationship of congruity with other life forms and phenomena that surround it. The animal grows from a puppy to a large dog, or from a baby to a tall human by maintaining its form but what surrounds it—from other dogs or humans to the air, earth, or water—is strictly external or contiguous to it. A human body can dive deep into water, for instance, but regardless of how close its skin gets to it, the water is always only adjacent to it. For Hegel this perseverance of animal form throughout its life, regardless of changes in body size, manifests the "real" unity of its "members" (organs and limbs). Both organs and limbs are thus "purely and simply moments of the form, perpetually negating their independence and bringing themselves back into their unity."[8] And even though limbs and organs are clearly delineated they are for Hegel not discrete since their form doesn't individuate them into an independent existence but merely entangles them in the form of the individual they constitute. Limbs and organs are endowed only with a quasi-discreetness, for they stop being if they stop being united with other organs. Hegel is thus aware that the animal unity of form can be violated and altered, since limbs can be amputated and organs removed, but on his account such a "removal" is never the removal of an individual's unity but only that of its "mere" member, so that "if a finger is cut off, it is no longer a finger, but a process of chemical decomposition."[9] This claim is strange and Hegel quickly passes over it for it suggests that in talking about the formal unity of the animal body he in fact has in mind an ideal unity of the animal's self or personhood, and that animal body's shape, which he declared to be its quintessential characteristic is merely phenomenal, and extraneous to it. What Hegel insists on, though—despite the problem imposed by the potential alteration of animal's shape—is that the unchangeability and continuity of the animal life's form must be accepted as the criteria of true identity. An animal acquires true identity in so far as it remains formally identical to itself and in relation of congruity to everything else around it, for it is the integrity of form that gives the animal "the veritable subjective unity, a unitary soul" or life,[10] which is the "filled center" of that form.[11] Subjectivity thus belongs to the animal thanks to the stability of its form.

Philosophically, there are at least two different ways of interpreting a life that, like the vegetal, lives by violating its formal integrity. One is Hegel's (which he also claims is the stance of mainstream naturalistic views of the early nineteenth century). As Hegel summarizes the botany of his day, "in plant-life ... growth is predominantly ... an alteration of form,"[12] since a root moves out of itself into a formally different stem, a flower leaves its form for a fruit, and a seed too becomes a root by violating its form. Because for Hegel, identity is based on the sameness of form, if one "moment" or "organ" of a plant becomes formally different from another it is because the same plant does not persevere through its different formal instantiations. Rather, plant life never constitutes a unity and is therefore never "taken up" into subjectivity; a plant is not an individual but a "multiplication of individuality"; it is never one but many. Plant "organs" are not therefore "moments" of the same organism; they are not "members" of a real unity, but are unities for themselves, which in their independence "fall asunder, because they are not related to each other as inner, qualitative differences."[13] For Hegel, the plant always "begins" as two, "the plant itself and the bud." By this somewhat enigmatic claim, he means that the bud from which a plant grows finds itself next to the plant it has fallen from and to which it no longer belongs, and that that "falling off" does not affect the plant in any way. The plant and its organ thus find each other in the relation of "nextness," completely indifferent to how their lives develop and grow. That is why on this reasoning, the plant is never less than "two independently existing individuals,"[14] even if it can be many more such individuals, for its "growth" only numerically multiplies rather than unifies it. And because everything that is on a plant at any single moment can be severed from it without affecting the plant itself, and turned into a new individual, plants are piles or heaps of matter; the logic of plant life is "nextness" or congruity but never continuity.

The other way of interpreting plant life is minoritorian; it is Thoreau's. For Thoreau, the fact that plant "organs" move out of their form into something formally dissimilar doesn't cancel the continuity of plant life; it doesn't make it a merely congruous plurality. And because this trust in the plant's continuity in fact claims that what is formally different is materially continuous, it faces him with both an ontological and an epistemological challenge. Ontologically, for plant life to maintain continuity while undergoing formal change allows it to be understood as the model of metamorphosis defined as the capacity of a life to literally transcend its form while also remaining continuous with the form this transcendence revises. By this reasoning, even if a root is formally different from the stem, the two are still vitally one, as are stem and leaf, flower and seed). But Thoreau also considers that what Hegel calls the plant's originary congruity or duality—the fact that the plant and the bud, which falls off it and begins a life completely different from it, which can occur at some spatial distance—doesn't testify to the plant's congruous nature, for despite the distance that perceptually separates them, he nevertheless understands them as continuous, as being really or materially related (that is the consequence of Thoreau's claim that plant life spreads laterally, shooting extremities out of its form and having roots connect with other roots in a vital continuous commons). For Thoreau, plant life is a continuity of metamorphoses; it suggests that different forms, which on the surface of things separate phenomena into unrelated multiplicities, can therefore be one.

And the suggestion that all life lives according to the logic of the vegetal—implied by the *Journal's* claim that "there is no doubt a perfect analogy between the life of the human being and that of the vegetable—both of the body & the mind" (*PJ* 3: 224)—would then mean that all life lives not only by moving in and out of form but also that through such incessant transformation it manages to maintain continuity with what is, formally and at least in appearance, numerically different. The claim comes as a shock to common sense best represented precisely by Hegel's argument about plant life as always being "asunder," for such being "asunder" of a plant is routinely supported by perception. Yet, Emerson systematically insisted on it, clearing the ground for Thoreau's vegetal ontology. As Emerson famously put it, all life "is becoming somewhat else; is in rapid metamorphosis," and the index of its universal logic is "vegetable life," for it moves from "palm" to "oak" "sprouting into forests ... and grasses and vines," always "exceeding" itself into something else, this "ecstasy" of its forms nevertheless never impairing its continuity.[15] According to the scenario of this vegetal ontology phenomena are individuated but the individual is not completely severed from what it is not; instead, what appears as discrete imperceptibly flips over its perceivable form, literally continuing outside itself into something else. On this plane, then, form is only the most "concretized" or perceptible shape of a being, not its firm, closed and stable shape; form is not composed of edges that sever what is enclosed within it, as it is on Hegel's account. A different way of putting this would be to say that between two formally discrete phenomena there is always a material relation that vitally connects them, even if such a relation isn't available to ordinary perception. If the eye doesn't observe the material relation, or continuity, between a plant and a bud for instance, that isn't because the two phenomena are congruent, separated by the spatial interval that separates them, but because the existing relation isn't perceptible.

And that is where the ontologically metamorphic and continuous nature of the vegetal, which for Hegel gave the appearance of what is asunder, posed for Thoreau an epistemological challenge. The challenge consisted in thinking and affirming relations where no relations were perceived, in order to "prove" that phenomena are connected rather than adjacent. Even if it is convincing to claim the continuity of vegetal life on the basis of its lateral expansion and generation of life in a continuous vital network of rhizomes, the question remains of how to generalize such a claim to all life. The question is this: how to claim seriously that there is a vital continuity between, for instance, a plant and an animal. It is easy simply to posit that life is a continuity of the heterogeneous, but how can such a claim be saved from reducing to mere fantasy, and what procedure grounds such a claim as non-trivial? To respond to the challenge of the vegetal and to think as continuous what is perceptually experienced as congruous, Thoreau rehabilitates analogy: "there is no doubt a perfect analogy between the life of the human being and that of the vegetable—both of the body & the mind" (*PJ* 3: 224).

Analogy: Epistemology of the Vegetal

But what does it mean to say that the analogy between man and plant is "perfect?" Or, since the force of the analogical thinking resides in the simile, what does it mean to say that man is like a plant? What does it mean to be "perfectly" like something while not quite being it, as if a phenomenon were neither completely itself nor something else since what it is in itself is said to gestate toward something else? What is Thoreau saying when on numerous occasions he declares that he would call one thing another ("I would call pasture flowers"),[16] or that phenomena are "as if" they are about to be something else ("the epigea looks as though it would open in two or three days at least"),[17] or when he declares it "fitting" that a phenomenon that is "almost" like itself should be colored in a certain way ("It is fit that this almost earliest spring flower should be yellow")?[18] How does one thing become itself only by becoming something else? Does this "identity" in transference confer some sort of insubstantiality on beings, making them evanescent subtleties without defined qualities, bringing them all close to non-existence or, at least, to non-identity? Yet, regardless of how evanescent phenomena might be, Thoreau's perception of them as being what they are only if they are like something else doesn't cancel their individuality, maintaining it instead in a counter-intuitive condition of what both is and isn't what it is. It does that by employing analogy, which could thus be understood as a linguistic and logical practice commensurate with Thoreau's ontology, which posits the world as composed of weakly individuated phenomena that continue into what they aren't. In fact, it is precisely because analogy depicts all phenomena as processual and unstable—eluding strategies of identification and classification—that it was resisted by nineteenth-century science.

Instead of analogy, the early nineteenth-century sciences of life favored homology, a form of reasoning that tended to collapse the similarities between differences into identity, thus abstracting them as the homogeneity of a type or the unity of an essence. As a quintessentially ideational way of thinking—ideational because it is predicated on synthetization, reduction, and abstraction—homology was thus a crucial discursive vehicle for achieving what Gillian Beer calls the "total and satisfying congruity"[19] on the basis of which stable denominations and classifications were made. As Mary B. Hesse argues, not only were Cuvier's or Agassiz's fossil theories centered on it, but even Goethe's morphology subscribed to it, often appearing as celebrating process and relationality of beings: "When homologies were first described in detail by Goethe, Cuvier, Saint-Hilaire and their successors, it was commonly suggested that community of type among organisms is based on an 'ideal type,' an archetype, or natural plan."[20]

On the other hand, when Thoreau in 1851 records in the *Journal* his dream "of a return to the primitive analogical & derivative senses of words" (*PJ* 4: 46), he is effectively welcoming analogy for the same reasons that science dismissed it. For in opposition to homology, analogy brings differences into relation without gathering them into an identity, thus establishing continuities while preserving individuations. It is because of analogy's ability to honor the specificity of phenomena while seeing them entangled in real or embodied relational networks that Thoreau issues an injunction, which insists that not just scientific but all thinking should be analogical: "Improve the opportunity to draw analogies. There are innumerable avenues to a perception of the truth. Improve the suggestion of each object however humble-however slight & transient the provocation ... It is not in vain that the mind turns aside this way or that. Follow its leading-apply it whither it inclines to go" (*PJ* 4: 41). In obeying analogical thinking, Thoreau suggests, the mind will refrain from imposing a priori criteria of unity on phenomena, as is the case with homology; instead thinking would follow the heterogeneity of "the transient," without knowing where it will lead ("whither it inclines to go"), and extending in diverse directions simultaneously ("this way or that"). Thought thus becomes analogical not only in how it thinks but in how it is: transient, not pre-determined by guiding concepts, taxons, or methods; instead, it is multi-directional, improvisational, and relational. Such a thought doesn't only think a plant-like world but does it in a plant-like way, moving through its forms into "innumerable avenues" of perception; thought thus is what it is analogous to. Thinking how things are it is also one of those things, which explains how it is possible that, on the basis of an analogical approach, something is what it is only if it is like something else.

Here is what this analogical thinking—preserving discreteness and thus heterogeneity while allowing for continuity and relationality—looks like in a series of analogical statements about flowers dating from various moments in Thoreau's life: "As I go up the hill beyond the brook, while the hyllodes are heard behind, I perceive the faintest possible flower-like scent as from the earth, reminding me of anemones and houstonias. ... Downy-swaddled, they lie along flat to the earth like a child on its mother's bosom";[21] "There is an abundance of low willows whose catkins are now conspicuous rising four to six or seven feet above the water. ... They look when you look from the sun like dead gray twigs or branches ... of bushes in the light. ... We sail by masses of these silvery buttons two or three rods long, rising above the water. By their color they have relation to the white clouds and the sky and the snow and ice still lingering in few localities;[22] "The blossoms of the sweet gale are now on fire over the brooks, contorted like caterpillars";[23] "The gold-thread up for a day or two, though few flowers compared with buds. Not at once referred to its leaf, so distant on its thread-like peduncle."[24]

Thus a scent is (perceived as) a "flower" that isn't quite vegetal but is of the "the earth," which is thought of as another flower ("anemone") itself accessible only if thought of as a "child"; or, the "blossoms" are "fire" which is caterpillars; or "low willows" are "dead gray twigs" are "branches of bushes" are "silvery buttons" are "white clouds" are "the sky" is "the snow" is "the ice still lingering." One phenomenon is at the same time identified and rendered transient by virtue of leading to its difference (a scent to a flower for instance), which is also the point of its evanescence, for once a scent transitions to a flower it is thought of as a flower. Thus, despite the transient nature of a phenomenon, which reveals itself only by moving into something different from it, each such phenomenon is thought in its fragile discreteness (scents, flowers, condition of the earth, all of that is named and thus identified). Each phenomenon is the "link" that establishes a relation of transference while also being a relate: the scent is not only what moves (perception) into the flower and what thus evaporates into the flower; it isn't only what becomes available to thought as the anemone, but also what is "like" the flower, and therefore an entity that isn't a flower. There is thus established a counterintuitive continuity of what is heterogeneous in nature (mineral, vegetal, human; fragile and hard; light and heavy; phenomenal and substantial) and discrete in existence. Respecting the concreteness of a singular instance as opposed to generalization and abstraction, the analogical thinking of phenomena brings them into continuity with what they are not, while simultaneously preserving them in their fragile individuation. In so doing, analogy also manages to think the world outside of a dichotomy between disorder and determinism. The world it thinks is decidedly not deterministic, pre-decided by a priori types, homologies, or regularizing laws into which phenomena must fit; nor is it a contingent world in which phenomena are disconnected and, because of this un-relatedness, disorderly. As Philippe Descola puts it, analogy "becomes the only means of introducing order, for this is a priori a chaotic and inflated world, since it contains an infinite number of different things, each in a particular place and each at the heart of an idiosyncratic network."[25]

But, if the resemblance that analogy establishes between phenomena were to be understood as claiming them to be "almost" the same, analogy would amount to a tool of reduction rather than differentiation; if a scent's being like a flower would in fact mean that it is a flower then two relata would be reduced to one, and their relation of continuity would collapse into identity. If analogy is opposed to homology it is because it precisely resists moving similarities into identity. In analogy each established relation is identified by a simile only in order to generate more relations, similes and differences; thus, the scent is like the flower which is like the earth only because the earth is like anemones that are like houstonias that are like a child. Analogy proliferates analogies and so produces differences, in contradistinction to homology, where an identification of similarities generates the sameness of types. As Descola put it, analogy would precisely "bring together through an operation of thought that which was previously separate," but only in order, through this new "togetherness," to redistribute differences, generating a plethora of phenomena.[26] Beings are rendered continuous—for instance, Hegel's bud and plant are no longer asunder but instead related by material relations, via the earth—yet that continuity only expands their difference (by growing them into another plant) and proliferates relations. Moreover, this expansion of differentiation through continuity of the analogous finally tends to multiply series into indefinite continuities (in Thoreau's example, for instance, the "scent" is only the beginning of a seven-term series that can in principle proliferate indefinitely). That is why, as Descola posits, "analogy is a hermeneutic dream of plenitude that arises out of a sense of dissatisfaction. Noting that the general segmentation of the world's components is based on a scale of small differences, it nurtures the hope of weaving these slightly heterogeneous elements into a web" of continuity.[27]

Yet, as Thoreau's examples of analogical thinking suggest, to say that analogy operates through "similarity" is somewhat misleading, since no two phenomena he relates are either morphologically or otherwise similar; even if he says that a plant is like a human or a flower like a child, it remains difficult to understand what kind of perception authorizes such similes, how a human body can be morphologically compared to a plant's when we all perceive them as formally incommensurable. The answer to that question lies in understanding analogy not as rhetorical, but as a logical tool. For analogy is neither allegorical (for there is no "one-to-one correspondence of object and meaning"), nor metaphorical (different entities are not considered simply similar, and "resistance as well as accord" persists),[28] nor emblematic (one phenomenon doesn't represent another). As Hesse explains, in analogy— hence its strangeness but also its allure for Thoreau—similes serve as forms of "analogical inference," by which she means that analogy doesn't search for formal similarities between phenomena in order to compare them, but concludes that there is a causal connection—a literal material continuity of influence—between co-occurring phenomena whose causal relations are not clearly visible.[29] The specificity of analogical thinking, which in fact led to its being discredited by scientists, is that the simile doesn't claim a resemblance but a causal connection between the phenomena it relates, despite the fact that such a connection is not observable, and despite the fact that phenomena remain morphologically disparate. Analogy is thus not predominantly a rhetorical or literary device meant to suggest fabulated connections, but a strategy of reasoning that uses simile to claim actual relations. For instance, in Thoreau's discussion of fish in *The Week on the Concord and the Merrimac Rivers*, the observable chromatic similarity among phenomena as different as metal, fish, and clouds is sufficient to claim their causal relation despite their morphological, material, and taxonomical dissimilarities: "fishes too, as well as birds and clouds, *derive* their armor from the [copper] mine. I have heard of mackerel visiting the copper banks at a particular season; this fish, perchance, has its habitat in the Coppermine river."[30] The mackerel's skin is not simply *like* copper and the mackerel doesn't look like metal; rather, the two entities are causally connected as the fish *derive* their armor from the copper banks, as if metal were bringing the fish-skin into being. By registering phenomenal but not substantial, biological or taxonomical similarities between phenomena (for instance, the similarity in color between skin, metal, and a cloud), analogy goes on to infer a real bond (it concludes that the sameness of color must be generated by the same cause). In that way it existentially bridges beings. Moving from what is visible (fish, birds, copper banks) to what is obscure and unknown (the existential and causal link between the fish, the clouds, the metal, and the banks), analogy claims an invisible agency (of copper on fish, flowers, birds, and clouds). In analogy, then, the "like" stands for "is." The simile that it uses thus less establishes formal semblances than it summons into visibility invisible causes and continuities. But since these continuities emerge not only through simile but as it the simile loses its nature of representation in order to be promoted into what it represents. That is why when Thoreau establishes copper as the cause of a fish's or bird's coloration he has no other testimony for it then his "sense" or discernment, which can be validated only by the simple "like." Analogical words are real bridges between material phenomena, the actual causes of their connection. Analogy thus casts doubt not only on the formal separation of phenomena but also on the distinction between thoughts (words) and bodies. Analogy affords thought and word the capacity to evoke beings and their relations, which means, as Gillian Beer argues, that it is aligned with magic:

> The shifty, revelatory quality of analogy aligns it to magic. It claims a special virtue at once incandescent and homely for its achieved congruities. A *living*, not simply an imputed, relation between unlikes is claimed by such discourse. The power of analogy to transform the homely into the transcendent or the lesser into the greater intensity draws on a formulation of experience learnt by Christians in the sacraments. Analogy requires transformation and implicitly claims transubstantiation.[31]

Thoreau precisely celebrates analogy as a sorcerer's tool, representing it as demonological in his *Natural History of Massachusetts*, a text he writes in 1842: "He has something demoniacal in him, who can ... couple two facts. We do not learn by inference and deduction and the application of mathematics to philosophy, but by direct intercourse."[32] A connection established (a "coupling" of facts) is thus predicated not on methodically organized observation or induction but on the immediacy of the force of seeing through what is here into what is not perceptible, shortening the distance between stating and enacting causations, or discerning continuity between what to Hegel appears as asunder. And since the "facts" Thoreau wants to couple are never simply imagined but are, as Walls underlines, always "*vital*," to couple them is to generate, in the manner of a sorcerer, real vital relations (what Beer refers to as a "living, not simply an imputed, relation").[33] If, then, Thoreau insists that "all perception of truth is the detection of an analogy" (*PJ* 4: 46), it is because the analogist, like the magician, "perceives" connections escaping observation, allowing them to be revealed as really related. His statement that there is a "perfect analogy" between a plant and human not only generalizes vegetal life onto animal life; it doesn't only mean that the human or any other animal lives in a vegetal way, porous and always entangled in literal continua or relations that materially change it, affecting also its form; nor does it suggest only that the human mind thinks according to the logic of the vegetal, its thoughts branching out simultaneously in multiple directions. Thanks to analogy's power to establish direct relations Thoreau also suggests that there is a literal continuity between plant and human life, which amount to rephrasing Emerson's claim that there is an "occult relation between man and the vegetable," something he confirms by claiming a direct communication between humans and plants: "they nod to me, and I to them."[34] Thoreau's vegetal ontology and analogical epistemology can thus be conceived of as an effort to understand how this occultism works, the way in which the plant both grounds the human and directly communicates with it, acknowledging it and nodding to it.

About This Collection: Concepts for Ecological Thought

That said, to maintain that Thoreau understood all life as obeying the logic of the vegetal, or to maintain, synonymously, that all life forms transcend themselves and are therefore unstable and porous, is to say that he understood all life forms as mutually dependent thanks to their literal connectedness, caught in networks of influences and mutual modifications. Or, synonymously again, it is to say that he imagines all life forms, selves and bodies, ecologically. If he can safely be called the first serious thinker of the ecological in the Western tradition, it isn't only because of his love of nature or desire to protect it, but because he invents a veritable ecological ontology (of continuity) and epistemology (of analogy), on which an ecological politics and ethics can be grounded. That is what makes his thought so contemporary and indispensable for us today, caught in the midst of the ecological crisis, a crisis that calls upon us to change how we think about identity, form, and individuation.

All of the essays included in this collection are written with an eye to our contemporary moment. In engaging with Thoreau in novel ways they also formulate new conceptual tools that can assist us in thinking about ecological ethics and politics, such as the simultaneity of the different, the co-dependence of the heterogeneous, the continuity of life forms, relationality, cohabitation, porousness, fragility, the openness of beings to incessant modification by other beings and phenomena, patience, waiting, slowness, and receptivity. While all of the contributions are concerned with such ecological politics and ethics, some approach it from ontological or epistemological perspectives, others through natural history, botany, or geology, whereas still others by locate Thoreau within an emerging field of plant studies.

And while the essays are not thematically grouped inasmuch as their topics overlap, neither is their succession contingent. The collection opens with essays that are concerned with ontological aspects of Thoreau's thought about the vegetal (such as influence, relation, process, heterogeneity, multiplicity). Following that, via a group of essays preoccupied with epistemological questions (nature of vegetal thinking in Thoreau, or how vegetal thinking influences his understanding of form and individuation), the volume advances to a series of contributions that relate Thoreau's plant-thought to the questions of the body. We thus begin with Jane Bennett's "Thoreau Experiments with Natural Influences," which, as its title indicates, investigates ways in which phenomena and beings affect and even influence one another. By "natural influence" Bennett means not only how humans or animals affect each other and so modify their psyche, but also how the vegetal and even inanimate can affect the human or how what is non-human affects various sensitive bodies. The claim that for Thoreau there is an "inner minerality and vegetality" in man, that man is thus a sort of plant, as he explicitly argued time and again, then allows Bennett to hold that such "interiority" is also porous, that in concert with the vegetal and the mineral it is open to surprises, excesses, or errancies influenced by surrounds that the human doesn't direct and control but through which it is reshaped.

Laura Dassow Walls's "A Material Faith: Thoreau's Terrennial Turn" is predicated on the premise that Thoreau's plant thinking is his vehicle for materializing, or making immanent or Earthbound, Emerson's millennialist transcendence. It is through plants that transcendence—the movement of forms out of themselves—remains literal or material, related to what Latour termed "terrestrial," but which Walls, in order to avoid Latour's "apocalyptic overtones," prefers to call "terrenial." By following the logic of the plant in Thoreau Walls is able to propose a new ecological ontology.

Staying close to the ontological force of Thoreau's thinking about the vegetal Michael Marder's "Auto-Heteronomy: Thoreau's Circuitous Return to the Vegetal World" investigates the way in which the vegetal brought Thoreau to a novel thinking about subjectivity. He argues that even if Thoreau's experiment of living life on Walden pond can be taken as emblematic of autonomous subjectivity grounded in the Cartesian subject's quest for absolute certainty—his other model for such Cartesian subjectivity is the idea of self-reliant personhood brought about by the American revolution and exacerbated by the frontier ethos—the writer's encounter with plants forces him to formulate and live a different subjectivity. This vegetal subjectivity is autonomous in only the very limited and fragile sense that it is individuated. But it is not autonomous in the sense of being self-sufficient and independent; instead, as vegetal it is co-dependent, communal and predicated on what Marder calls "sympathetic companions." Marder's concept for this new subjectivity that is both individuated and dispersed, both singular and heterogeneous, is "auto-heteronomy," which references selfhood as "a tortuous framework for every life-altering experiment— the framework that, in light of vegetal heteronomy, is at its clearest in this engagement."

Still thinking about ontology or, as he calls it, the "metaphysics" of plants, Antoine Traisnel ("Thoreau's Garden Politics") puts Thoreau into dialogue with contemporary thinking of the vegetal. He does so in order to argue that Thoreau's plant-ontology—with its emphasis on porousness, immersion, instability of forms—reveals vegetal forms as agents and these agents bear within them a lesson in politics. Whereas contemporary philosophy of plants, as Traisnel acknowledges, unsettles the "zoocentric bias toward autonomy and subjectivity, favoring instead a notion like ... susceptibility" it doesn't address the ethics and politics of such unsettling. To develop such a politics out of ontology, such that plants become active and plant becomes a verb, Traisnel investigates Thoreau's theoretical and practical engagements with plants, paying special attention to how such engagements were formulated in *Walden*.

Both Marder's and Traisnel's arguments bridge the gap between the ontology of plants and a subjectivity based on it. Michael Jonik's "'Wild Thinking' and Vegetal Intelligence in Thoreau's Later Writings" moves us entirely onto the terrain of the vegetal image of thought in Thoreau. As if extrapolating Traisnel's argument, Jonik claims that to talk about vegetal agencies isn't enough. The key to understanding vegetal agency is found in vegetal intelligence. Plants act, but is their acting to be understood "merely as deterministic modes of self-organization" or is it rather intelligence; is it a "mechanism" or is it an "integrated self-aware system." To answer this question Jonik brings a group of Thoreau's writings—"The Succession of Forest Trees," "Wild Apples," "Autumnal Tints," and selections from his journals and his unfinished manuscripts *The Dispersion of Seeds,* and *Wild Fruits*—into conversation with current discourse regarding plant intelligence, distributed cognition, and collective natural agency.

Monique Allewaert's "Green Fire: Thoreau's Forest Figuration" stays with *The Dispersion of Seeds.* Her argument is that the "mode of registering" transformations and the mobility of the vegetal that is applied in *Dispersion* was to serve as a method for reading forests and the natural more generally. And while such a method anticipates what later critics have called biosemiosis ("in signs given off by life forms and read by other life forms"), Allewaert's main interest is less in "emitting" and reading than in the problem of figuration, which, she argues, Thoreau conceives as "shape-making." Forms are thus shaped by the mutual engagement of trees, birds, winds, and humans, but "far from bearing the sorts of meanings prioritized by scholars focused on biosemiosis," they testify only to "the transit of a formative impulse that gives on to engendering relations but that has no meaning as such."

Staying with Thoreau's late work, Mark Noble's "The Riddle of Forest Succession" investigates Thoreau's self-conscious efforts to change the epistemic boundaries of contemporary science and to direct scientific epistemologies toward the realm of the ecological. What exactly such redirection might mean is something Noble unfolds by attending precisely to concepts such as "succession," or procession, concepts that, once they are transferred into the realm of modern scientific practice, raise questions about conceptual boundaries. In Noble's reading the logic of forests reveals to Thoreau the direction of a dissolution of the way science thinks and suggests how to think ecologically, that is to think relations and co-dependencies.

Jason Gladstone's "Low-Tech Thoreau; or, Remediations of the Human in *The Dispersion of Seeds*" stays with the text that was Allewaert's main focus too but reads dispersion as "underwriting a sustained consideration of the relationship between humanity, technology, and nature." According to his argument, though, the vegetal in question for Thoreau displays neither the agency that Traisnel talks about nor the intelligence recognized by Jonik; nor is the force of a "formative impulse" as it is for Allewaert, and still less the source of sympathetic influences as it is for Bennett. Instead, his claim is that the non-vibrant vegetal is simply operational; it works, it is machinic. By operating in that way "the vegetal emerges as an aspect of a nature that both coopts human actions and serves as the unacknowledged basis of the bulk of human technologies."

Cristin Ellis remains invested in Thoreau's later writings in her essay "On Thoreau's Ecoerotics," investigating how Thoreau conceives (his) sexuality as plant-like. Her essay is not only about Thoreau's sexuality (about which much has been written) but, more broadly, about how vegetal-sexuality—features of which were, as Ellis also reconstructs, familiar to writers of the eighteenth and the nineteenth centuries—enabled Thoreau to completely "re-theorize sexuality starting from plants rather than humans." To explain the features of this retheorized vegetal sexuality Ellis coins the term "ecoerotics," grounded on the idea of radical metamorphoses and understanding bodies as more volatile than the twentieth century was accustomed to think.

Vesna Kuiken's "Chance Encounters: Thoreau's Pomontology" investigates Thoreau's interest in chanciness in "Wild Apples" as an ontology. She reads Thoreau's lifelong obsession with wild apples as an ethics of leaving behind—of running wild from—the classificatory stability imposed by familial lineage and botanical variety. While Thoreau's research of wild apples coincides historically with Darwin's theory of survival as genetic modification, Kuiken concludes that in Thoreau's thinking wild apple's variability isn't reducible to Darwinism. Instead, for Thoreau wild apple becomes a model for how to understand life as such: an embodiment of idiosyncratic relations and environments that craft every wild apple and every one of us—embodiment by way of which we too become new environments for other entities.

Mary Kuhn's "'Wild Only Like Myself': Thoreau at Home with Plants" investigates the introduction of new plants to America and how they influenced Thoreau. Her argument is that those new plants profoundly influenced the politics of the American mid-nineteenth century. How such an influence worked is demonstrated through Thoreau's engagement with plants that blur the distinction between the domestic and the imported, between wild and cultivated, known and unknown. The disturbance of these dichotomies, Kuhn demonstrates, had a larger impact, unsettling the divide between familiar and strange in both the ethical and political realms, especially when it came to understanding the meaning of naturalization and indigeneity.

While all the essays assembled in this collection engage with current conversations relating to ecological ways of thinking, the last one moves explicitly from Thoreau to contemporary aesthetics. Gillian Osborne focuses on how Thoreau and his contemporaries understood poetry as material and entwined with the vegetal, and how such an understanding can help us approach the materialist aspirations of contemporary eco-poetics.

However seriously this collection engages Thoreau's plant-thinking, it is not intended for Thoreau scholars only. For the series of novel concepts that these essays introduce—sympathetic influence, terreniality, auto-heteronomy, diversion, astrality, vegetal technology, ecoerotics, vegetal eco-poetics, or pomontology—in fact constitute a novel set of additions to the vocabulary of our ecological thinking more broadly, and their novelty aids our efforts to conceptualize and name ecological problems—both philosophical and empirical—more astutely.

1

Thoreau Experiments with Natural Influences

Jane Bennett

Henry Thoreau was a man of influence. I don't mean that he wielded political or literary influence over his neighbors or future readers, although that is also the case. I mean that he seemed to be "more than usually sensitive to influences operating around him,"[1] to the vibrancy of shapes, sounds, rhythms, and moods in his vicinity. Like Whitman's "I," Thoreau was dilated, and dialed into, the "vibrating speech" of things. Thoreau, however, was more vocal about the need for discrimination, for letting some but not all "influences" in. He is, most famously, presumptively wary of those originating from people: "Yesterday I was influenced with the rottenness of human relations. They appeared to me full of death and decay."[2] The default trajectory of inter-human encounters was a dull social conformity: "I am but too ready to conform. ... I find myself disposed to review the acts and position of the general and state governments, and the spirit of the people, to discover a pretext for conformity."[3] In contrast, Thoreau was presumptively welcoming to the influence of nonhuman things: "Open all your pores and bathe in all the tides of Nature. ... Miasma and infection are from within, not without."[4] "If I am too cold for human friendship, I trust I shall not soon

Reprinted from Bennett, Jane. *Influx & Efflux*. Copyright © 2020 Duke University Press, with the permission of Duke University Press. The essay has been shortened for inclusion in this volume.

be too cold for natural influences."[5] Like Whitman's joyful proclamation of an inner minerality and vegetality—I find I incorporate gneiss, coal, long-threaded moss, fruits, grains, esculent roots,[6] Thoreau too celebrates the nonhuman within—"Am I not partly leaves and vegetable mould myself?"[7]

Thoreau insists that the influx of "natural influences" is a beverage that refreshes: "Let me have a draught of undiluted morning air," he exclaims in the "Solitude" chapter of *Walden*, "Morning air! If men will not drink of this at the fountainhead of the day, why, then, we must even bottle up some and sell it in the shops."[8] But even here, the "undiluted" air calls for some filtering: it is put through the sieve of words as Thoreau *stages* his encounter in ways designed to maximize the refreshment-effect. The beverage of morning air needs to be, shall we say, *decanted* in prose: to be written up in journals, essays, books in ways designed to highlight, exaggerate, and intensify its salutary effects. Poetics allows the flavors of natural influences to bloom.

The figure of "natural influence" is one way that Thoreau marks this not-fully-human effort to enter and affect sensitive bodies. His figure of "the Wild" is another.[9] Defined as the surprise, excess, or errancy simmering within every object of encounter, the Wild disrupts human habits of perception, alters the usual targets of one's affection, and derails trains of thought. There is wildness in old books, the railroad, foreign tongues, and even one's own "winged thoughts," whose "current" makes "as sudden bends" as does the Merrimack river.[10] But the Wild is most readily experienced in engagements with *uncultivated* things, such as the relentlessly buzzing mosquito, the disconcerting geology of Mt. Ktaadn, the dank fecundity of swamps, the bracing "tonics and barks" of trees.[11] People are attracted to the Wild; the Wild is a lure because it not only disrupts but *refreshes*: "We need the tonic of wildness,—to wade sometimes in marshes where the bittern and meadow-hen lurk ... ; to smell the whispering sedge where ... the mink crawls with its belly close to the ground."[12]

When Thoreau invokes "natural influences," he is again pointing to a power of disruptive refreshment. But whereas "the Wild" tends to call attention to the power as it is operating through individualized entities, the figure of "natural influences" highlights the effusive/infusive efforts of an ongoing process. This processual flow is like Quebec's "Great River" (the St. Lawrence), which Thoreau visited in the fall of 1850 and depicted in "A Yankee in Canada." Thoreau says he had initially apprehended Quebec under the influence of its given names—"St. Lawrence River," "Plains of Abraham," and "Cape Diamond" (so named by Champlain because of its quartz crystals). But that kind of history, proceeding by reference to "human relations," is soon "swept away ... by an influence from the wilds and from nature, as if the beholder had read *her* history,—an influence which, like the Great River itself, flowed ... with irresistible tide over all."[13] There exists, Thoreau insists, a tale told by rivers, plains, promontories—a riparian history, a fluvial history, a limnological history, a sweeping-grasslands history, a mineral history. Natural bodies speak and impress upon Thoreau, entering into and inflecting his postures and moods (to be, in turn, adjusted and expressed as the stories he writes up). It would thus be inaccurate to describe Thoreau's nature-writing as poetic but not historical: the presence of the past is *always* on his radar. When he historicizes, however, he goes beyond the "muddy and dusty ruts"[14] of human acts and artifacts, in order to highlight the ongoing past—the present influence—of rivers, ponds, mountain, plants, stars, woodland animals, and the living landscapes they compose with and upon us.

Influence: a tendency for outsides to ooze, drift, seep, incur across the perimeter of insides; the propensity to cross over an edge; to cause to flow in; to infuse, inspire, instill, as emanation from the stars or the inflow of water. In this chapter, we will examine three occasions when Thoreau wades deep into the great river of natural influence—into what he also calls the "circulation of vitality beyond our bodies."[15] We will follow him as he is impressed by, digests, and decants that vitality. In the first occasion, the influences of the summer sun and of a field of rye elicit in Thoreau an inner faculty that is usually eclipsed by the ordering activity of thinking. Too hot to think, what is activated instead is his capacity to receive outside impressions with equanimity and without judgment: he abides them without rushing to name or process them intellectually, he lets them breathe, he "nod[s] like the ryeheads in the breeze."[16] If in this first occasion, Thoreau's experiment is to assume a stance akin to Whitman's "nonchalance," in a second occasion of natural influences, Thoreau posits the presence of a cross-species current of "sympathy" conjoining him to pine needles and alder leaves. The effect here is that the hold of Thoreau's species-specific identity is relaxed; he now comes to feel himself to be less a human individual than a natural element within an ecological process. In a third kind of encounter with natural influences—including dentistry-grade ether, a hallucinatory plant called the thorn-apple, and repetitive sound and shape of drops of rain—Thoreau experiments with intoxication. What he stages now is the non-benevolent, even toxic potential of natural influences. As Thoreau drinks up some of them to the point of intoxication, he imbibes a vitality that can not only disrupt the urge to conform to society and refresh stale thoughts, can not only expose mimetic relays between people and plants and relax the borders of individuation, but can also be quite indifferent to human ideals, disciplines, or even survival.

"Significant but Not Efficient" Efficacy

One final philosophical stop before we turn to each of Thoreau's experiments in more detail: a brief discussion of the peculiar kind of efficacy that is "influence." It is a capacity to induce effects quietly, without fanfare, and often at the very margins of cognitive or even sensuous detection. It is, for example, the unexpected potency of "Night and Moonlight," whose mechanism, writes Thoreau, is just too delicate to be fully detailed:

> It must be allowed that the light of the moon ... is very inferior in quality and intensity to that of the sun. But the moon is not to be judged alone by the quantity of light she sends to us, but also by her influence on the earth and its inhabitants.[17]

In distinguishing between a bright "quantity of light" characteristic of the sun and the qualitative luminousness of "influence" characteristic of "moonshine," the effort of Thoreau's words is to acknowledge the everyday presence of streams of inflow that make their mark through a gossamer persistence. He reiterates the point later in the essay when he cites Sir Walter Raleigh's claim that the stars are "significant but not efficient": that is to say, stars have an indirect and ethereal, *but not therefore negligible*, power to produce effects. Other examples of this sly efficacy include the "secret of influence" of a "crimson cloud on the horizon" that "boots" the imagination of the observer—"this red vision excites me, stirs my blood—makes my thought flow" by means of "something unexplainable—some element of mystery,"[18] or "the silent influence which flowers exert, no less upon the ditcher in the meadow than the lady in the bower,"[19] or "the finest influence" of "electricity in the air."[20] Or "the occult relation implied" between skunk cabbage and man:

> What a conspicuous place nature has assigned to the skunk cabbage—first flower to show itself above the bare ground! What occult relation is implied between this plan & man? ... Why should just these sights & sounds accompany our life? Why should I hear the chattering of blackbirds—why smell the skunk each year? I would fain explore the mysterious relation between myself & these things.[21]

In general, Thoreau will use the word "influence" when he wants to highlight a recursive causality whose operation is elusive but whose effects are salient. Thoreau affirms the real presence of natural influences and iterates them: he translates them into words that decant—ex-plicate, inflect, redirect—their disruptive refreshment.

Experiment 1: "Light Ethereal Influence"

One hot day in late July, Thoreau really *feels* the weight of the atmosphere. Here is what he writes up in his journal after he goes back inside:

You must walk so gently as to hear the finest sounds, the faculties being in repose. Your mind must not perspire. True, out of doors my thought is commonly drowned as it were & and shrunken, pressed down by stupendous piles of light ethereal influence—for the pressure of the atmosphere is still 15 pounds to a square inch—I can do little more than preserve the equilibrium & resist the pressure of the atmosphere—I can only nod like the ryeheads in the breeze. I expand more surely in my chamber, as far as expression goes, as if that pressure were taken off; but here out-doors is the place to store up influences.[22]

The pressure of the 15 pounds (which has the weird heft of "stupendous piles" of "light ethereal" layers) would in another season have gone unnoticed, encountered not as an active force but only a background condition. On that particular summer day, however, Thoreau does sense the vitality of atmosphere: it feels heavy on his skin, and it passes through his pores to alter the relative strengths of his "faculties." One of these, the power to form "thoughts," is "shrunken" by the influx of atmosphere, leaving him in a kind of vegetal state. At this point, he "can only nod like the ryeheads in the breeze."[23] Writing in his journal later that day, Thoreau revisits his vegetal experience. Out in the heat, he could "do little more than preserve the equilibrium," and because he was expending *so* much of his energy on boundary-maintenance, he couldn't think. He is now able to discern how much *effort* it takes to maintain the boundaries of individuality in the face of atmospheric pressures always clamoring to get in.

A suspension of the power of thought is not, however, the only adjustment of faculties induced by that ethereal influence. There is also an *enhancement* of a non-cognitive power. We can see this if we attend to the first line of the journal entry: if you want "to hear the finest sounds" that the world has to offer, you must walk "gently" and have faculties that are "in repose." And *that* is precisely the gait and comportment of "the ryeheads in the breeze." Thoreau's own nod, a mimetic response to ryeheads, is both a cognitive *disability* and a *boost* in his capacity for refined hearing, for a mode of receptivity that acknowledges without rushing to judge, that listens without filtering the sounds through conventional standards of good and bad. Thoreau couldn't think, but he could "store up influences." There is a shift in the balance of his faculties, away from cognitive judgment and toward a non-discriminating equanimity.

Once back inside, however, the balance again re-adjusts. "I expand more surely in my chamber, as far as expression goes."[24] Thoreau expands the outdoor impressions into poetic expression: he writes them up. Later that year, in a journal entry from September 1851, Thoreau returns to the question of the difference between outside and inside, and again notes that each locale encourages a different arrangement of human faculties. To stay outside too long is to nod off; to stay inside too long is to overthink, to have a head that "stands out too dry, when it should be immersed. A writer, a man writing, is the scribe of all nature; he is the corn and the grass and the atmosphere writing."[25] For Whitman too, there was such a thing as too much thinking: "Too incessant a strain of the Mind—continual alacrity of thought-a never-quiet lambency of brain—too restless an Intellect—That is it—'too restless an intellect'—the wearer out of life—It is not Soul—it is Intellect—Soul is longeve, good—it helps, sustains, makes sane—but too restless an Intellect and Brain action wears out life."[26]

Thoreau takes up a nodding attitude once more on August 23, 1853, when he counsels himself to "resign" to "the great influence that Nature is"—here the great influence of the changing seasons. To "resign" can mean to submit, or to re-sign—and Thoreau's texts often do the latter. Here he resignifies himself as one creature among others, as not above but "part and parcel" of nature. To "resign yourself to the influences" of each season and "drink of each season's influence as a vial" is to acknowledge the extent to which *you yourself* are a fruit of the season, as are berries, herbs, goats, and pigs:

> Live in each season as it passes; breathe the air, drink the drink, taste the fruit, and resign yourself to the influences of each. ... In August live on berries. ... The invalid ... instead of imbibing only the great influence that Nature is, drinks only the tea made of a particular herb, while he still continues his unnatural life. ... Grow green with spring, yellow and ripe with autumn. Drink of each season's influence as a vial, a true panacea of all remedies mixed for your especial use. ... Drink the wines ... not kept in goat-skins or pig-skins, but the skins of a myriad fair berries. ... For all Nature is doing her best each moment to make us well. She exists for no other end. Do not resist her.[27]

Himself a natural body, Thoreau is porous and sensitive: he receives and exudes influences, he drinks in impressions and expresses a life in-formed by them. Such a *receptive creativity* pertains as well to other organic bodies: a fox running "across the pond in the snow" reveals its "visible sympathy" with sun and earth;[28] a pond, "sensitive" to the stormy weather, responds with a "thundering" of its own;[29] air, even "more fine and sensitive" than water, is shaken by the sound of voices;[30] "the wind has fairly blown me out doors—the elements were so lively & active—and I so sympathized with them that I could not sit while the wind went by";[31] the earth itself "is all alive and covered with papillae."[32] Indeed, for Thoreau, "there is nothing inorganic."[33]

It is good to give Nature the nod, Thoreau counsels—even if that nod, unwitted and unwilled, is something induced by the atmosphere and thus not exactly his to give. But then again, it *is* his: the nod, *induced* rather than *produced* by atmosphere, relies upon the fact that nodding is one of the potential postures belonging to the configuration of "fresh and blood and bones"[34] that is Thoreau. In sum: the nod is Thoreau's, even if not an act of will in the strong sense; the nod is the atmosphere's, even if it activates a plant-like posture already within Thoreau's somatic repertoire. Thoreau and atmosphere each contribute strivings and tendencies to a much larger recursive, creative process. At work in the scene of cognition-suspension and nod-activation is an agency distributed across a variety of bodies and forces.

Experiment 2: Cross-Species Sympathy

A second encounter between Thoreau and natural influences occurs not on a hot day but a cool, cloudy, windy evening; it involves also alder and poplar leaves. When Thoreau writes up the event in the (ironically named) "Solitude" chapter of *Walden*, what comes to the fore is the presence of an invisible current of sympathy that had also been there:

> This is a delicious evening, when the whole body is one sense, and imbibes delight through every pore. I go and come with a strange liberty in Nature, a part of herself. As I walk along the stony shore of the pond in my shirt sleeves, though it is cool as well as cloudy and windy, and I see nothing special to attract me, all the elements are unusually congenial to me. ... Sympathy with the fluttering alder and poplar leaves almost takes away my breath; yet like the lake, my serenity is rippled but not ruffled.[35]

Thoreau's sympathy with the fluttering leaves "almost takes away my breath": his gaspy shortness of breath mimetically salutes the quick back-and-forth movement of vegetal flutter. The mimesis continues as Thoreau finds that his own "serenity," like the contour of the lake's surface (which itself repeats the waves of wind) is "rippled but not ruffled."[36] As the walk proceeds, we are free to imagine that Thoreau's gait too starts to keep pace with the rhythm of flutter or lap of waves,[37] just as "the note of the whippoorwill" repeats the tempo of "the rippling wind."[38] The stances, rhythms, and paces of Thoreau's sympathize with other natural bodies. But the current of sympathy also flows the other way: "Every little pine needles expanded and swelled with sympathy and befriended me."[39]

In play here is a non-species-specific current of sympathy, a rhythmic process of rippling repetition. Thoreau's lyrical description in that passage helps us glimpse a sympathizing that is more-than-personal, a kind of ontological infrastructure that makes possible the subjective experience of one Henry Thoreau. Thoreau eschewed person-to-person sympathizing because the risk of infection by the moral sentiments of the day was therein dangerously high.[40] Such "compassion is a very untenable ground," he writes, and ought to be rendered as brief or "expeditious" as possible.[41] The kind of sympathizing Thoreau prizes instead is an apersonal current of attractions and iterations. What repeats are less societal ideals or moral values than bodily postures, movements, sounds, and rhythms. These less normalized, more physical repetitions sweep across humans and nonhumans alike: "I warn you, my sympathies do not always make the usual phil-*anthropic* distinctions."[42] What prompts any deliberate effort to sympathize, then, is this apersonal mimesis, always already in play.

This process, at work in the walking scene in "Solitude," cannot be reduced to a purely imaginative act of projection made by Thoreau (or to a psychologized "sympathetic identification"). The resonance between vegetal flutter and human breath does not begin and end with the man's projections. Thoreau makes it clear, for example, that the plant's sympathies come to his notice only *after* his breath is taken and his serenity is rippled by outside forces. Thoreau, in other words, lets us know that he has *already been affected by* an independent vitality *prior* to having registered a thought about them or a personal sentiment of sympathy for them.[43] As Branka Arsić says, "we are in the midst of things that affect us even before we get to know them, and things continue to affect us even though they remain unknown to us. We are, in other words, affected by the world and through this affection we acknowledge the world before, or independently, of our knowing it."[44] Thoreau's walking body had already gravitated toward—and mimetically responded to—the fluttering leaves, just as the whippoorwill's note had repeated the ripples of wind. Every act can only emerge from, even as it adds something to, an eco-morphic process of mimesis: "'How vast and profound is the influence of the subtle powers of Heaven and Earth!'"[45]

Material Leanings

Is there a *purpose* behind these unsolicited, unwitted attractions and repetitions? It is true that Thoreau often presents "natural influences" as signals of divine providence: "The indescribable innocence and beneficence of Nature,—of sun and wind and rain, of summer and winter,—such health, such cheer, they afford forever! and such sympathy have they ever with our race."[46] Or again: "My profession is always to be on the alert to find God in nature, to know his lurking places."[47] And so when he says that "every little pine needle expanded and swelled with sympathy and befriended me. I was so distinctly made aware of the presence of something kindred to me,"[48] the reader may be justified in concluding that pine trees and people are kin because each is a creature of the same divine parent. But it is also noteworthy that there are times when Thoreau does not seem particularly interested in the question of purpose or divine design: he is content simply to give natural influences the nod, or to enjoy the sensations they induce, or to acknowledge that they affect him in ways too subtle to analyze. On these occasions, Thoreau heeds his own prayer to "not be in haste to detect the universal law, let me see more clearly a particular instance."[49] One might say here that he allows his creationism to become "ruffled" by the idea of a *material* creativity.

An example of this is when Thoreau, right after effusing about Nature's sympathy with the human race, explains his kinship with nonhuman bodies in these more physical terms: "Shall I not have intelligence with the earth? Am I not partly leaves and vegetable mould myself?"[50] The "intelligence" between man and pine needles now appears, perhaps, as a function not of divine design but of a certain overlap in *materials*. Indeed, it is as if, as Thoreau walked along the stony shore of the pond, the vegetal within him— all the plants he has eaten, breathed in, or otherwise incorporated over the years, and from which he has absorbed nutrients, colors, textures, tempos, scents[51]—leaned toward and gave a nod to its counterparts on the outside. Here "sympathy" appears as an apersonal material process where like seeks, meets, and greets like. Sympathy now names the encounter of amen-able materials. Here the *materialist* strands in the fabric of Thoreau's (always nature-loving) "transcendentalism" come to the fore, and the edges of his pantheism blur into a philosophy of vibrant matter.

If we were to expand upon Thoreau's half-winking claim that his inner "mould" has "intelligence" with vegetal kin living abroad, we might describe what happened that delicious evening as a *trans-species nod*. This is not the inter-subjective recognition pursued by Hegel, wherein two human individuals become self-conscious of themselves in the process of recognizing "themselves as mutually recognizing" that the other being is, like itself, more than an object in its capacity to reflect upon its own existence.[52] We would have here instead a species-crossing acknowledgment that gives witness not to shared personhood but to asubjective affinities between resonant materials. This "recognition" is more like heliophilia than an inter-human recognition initiated and enacted in psyches.

Literary Influences

Thoreau was sensitive to plants. He lifted the presence of vegetal influences out from the oblivion of the ordinary, highlighting the subtle causality by which a potato farmer is affected by his "long intercourse with potatoes."[53] There is also at work a literary effort and effect. Thoreau walks a fine line between, on the one hand, affirming a pre-literary existence of natural *influences*, and, on the other hand, using words to conjure it up. The verbs to evoke and to invoke are also apt here, for they suggest a shared and distributed kind of agency: Thoreau *evokes* a reader's memory of occasions when she too may have sensed the presence of natural influences, as he *invokes* an enchantment-power proper to the literary images he crafts in honor of those occasions. The latter appears in such lines as these: "Sympathy with the fluttering alder and poplar leaves almost takes away my breath," "Every little pine needle expanded and swelled with sympathy," "Am I not partly leaves and vegetable mould myself?" Thoreau's ecopoetic compositions encourage himself and his readers to linger a bit longer with any vague feelings of vegetal friendship that may arise, and to entertain the thought of an earth that "is not a dead inert mass" but "the most living of creatures."[54] Such a rhetoric allows these kinds of questions to arise: What if pine needles really do sympathize? Is it not quite ordinary to befriend and be friended by alder leaves?[55]

If for a long time in literary criticism such claims would be dismissed as instances of the pathetic fallacy, today that "anti-pathetic reaction to the Romantic investment in the vitalism of the natural world"[56] faces a renewed affirmation of the creative agency of bodies and forces. This new materialism highlights a vitality that need not rely upon divine design, though it may for some. The reading of Thoreau I am offering is part of such an effort: it tries to pull the materialist threads out of the creationist fabric, weaving them into an onto-ethics of a nature that is wondrous and mimetic, all alive with papillae, even if the human species is not its center or apex. Thoreau too flirted with this idea. But even when he relies upon providence, his depictions of trans-species nods work to enhance our sensitivity to a less guaranteed kind of material vitality. "If it is *possible* that we may be addressed, it behooves us to be attentive," Thoreau says in his journal.[57] Once such vitality is brought to the foreground of attention, even if by way of a religious transcendentalism that one may not share, it is difficult to un-see it. Thoreau reminds us that there is something amazing about physicality. His nature-writing is also valuable because it shows that there is no need to *understate* the efficacy of "natural influences" in order to celebrate the creativity ("genius") of humans: "What is called genius is the abundance of life or health," genius is itself a function of the "circulation of vitality beyond our bodies."[58]

Experiment 3: Psychedelia

In a third kind of encounter between Thoreau and natural influences, the "natural vitality" at work around and upon him is more intoxicating than comforting, and more difficult to link to divine benevolence.[59] As Thoreau takes swigs of these, his thoughts become "winged": they fly off into psychedelia. If the 15 pounds to a square inch of air pressure had "drowned and shrunk" Thoreau's thought, we now encounter nonhuman influences that wildly accelerate its flow.

As Mary Elkins Moller has noted, Thoreau was both an advocate of clean living (preferring a "draught of undiluted morning air" to alcohol or tea) and also fascinated by intoxication:

> We know that Thoreau usually deplored drunkenness, or even a moderate use of alcohol, that he advocated abstinence and simplicity of diet, ... believing ... that one could be more truly intoxicated by the marvels of Nature and day-to-day experience. But it is important to recognize that he did not deplore "intoxication" itself. Indeed, a kind of intoxication—euphoria, ecstasy—was valued by Thoreau above all things.[60]

As an example of his fascination with intoxication, Moller points to Thoreau's experience with ether during a dental procedure, described in a journal entry of May 12, 1851. What is revealed while under the influence of ether, says Thoreau, is the existence of a part of himself able to separate from his "organs" and from the usual repertoire of "sense" they afford. In this drugged state, "You are a sane mind without organs,—groping for organs,—which if it did not soon recover its old sense would get new ones." The gas exposes "an interval between one life and another," an interval always there if not always noticed. Moller, accenting Thoreau's mention of a "mind" that can travel to "another life," reads Thoreau as flirting with mysticism. Even more notable to me is the way Thoreau presents this mind as plant-like: "You are a sane mind without organs,—groping for organs,—which if it did not soon recover its old sense would get new ones. *You expand like a seed in the ground. You exist in your roots, like a tree in winter.*"[61] Under the influence of ether, the mind again reveals its inner vegetality. Its "groping" toward the plants outside is a nod of affinity: under the pressure of atmosphere, under the spell of pine needles, and now under the influence of ether, Thoreau's inner plant rises to the surface. One could say that on May 12, 1851, Thoreau wrote up what Richard Doyle calls as an "ecodelic" experience: the ecodelic is that which provokes in people a sharper sense of the "inhuman or transhuman presences in ... consciousness."[62]

Later that year, on September 7, Thoreau mentions another "pot of ether," this one administered not by a dentist but by some fruits: "the juices of the fruits which I have eaten the melons & apples have ascended to my brain—& are stimulating it. They give me a heady force." These "force-ful" plants, which leave an "indelible impression," produce in Thoreau an "exstatic" state wherein he is infused with a "fulness of life" that seems to have no purpose. But like a "pot of pure ether," this "superfluity of wealth" nonetheless has great value—for poets: it induces a kind of writing that can "overrun and float itself," that gets at the truth by virtue of "exaggeration."[63]

As an example of such writing, we might turn to Thoreau's account, in *Cape Cod*, of another intoxicating plant, the thorn-apple:

> The *Datura stramonium*, or thorn-apple, was in full bloom along the beach; and, at sight of this cosmopolite,—the Captain Cook among plants,—carried in ballast all over the world, I felt as if I were on the highway of natures. ... This Viking, king of the Bays ... is not an innocent plant; it suggests not merely commerce, but its attendant vices, as if its fibres were the stuff of which pirates spin their yarns. I heard the voice of men shouting aboard a vessel, half a mile from the shore. ... As I looked over the water, I saw the isles rapidly wasting away, the sea nibbling voraciously at the continent. ... On the other hand, these wreck of isles were being fancifully arranged into new shores ... where everything seemed to be gently lapsing into futurity.[64]

The thorn-apple, itself having been subjected to the influences of human traders and explorers, repeats and transmits those "not innocent" tendencies back to Thoreau: in their presence he hears voices and is provoked into a hallucinogenic vision of Vikings, pirates, a "sea nibbling voraciously at the continent," and a cosmos of multiple forms morphing and "lapsing into futurity." Further evidence of the psychotropic inspiration of this plant is provided in a footnote, where Thoreau cites Beverly's *History of Virginia*: "being an early plant," the thorn-apple was gathered for a salad by soldiers in Virginia who, after eating it, "turned natural fools":

> One would blow up a feather in the air; another would dart straws at it with much fury; and another, stark naked, was sitting up in a corner like a monkey, grinning and making mows at them; a fourth would fondly kiss and paw his companions, and sneer in their faces. ... A thousand such simple tricks they played, and after eleven days returned to themselves again, not remembering anything that had passed.[65]

Another instance of intoxication is the "mesmerizing" effect of a woodchuck whose path Thoreau crosses. Alongside the natural influences of atmosphere, vegetal sympathies, and the "influence of gravity,"[66] there is also the current of "mesmeric influence." It was the latter that bound him and a woodchuck together on April 16, 1852:

> As I turned round the corner of Hubbard's Grove, saw a woodchuck ... in the middle of the field. ... When I was only a rod and a half off, he stopped, and I did the same. ... We sat looking at one another about half an hour, till we began to feel mesmeric influences. ... I walked round him; he turned as fast and fronted me still. I sat down by his side within a foot. I talked to him quasi forest lingo.[67]

As a final example of Thoreau's poetic encounter with intoxicating natural influences, let us consider his preoccupation with dripping drops in *Walden*. One rainy day, Thoreau becomes "suddenly sensible" of an "unaccountable friendliness" between himself and the "pattering of the drops."[68] In a long and famous passage in the "Spring" chapter Thoreau stages a psychedelic encounter with sand, leaves, and clay on the side of a railroad embankment, again taking "delight" in Nature's practices of repetition and iteration. This time the mimesis is more volatile than the friendly resonances between Thoreau and pine needles, or the sympathetic redounding of pond and thunder. It is the weirder and wilder repeat of a *shape*—of lobe or drop that repeats in the way an image multiplies in a fun-house of mirrors. As the lobe or drop repeats itself with a twist, a series of strange and inexplicable "hybrids" take shape.

"Few phenomena gave me more delight," writes Thoreau, "than to observe the forms which thawing sand and clay assume in flowing down the sides of a deep cut on the railroad through which I passed on my way to the village." It was an early spring day, and the snowy banks were starting to give way to ejaculates of sand, which "flow down the slopes like lava. ... Innumerable little streams overlap and interlace ... exhibiting a sort of hybrid product, which obeys half way the law of currents, and half way that of vegetation." These drops or globules of water-sand continue to morph, now into "the forms of sappy leaves or vines, making heaps of pulpy sprays a foot or more in depth."[69] Both the water-sand and "sand foliage" had erupted suddenly, as if Thoreau has witnessed an "excrementitious" bursting of the vitals of the earth.[70] Thoreau here witnesses a repetition that is fractal without being a *perfect* (what Gilles Deleuze will call "bare") repetition:

> Innumerable little streams overlap and interlace. ... As it flows it takes the forms of sappy leaves or veins ... resembling, as you look down on them, the laciniated, lobed, and imbricated thalluses of some lichens; or ... coral ... leopard's paws or birds' feet, of brains or lungs or bowels and excrements of all kinds. It is a truly grotesque vegetation ... a sort of architectural foliage ... destined perhaps ... to become a puzzle to future geologists. ...
>
> What is man but a mass of thawing clay? The ball of the human finger is but a drop congealed. The fingers and toes flow to their extent from the thawing mass of the body. ... The nose is a manifest congealed drop of stalactite. The chin is a still larger drop, the confluent dripping of the face. The cheeks are a slide from the brows into the valley of the face. ... Each rounded lobe of the vegetable leaf, too, is a thick and now loitering drop ... the lobes are the fingers of the leaf.[71]

These mimetic repetitions, which ignore distinctions between animal species, or between animals and plants, or between biology and geology, remain linked to a divine source. But in contrast to what Thoreau experiences while nodding and sympathizing, this source appears less as a God-person than as an onto-experimental "divine" *process*—it is, one could say, creativity *per se* not bound by a design that would have preceded it. "I am affected as if I stood in the laboratory of the Artist who made the world and me—had come to where he was still at work, sporting on this bank, and with excess of energy strewing his fresh designs about."[72] In this passage, says Michael Ziser, "natural phenomena are viewed as the fruit of experimental aesthetic labors."[73] Thoreau encounters an open-ended, "sporting" creativity, of an Artist *in the midst* of making, who, overtaken by the creative process, allows new inventions to proliferate on the fly. His text here raises the question of whether *this* process can still be described as reliably "beneficent," as reducible to a divine agent of an overriding intentionality.

Clay, water, sand, vines, lichens, coral, leopard paw, birds' feet, brains, the flesh of fingers and toes and noses—all these materials repeat the shape of the droplet or "moist thick *lobe.*" What at first appears to be a discrete entity—a nose, a chin, a leaf—reveals itself to Thoreau to be a congealed drop of the flow of nature. Thoreau goes so far as to say that the letters of the *word* "lobe" re-iterate the shape of "moist thick lobe": "the radicals of lobe are lb, the soft mass of the b (single lobed, or B, double lobed), with the liquid l behind it pressing it forward."[74] As if on an LSD trip, Thoreau finds that alphabetic letters are "suddenly severed" from their conventional context,[75] as everything becomes a riff on the phenotype of a drop falling out of a protean, viscous substance.[76] It is thus better described as iterative rather than fractal, as Thoreau moves closer to Bersani's notion of "inaccurate repetition," a "replication" that is both universal in scope and imperfect, insofar as each thing "reoccurs [slightly] differently everywhere."[77]

At the embankment, Thoreau's thoughts became truly "winged": they take psychedelic flight: "You find ... in the very sands an anticipation of the [shape of the] vegetable leaf"; the leaf "sees its prototype" in the shape of a "moist thick lobe"; "the ball of the human finger is but a drop congealed"; "the chin is a still larger drop, the confluent dripping of the face"; "what is man but a mass of thawing clay?"[78] Natural influences, emanating from the sandy bank on the side of the railroad as well as from the shape of the letters of the alphabet, start to loosen the links of a Romantic order of nature: thoughts run wild and sympathies go mad. Thoreau invites us to experience a ruffled conjunction between reflective subjectivity and vegetal nonchalance. Once you become so sensitized to human-plant resonances, there is a kaleidoscopic shift in everything you see, hear, smell, touch, taste, and think. At least for a time. One may start to experience oneself less as an intersubjective being and more as an *intra-twined shape.* By means of these trips, Thoreau allows himself to glimpse not only his inner vegetable, and not only his ecodelic connection to a grander scheme of Nature, but also a cosmos that exceeds "beneficence." Like Whitman, Thoreau fronts an affectivity that is not only profound but also impersonal—*not predisposed first and foremost toward humans.*

To Thoreau and me, it is worthwhile to experiment with different styles of encountering natural influences—to find out how they work upon our moods, propensities to action, and tendencies toward judgment even before we become attentive to them. This helps to quiet the human conceit that everything said or felt about the nonhuman is but a product of our imagination, or construction, or projection, or deployment of metaphors. It is unlikely that our attentiveness will ever be equivalent to or capable of mastering the flows of influence. Nonetheless, Thoreau, writing in ways that decant or exaggerate or dramatize those influences, can encourage the "beneficent" ones to play larger roles in our lives.

2

A Material Faith: Thoreau's Terrennial Turn

Laura Dassow Walls

Thus we must indeed place things in the center and us at the periphery, or better still, things all around and us within them like parasites.

MICHEL SERRES, *THE NATURAL CONTRACT*

Materialism and the Terrennial Turn

My title links two terms, one ancient and beridden with controversy, the other still unborn, my audacious attempt to name a movement for which we lack a stable vocabulary. In what follows I attempt to tie both the ancient and the not-yet-born to Thoreau's turn toward "terra," the terrain, to an Earth then just coming into view, conceived through the tracings of plant life which, in Thoreau's immersive philosophy, transmuted into a wild nature whose resistance could anchor a new faith, a material faith. This is the sunrise that Thoreau in *Walden* anticipated and assisted, as he said, "materially" in its rising[1]—a turning of the Earth, that is, a Terrennial turn.

Materialism competes with *nature* as a keyword of such confusion as to approach the limit of usefulness. As Raymond Williams informs us, the word's long history unfolded from the root of *matter* as L. *materia*, "building material," evolving into three variously related senses: matter as the primary substance of the universe; the related complex of judgments moving materiality into "mental, moral, and social activities"; and the recent devolution into mere getting and spending. In today's critical theory, "materialism" descends from the second of these senses, taking two opposite directions. Traditionally, it names half of the theological arrangement conferred upon us by René Descartes, who settled the anxieties of his own time by dividing "soul" from "body." As Descartes argued, "the rational soul … cannot be derived in any way from the potentiality of matter, but must be specially created."[2] Descartes's conclusion, that the body must be an ingenious machine into which God has emplaced, in humans only, a rational soul, still arranges the furniture of our thought: one sees such Cartesian afterlives in the assertion by Mary Baker Eddy, the founder of Christian Science, that "Spirit is the real and eternal; matter is the unreal and temporal." One sees it also in Thoreau's friend Emerson, who, echoing Descartes, opened his landmark essay *Nature* by separating "ME" from "NOT-ME," "Soul" from "Nature," followed by a heroic struggle to reintegrate them. For once one evacuates the ghost from the machine, how does one put it back?[3]

But recently the polarity has reversed: "materialism" has been revived to recover the very stance that Descartes sought to suppress, as in the "new" or "vital materialism" that sees all matter in some sense as vital, vibrant, agential, and self-organizing, what Jane Bennett calls "a heterogeneous monism of vibrant bodies."[4] But confusingly, the term "vitalism" can also refer back to Descartes's original solution, the infusing of dead matter with living or "vital" spirit as a kind of breath or animating current—the sort of superadded animating force by which Mary Shelley imagined Dr. Frankenstein shocking a patchwork corpse into life, animating dead body into living monster. This tells us that to animate dead nature with living spirit is a monstrous thought, for its foundation lies in the deanimation of all nature itself. Worse, it tells us that the instrumentality of the mind, applied to the body of nature-as-dead, breeds monsters. Thus, *Frankenstein* becomes the Ur-myth of technological modernity, but more, of a habit of mind that still sheds horrors upon the living world.

Thoreau is not captured by either side of this dualism. Instead, he swerved to a newly emergent alternative tradition that was, depending on how one tells the history, either repressed by Cartesianism, or emergent as a response to the problem Descartes created but could not solve: life's evident self-creation and hence its persistent ability to invent for itself its own history. As natural historians began to recognize starting in the 1780s, this "natural" history not only outstrips human history by orders of magnitude but is integrally part of the self-making of the very planet we inhabit, threatening human exceptionalism on the most visceral level. This is the threat, emerging from terrestrial science, that Emerson must work to contain. Thoreau, by contrast, exults that "man is but the place where I stand," and the view thence is "infinite"; as he adds, "I find that there is other than me." This is nothing less than an epistemic break, a paradigm shift that allows, as Thoreau says, any eyes to "see new worlds at once."[5]

How to name this new paradigm? Two decades ago I titled my collection of Thoreau's writings on science *Material Faith* (1999), intending to highlight the peculiar tension between "materialism" as soulless or disenchanted, and Thoreau's reenchanted vision of materiality, a vision whose spiritual faith made him, as Catherine Albanese observes, the progenitor of an American tradition of nature religion.[6] In *Seeing New Worlds* (1995), I suggested a genealogy for this paradigm under the phrase "empirical holism," by which I designated an approach to the world through what we now call an "ecological" sensibility: rather than divide nature from the human, then agonize over our resulting sense of alienation, empirical holism (I now rather wish I had called it, in line with the Pragmatists, "experiential" holism) instead tracks the identities and interconnections of individual, constituent parts, as their interactions generate ever-ramifying couplings, loops, and networks which can be traced only experientially or, in the more technical term, empirically.[7]

The empirical researches of today's terrestrial or "earth system scientists" have given us a name that has stuck: the Anthropocene. This term implicitly recognizes that a new player has lately entered the field: Earth itself.[8] As a result, the emergent realization that humans have assumed geological agency on a reactive planet—what one could call the conceptual Anthropocene—is finally blowing apart Descartes's centuries-old world. No wonder we feel a rumble of apocalypse! Yet who is this "we"? One virtue of the contested term "the Anthropocene" has been its ability to destabilize the *Anthropos*: are "we" central, and, thanks to our technological prowess, in control? Or have our unintended consequences spun us out of the illusion of control altogether? This points to the further problem: how can there be a unified Anthropos at all, given that technological modernity achieved dominance only by dehumanizing all non-white peoples into either labor or gold?[9] For it turns out that Earth isn't the raw material out of which we are given special license to build humanity's heaven; it's *Earth*. It's an ancient planet that has been writing its own story for billions of years, a story written in the most intimate reciprocity with all life, which discovered billions of years ago a talent for engendering, out of the material matrix of matter, its own living matrix, its so-called "environment." It turns out we're not so special; life has been a geological agent ever since the very beginning of life itself. How did we ever imagine we were excluded from this talent, or exempted from its perilous consequences? Or that we could shield ourselves from this fact by naming all beings other than ourselves "nonhumans," designating them in the usual Cartesian fashion by what they are not?—not ensouled, not language-bearing, not carriers of meaning, not of our world. By naming everything not-me, not-us, as effectively "out of our world," is to say, in effect, that we still imagine ourselves living "out-of-*this*-world," in a bubbled spaceship fantasy that hides how intimately embedded we are, body and soul, in this world, *in* this planet not "on" it, at the most cellular, elemental, levels—the infrastructural levels beneath the level of our very consciousness.

Until now.

Our task, we who ride the cusp of our epistemological and ontological break, is to find our way to a post-dualistic world. True, this "we" leaves out most of the actual Anthropos, for as the French anthropologist Phillipe Descola shows in immense detail, the Cartesian tradition, what he calls "naturalism," characterizes only a small portion of the world's peoples, none others of whom isolate "nature" as the deanimated ground for human self-fulfillment. We who do, who have ended so many other worlds only to find we are now ending our own as well, can move forward only by forging an effective post-dualism. This, as Hans Jonas remarks, will not mean we cease to be marked by dualism: "any postdualistic theory of being [has] inescapably to deal with the two pieces which dualism left behind," those dueling monisms of matter and mind, materialism and idealism.[10] Yes, the break that powered modernity must be healed, but the scar will remain visible so long as our heritage leaves traces in futurity.

The first step toward post-dualism is to turn back to Earth, to reground ourselves in terrestrial existences. This is Bruno Latour's call in *Down to Earth*, his recent political analysis of the new climate regime, in which he seeks to redirect attention away from "nature" and toward "the Terrestrial," centered on the wholly singular fact that we do dwell on Earth, a planet whose "system of engendering brings into confrontation agents, actors, animate beings that all have distinct capacities for reacting." Orienting ourselves as "Terrestrial" allows us to see "that not only points of view but also points of life proliferate," that "the Terrestrial" itself is an independent actor with a wholly different political role than that of our ancient arbiter, Nature.[11] But I sense a hopeful, bracing futurity to this orientation not captured by that quotidian word *terrestrial*: will this not be the work of the newest generation, the generation of Greta Thunberg, Extinction Rebellion, and Black Lives Matter? Can we accede to their bitter hopefulness, their angry demands for a livable future? We speak of a "Millennial" generation. But the last thing we need is the old millennial promise of heaven-on-earth; that was the project of modernity, which stranded us on a heating planet, 97 percent of whose biomass has been converted into human beings and their domesticates, precipitating mass extinction, acidifying oceans, melting poles, microplasticized waters, and all the rest. So might we call this turning "Terrennial"? Instead of imagining yet another heaven-on-earth, another paradise-to-be-regained, just around the corner, with just a few more turns of the technological crank, let's imagine this Earth as heaven already, were we to unblind ourselves. This is, of course, the thought that motivated Thoreau when he exclaimed, in *Walden*, "Heaven is under our feet as well as over our heads."[12]

Thoreau's Material Faith

This crisis may feel new to us, but in fact it has been visibly percolating since well before Thoreau's lifetime; it takes generations to shift a paradigm with such historical and ideological tenacity.[13] Anomalies began to emerge by the mid-1700s, when the field then called "physical geography" introduced global comparative natural and cultural histories to the European metropole. Over the next hundred years, geology became the great engine of anomalies as emergent industrialization called for endless supplies of mineral wealth, above all coal—ancient solar energy captured by millions of years of plant life, compacted by the weight of Earth into solid, burnable carbon that had only to be mined. "Fossil fuel," we say without thinking. The quest to divine where such resources could be found, and the labor of miners whose excavations revealed deep patterns of stratification, produced the most disquieting anomaly of all, the realization that only an Earth immensely older than Genesis could have produced such fossilized energy; Earth was not a created object but an ongoing, unfolding historical event. Even as Thoreau moved to Walden Pond, the discovery of Earth as a self-organizing, evolving planet, one stellar body among the uncountable others taking shape in what Alexander von Humboldt called "the great garden of the universe," was ripping apart biblical certainties.[14] The further discoveries that geological strata are packed with relics of once-living beings, and that Earth's surface is everywhere alive and inhabited, from subterranean depths to atmospheric heights, by everything from microscopic infusoria to those immense mobile caskets of oil called whales—even life itself was inhabited by life, in the form of bacteria—were forcing not just a reorganization of knowledge but a reimagining of the entire ontology of human existence. As the old paradigm began undoing itself from within, Thoreau jumped to the new with sheer exhilaration. But the early adopters—Humboldt, Darwin, Thoreau, Melville, among others—were exceptional. The "new worlds" they saw by the 1850s remain unseen by most of us even today; the paradigm shift they propelled has still failed to reorient politics, or economics, or philosophy, or the social sciences, or the humanities, all of which developed their modern forms by underscoring, in the face of the ominous new findings, the reactionary priority of human exceptionalism, maintained by an uncrossable barrier dividing humans from nonhumans.[15]

Which raises an important question: how did Thoreau become post-dualist? What anomalies induced him, a Harvard-trained humanist deeply imbued with Emerson's foundational division between "Soul" and "Nature," to engage this new, vitalized form of materialism? This query is aided by Lorraine Daston's recent book *Against Nature*, which offers a three-part taxonomy: specific natures, local natures, and universal natural law. First, "specific natures" are inborn natures, "species," and as such, they underlie all taxonomic systems; by faithfully reproducing themselves, they thus reproduce the given order of the world. Inquiries into specific natures investigate the "nature" or "essence" of a thing, "its ontological identity card," according to its inborn traits. This most ancient concept of nature underlies our most basic vocabulary, including the words *physics* via the Greek root *phusis*, or "growth," and *nature* via the Greek *natura* or "to be born."[16] Second, "local natures" are tied to the power of place. Inquiries into the distinctiveness of any given place examine nature's customs in that place, patch by patch, together with the resulting interplay of natural and human customs as they generate coherent communities. As Daston observes, this ancient integrative model (she dates it as far back as Herodotus) was dramatically updated in the nineteenth century into a vast new scientific research program, first inspired by Humboldt's *Views of Nature*—a book that shaped the youthful Darwin's founding conception of nature, and that Thoreau not only read but claimed as the model for his own work.[17] Humboldt introduced Thoreau to plants not merely as static taxonomic species, but as the structuring elements of what he called "the physiognomy"—or face—"of nature"; the outcome of Humboldt's research program was the integrated approach to natural/ human systems captured in the nineteenth-century word "ecology" (coined by a follower of Humboldt), and more recently by Earth system scientists' research into what they are calling "critical zones," a further outgrowth of Humboldt's scientific innovations.[18]

Finally, "universal natural law" emerged in the early modern era of seventeenth-century Europe, thanks to Descartes's pioneering work, as the "uniform, universal, and inviolable" laws instituted by God, envisioned as a "divine legislator" imposing laws on nature exactly as a monarch upon his kingdom, laws which nature "obeyed" exactly as a clock might be said to obey the laws built into it by the clockmaker. Hence the power of Descartes's innovation: nature, like the clock, is a machine with no agency of its own. To grant nature any degree of agency, intelligence, or rationality—that is, to imagine nature as a clock that not only *tells* the time, but *knows* the time it tells—was to risk idolatry and charges of heresy, charges which, in an era of religious warfare, were not trivial.[19]

Thoreau participated in all three taxonomies of "nature." His formal journey began with his era's standard schooling in "universal nature" coded through training in Newtonian celestial mechanics, by which students learned the order of natural law. As Daston explains, the quest for an equivalent order in the political realm "enlisted the language of rights guaranteed by nature and therefore universal and inalienable"—an Enlightenment discourse heralded by every American reader of Thomas Jefferson's Declaration of

Independence, which based the right of revolution on "the laws of nature and of nature's God." Thoreau also imbibed the updated Christian Romantic form of universal natural law through Emerson's Neoplatonic theology in *Nature* (1836), which, after opening by dividing soul from body, concludes by suggesting that material nature does not actually exist except as a carrier by which divine law might reach the human heart: "When a faithful thinker, resolute to detach every object from personal relations, and see it in the light of thought, shall, at the same time, kindle science with the fire of the holiest affections, then will God go forth anew into the creation." The hallmark of Transcendentalism was this elevation of the human from God's mere likeness, to God's literal embodiment, walking forth anew in his creation in human form, not merely "seeing" new worlds but "building" them out of the raw and passive resource offered by nature as commodity. "Build, therefore, your own world," commands Emerson in his final paragraph: "As fast as you conform your life to the pure idea in your mind, that will unfold its great proportions. A correspondent revolution in things will attend the influx of the spirit," bringing "the kingdom of man over nature ... a dominion such as now is beyond his dream of God."[20]

Thoreau, taking Emerson's cue, went to Walden Pond and did just that, converting the matter or "building material" of nature into his model house. Note that Thoreau's initial inquiry at Walden was not into the nature of *nature*, but, as his opening chapter "Economy" shows, into the specific nature of the *human*: "When we consider what, to use the words of the catechism, is the chief end of man, and what are the true necessaries and means of life, it appears as if men had deliberately chosen the common mode of living because they preferred it to any other." This query initiated the classic Transcendentalist quest, pursued in solitude in the classic Emersonian way, for only in solitude could one live deliberately, perfecting one's inner character and drawing ever closer to union with God. Emerson's call for this "upbuilding of a man" was Thoreau's catalyst for *Walden*, a staged demonstration of self-culture, or the deliberate, intentional cultivation of the inner self, by which the soul, like a plant, would grow organically into full self-realization. It was this impulse toward intellectual *phusis*, or humanist self-directed growth, that gave birth to the Transcendentalist movement.[21]

But Thoreau's inquiry into the specific nature of the human was complicated by the very setting he chose: the distinctive local place marked off and known as Walden Pond. Thus, his project unfolded within "local nature," the beloved New England landscape of his home and birthplace, to which he'd recently returned after an excruciating period of exile in New York City. All the while Thoreau was *building* his new selfhood through the literal building of his Walden house, and *cultivating* his selfhood further through the literal cultivation of his bean-field—tropes he milks in the first half of *Walden*—he was also enjoying a growing acquaintance with the wild, unconstrained and unscheduled local natures that surrounded him, that even moved right into the house with him: the air, sounds, and smells; the wasps that took up winter residence, disappearing into the crevices; the little mouse who appeared out of those crevices to explore his Spartan pantry and share his meals; the woodchuck who ate his beans; the rabbit who spurned his charity; the loon who gamed him on the surface of the pond, then withdrew, uttering "one of those prolonged howls, as if calling on the god of loons to aid him."[22]

Thoreau's interest in natural history, originally inspired by his beloved, and deceased, elder brother John, grew as he worked natural historical details into the book he'd come to Walden to write, a memorial to their journey together up the Concord and Merrimack Rivers. Thoreau's independent study of natural history, initially modeled on the British parson-naturalist Gilbert White and deeply researched in local town histories, intensified during his third and final summer at the pond. For during that summer of 1847, Thoreau became a field collector for Louis Agassiz, the Swiss natural scientist who'd been befriended by Humboldt and who, thanks to Humboldt's assistance, had recently arrived in Boston, where he took up a professorship at Harvard's new Lawrence Scientific School. The charismatic Agassiz introduced himself to Boston by giving a series of lectures at Tremont Temple to audiences numbering in the thousands, who gathered to hear him declare the "Plan of Creation in the Animal Kingdom." So taken was Thoreau by this new form of natural science—this local manifestation of the new global research program—that he planned to join the scientific expedition to Lake Superior organized by the geologist Charles T. Jackson, Emerson's brother-in-law, even writing a publisher that the printing of *A Week on the Concord and Merrimack Rivers* must be finished soon, for he planned to be away on "a journey of considerable length."[23]

Jackson did not select Thoreau for his expedition. Instead, after leaving Walden in September 1847, Thoreau stayed in Concord and worked up *A Week* for publication. When finally published in 1849, Thoreau's debut book precipitated a complicated legacy, troubling his friendship with Emerson (who failed to support it in public) and upsetting his hopes for a conventional literary career. As the book's poor sales forced Thoreau into debt, he shelved the growing manuscript of *Walden* and reinvented himself as a land surveyor. It was exactly at this moment, when Thoreau the disillusioned ex-Emersonian was learning how to take transepts across the fields, swamps, and forests of Concord, stomping through the underbrush, hacking away at plants, that he took up Humboldt's writings, newly available in English, starting with *Views of Nature*.

From this, Humboldt's most popular book, Thoreau worked his way through several other Humboldt titles, and thence out to other practitioners of the new Humboldtian paradigm, starting with the South American explorations of Charles Darwin and the botanical studies of the American botanist Asa Gray. (Gray, notably, was one of the few privy to Darwin's ongoing work on evolution, for which Gray was supplying botanical data. In turn, Darwin helped Gray establish that plant distribution was not the fixed result of divine creation but the dynamic result of climate change and the migration of species across continents.) Through Gray's cutting-edge botany guides, Thoreau learned how to discipline and inform his intensifying study of *local* nature by deploying the taxonomies devised to study *species* nature. At the same time, his reading in the scientific exploration narratives of Humboldt, Darwin, John C. Frémont, and others taught him how to set his own local nature into the new global Humboldtian paradigm by which each local place gained new meaning—that is, gained significance as the planetary Earth realized in its fullness in this one specific place—through comparison with other specific local places, generating the patchy geographies that later generations would learn to call ecosystems. Thoreau pursued ecological field studies for the rest of his life, gathering comparative data whenever he could afford to travel—across Massachusetts, up into the White Mountains and the Maine Woods, out to Cape Cod, along the Canadian seaway, into New Jersey pine barrens and Minnesota prairies. And everywhere, along beaches and up mountains and down rivers, what he saw was—*plants*. What had once been undifferentiated green diversified, through the 1850s, into an ever more precise index to local ecologies and environments, from microclimates to regional differences to the broad cyclicity of nature. Plants became more than objects to identify and name; they became, in Thoreau's rewriting of "views of nature," modes of *thinking*. And that changed everything.

Thoreau's Plant Thinking

Think back to the opening chapter of Walden, "Economy," in which Thoreau addresses the nature of man by defining, as a first step, the "gross necessaries of life and what methods have been taken to obtain them." First, food: for many creatures, he observes, this is all they need, with perhaps a little shelter; "None of the brute creation requires more than Food and Shelter." To these, man (at least its New English subspecies) adds "Clothing, and Fuel," which are all, Thoreau further postulates, nothing more than the means toward the one, sole "grand necessity" for our bodies: "to keep warm, to keep the vital heat in us."[24] These are, notably—Thoreau notes it—the conditions for animal life only. He doesn't think to add, say, sunlight and water, the two absolute requisites for plant life. At this early stage of *Walden*, plant life figures only as food, the "few inches of palatable grass" needed by the bison of the prairie (or, later, the few leaves of palatable bean plants needed by the woodchucks of Walden).

But of course all of *Walden* is predicated on plant life: it is, after all, subtitled "Life in the *Woods*." But how many plants exist in *Walden* in and for themselves? They exist as building materials, like the pines Thoreau cuts down for his house frame, or as food like his beans, or as stage settings like the two great chestnut trees shading his house, or as furniture both mental and physical—as in the delightful moment when, to clean his floor, he sets his things outdoors and marvels to see his three-legged table, still stacked with books, pen, and ink, "standing amid the pines and hickories," with "blackberry vines run round its legs; pine cones, chestnut burs, and strawberry leaves ... strewn about," as if the forms decorating his furniture had found their originals. Plants are everywhere in *Walden*, but they exist as unconscious elements of his experience, part of the overall plenitude of his Walden experiment. Notably, though, they are already entering the text as agents of interaction, as when the blackberry vines entwine the legs of his writing table, or when a rainy day keeps him indoors and, in his solitude, he became "suddenly sensible of such sweet and beneficent society in Nature ... an infinite and unaccountable friendliness all at once like an atmosphere sustaining me. ... Every little pine needle expanded and swelled with sympathy and befriended me." As he asks a few pages later, "Shall I not have intelligence with the earth? Am I not partly leaves and vegetable mould myself?"[25] This vegetal communion is friendly, even companionate. Plants are beginning to compose an alternative society, a welcoming society whose existence he never suspected until he found himself housed within it.

Plants may not figure centrally in *Walden* itself, but outside its pages they figure ever more centrally in Thoreau's thoughts, until they emerge in his post-*Walden* years as the structure of thinking itself. One must turn the pages of the *Journal* to see how fully this is true, how over the months and years plants move from the periphery of Thoreau's vision to its center. Whether causally or coincidentally, this process began exactly as Thoreau was articulating his break with Emerson, and exactly when, immersed in *Views of Nature*, he began to quote Alexander von Humboldt in his *Journal*, as he does in April 1850 on the transmission of sounds in the night air, exactly as he's noting, for the first time, the blooming dates of the earliest flowers, an act of knowing that reveals new relationships: "A name enriches your associations wonderfully." By summer's end he has acquired a botany text—likely Asa Gray's *Manual of Botany* (1848)—and is identifying plants by their scientific name: the choke cherry, *Pyrus arbutifolia*; the cymes of "one of the Viburnums" (he's unsure which one); the spotted "Polygonum Persicaria." He is now listing flowers in the back of the volume as well.[26]

Through the following winter of 1851, Thoreau's reading expands from Humboldt to his associates: in May 1851 he downloads extensive notes from Francois André Michaux's *North American Sylva* (1819) on the ranges, uses, and leafing times of trees, which tells him, for instance, the southerly range of the canoe birch and how to identify "the turning point between winter & summer." His reading in Asa Gray inspires a rambling essay on how the

mind develops, like the plant, simultaneously "in two opposite directions—
upward to expand in the light & air; & downwards avoiding the light to
form the root. One half is aerial the other subterranean ... send[ing] down
a tap root to the centre of things." Two weeks later, he is annotating Charles
Darwin's *Voyage of a Naturalist round the World*, with particular attention
to the distribution of species and insights into ecological interrelatedness.[27]
What would it mean, Thoreau wonders after a long session with Darwin,
to travel "in your own country even in your own neighborhood" with the
eyes of a Darwin? It would mean combining the virtues of dwelling with the
virtues of travel: "You would be so thoroughly prepared to understand what
you saw."[28] Naturally, whenever he's on the road he stops off in Boston or
Cambridge to consult with his new friends Édouard Desor and James Elliot
Cabot, the naturalists working with Louis Agassiz. Thoreau's program of
re-education advances rapidly: by summer's end he is ready to pronounce on
"the precision and copiousness of botanical language," adding the wish that
it could be applied "to the description of moral qualities!"[29] "No doubt," he
ventures two weeks later, "like plants we are fed through the atmosphere &
the varying atmospheres of various seasons of the year feed us variously."
Plant thinking has now become his model for the human body as well as
the human mind: this, he adds (quoting James Wilkinson), "is the office of
the lungs—to drink the atmosphere with the planet dissolved in it." And
plant thinking has now become both the method and the goal of his artistry:
"Often I feel that my head stands out too dry—when it should be immersed.
A writer, a man writing is the scribe of all nature—he is the corn & the grass
& the atmosphere writing."[30]

The following year, 1852, would consolidate this turn in Thoreau's
thought and practice. This was, he said, "my year of observation," the year
he vowed to refuse newspapers and lectures and even his friends to devote
himself entirely to the phenomenal world. That January he took out the
shelved manuscript of *Walden* and began to write it from a good book into
a great one, deliberately cultivating his moral and artistic development on
the model of the farmer cultivating his crops, or the poet courting his lover.
"Obey—report," he admonished himself in his *Journal*.[31] This could be
no mere parlor exercise. All that year his daily walks—ten miles or more,
virtually every day—structured the daily rhythm of his writing, in a practice
that swelled his *Journal* into a minute phenomenological record that would
not cease until death. Through the 1850s, as Emerson moved deeper into the
austerity of universal natural law, Thoreau moved deeper into the romance
of "corn, grass, and atmosphere." "Simply our paths diverge," he wrote in
a reflective moment.[32] By 1860, Emerson would end his great, dark essay
"Fate" by counseling us to

> build altars to the Blessed Unity which holds nature and soul in perfect
> solution, and compels every atom to serve an universal end. ... Let us

build altars to the Beautiful Necessity. ... which rudely or softly educates him to the perception that there are no contingencies; that Law rules throughout existence, a Law which is not intelligent but intelligence.[33]

Thoreau, by contrast, lived by the vow he gave himself on Christmas day, 1851: "Ah give me pure mind—pure thought. Let me not be in haste to detect the *universal law*, let me see more clearly a particular instance. ... Perchance it may convince such that there are more things in heaven & earth than are dreamed of in their philosophy."[34] The impulse that took Emerson to the dissolution of particular facts in the great menstruum of Idea, the intelligence of the Law, took Thoreau ever deeper into the great flux of the phenomenal world, the intelligence of the Earth. By April 1852 he was ready to ask,

> Why should just these sights & sounds accompany our life? Why should I hear the chattering of blackbirds—why smell the skunk each year? I would fain explore the mysterious relation between myself and these things. I would at least know what these things unavoidably are— make a chart of our life—know how its shores trend—that butterflies reappear & when—know why just this circle of creatures completes the world. ... As Cawley loved a garden, so I a forest. Observe all kinds of coincidences—as what kinds of birds come with what flowers.[35]

This project would consume Thoreau's energies through the last decade of his life, which he devoted to a particularist investigation of "all kinds of coincidences" and their various correlations and couplings across seasonal time, tracked across the narrative form of his travel writings as well as in such localized nature essays as "Autumnal Tints" and "Wild Apples" and across reams of seasonal notes, lists, and charts.[36]

In later years, Emerson admired Thoreau's uncanny ability to tell, from the flora alone, the date of the year within two days. In Emerson's telling, the plant world became a living sundial relating the time of the day and the seasons of the calendar to the grand mathematical cycles of celestial mechanics: a lawful universe, governed from the greatest nebulae to the very blackbirds and skunk cabbages, in a formula Emerson imagines could be written on a thumbnail.[37] But Thoreau's own practice animates the sundial of the Earth quite differently. Emerson's clock of the universe can *tell* the time, but only superadded Intelligence can *know* it; by contrast, Thoreau's living sundial is composed of vital beings who not only *know* the time but *generate* it, "fetch the year around." Instead of passive expressions of universal laws governing temporality, plants become time's active and generative agents—Thoreau's guides to an emergent planetary reality, his models of counter-friction to an industrial modernity which remakes *humans* into passive expressions, not of planetary but of "railroad" time, artificially bound to the industrial, globalizing machine by its relentless demands and mechanical clockwork rhythms. Thoreau pressed back by elaborating seasonal time instead, what he called "living in season," by which humans could recapture their own living agency by dwelling amidst that "mysterious relation" between self and nature. Thus we, too, might produce time, produce life rather than death, in symbiotic engagement with the material beings who, like us, both produce, and drink, the atmosphere with the planet dissolved in it.

Beyond Bifurcation: Either Death or Symbiosis

In sum, Emerson's "Beautiful Necessity" is a direct descendent of the seventeenth-century "Universal Natural Law," a Christian theology that, as Lorraine Daston explains, mutated during the Enlightenment into a secular metaphysics in which the only loopholes were the exercise of free will: "Acts of divine will produced miracles; acts of human will, moral freedom."[38] While Thoreau has not left that formation entirely behind, he does invert it through a disciplined combination of the taxonomic work characteristic of "species nature" with the new ecological research program initiated by Alexander von Humboldt, whose roots in the "local nature" of place studies hearken all the way back to ancient Greece. The result is an entirely different cosmology from the clockwork universe instantiated by Descartes, who by denying intelligence to nonhuman nature defended the human against the threat of a nonhuman nature with will, agency, and self-direction—a self-willed nature, a "wild" nature beyond the human, whose heresies of chance and contingency both Emerson and Descartes longed to master and control.

What scientific process could have reopened such an awareness of the "mysterious relation" between subject and object? Descartes's canonical deanimation of life was challenged around 1800 by German empirical investigations into the material processes that characterize living beings, processes that bely the very boundary between organized, or "organic," beings and the "inorganic" elements of which they are composed. These investigations were triggered in part by Humboldt's early experimental work on the relationship between galvanic, or electrical, currents and the animation of living bodies. As Joan Steigerwald has written, these "instrumental explorations of organic bodies expanded the domain of organic vitality and its boundary with the inorganic, confusing any clear delineation of the living and the nonliving." The German investigations into the nature of life were not, for the most part, available to Emerson and Thoreau except through the work of Humboldt, who in his popular book *Cosmos* (1845–7) dismissed the division between organic and inorganic, life and nonlife, as useless for understanding Earth's living processes.[39] As he wrote (in a volume of *Cosmos* which Thoreau annotated), "knowledge of the reciprocal action of air, sea, and land teaches us that great meteorological phenomena cannot be comprehended" apart from the structure and nature of Earth—or what, in *Views of Nature*, Humboldt called the "planetary organism."[40]

One of the outcomes of such thinking was the work of Humboldt's colleague Justus von Liebig, whose book *Animal Chemistry* (1842) Thoreau cited in *Walden* as his source for the notion of "animal heat." The connection might seem obscure, but Liebig's groundbreaking work on soil composition and plant growth was just then making the rounds of the practical farmers of Concord, for his earlier book, *Organic Chemistry* (1840), had established the previously unsuspected fact that plants derive nutrients not only from organic sources—such as the manure farmers used to fatten their lean soils—but also from inorganic sources: water, air, minerals in the soil. Plants, then, literally do drink the atmosphere with the planet dissolved in it. By demonstrating that the boundary between life and nonlife was permeable and eternally circulating, Liebig proved the utility of artificial fertilizers, a discovery that was swiftly revolutionizing agricultural science, including the practices of Concord's struggling farmers.[41]

In both cases—animal heat, plant flourishing—Thoreau's reading in Humboldt and Liebig opened up the old interface between organism and environment into an expanding ecological realm that gathered up everything on Earth, from the coal seams underground through the forests of New England to the atmosphere swirling above, transforming them all into parts of an ongoing process of mutual consumption and production that blurred any boundary between life and nonlife. As Humboldt wrote, "Metamorphosis, union, and separation afford evidence of the eternal circulation of the elements in inorganic nature no less than in the living cells of plants and animals." Earth might appear to be "a laboratory of death and decay ... but that great natural process of slow combustion, which we call decay, does not terminate in annihilation. The liberated bodies combine to form other structures, and through the agency of the active forces which are incorporated in them a new life germinates from the bosom of the earth."[42]

That is, agential matter, in Humboldt, is eternally producing and circulating life through the grand processes of decay and regeneration. The empirical study of living, phenomenal nature literally deconstructs not merely the founding dualism of me and not-me, subject and object, or man and nature, but between spirit and matter, life and death. In Humboldt's vision, the human spirit itself dissolves into the soil, to become planetary compost: "But with the wilting of each blossom of the spirit, whenever, in the storm of the times, the works of creative art are scattered, so forever will new life sprout forth from the womb of the Earth."[43]

Whither, then, the human? Thoreau first framed this boundary zone as a crisis in the summer of 1846, when he left his Walden home to climb

Maine's Mt. Katahdin. High on the mountaintop he felt the ghost falling away from the machine:

> What is it to be admitted to a museum, to see a myriad of particular things, compared with being shown some star's surface, some hard matter in its home! I stand in awe of my body, this matter to which I am bound has become so strange to me. I fear not spirits, ghosts, of which I am one,—that my body might—but I fear bodies, I tremble to meet them. What is this Titan that has possession of me?[44]

Thoreau's sense of slippage followed him back to Walden Pond, where he was already thinking about Liebig's notion of "animal heat" by which food "is the fuel which keeps up the internal combustion" of the body. In the fall of 1846, Thoreau brought together the implications of Liebig's science with his own uncanny experience on Katahdin:

> All material things are in some sense man's kindred, and subject to the same laws with him.
>
> Even a taper is his relative—and burns not eternally, as some say of lamps found burning in ancient sepulchers—but only a certain number of his hours.
>
> These things belong to the same dynasty or system of things. He witnesses their wasting and decay as well as his own[.] What man's experience does not embrace is to him stationary and eternal[.] Whether he wakes or sleeps the lamp still burns on and burns out—completing its life within his own.
>
> He sees such objects at a very near angle. They have a very large parallax to him—but not so those tapers the fixed stars which are not both lit and burnt out in the life of a man—yet they too are his distant relations.[45]

Here, material bodies become "burning tapers," "distant relations" subject to the same universal rules of combustion and decay as every one of us. Nevertheless, Thoreau is still speaking from the perspective of an animal body, newly aware of his kinship with all the other bounded and material bodies that must burn, and keep burning, to stay alive. While this extends human kinship to all fellow bodies bonded in shared mortality, plants would figure here—had he included them—only as "fuel," like the bison's few inches of grass. Thoreau has decentered his humanity, but his is still a metaphysics of self and other, body and environment, in which plants figure as background elements, the invisible support staff. Thoreau is still plant blind. He is not being ecological—not yet.

Only after Thoreau's years at Walden, starting with that remarkable turn in 1850, does he start being ecological, as he becomes aware of plants as beings in themselves, worthy of naming and identifying, with histories, even individualities, of their own—as when he details the history of this or that significant tree, or follows the tragic death of favorite trees as they fall to the woodchopper's ax. And the more that plants emerge in his awareness, the less he sees them as objects—solid bodies analogous to his own, only rooted in place—and the more he experiences them as a special, even an uncanny, *kind* of object: not burning, combusting body-objects, but objects-that-are-really-events; and as events, objects that are ongoing, hence *phenomenal*. That is, plants first enter Thoreau's thinking as indexical, dials that point to time, whether daily or seasonal or measured in centuries, by merging their very corporeality with time's passing. Yet how could such phenomenal events be so wholly real and solid, so ontologically present, even commanding, as the plants he was learning to see? On the taxonomic level of species, science was teaching him that the proper question was not about the single, individual plant, but how to abstract it into its species kind; yet the Thoreau who jests about making appointments with this or that individual flower is learning to see each one as also a unique, historical being in itself—a biographical being, simultaneously individual and social; unique and representative; solid and phenomenal. This new kind of object utterly defies the bifurcation that had, since Descartes, separated the primary "real" from the secondary "phenomenal." These objects, these bewildering eternally emergent plant beings, were both real and phenomenal, simultaneously: this was seeing a whole new world indeed.

Thoreau's dawning realization brought into visibility an entire new realm of problems. The classic explication of Cartesian bifurcation, given by John Locke, imagined a grain of wheat being divided and divided again, until all its secondary, phenomenal qualities (such as color, texture, and flavor) were gone; yet it remained wheat nevertheless by virtue of its primary qualities (such as solidity, extension, figure, and mobility) which alone were "real."[46] Plants posed two problems with Locke's assertion: first, the grain of wheat is a seed. Divide the seed and you get not two seeds, but no seed; the generative principle that is its reason for being is destroyed. What remains of the operation is not "wheat" at all, but something else. Second, imagine the wheat grain is planted and grows until it sows a field of wheat: the farmer cuts down half the wheat, then another half, then another half; at some point it is no longer a field of wheat, but, again, something else. This was exactly the situation Thoreau faced in the winter of 1852, as he revisited Walden Pond with his renewed interest in writing *Walden* only to discover how radically, in the five years since he left, it had been deforested. There were no trees left; even the two great chestnuts that had shaded his house and scented the spring air were gone. How many trees could one remove from the woods until it was no longer a woods, but something else? Was a Walden without trees still Walden?

The rest of Thoreau's life was devoted to unpacking these insights. The seed became not merely a metaphysical problem but an actual, material body which carried, and alone carried, the principle of life to the next generation. Any future succession depended, he insisted, on that material embodiment. How each kind of seed formed itself—winged like maples, or plumed like milkweed, or husked like acorns, or carried like cherries in juicy, edible casings—was one set of concerns, relevant because, as Thoreau realized, the material body of each seed actively anticipated its phenomenal future. The winged maple seed that spiraled away from its parents' shade, the plumed willow seeds that floated over water to be captured and carried to the riverbank where they might lodge in the perfect situation for the flourishing of willows, the acorn or chestnut buried by a squirrel, the cherry carried by a robin, or the apple by a crow. ... Each seed not only embodied the entirety of its history and future, but transported that history and future with it. Every seed, even the least, was the carrier of *Kairos*, all time coiled into presence. As Thoreau says, marveling at the prismatic milkweed seeds he releases rising to the winds, "for this end these silken streamers have been perfecting all summer, snugly packed in this light chest—a perfect adaptation to this end—a prophecy of the fall & of future springs. Who could believe in prophecies of Daniel or of Miller that the world would end this summer while one Milkweed with faith matured its seeds!"[47] Each seed, and every plant that lives, is a standing refutation of the apocalypse.

His second set of concerns became the immeasurable totality of all the worlds into which the seed projects itself: the flowing water of river or the percolating water of swamp, the winds that carry birch seeds onto the snow and the juncos that survive the New England winter by eating them, the pine cones whose winged seeds carry them far from the smothering shade of the pine forest, and the squirrels who bury the nourishing acorns under the pines, assuring the succession of New England's unique forest ecology. As Thoreau's studies lengthened, the links multiplied, generating connective loops that grew until their ligatures tied the planet together. Thoreau's "faith in a seed" insisted (against prevailing doctrine) that seeds and successions were all material; it was materiality all the way down; but now, materiality figured not as passive carrier of spirit or transparent embodiment of Idea, but as active agency, self-forming, self-acting, self-organizing.[48] Thoreau's endlessly ramifying plant lists and multiplying charts of seasonal events were not merely barren collations of dry facts, as they once seemed to generations of literary scholars, but vibrant indices to entire complexes of interwoven lifeworlds, whose interrelationships became Thoreau's obsessive study.

Plants, in short, queered Thoreau's inherited metaphysics.[49] Bounded bodies could still be imagined within the traditional framework as actors on a stage, centers of being surrounded by a supportive environment. But plants-as-events became entire intersecting and overlapping temporalities, from the mushroom that appeared and disappeared in a day to the enduring oaks, hundreds of years old, Thoreau discovered in Inches Woods. (They barely survived him; soon after his death they were cut down to fuel the Civil War.) By 1857, Thoreau's insights had matured enough to define his field of interest against the objectifying path of both modern science and modern expansionist consumer economies, which, in a long and still-unpublished *Journal* passage, he linked as two aspects of a single, destructive historical moment:

> I think that the man of science makes this mistake—& the mass of mankind along with him, that you should coolly give your chief attention to the phenomenon which excites you—as something independent on you—and not as it is related to you. The important fact is its effect on me. ... With regard to such objects I find that it is not they themselves—(with which the men of science deal) that concern me. The point of interest is somewhere <u>between</u> me & them [i.e. the objects]. What beavers these men are! They have rushed up the streams like a colony of beavers have dammed all the large lakes ... thus turning [the] forces of nature against itself that they might float their spoils out of the country[.]
>
> ... Think how much land they have flowed without asking Nature's leave. It is as when an army of mice girdles a forest of pines. ... [Nature] feels 10 000 vermin gnawing at the base of her noblest trees ... till the work of destruction being complete—they scamper off to ransack some other wilderness. ... Whose houses does it build? ... For a man to pride himself on this kind of wealth as if it enriched him—is as ridiculous as if one struggling in the ocean with a bag of gold on his back should gasp out—"I am worth a hundred thousand dollars." I see his ineffectual struggles just as plainly—& what it is that sinks him.[50]

This long meditation, a response to the clearcutting of Maine's white pine forests, reminds us that Thoreau learned how to think "somewhere <u>between</u>" himself and "the objects"—that is, how to think beyond three centuries of mind/body dualism—by following out, with all the precision conferred by botanical terminology, the implications of plant-thinking for the relational realm, the *moral* realm, the very project begun with his first reading of Asa Gray's botany.

Thoreau had also read Humboldt's several accounts of the role forests play in generating moisture and moderating temperatures, such that plant-life was demonstrably a major component of climate. Humboldt documented the calamity prepared for future generations by clearcutting, which desiccates the land, lowers water levels, raises local temperatures, and destroys topsoil cover, all of which added urgency to Thoreau's call that the town of Concord appoint forest wardens to protect its green commons.[51] But he also had in mind what Humboldt called "the influence of the physical world upon the moral, the mysterious interworking of the sensory and the extrasensory." As Humboldt asked, "Who does not feel a different mood in the dark shade of a beech tree, upon hills crowned with lonely firs, or in the middle of a grassy meadow, where the wind rustles in the trembling leaves of a birch?" In this way, the natural character of each region, its "climatic conditions," will affect the character of a people; furthermore, insists Humboldt, the primary factor in this

> impression is the covering of vegetation. The animal organism lacks the mass; the mobility of individual creatures, and often their small size, keeps them from our view. The plant kingdom, however, impresses our imagination through a constant immensity. Its massive dimensions indicate its age, and in individual plants, age and the impression of a constantly renewing strength are paired with one another.[52]

As Thoreau affirmed in response, "I believe that climate does thus react on man"—good news for America, for it opened a pathway beyond environmental guilt toward healing and renewal. This insight grew out of Thoreau's own personal experience, as the regenerative capacity of Concord's damaged forests offered moral encouragement in the face of his own bleakest moment of environmental sin: "In the spring I burned over a hundred acres till the earth was sere and black—& by mid-summer this space was clad in a fresher & more luxuriant green than the surrounding even. Shall man then despair? Is he not a sproutland too after never so many searings & witherings?"[53] One cannot separate Thoreau's study of forest succession and the regenerative capacity of the seed from the narrative he told of his own life; as his late autobiographical essay "Wild Apples" demonstrates, Thoreau understood himself in these very terms.

All this comes together in the climactic passage of *Walden* in which Thoreau encounters the "sand foliage" formed by the melting earth of the Deep Cut, the gully next to Walden Pond sliced open by the railroad workers while laying the tracks across the water from his Walden house. Every year Thoreau watched for this phenomenon, fascinated by the way the thawing earth "flowed into the forms of foliage—before plants were produced to clothe the earth." As he wrote in 1851, "The earth I tread on is not a dead inert mass. It is a body—has a spirit—is organic—and fluid to the influence of its spirit—and to whatever particle of that spirit is in me. ... Even the solid globe is permeated by the living law." In these few pages of *Walden*, Thoreau condenses years of these observations, folding Humboldt's sense of plants as a visual language into his own sense of the word as embodying breath or "spirit," as green leaf becomes the word "leaf," as the sounding breath of speech and the forming force of life simultaneously figure the sand that "organizes itself as it flows." Thoreau insists on the very materiality of speech, of language:

The overhanging leaf sees here its prototype. *Internally*, whether in the globe or animal body, it is a moist thick *lobe*, a word especially applicable to the liver and lungs and the *leaves* of fat ... *externally* a dry thin *leaf*, even as the *f* and *v* are a pressed and dried *b*. The radicals of lobe are *lb*, the soft mass of the *b* (single lobed, or B, double loved,) with a liquid *l* behind it pressing forward. ... The feathers and wings of birds are still drier and thinner leaves. ... The very globe continually transcends and translates itself, and becomes winged in its orbit.

(W, 306–7, 309)

Off he goes, in an excrementitious delirium of sound and sensuality that takes several pages to find its target: "The earth is not a mere fragment of dead history, stratum upon stratum like the leaves of a book ... but living poetry like the leaves of a tree, which precede flowers and fruit,—not a fossil earth, but a living earth; compared with whose great central life all animal and vegetable life is merely parasitic."[54]

We can't say we weren't warned. "This is history's bifurcation," Michell Serres told us long ago: "either death or symbiosis." Parasites who kill their host put themselves "in mortal danger, for dead hosts can no longer feed or house them." Thus, our precious word "environment" has gotten things exactly backward: "It assumes that we humans are at the center of a system of nature," the "excellent culmination of all things," when it is we who cannot exist without the Earth. "Thus," chides Serres, "we must indeed place things in the center and us at the periphery, or better still, things all around and us within them like parasites."[55] Thoreau presses still farther: all merely organic life is "parasitic" on that "living earth," that great central trunk whose ramifying life is carried outward and inward simultaneously from extremities to core and back again in the flow of waters, the weight of soils, the folded plentitude of leaf forms across the spectrum of life, the breath that carries form into language from leaf to lungs to tongue to palate and lips to script and leaf again, an atmosphere materialized, materiality vitalized, depths inverted into surfaces, universal law into a feather, a sandbank, slag, ice and excrement, lungs, lobes and bowels mingled as in the laboratory, as if Gaia, our home, were some cosmic Frankenstein's monster. What are these monsters, asks Thoreau by moonlight, resting on Fairhaven Cliff,

these rivers and hills—these hieroglyphs which my eyes behold? There is something invigorating in this air which I am peculiarly sensible is a real wind blowing from over the surface of a planet—I look out at my eyes, I come to my window, & I feel & breathe the fresh air. It is a fact equally glorious with the most inward experience. Why have we ever slandered the outward? The perception of surfaces will always have the effect of miracle to a sane sense.[56]

Planet and plant: the wandering star that is our home, the wandering monsters that we are: our own languages tell us we must return, we must plant ourselves, impress our souls deep into the answering Earth.

Plunging into the ground, "launched into the air, a plant might be said to palpate the world," suggests Jean-Christophe Bailly; plants develop as "nonfinite forms," unfolding in the totality of space "in superimposed parabolas, forms full of curves and angles, narrowings and expansions, interlacings and protrusions, trembling in the wind, through all their countless leaves, however free they may be, remain unfailingly attached to a common trunk, to a nourishing channel that comes from the earth."[57] Thoreau no longer merely writes about plants but has, in the structure of his imagination, become one. Becoming plant is a standing refutation of the apocalypse. Thoreau, like Buddha, when asked the meaning of life, simply points to the Earth at his feet: the only viable response, the Terrennial response, to the terror of our time.

3

Auto-Heteronomy: Thoreau's Circuitous Return to the Vegetal World

Michael Marder

While working with Luce Irigaray on *Through Vegetal Being*, I've had Henry David Thoreau at the back of my mind with much greater frequency than the number of pages opposite his name in the book's index would lead readers to believe.[1] Our respective returns to vegetal and elemental realities were certainly distinct from his. I would say that they were both less and more radical: less, because they neither began with, as *Walden* did, nor involved economic considerations and activities; more, because their ecological objective was to reimagine relations to ourselves and to other humans through relations to plants. Although Thoreau eventually came to experience vegetal life otherwise, that life was neither his point of departure nor a medium/mediator—signaled in our title by the word *through*—for his daring experiment.

Thoreau characterizes his stay at Walden Pond as solitary: "My nearest neighbor is a mile distant. ... I have my horizon bounded by woods all to myself."[2] The woods themselves are not his neighbors. They delineate, instead, the rim of a horizon, which, unlike the open vistas of the seas, high mountains, or deserts, is intimate, close, enclosed, sheltered there. At the same time, the *textual* horizon for the passage in question is itself bounded on two sides by admissions of Thoreau's sympathy with plants. Before the rather dry remark on solitude I have cited, he writes: "Sympathy with the fluttering alder and poplar leaves almost takes away my breath" (125). After that remark, he acknowledges that every little pine needle expanded and swelled with sympathy and befriended me. I was so distinctly made aware of the presence of something kindred to me, even in scenes which we are accustomed to call wild and dreary, and also that the nearest of blood to me and humanest was not a person nor a villager, that I thought no place could ever be strange to me again.

(128)

My brief text is an attempt to make sense of this experiential contradiction, this blatant contrast between solitude and human-vegetal sympathy.

I take the reflections that follow as an occasion for exploring the formal paradox of Thoreau's experiment at Walden Pond as it bears on plants. On the one hand, the list of motivations for his retreat from human society (fictitious as it might have been: far from being a hermit, Thoreau often welcomed visitors in his cabin and ventured out into town) is of a piece with the Western values of a heroic and tragic, autonomous subjectivity, nourished and exacerbated by the American revolutionary and frontier ethos.[3] His self-reliance, a sweeping reduction of the ostensibly superfluous, and the very desire to start life anew on the foundations of a previously obscured truth are all recognizable as gestures of an essentially modern Cartesian subject on a quest for absolute certainty. On the other hand, his encounters with plants (those he cultivates—for example, the beans; those he fleetingly sees in the woods; those that he needs to uproot in order to clear the space for his crops and that keep haunting him) reveal the limits of human autonomy and, immediately beyond these limits, the law of the vegetal other as a master to learn from or a sympathetic companion. My working hypothesis is that, rather than a contradiction limited to Thoreau's engagement with plants, auto-heteronomy is a tortuous framework for every life-altering experiment—the framework that, in light of vegetal heteronomy, is at its clearest in this engagement.

It is worth noting with respect to the objects of Thoreau's sympathy that they are, in each case, specific plant organs, namely the leaves. The leaf is an archive of vegetal identity, so much so that systems of plant classification often rely on the shape of this organ for their enunciation. It would, therefore, come as no surprise that one's identification with plants would bind to that which provides them with their identity, at least from the standpoint of a contextually and historically embedded human observer. Affect and cognition intertwine: sympathy is allied with discernment, which is a hallmark of intelligence. Thoreau will announce that "the highest we can attain to is not Knowledge, but Sympathy with Intelligence,"[4] a formulation which could provide us with a good working definition of philo-sophy. Accordingly, the highest we can attain to is not the knowledge of plants but an intelligent sympathy (in a word: a way of philosophizing) with them.

A curious feature of the vegetal archive is its seemingly unessential, superficial nature, whether to do with the physical shape of leaves or their detachability, the fact that they are shed each year in the fall. That Thoreau's sympathy is addressed to them is a sign for the pulsing-together, the infinite echoing and reverberations of his fragility and finitude with theirs—hence, the exact opposite of the heroic and autonomous stance he adopts as he leaves for Walden. The solitude of a maple, whose leaves turn red in the fall, is "brave" but not heroic: "It has finished its summer's work before all other trees, and withdraws from the contest,"[5] just as Thoreau withdraws from the comforts of civilization. However negative, the autumnal turning of leaf colors is a *decision*, one that both presages and confirms Thoreau's own resolve to turn over a new leaf and start his life afresh in the woods. It is solitude that paves the way to another kind of engagement, another sympathy, the act of withdrawing that draws a voluntary exile into a new time and place of existence.

To be sure, Thoreau identifies not only with alder, poplar, and maple leaves but also with pine needles, the ever-green symbols of eternal life. Yet, what he highlights is the diminutive size of these modified leaves, pointing in their prickly style toward his own insignificance. The size of the needles is ontically small and ontologically great: "Every little pine needle expanded and swelled with sympathy and befriended me." Through a micro-level sympathy with parts of a plant, Thoreau makes contact with a much vaster nonhuman "presence," which "heals my cuts,"[6] not least the cut of having alienated oneself from an alienated society.

In this, too, his method has much in common with plant-thinking. As I've confessed on several occasions, for me, plants are singular universals, the miniature mirrors of and gateways to what is usually called nature and, ultimately, being itself. To start—moved by an oceanic feeling or some other sort of universal sympathy—from an identification with the whole, with the world, with the vast unknown would result in betraying the identifying subject and that with which she identifies. The scale matters: the world and even the woods are realities that are thought but not experienced, any direct identification with them bound to remain abstract. Perhaps for this very reason Thoreau relates to the woods as the frame of his horizons, within which the experience of vegetal sympathy germinates.

We should not skip over the mundane word *experience*, either. There is, I would suggest and Thoreau would agree, no experience without sympathy, without a *pathos* with ..., a suffering with, the attitude of a patient awaiting and passive reception. Nothing could be further from a tragically heroic, autonomous subject than that. A true hero loses the capacity to experience the world as a consequence of the inability to tarry and suffer with it. To be a hero is to become utterly insensitive. Thoreau's retreat from civilization is not the end of the road; it merely paves the way to a cultivation of sympathy and a rediscovery of the capacity to experience the world. The act of detaching oneself from human society is a negative precondition, similar to the separation of a maple leaf from its branch in the fall, a minimal prelude to the revitalization of experience. It is an act that, independent and courageous (or, some would claim, misanthropic and defeatist) as it may be, cuts autonomous activity short in order to awaken the receptive capacity in sympathy with certain aspects of plant life. Such will have been the sequential arrangement of Thoreau's auto-heteronomy, initially giving the law to himself in order to then receive it from the vegetal other.

Thoreau juxtaposes his version of sympathy to that he finds in philanthropic conduct. "The philanthropist," he writes, "too often surrounds mankind with the remembrance of his own cast-off griefs as an atmosphere, and calls it sympathy. We should impart our courage, and not our despair, our health and ease, and not our disease, and take care that this does not spread by contagion" (74). Sympathy is not (more accurately, should not be) a projection of one's own suffering onto the other, human or not. Such a projection would spread one's griefs as though by contagion, to which even plants are not immune. In Thoreau's version, the resonance of *pathê* occurs on the basis of positivity, of plenitude and excess, of courage and health, the abundance of leafy green received by and receiving into its presence a human apprentice in the art of living with oneself and with others. The atmospheric backdrop of his sympathy is not permeated by a one-sided remembrance of suffering generalized; rather, it is jointly created thanks to a bidirectional swell, a non-imperialistic expansion of the human toward the vegetal and vice versa. Experience is impossible unless it twists free from the overwhelming projection of oneself onto the world as much as from one's totally passive subjection to the world. The renaissance of experience happens owing to a two-fold approach, whereby human and vegetal health (a word that needs to be heard not so much in its physical as in the existential register) overflow toward one another. The sympathy of plants "with our race" (133) is thus indispensable to the dramatic hero of *Walden*, who will identify with them so deeply as to ask: "Am I not partly leaves and vegetable mould myself?" (134).

With subtle irony, Thoreau goes on to saddle reactive philanthropic sympathy with vegetal connotations. Allow me to cite the relevant excerpt at length.

> If any thing ail a man, so that he does not perform his functions, if he have a pain in his bowels even,—for that is the seat of sympathy,—he forthwith sets about reforming—the world. Being a microcosm himself, he discovers, and it is a true discovery, and he is the man to make it,—that the world has been eating green apples; to his eyes, in fact, the globe itself is a great green apple, which there is danger awful to think of that the children of men will nibble before it is ripe; and straightway his drastic philanthropy seeks out the Esquimaux and the Patagonian, and embraces the populous

Indian and Chinese villages; and thus, by a few years of philanthropic activity, the powers in the mean while using him for their own ends, no doubt, he cures himself of his dyspepsia, the globe acquires a faint blush on one or both of its cheeks, as if it were beginning to be ripe, and life loses its crudity and is once more sweet and wholesome to live.

(74)

The seat of sympathy is in the bowels, that is, in the digestive system, which serves the classical faculty of *tō threptikon*, the nutritive or vegetal soul in Aristotle. The cause of sympathy, however, is indigestion, the consumption of green apples, fruit not yet ripe. And its object is equally vegetal—"the globe itself [as] a great green apple." What troubles a reactive philanthropic sympathizer is not the destructive consumption of the world *per se*, not biting into the apple that the globe is, but doing so prematurely, before it has ripened enough to be digested. Philanthropic activity takes it upon itself to contribute to the world's ripening, or at least to the perception that it is on a good path toward its final state. A philanthropist aims to bring the world to its proper (timely, nutritionally adequate, easy to digest) end. Thoreau construes this state of affairs as a carefully manufactured, if likely unconsciously produced, perception, intended to placate the philanthropic sympathizer, who thereby "cures himself of his dyspepsia." The globe "acquires a faint blush ... *as if* it were beginning to be ripe, and life ... is once more sweet." What is missing from this reactively sympathetic attempt at reforming the world? Why the thin line of the "as if" separating an actual development from a fictitious process?

Compare the stance of a philanthropist to Thoreau's cultivation of his bean field. An obvious difference is that philanthropy hastens the maturation of the world with money, whereas the beans are ripened by the sun and that "the same sun which ripens my beans illumines at once a system of earths like ours" (10). The light of finance eclipses and pretends to have replaced that of the solar blaze. At stake is not so much a contrast between the metaphoric ripening of green apples and the literal ripening of the beans as between a highly symbolic, monetary intervention into the course of the world and care for the conditions that promote its self-expression: "Removing the weeds, putting fresh soil about the bean stems, and encouraging this weed which I had sown, making the yellow soil express its summer thought in bean leaves and blossoms rather than in wormwood and piper and millet grass, making the earth say beans instead of grass,—this was my daily work" (152).

With Thoreau's encouragement, the earth itself expresses its "summer thought" in beans, even though it could have said wormwood or piper or millet grass. Here, the second difference from philanthropy leaps into our field of theoretical vision: a philanthropic sympathizer does not question the end of philanthropic activity, whereas Thoreau's sympathy goes along with an interminable interrogation of his choice of beans over the grasses native to the place and, wrapped in this choice, of the sovereignty he asserts by means of his work. Thoreau is not afraid to refer to his crops as weeds, relativizing tacit presuppositions regarding their uselessness or usefulness (to human beings, not to mention to *this* particular human known as Henry Thoreau). The cultivator's autonomous gesture is critically self-undermining; he unsays what his actions make the earth say and imagines the earth saying its plant thoughts otherwise. Letting go of his sovereignty—if only as an afterthought included in a book—he approximates vegetal heteronomy, the freedom of botanical being.

Another important motif of Thoreau's paradoxical auto-heteronomy is time. The nation, he complains, "lives too fast" (89). A break with civilization slows the pace of life down and allows it to abut that of plants.[7] Once again, the acquaintance with beans nicely reflects this point: "As I had little aid from horses or cattle, or hired men or boys, or improved implements of husbandry, I was much slower, and became much more intimate with my beans than usual" (152). The indicators of our dependence on the benefits of civilization include technological artifacts (the "improved implements" Thoreau is citing) and a division of labor that makes work faster and more efficient. By refusing to divide his agricultural labor either with other humans or even with animals and by using the most rudimentary of implements, Thoreau slowly planted, hoed, harvested, and threshed his beans at a hybrid rhythm of human-vegetal existence that allowed him to become "much more intimate" with them than usual.[8] The ultramodern instant of his autonomous decision—"It is never too late to give up our prejudices" so as not to "lead lives of quiet desperation" (7)—catapulted him to a decidedly non- or unmodern way of life at the mercy of the seasons and the elements, attuned to the place and its animal and plant inhabitants. It was, indeed, a sweeping decision, but also one that, through its ramifications, transferred the power to decide to others: to the soil and the rain, to the seedlings and the birds and the insects. We might say that, going against the historical tide, consciously refusing the poisonous benefits of his epoch, Thoreau made a metadecision on the temporal form of his "sojourn," which, from that moment on, slipped from his own hands and was entrusted to plants, above all.

If, with a greater or lesser dose of irony, the anatomical seat of sympathy is the bowels, then its time is the period between the moment of ingestion and the excretion of the bowels' contents. Indigestion, as we have seen, renders the process more protracted and convoluted, interfering with the digestion and metabolic health of sentiments and relations, to others and to oneself. Often neglected, the excretory function of the nutritive process is, on a par with ingestion, a component of *tō threptikon*. With the exception of a couple of allusions, Thoreau, too, does not draw the readers' attention to that function.

These exceptional instances, however, are quite telling, in that they militate against the conventional interpretations of nature and culture alike.

In the first reference to the by-products of the digestive process, Thoreau announces: "I put no manure on this land, not being the owner, but merely a squatter" (52). The tongue-in-cheek comment on squatting carries a double meaning: (1) temporarily occupying a site and (2) physically lowering oneself into a pose appropriate for the act of defecation. Property relations and ownership, Thoreau insinuates, mean that one is holding onto one's shit, not letting it go, and, in the case of a "model farm," is surrounding oneself with and drowning in it. The farm house "stands like a fungus in a muck-heap," with the land "under a high state of cultivation, being manured with the hearts and brains of men" (190). While property becomes indistinguishable from the excremental excess it does not let go of, the landowner's sympathy with the earth and its produce is predicated on the conversion of thought and emotion—that is, of every facet of one's inner life—into piles of manure.

Should we transpose these ideas back onto the terrain of the vegetal soul, we would realize that they amount to a glitch, if not a perversion, in the operations of *tō threptikon*: the end result of the nutritive process grows to be more valuable than either the beginning or the middle. On the contrary, living as a squatter is defined by the nomadic possibility of moving on and moving away from one's excrement, distributing it evenly and randomly over the terrestrial plane, and refusing to dedicate one's heart and brain to serving, in the shape of possessive individuality, as manure for the institution of property. Squatting opposes the feigned autonomy of a property holder, who in fact depends on being constantly surrounded by and filled with physical and psychic manure, to the autonomy of sojourners, who are as mobile as they are aware of their heteronomy, of dependence on yet another plot of land and the crops it yields.

Second, in his ruminations on the spring, Thoreau constructs a complex analogy between the thaw and the universal shape of a leaf constitutive of inorganic phenomena (such as sheets of ice) as much as of human forms, from earlobes to the palms of hands. It follows from this multifaceted analogy that the physiological blueprint for expression is excretion, specifically as regards the earth's self-expression in vegetal growth: "You find thus in the very sands an anticipation of the vegetable leaf. No wonder that the earth expresses itself outwardly in leaves, it so labors with the idea inwardly" (295–6). Springtime, when everything sprouts into existence, is, therefore, the most excretory of seasons, the earth exuberantly releasing what it has been digesting during winter as it "labor[ed] with the idea inwardly."

Thoreau admits, moreover, that his theory "is somewhat excrementitious in its character, and there is no end to the heaps of liver lights and bowels, as if the globe were turned wrong side outward; but this suggests at least that Nature has some bowels, and there again is mother of humanity. This is the frost coming out of the ground; this is Spring" (297–8). It is as though, he suggests, everything that surrounds us, ourselves included, is the contents of "Nature's bowels" externalized. The transition from a merely abstract idea to an actuality is none other than the act of excretion, most evident in the spring. And, seeing that the bowels are the organ of sympathy, life itself is the product of the earth's sympathy with the living, who *exist* as *ex*creted at the confluence of ontology, biology, phenomenology (experience), and a certain ethical comportment.

Some will protest that the mode of a tree or even a bean plant existence bears a greater resemblance to Thoreau's depiction of a propertied farmer, whose dwelling he compares to a fungus, than that of a squatter. Aren't squatters, insofar as they are similar to nomads, akin to animals, roaming in search of food and running away from their waste? That said, the tree produces manure from the remnants of its own life processes, the roots partly feeding on the decomposing matter of its leaves and fruit. It is autonomous in its heteronomy, in its being an autotroph *and* reliance on the elements, pollinating insects, other plants, animals, and humans, whereas propertied farmers are heteronomous in their autonomy, able to secure their possessions only at the price of transforming their innermost core into manure and utilizing the excrements of others to "fatten the soil," as Thoreau puts it at some point in *Walden*. In addition, vegetal metabolism is ensconced in the seasonal cycle, which Thoreau elucidates in a creative vein when he considers the spring as the time of excretion from the bowels of the earth. Farming simultaneously depends on this cycle and, as a harbinger of possessive rationality, breaks it or overrides it, putting vegetal growth and decay, plant excretion from and ingestion back into the soil, at the service of the malignant institution and its augmentation. As a form of property, the farm translates the world around the farmhouse into shit, not sparing the property holder either.

Assuming, in line with my plant-thinking, that human cognition is nothing but a rarefication, sublimation, or thinning-out of the vegetal *tō threptikon*, it is necessary to concentrate not only on the nutritive or reproductive dimensions of this faculty but also on their excretive and decaying underside.[9] The civilization Thoreau flees from in the nineteenth century, its logic exacerbated in the twenty-first, worships growth without decay (i.e. progress), ingestion without excretion (i.e. limitless appropriation), all the while staying mired in nondecomposable, unthought, environmentally, socially, and physically noxious residue of its agricultural and industrial activity. To begin thinking, finally, is to think through, without ever reaching its bottom, a *general metabology*, the metabolism that traverses every domain of being, as well as being as such, and that, after two hundred years of rupturing, is now coming to a grinding halt. Thoreau, like Marx albeit in another sense, espied in the accumulation of (private) property the root cause of the rupture, a blockage of metabolic relations tantamount to a large-scale societal indigestion. With the view to securing the future, mistaken for a life without death or for growth without decay, such an accumulation nips the future in the bud. Hence, Thoreau's statement: "It may be guessed that I reduce almost the whole advantage of holding this superfluous property as a fund in store against the future, so far as the individual is concerned, mainly to the defraying of funeral expenses" (31) and, I should add, so far as *Homo sapiens* is concerned, to defraying the funeral expenses of humanity.

The prototype for Thoreau's auto-heteronomy is learning. Succinctly, all learning is an auto-didacticism facilitated by the other, mediated by sympathy, the *pathos*, passion, and experience with the other: "We do not learn by inference and deduction and the application of mathematics to philosophy, but by direct intercourse and sympathy."[10] Within the paradigm of a sympathetic pedagogy, Thoreau's proposal for a mutual learning from and with plants is imbued with meaning.

"What shall I learn of beans or beans of me?" he asks in *Walden* (150). Metabolically astute learning would, without a doubt, follow the movement of growth, but it likewise cannot be remiss about metamorphosis and, especially, decay. To cherish the crops, as Thoreau reports he does, is also to accompany their digestion or ingestion, be it by the soil, by the cultivator himself, the worms or the woodchucks. Learning itself is lop-sided unless, consistent with the principles of a general metabology, it supplements the incorporation and assimilation of the learned with the expulsion of its by-products, which, having decomposed and decayed, may fecundate the ground for further learning and experiential growth. Then, in keeping with Thoreau's "somewhat excrementitious" theory, a learner may learn that experience itself is excremental, the spring of psychic life mimicking the time of the year when plants spring from the earth that excretes them toward the expanses of the warming skies. A sympathetic experience, in its turn, would entail being excreted-with parts of others: stalactite formations, pine needles, Schnauzer fur, those imploring probing eyes that stare at me.

*

P.S. Are we writing and thinking about plants, in this collection and in numerous others, with such intensity and dedication because the forests are receding? Because we are losing vegetal variety, the biodiversity of the flora, in actuality? Are we trying to commemorate in thought what is disappearing in deed? If so, then our endeavor is at odds with that of Thoreau, who combined the thinking and the living (a thinking-living) with plants. Should this realization not shadow our every reflection on "Thoreau and the vegetal"?

4

Thoreau's Garden Politics

Antoine Traisnel

If a plant cannot live according to its nature, it dies; and so a man.

THOREAU, "RESISTANCE TO CIVIL GOVERNMENT"

This essay responds to the emergence of a new subject in critical theory: the plant. The recent turn to plants in the humanities has already produced a robust body of work that branches out across a number of disciplines, from indigenous philosophy to anthropology to metaphysics.[1] Beyond their significant differences, these works share the belief that the ecological calamities we face today are in no small measure a byproduct of Western modernity's epistemological indifference to the life of plants. Re-focusing our attention on vegetal life, they propose, might remediate the harm inflicted, not just to plants themselves but more broadly to entire ecosystems and to the populations who have historically entertained a more reciprocal, less exploitative relationship to the land and its productions. Yet despite the incontestable urgency of its concerns, and despite the clear ethical and political motives that animate it, this new "plant theory" is at first sight surprisingly *demobilizing*. Both Emanuele Coccia's *Life of Plants* and Jeffrey Nealon's *Plant Theory*, for instance, call for a suspension of action: the former enjoins his readers to cultivate a more "contemplative" disposition, and the latter to "slow down" in order to reconsider the question of life "from the ground up."[2] How are we to understand these odd injunctions in the face of accelerating and irreversible environmental disasters?

To account for this paradox, I look to Henry David Thoreau's botanical ruminations in *Walden; or, Life in the Woods* (1854).[3] Thoreau's reflections on plant life trouble Nealon and Coccia's claim that plants were being thoroughly expunged from Western scientific and political thought in the nineteenth century. Far from ignoring them, Thoreau explicitly asks himself whether he has the "right" to kill and use certain plants for his own benefit, and (not unlike our plant theorists) he invites his readers to adopt a "much slower" pace if they want to entertain a "much more intimate" knowledge of plants.[4] But beyond a speculative epistemology and ethics of vegetable life, *Walden* devises a *pragmatic politics of planting*. This politics is largely specific to Thoreau's time and place, responding to antebellum agricultural reforms and other governmental initiatives, but I will argue that it also models what a biopolitics attuned to plant life might look like.

Thoreau's horticultural experiments at Walden Pond, I propose, make it clear that biopolitics—broadly conceived as the government of the living— does not renounce the sovereign "right to kill" so much as it subordinates it to a different calculus of power. As such, what Leo Marx called Thoreau's "experiment in transcendental pastoralism" can be seen to complement Michel Foucault's reflections on "pastoral power."[5] In his 1977–8 lectures at the Collège de France, Foucault borrows the concept of pastoral power from the archaic model of the Christian pastorate to account for the profound mutation in the art of governing that occurs when technologies of power and knowledge take life as their subject. Predicated on the theological (and zoopolitical) example of the shepherd in charge of safely leading his flock to pasture, pastoral power "is not exercised over a territory," Foucault asserts, "but, by definition, over a flock, and more exactly, over the flock in its movement from one place to another."[6] While the category of "territory" was key to the conceptualization of the older regime of sovereign power, it becomes much less central when Foucault turns his attention to the biopolitical management of populations, or "governmentality." Government "in no way refers to territory," Foucault asserts: "One governs things."[7] Thus, as Daniel Nemser observes, "space seems to disappear from Foucault's work at almost exactly the moment that the biopolitics of population emerges."[8] In fact, the territory does not entirely "disappear" from Foucault's lectures; rather, it becomes incorporated as one variable among many others into a complex network of relations that governments administer for the benefit of (certain segments of) the population.[9]

What Thoreau offers, I propose, is precisely a consideration of the territory that quite literally underlies Foucault's "government of the living." Thoreau shifts our attention from the mobile flock to the pasture, from the zoological to the botanical, making clear that pastoral power always implies what we could call *pasture power*: specific forms of care and knowledge and a certain notion of politics that address the life of plants, and not simply the longevity and health of (some) human lives or the mass-reproduction and management of (some) animal lives. Not only does Thoreau's experimental gardening at Walden Pond help us assess the role that plants have always, if inconspicuously, played under biopolitics, but it unsettles the Eurocentric perspectives that subtend Nealon and Coccia's lapsarian narratives, inviting us to amend certain assumptions in dominant biopolitical discourses by inscribing them within a broader imperialist landscape—specifically, if obliquely, within the context of settler-colonial implantation and the slave plantation economy.

The first section of this essay, "Planting," is a brief overview of the theoretical tenets and political promises of plant theory. I focus primarily on Nealon and Coccia, whose work best illustrates the belief that altering the fundamental "unit of thought" of the sciences and philosophies of life—that is, shifting their attention from animals to plants—would be ecologically less detrimental, or at least would offer a more apt heuristic for diagnosing the condition of our biopolitical age. The second section, "Hoeing," reads Thoreau's "Bean-Field" chapter in *Walden* as a meditation on the ethics of weeding in order to consider what becomes of the sovereign "right to kill" when plant life is taken into account. The last section, "Harvesting," shows how Thoreau's acknowledgment of the violence inherent in tending his bean plot informs both his political critique of the alienation from the land wrought by settler biopower and his twin theories of resistance and civil government.

Planting

On the face of it, the recent surge of theoretical consideration for plants is but the latest offshoot of posthumanist efforts to decenter the universalizing category of "the human" in humanistic discourses and epistemological practices by focusing instead on liminal figures like "the cyborg" and "the animal" or by attending to hyperobjects like global warming or the Great Pacific Garbage Patch. Yet plant theorists do not view the turn to plants as a mere evolution, a new ground for the same old posthumanism; rather, they present it as a radical departure from its previous ventures, as an entirely new project that promises to remake the world "from the ground up."

Two recent books in particular have put "vegetable life" at the center of their analyses to rethink radically the political landscape of Western modernity. Emanuele Coccia's *Life of Plants: A Metaphysics of Mixture* (2016) takes modern Western thought to task for its inveterate zoocentric bias, and Jeffrey Nealon's *Plant Theory: Biopower and Vegetable Life* (2015) laments that at the advent of biopower, animals eclipsed plants as the "image of life" and thus as the focus of politics. Coccia's and Nealon's books are very different, but they share the conviction that amending modern (bio)politics demands that we shake up the metaphysical or epistemological ground in which it is rooted. Both authors, moreover, have in common a strong aversion toward the recent field of animal studies, which they see as little more than a continuation of the old humanist project by other means. Concern over animal suffering, for Coccia, grows out of "an extremely superficial moralism" and a narcissistic inability for humans to empathize with such dissimilar beings as plants: "No one has ever wanted to question the superiority of animal life," he bluntly asserts, "and the rights of life and death of [animals] over [plants]."[10] Nealon is less hyperbolic, but he too asserts that animal studies, "far from constituting a critique of an all-too-humanist biopower (exposing the imperialism of human life over animal life), tends to function in fact as an intense extension of that very biopower." Animal studies scholars, he contends, assume that animals became utterly marginalized in nineteenth-century Western cultures when in fact the role of "abjected other" was "played throughout the biopolitical era not by the animal, but by the plant."[11] Coccia and Nealon, in sum, embrace a lapsarian script according to which animals, over the last two centuries, have unduly upstaged plants in the natural sciences, and by extension in the cultural and political imaginaries of the West.[12] Both lament that the paradigmatic subject of our philosophical, scientific, and political discourses is all too individuated, action-driven, and nomadic—in other words, all too *animal*.[13]

Coccia and Nealon hope to bring plants back into the picture in order to promote an entirely different economy of relations with the natural world, inviting their readers to think and act *botanically*. Coccia, for instance, advocates vegetal values such as "immersion" over autonomy, "exposure" over immunity, and "contemplation" over action. He explicitly suggests that the plant is an ideal model for a more holistic eco-philosophy, for he describes plants as essentially *non-critical beings* that perfectly adhere to their surroundings. In fact and effect, for Coccia, plants are immersed in the world and thus *make* the world simply by existing: "Immersion," he writes, "is first of all an *action* of mutual compenetration between subject and environment."[14] For plants, in other words, there is no clear distinction between being and acting. Coccia contends that this lesson is generalizable to all living organisms, but that animals have forgotten it, mistaking mobility for independence. The moral, for him, is that "organisms do not need to go beyond or outside themselves to reinvent the face of the world [because they are *part and parcel* of it]; they have no need to act."[15]

As for Nealon, he proposes that plants' rhizomatic territoriality is better suited to address the complexities of biological life than the projected and overly *organized* human or animal "worlds" ("organized" in the sense of built and inhabited by bodies with organs). For Nealon, plants offer a more productive paradigm for resisting various forms of control, especially as power has grown increasingly reticular and decentered under late capitalism. Yet if he urges us to "follow the plants" (Deleuze and Guattari's formulation), he recognizes that the rhizome is little more than a diagnostic template that "doesn't guarantee anything politically."[16] Here lies the main difference between Nealon and a thinker like Cary Wolfe, the only representative of "animal studies" with whom he engages in any depth. Nealon repeatedly rebuts Wolfe's argument at the end of *Before the Law* that legal protection cannot indiscriminately be extended to all living beings. Wolfe is particularly wary of thinkers of biopolitics like Roberto Esposito who refuse "to take seriously the differences between different forms of life—bonobos versus sunflowers, let's say—as subjects of immunitary protection."[17] Esposito's proposition that all lifeforms are equally deserving of protection seems impracticable to Wolfe, who insists that we "*must* choose, and by definition we *cannot* choose everyone and everything at once."[18] This requirement of choice, or decision, is precisely what Nealon challenges, especially as it involves, in Wolfe's example, choosing animals over plants ("bonobos versus sunflowers");[19] Nealon concludes *Plant Theory* with a plea for more "undecidability," arguing somewhat cryptically that "undecidability complicates decision; it doesn't make decision impossible."[20]

On the one hand, Coccia theorizes a mode of action that does not look like action but that is not reducible to inaction; on the other hand, Nealon advocates a form of decision that does not look like decision but that is not reducible to indecision. In other words, our plant theorists invite us to conjugate differently two of the most important verbs in the political idiom of Western modernity: *decide* and *act*. This demand seems oddly paralyzing, even defeatist at times, but it offers a powerful counterpoint to the proprietary conceptions of life that prevail in classical biopolitical narratives. The invitation to amend the grammar of modern political thought is most useful when politics concerns itself not merely with human affairs, nor even with discrete living beings, but with the mesh of life itself. And in our age of ecological peril, it is imperative to heed one of the most important lessons of biopolitics: that modern power is no longer predominantly expressed as the decision to interrupt life—which, once taken away by the sovereign, paradoxically and retrospectively appears as an individual's unalienable property—but rather as an investment in "life itself," construed as a transindividual, unownable force. As we move toward pastoral power and away from the sensational and discontinuous violence of the sovereign, decisions and actions become more distributed and less localizable. This reconfiguration facilitates the institution of gradual, unspectacular forms of what Rob Nixon calls "slow violence," which disproportionally aggravate the vulnerability of already disempowered populations. Under pastoral power, lives can be inhibited or encouraged by techniques that target not individuated living beings but rather "populations";[21] these techniques work less visibly because indirectly, by altering the "milieu" in which these populations (are forced to) live.[22]

Plant theory usefully reminds us that the milieu—of which plants make up a significant portion—is neither an inert background nor an abstract notion but rather, as Foucault defines it, "a set of material elements that act on [living individuals] and on which they act in turn."[23] Yet recognizing this runs counter to Coccia and Nealon's respective claims that vegetable life became thoroughly jettisoned under biopolitics.[24] I take issue with this botanical "repressive hypothesis" because assuming that plants were forgotten or neglected makes it difficult to account for what was effectively done to and with plants under biopolitics. Ironically, this is a point Nealon makes about animals: "Modernity is not, as some animal studies thinkers would have us believe, born by jettisoning or abjecting animality but rather by fully incorporating animal desire into our definition of the human."[25] I would similarly argue that plants were not forgotten or abjected when life made its entrance on the political stage but rather made to play a vital if underrecognized and undertheorized role. It is more fruitful, I suggest, to understand biopolitics not as spurning plant life so much as assimilating its logic as a way to subject individuals to the dispersive logic of the population. In other words, biopolitics does not disappear plants; it vegetalizes animal bodies.

Tellingly, Foucault discerns the lineaments of a concept of milieu in the writings of eighteenth-century demographer Jean-Baptiste Moheau, who states that it is "up to the government to change the air temperature and to improve the climate." For Moheau, "a direction given to stagnant water, forests planted or burnt down, mountains destroyed by time or by the continual cultivation of their surface, create a new soil and a new climate," which in turn create new subjects. Reflecting on how the Italian weather has become warmer since Virgil's time, Moheau oddly attributes changes in climactic conditions not to natural phenomena but to political transformations: "If there has been so much change" between Virgil's time and ours, "it is not the climate that has changed; the political and economic interventions of government have altered the course of things to the point that nature itself has constituted for man … another milieu."[26] We understand how inconceivable an "event" like climate change becomes when nature has been fully translated into a milieu (when nature is politicized through and through, the idea that it could "change" of its own accord is heresy[27]). But when it is being rendered into a governmental technology, nature also becomes a privileged site of "resistance" for thinkers of civil government. Enter Thoreau.

Hoeing

In *Walden*, Thoreau conducts biopolitical experiments that *actively* and *decisively* engage plants, not as an inert backdrop for human life, not simply as a means by which power acts on its subjects, but as subjects of knowledge and power in their own right. In a famously tedious chapter of *Walden*, Thoreau describes the cultivation of his bean-field in painstaking detail, framing his experiment in husbandry as an economic project: "Before I finished my house, wishing to earn ten or twelve dollars by some honest and agreeable method, in order to meet my unusual expenses, I planted about two acres and a half of light and sandy soil near it chiefly with beans" (36). Significantly, his beans are introduced from the start as a form of currency (although one that does not suppose the abstraction of something like a gold standard, as Thoreau's beans derive their value from being worked by his own hand). His is not a dream of self-sufficiency and retreat from the world of commerce; he makes it clear that he does not plant in order to eat. He claims he will not partake of his beans because of his Pythagorean allegiances,[28] but he will happily exchange them for rice or grow them for their poetic yield ("for the sake of tropes and expression, to serve a parable-maker one day," 108).

For Eric Sundquist, the tie Thoreau establishes between writing and cultivating is far from innocent: "Thoreau's cultivation of Nature yokes literal seeding with insemination by the letter in a precise way, for his whole project involves implanting himself in the midst of Nature while at the same time concealing the injury generated by that act."[29] Yet Thoreau does not conceal the injury he is inflicting on the land and its occupants; in fact, he draws attention to the violence inherent in his agricultural enterprise on multiple occasions. He describes battle after battle with weeds, fought to protect his cherished bean-crop: "A long war ... with weeds, those Trojans who had sun and rain and dews on their side. Daily the beans saw me come to their rescue armed with a hoe, and thin the ranks of their enemies, filling up the trenches with weedy dead" (108). Thoreau acknowledges that his annexation of the bean-field entails the conquest of the "native" plants that grew there before, and he explicitly asks what "right" he has to kill some plants (weeds) to the benefit of others (beans). He is equally aware of the collateral damage occasioned by this interminable war, knowing full well that the weeds serve as a "granary" for the local birds, and that his gardening is destroying that resource (111). Not only does he relish describing his mock-heroic war on weeds, but he implicitly compares his own conquest of the bean-field to the Europeans' conquest of the land. He repeatedly notes the arrowheads he turns up while hoeing his beans, which he reads as living indices of an "extinct nation" that planted beans long before he did (104). And after all, what is *Walden* if not a narrative of settlement? As Stanley Cavell notes, Thoreau recounts "the building of a house, that is, the finding of one's habitation,"[30] while knowing well that one's entitlement to the land is never that of a rightful "owner" but always of a temporary "squatter" (34). In contrast to settler colonialism, which rhetorically and materially attempted to "naturalize" its legitimacy,[31] Thoreau plainly admits that his agricultural labor displaces people and plants indigenous to Massachusetts—in his own words, his hoeing amounts to "levelling whole ranks of one species [to] sedulously cultivate another" (108).

He kills and displaces weeds *even as* he questions his license to do so: "what right had I to oust johnswort and the rest, and break up [worms and woodchucks'] ancient herb garden?" (104). The question remains unanswered, but it is not rhetorical. His decision to remove the weeds in no way annuls their right to flourish. This right is simultaneously recognized and violated by the farmer, whose decision is shown to be rooted not in a pre-established hierarchy of value but in a set of relative interests: What can I grow in his climate? What can I sell to my neighbors? What crop will make a worthy parable? As such, Thoreau's horticultural experiment effectively reconceives *decision*, which is neither a wholly volitional or proprietary act that presumes an autonomous subject nor a legal verdict predicated on abstract principles of equality; rather, decision here involves a pragmatic, economic calculation. To the repetitious monotony of Jacksonian agriculture, which purposely prevents any true kinship with the land and its productions,[32] Thoreau opposes the no less tedious iteration of his hoe, which demands intimacy with what will be recognized a weed: "Consider the intimate and curious acquaintance one makes with various kinds of weeds,—it will bear some iteration in the account, for there was no little iteration in the labor,—disturbing their delicate organizations so ruthlessly, and making such invidious distinctions with his hoe" (108). Decision—epitomized by the incision of the hoe, the critical instrument par excellence—ought for Thoreau to be local and finite, lest it alienate the farmer from his land and from his own self.

Heeding the contingent nature of hoeing is a way for Thoreau to acknowledge the ordinary violence inherent in his practice. There is no ontology of the weed; weed is what has been designated as such. Case in point: Thoreau calls beans "this weed which I had sown" (105). Likewise, there is no fixed essence of the plant, no such thing as "the plant."[33] Is plant what is planted; for Thoreau, plant is a verb before it is a noun.[34] And plant is a verb whose ostensible transitivity Thoreau likes to call into question, as he does when he writes that his hoe makes "the earth say beans instead of grass" (106). Thoreau's planting is a perlocutionary act, to borrow from J. L. Austin's typology of performatives, insofar as it brings something about without addressing a direct order or a request to an interlocutor interpellated as a fully intentional subject (the perlocutionary act can be seen as a linguistic counterpart to Foucault's conception of pastoral power, a form of government that does not act directly on subjects but "acts upon their actions," as I will discuss shortly[35]). Thoreau's performative gardening finds an echo in Potawatomi biologist Robin Wall Kimmerer's description of a vegetable garden as a place where "you can't say 'I love you' out loud, [but] you can say it in seeds. And the land will reciprocate, in beans."[36] In both Kimmerer and Thoreau, speaking in seeds entails having faith in the soil and the countless determinants that contribute to the beans' growth. Thoreau continually evokes the participatory nature of husbandry, which requires not acting directly on something so much as *activating* it by controlling its environment. The true farmer does not rule by fiat but must acknowledge the limited and ancillary role he plays in the economy of nature. He will not be tempted to turn nature into his garden unless he ignores that "the sun looks on our cultivated fields and on the prairies and forests *without distinctions.* ... In [the sun's] view the earth is all equally cultivated *like a garden*" (111, emphases added).

Hence Thoreau's determination to refute the notion of spontaneous generation in his late study on "The Dispersion of Seeds," which attends to the unlikely phenomenon of vegetable locomotion (seeds "run," "fly," "sail," "go off like pistols on the slightest touch").[37] This work can be classified alongside Eadweard Muybridge's protocinematic experiments on "animal locomotion" a decade later, except instead of slicing up a movement too rapid for the human eye, Thoreau reconstitutes the invisible journey of seeds too slow, too small, or too dispersed to be registered in real (human) time. Wind, water, jays, and rodents count as "the principal agents in this planting."[38] The desire to connect the growth of plants to a multiplicity of unheeded causes is present already in *Walden*, for Thoreau catalogs the cultivator's many "auxiliaries"—the sun, the dew, worms and squirrels, etc.—to advance a more distributed, less individuated but still "invidious" understanding of his own farming practice. He insists on seeing the farmer as a transitory means in the larger "economy of living," which has little to do with the "*political* economy" taught in New England colleges (35). He concludes the bean-field chapter with a homily about the "sacred" labor of the "true husbandman" (etymologically, the one who is "house-bound," the manager of an estate), who never works *solely* for his private interests. Lamenting the deritualized economization of modern agriculture, which sacrifices to Plutus instead of Ceres or Jove, Thoreau condemns the "grovelling habit, from which none of us is free, of regarding the soil as property" (111). This is not a moral judgment so much as a pragmatic call for de-habituating oneself, for re-forming oneself so as not to "deform" the landscape (111).

Concluding on the farmer's duty to be more squirrel-like and "relinquish all claim to the produce of his fields" (112) seems at first sight to contradict his whole enterprise, which started as a means "to earn ten or twelve dollars by some honest and agreeable method" (36). Turning a profit, however, is not incompatible with the cosmological perspective Thoreau adopts at the end of the bean-field chapter so long as it does not become the farmer's primary motivation. The true husbandman's operations must not be construed as a series of discrete acts aimed at accumulating private wealth but instead as a laborious, iterative, and endless praxis with countless beneficiaries:

> It was a singular experience that long acquaintance which I cultivated with beans, what with planting, and hoeing, and harvesting, and threshing, and picking over and selling them,—the last was the hardest of

all,—I might add eating, for I did taste. I was determined to know beans. When they were growing, I used to hoe from five o'clock in the morning till noon, and commonly spent the rest of the day about other affairs.

(108)

The polysyndeton and the accumulation of gerunds ("planting, and hoeing, and harvesting") perform the very grammar of action that Thoreau puts into practice in his bean-field: sporadic but continuous, finite but interminable.[39] This chapter does not simply critique the agricultural innovations promoted by the Federal Government, as Robert A. Gross has argued;[40] rather, it effectively *rehearses* (from the Old French *rehercier*, to re-harrow) a different type of culture as cultivation—a cultivation, remarkably, not of the beans themselves, but of his "long acquaintance" with them. This new type of cultivation, I will now argue, is best understood within a biopolitical frame, for it involves both a reconception of the exercise of power (from a right *over* the living to a right *of* the living) and a transformation of the self (from subject of law to subject of interests). But it is crucial not to reduce the bean-field to a metaphorical training ground for what Jane Bennett calls, in Foucauldian fashion, a "technique of self."[41] The bean-field is primarily a living milieu in which humans, animals, and plants are all "equally," albeit differentially and invidiously, subject to forms of gardening, or "governmentality." In Thoreau's (writings on his) farming experiment we find the lineaments of a biopolitics attentive to plant life.

Harvesting

In her magisterial *Bird Relics*, Branka Arsić contends that Thoreau's idiosyncratic vitalism has "nothing to do with what, in the wake of Foucault's analysis, became known as the biopolitical organization of power." The early architects of biopolitics, she explains, were not philosophers of life but political thinkers primarily invested in the preservation of the liberal body politic. When they invoked life as a model for their politics, these thinkers construed it in immunological terms, as that which "protect[s] itself from what is foreign and ... unsafe"[42]—an approach that implies a deeply normative and hierarchized perception of life used to justify the killing (or letting die) of deviant lifeforms. Ultimately, Arsić shows biopolitics to be overly *organized*, and centered around individuated units, whereas life as Thoreau conceived it defies organicity and troubles established boundaries between species (human/animal) and kingdoms (animal/plant/minerals).[43] The only way to reconcile Thoreau with biopolitics, she posits, is to embrace what Roberto Esposito calls "affirmative biopolitics," a politics "no longer *over* life but *of* life, one that doesn't superimpose already constituted (and by now destitute) categories of modern politics on life, but rather inscribes the innovative power of a life rethought in all its complexity."[44] From this perspective, "any thing that lives needs to be thought in the unity of life," Esposito asserts, which means "that no part of it can be destroyed in favor of another."[45]

What, then, of Thoreau's deliberate destruction of weeds in favor of his beans? How can we reconcile Esposito's nonsacrificial injunction with Thoreau's oblative recommendation? I do not think that Thoreau's decision to oust weeds (and the justificatory violence of designating some plants as *weeds*) is incompatible with his vitalist proclivities, but I do think it reveals him to be a biopolitical thinker. At the end of *Plant Theory,* Nealon remarks that Esposito's affirmative biopolitics is in principle hospitable to plants, but he immediately concedes that it "contains no particular policy implications." The value of Esposito's trans-individual ontology of life is primarily heuristic, only giving "a picture of how something like life works": life can no longer appear as the "property of an individual organism," as biopower "seems to have decided";[46] instead, when we "follow the plants," we are able to think biopower beyond the immunological model. We realize that life "is not something that's owned by an organism, something hidden deep within it, to be protected against the outside at all costs; rather, life is the territory for the emergence of ... assemblages of heterogeneous processes."[47]

Thoreau knew this. His philosophy of life was deeply informed by his understanding of plants—his avid engagements with the major botanists of his time,[48] and more importantly his experiments in husbandry ("I did not read books the first summer; I hoed beans," 75).[49] More than a speculative epistemology of plant life, *Walden* sketches a pragmatic politics of planting—a method of husbanding a new "generation" (indeed, a new type) of citizens:

> I will not plant beans and corn with so much industry another summer, but such seeds, if the seed is not lost, as sincerity, truth, simplicity, faith, innocence, and the like, and see if they will not *grow* in this soil. ... Why concern ourselves so much about our beans for seed, and not be concerned at all about a new *generation* of men? We should really be fed and cheered if when we met a man we were sure to see that some of the qualities which I have named, which we all prize more than those other productions, but which are for the most part *broadcast and floating in the air,* had *taken root and grown* in him. ... We should never cheat and insult and banish one another by our meanness, if there were present the *kernel* of worth and friendliness.
>
> (110, emphases added)

These new citizens would, in turn, create a new kind of political garden. Indeed, Thoreau uses this image for American politics, urging ambassadors to import the seeds of "truth or justice" to US soil and distribute them freely. As with most of Thoreau's ideas, this one is rooted in empirical observation, for he knew that John Quincy Adams had requested ambassadors to send rare seeds to Washington and that the Congressional Seed Distribution Program, begun in 1839, dispatched seeds to farmers to stimulate and diversify US agricultural production.

Thoreau's germinal imagery points toward the future—the political harvest produced by proper planting and diligent hoeing—but it is rooted in the long imperial history of "planting," in the archaic sense of establishing a colony. Indeed, the word "plantation" should be heard *literally* in the Puritans' "Plantation of the Lord" and the plantation economy, as both imply transplantation of deracinated populations, the former semi-voluntary, the latter forced. Cotton Mather's lament that "never were more Satanical Devices used for the Unsettling of any People under the Sun, than what have been Employ'd for the Extirpation of the Vine which God has here *Planted*," for instance, takes on a more factual dimension when we consider Mather's pioneering work on plant hybridization, and even more so when we situate the Puritan jeremiad in the larger context of New World colonization.[50] Indeed, the colonies were literally "'planted' with people," as Sylvia Wynter observes, "not in order to form societies, but to carry on plantations whose aim was to produce single crops for the market."[51] For economic reasons, plantation zones were structured in ways that favored monocultures and proscribed the formation of "societies," nipping in the bud anything that looked like a diverse culture. "That is to say," Wynter continues, "the plantation-societies of the Caribbean came into being as adjuncts to the market system; their peoples came into being as an adjunct to the product, to the single crop commodity—the sugar cane—which they produced."[52] Anna Tsing also chooses the example of the sugarcane to correlate the treatment of plants and persons in the colonies. Just as the sugarcane, "imported to the New World, had few interspecies relations," so too the enslaved Africans working in plantations "had no social relations and thus no established routes for escape." This represented a great advantage from the planters' perspectives: "Like the cane itself which had no history of either companion species or disease relation in the New World, [African slaves] were isolated. They were on their way to becoming self-contained, and thus standardizable as abstract labor."[53]

Thoreau knew well that plants are not simply resources for governments (colonial or modern) to accumulate but "actants" that have significant effects on the land's occupants. And he was well aware that agriculture was a powerful instrument of colonial domestication when he referred to the seventeenth-century horticulturist John Evelyn's treatise *Terra: A Philosophical Discourse of Earth, Relating to the Culture and Improvement of It for Vegetation, and the Propagation of Plants*, which advised members of the British Royal Society on how best to "endenizon" plants to the cold climes of England.[54] Altering landscapes and climates was theorized by Evelyn as an efficient and necessary (if indirect) mode of governing colonial subjects. Thus the lexical field of seminality cultivated by Thoreau harkens back to the botanical model by which the premodern era theorized the influence of the climate on mores and customs. "Men are like plants," Crèvecoeur famously wrote in his *Letters from an American Farmer* (1782): "The goodness and flavour of the fruit proceeds from the peculiar soil and exposition in which they grow. We are nothing but what we derive from the air we breathe, the climate we inhabit, the government we obey."[55] The economic stakes and ideological underpinnings of Crèvecoeur's analogy—a well-known feature of late Enlightenment epistemology—are more discernible when viewed from the colonies.[56] The correlation between people and plants, however, was more or less strict depending on the "kind" of population it referenced, as Daniel Nemser observes. Certain bodies were believed to be more susceptible to environmental determinants, which led to the construal of racial difference as a function of a population's assumed vulnerability to external factors. The differential analogy between "plants and (certain kinds of) people," Nemser argues, implied the invention of an imperial "program of research" with far-reaching epistemological, political, and economic implications.[57] This program did not simply inventory plants in tidy classificatory tables to apprehend the "things themselves," as was the ideal of classical taxonomy according to Foucault;[58] rather, it understood plants to be dependent on a number of environmental factors (type of soil, temperature, altitude, humidity, etc.). For Nemser, this attunement to what specific conditions nonnative plants—and, by extension, displaced populations—needed in order to thrive or simply survive was forged in the colonies and first theorized in Alexander von Humboldt's early work on plant geography, not in the Paris laboratory of Georges Cuvier.[59]

Although at first sight Thoreau's parable of the sower appears to recycle an obsolete colonial epistemology, it bespeaks an attention to the discreet persistence, indeed the becoming "infrastructural," of the logic of what Nemser calls "imperial botany." If Thoreau recognizes humans' constitutive susceptibility to environmental management, however, he rejects any kind of predetermined racial hierarchy or climactic fatalism, demanding instead that space and time must always be left for indetermination (which is why he refuses to use manure to hasten the growth of his beans, favoring instead the "continual motion" of the hoe). Thoreau insists that government should not force men against their nature precisely insofar as this "nature" is pervious to external influences and never fully fixed in advance. Hence in his most explicitly political essay, "On Civil Disobedience," which he composed at the same time as *Walden*, Thoreau writes:

I perceive that, when an acorn and a chestnut fall side by side, the one does not remain inert to make way for the other, but both obey their own laws, and spring and grow and flourish as best they can, till one, perchance, overshadows and destroys the other. If a plant cannot live according to its nature, it dies; and so a man.

(237)

The word "destroys" denotes a degree of violence, though speaking of violence seems absurd since there is no conscious decision involved in the destruction; there are only seeds following their natural dispositions as they interface with external events and "perchance" managing to thrive at the expense of another seed. Yet if we take Thoreau at his word, as Arsić has taught us, the form of "government" he calls for is one that ought to be observant of the internal "laws" of every one of its human and nonhuman constituents, even though it will ultimately prove unable to guarantee "that no part of it can be destroyed in favor of another," as Esposito has it.

In the first sentence of "Civil Disobedience," Thoreau famously declares that he "heartily accept[s] the motto,—'That government is best which governs least,'" a motto he immediately glosses as "That government is best which governs not at all" (224). This is, in a way, a restatement of Thoreau's ideas about garden politics, and in it I hear an echo to Foucault's analysis of pastoral power, which he defines as "the art of not being governed quite so much."[60] The governmental formation that Foucault names pastoral power, whose establishment in the West he situates at the end of the eighteenth century, embraces this idea of the "least state"[61] by positioning itself as temporary, as a stopgap; acting as a mere "intermediary between the flock and pasture," pastoral power offers itself as a power working toward its own abolition insofar as it does not exercise any authority "imposed from above" but "pegs its action to the truth."[62] If "men were to govern according to the rules of evidence," Foucault argues, "it would be things themselves, rather than men, that govern."[63] As such, pastoral power appears to be in keeping with Thoreau's notion that "government is best which governs not at all" (note that Thoreau does *not* advocate the suppression of government but calls for the advent of an idle or nongoverning government, a government that "governs not at all"[64]).

Does this mean that Thoreau falls prey to the lure of this new governmental reason that operates by enlisting "the truth" (e.g., that purports to do nothing but follow the "natural" laws of the market)? Does Thoreau believe that there could exist a form of government that would truly conform to the "nature" of its subjects? Here we must remember that for both Foucault and Thoreau, "resistance" is never external to the practice of government but an integral part of it, necessary for the health of both government and those it governs.[65] In other words, subjects must *labor* to produce a government in harmony with "their own laws." This is precisely what is at stake in "Resistance to Civil Government"—the alternative title for "Civil Disobedience."[66] Thoreau's "best" government is one whose laws conform with the nature of its subjects. But these subjects are not *naturally* disposed to accept this government, as is demonstrated by the majority's acceptance of a government that enslaves a sixth of the nation's population (227); they need to be "prepared," they need to "*cultivate* a respect" not just for the law but "for the right" (225, emphasis added). The men who best "serve" their government are those who actively "resist" its tendency to conflate the right and the lawful and to pass off as natural fact a fiction sanctioned by colonial interests.[67] The very last sentence of Thoreau's essay aligns the proper state with the vegetable action of nature, asserting that a "State which bore this kind of fruit, and suffered it to drop off as fast as it ripened, would prepare the way for a still more perfect and glorious State, which also I have imagined, but not yet anywhere seen" (243). Conjuring up a government that would treat each individual as a "higher and independent power, from which all its [the government's] own power and authority are derived" (243), Thoreau sums up the aporia of pastoral power as a power caring equally for each and all of its subjects *at the same time*.[68] This impossible equation begins with the care of the living, not from sovereign right to take life.

As mentioned in passing in the introduction, Foucault's model for this fundamentally "benevolent" form of power is not vegetable but zoopolitical. Pastoral power, he writes, "is not exercised over a territory but ... over a flock, and more exactly, over the flock in its movement from one place to another."[69] However de-territorialized, Foucault's flock is still reliant on "fertile grasslands," "prairies and pastures"—the temporary but necessary *stations* sustaining the mobile flock.[70] The advent of pastoral power, Foucault suggests, reconceptualizes the rather static category of territory into the more dynamic concept of "milieu," the space to which populations are "biologically" tied, but which itself is susceptible to change and management. Granted, Foucault pays more attention to the flock than to the pasture, but he does warn against the shepherd who treats the pasture only as a resource to feed his flock (and by extension his wallet): the "bad shepherd only thinks of good pasture for his own profit, for fattening the flock that he will be able to sell and scatter."[71] Similarly, Thoreau concludes the bean-field chapter by lamenting that the bad farmer sacrifices to Plutus instead of Ceres and treats nature "as a robber" would (111). Both thinkers invite us to integrate plants in our thinking as part of the modern imbrication of life and of politics. Foucault does this implicitly by relating modern governmentality to the regulation of milieus (not an isolatable element or a constant but a living "field of intervention"[72]); Thoreau more literally by championing constant renegotiation between the cultivator and the land. This interminable process of mutual cultivation is emblematized by his preference for the hoe, which links him intimately to the land and his beans. Thoreau's "continual motion, repastination, and turning of the mould with the spade" are not without violence, not without decision; the hoe still represents the gardener's power to spare life or decree death. But

Thoreau estimates that it allows for a more truthful and commensal relation to the pasture, which is neither a passive backdrop for human action nor a mere fund awaiting extraction, but an invaluable "auxiliary" that actively contributes to the squatter's temporary implantation.

Reading *Walden* as a practical counterpart to "Resistance to Civil Government" helps us understand plant theory's recommendation to "slow down," even in the face of climate emergency, indeed *because* the situation is so critical, and has always been critical for some more than others. Potawatomi philosopher and environmental activist Kyle Powys Whyte warns against wielding the discourse of emergency because it is likely to "justify solutions that ultimately harm indigenous peoples." He is fully aware that developing relationships of trust and reciprocity between indigenous nations and other parties takes time, and that "the slow onset of achieving these relationships forecloses the global capacity to avoid climate disruptions." Yet he also knows that it is "the establishment of kinship that will make it possible, at some point in the future, to behave urgently when the need arises."[73] Accounting for vegetable life, likewise, prepares the way for a more capacious and rightful, though no less decisive biopolitics. But we must refrain from adopting lapsarian narratives that overlook the discreet yet foundational place that plants have occupied in the settling of Western politics. Recognizing planting, hoeing, and harvesting as critical features of modern governmentality is the condition for activating resistance to unjust governments.

And perhaps, despite the enduring perception that Thoreau is an individualist thinker, for *organizing* resistance. For upon his release from jail, after being incarcerated for refusing to pay his taxes in protest against slavery and the Mexican-American War, Thoreau writes that he "joined a huckleberry party, who were impatient to put themselves under my conduct" (239). The political dimension of the word "party" eludes Emerson, who laments that his friend's "contemplative" genius prevented him from having any political ambition. "Wanting this," Emerson deplores, "instead of engineering for all America, he was the captain of a huckleberry-party. Pounding beans is good to the end of pounding empires one of these days; but if, at the end of years, it is still only beans!"[74] But beans are never just beans for Thoreau, and his flight from the city to the huckleberry field, where "the State is nowhere to be seen" (239), is not a desire to return to some utopian pastoral state; rather, it should be read as a necessarily oblique indictment of the pastoral nature of the modern State, and as a radical act of resistance.[75]

5

"Wild Thinking" and Vegetal Intelligence in Thoreau's Later Writings

Michael Jonik

The idea of vegetation is irresistible in considering mental activity.
Man seems a higher plant.

EMERSON, *NATURAL HISTORY OF INTELLECT*

If you would make acquaintance with the ferns you must forget
your botany.

THOREAU, *JOURNAL*, OCTOBER 4, 1859

Radicle Thinking

From within such varied domains as cognitive psychology and neurobiology, anthropology and ecology, informatics and computer science, and philosophy and literary theory, many researchers have begun to challenge not only the anthropomorphism of intelligence, but also its zoomorphism. They have posited how cognition, sensation, embodied perception, memory, learning, problem-solving, decision, or judgment might take place without a human or nonhuman animal brain or phenomenological subject of consciousness.

To some, this is tantamount to nothing short of another "Copernican revolution."[1] While many studies now focus on the implications of such a revolution for the relation between human and artificial intelligence, others have asserted the importance of plant intelligence, a field of study that traditionally has been sidelined not only by those who privilege human and animal minds, but also by plant biologists themselves. This situation has changed with the recent publication of works such as Michael Marder's *Plant-3 A Philosophy of Vegetal Life* (2013);[2] Anthony Trewavas's textbook *Plant Behaviour and Intelligence* (2014);[3] Eduardo Kohn's *How Forests Think: Toward an Anthropology Beyond the Human* (2013);[4] Stefano Mancuso and Alessandra Viola's *Brilliant Green: The Surprising History and Science of Plant Intelligence* (2015) and Mancuso's *The Revolutionary Genius of Plants: A New Understanding of Plant Intelligence and Behavior* (2018);[5] as well as more critical-theory oriented studies like Jeffrey T. Nealon's *Plant Theory: Biopower and Vegetable Life* (2016)[6] and Monica Gagliano, John C. Ryan, and Patrícia Vieira's collection *The Language of Plants: Science, Philosophy, Literature* (2017),[7] all of which have shown how plant intelligence, communication, and behavior challenge traditional understandings of the vegetal as passive, sessile, or deterministic. What is more, they call into question how anthropo- and zoo-centric biases implicitly shape how we think about plant intelligence. Plant intelligence, that is, might be radically different than animal intelligence, and demand an altogether different understanding of what might constitute intelligence.

Likewise, although her focus is primarily on the relation between technical and human nonconscious cognition, N. Katherine Hayles, in her *Unthought: The Power of the Cognitive Unconscious* (2017),[8] offers a brief discussion of "complex plant cognition" (a description which she prefers to call "the anthropocentrically laden word 'intelligence'").[9] She glosses the "ways plants sense information from their surroundings, communicate within themselves and to other biota, and respond flexibly and adaptively to their changing environments."[10] Following Michael Pollan, Hayles details "more than a dozen plant senses, among them kin recognition, detection of chemical signals from other plants, and the manufacture of chemicals that deter predators and release others that have psychotropic effects for pollinators so encouraging them to revisit that plant again" (20). Each of these forms of plant cognition implies a communication network that functions through the "sessile life style" of plants, namely, one that operates through the material substrates to which they are attached.[11] Plant cognition serves for Hayles as an example of an extended, cognitive ecology, dependent on a series of complex symbiotic relationships and concatenated agencies, and in which "plants interpret a wide range of information about their environments and respond to challenges in remarkably nuanced and complex ways."[12]

Plant intelligence is not a new idea, however, despite this noteworthy resurgence of interest in the topic. In his 1880 *The Power of Movement in Plants*, Darwin remarks that, although "plants do not of course possess nerves or a central nervous system, we may infer that with animals such structures serve only for the more perfect transmission of impressions, and for the more complete intercommunication of the several parts."[13] Like Hayles's nonconscious plant cognition, this intra- and inter-organism transmission of materials and impressions entails an integrated system of sensation or a self-awareness within the plant. Yet Darwin focuses on the tip of the radicle —the primary root; the first organ to appear when the seed germinates—as the dynamic site of the plant's haptic sensations and phototropisms. The radicle is, for Darwin, the "helmsman" of the plant's directed movements: "It is hardly an exaggeration to say that the tip of the radicle thus endowed, and having the power of directing the movements of the adjoining parts, acts like the brain of one of the lower animals; the brain being seated within the anterior end of the body, receiving impressions from the sense-organs, and directing the several movements."[14] For Darwin, that is, plants might not have a central nervous system, but they nonetheless have a built-in system to communicate sensations, and a primary site from which, on the basis of these sensations, motion can be controlled.

Like Darwin and these more recent scientists and theorists of plant intelligence, Henry David Thoreau does not begin with the premise that plants are insensate and immobile, but rather that they are able to sense, communicate, and self-distribute across territories. From his bean-field meditations in *Walden*, his journals (including the phenological charts which comprise his "Kalendar" project), to his later natural historical writings such as "The Succession of Forest Trees," "Wild Apples," and "Autumnal Tints," he tirelessly investigates the scientific, philosophical, literary historical, poetic, and cultural implications of botanical life for humans. Vegetable genius, organic intellectual growth, and the teleology of metamorphosis (in which embodied forms aspire to higher ideal forms) form the familiar phototropism of Thoreau's materialist/idealist philosophy: how facts flower into truths, and how embodied life seeks the morning light of higher thoughts and "higher laws."

But if Thoreau encourages humans to think like plants and seeks out human-vegetal analogies, in his published and unpublished writings, he compiles a vast archive of encounters with plants that enable us to recognize different modes of plant intelligence without imputing to them our anthropocentric biases and suppositions. If, as Sharon Cameron writes, Thoreau's work in his journal is to dissociate the thinking of nature from "the background of human concerns" and "human significance,"[15] one modality of this is how Thoreau opens a space to explore plant intelligence beyond its analogies to human (and animal) intelligence. This happens, I argue here, in both direct and indirect ways. Thoreau could be said to prefigure Stanley Cavell who, in *In Quest of the Ordinary,* when considering the intelligence or sentience of plants, prompts us not to understand flowers as thinking or feeling as humans do, but to act *as if* they think and feel in their own way, a way different than we do.[16] Yet, more specifically, as Thoreau rigorously transcribes his perceptions of vegetable phenomena in the seasonal meditations in his journals, he often organizes his botanical observations around key themes such as plant blooming and growth, swamp ecology, forest transmission and "succession," the dispersion of seeds, or the relation of wild to cultivated plants—all of which collectively he calls, after Emerson's essay of the same name, the "method of nature."[17] Thoreau diagrams the method of nature, however, as a collectivity of natural agencies, in which plant actants conspire with human and nonhuman animal actants, as well as with aleatoric material agential phenomena such as sunlight, the wind, the rain, or intensive temperature differences.

What is key is to ask to what extent we can explain these themes in terms of intelligence, and not merely as deterministic modes of self-organization. It is to ask to what extent the method of nature might serve as a figure of collective or distributed intelligence or as an integrated self-aware system. To better see this, I will put Thoreau's "The Succession of Forest Trees," "Wild Apples," "Autumnal Tints," and selections from his journals and unfinished manuscripts *The Dispersion of Seeds* and *Wild Fruits* in conversation with the current discourse regarding plant intelligence, distributed cognition, and collective natural agency. What emerges is a Thoreau who thinks not just in ponds and rivers, but in swamps and forests; in which the soil expresses its summer thought in beans, and in which the tart apple and the acrid cranberry become potent examples of the nonhuman semiotics of taste.

Intelligence with the Earth

Before exploring how Thoreau describes plant intelligence on its own terms, it is important to note how the relation of human and vegetable intelligence works as a recurrent motif in his work, to the extent that it forms a key epistemological and ontological ground for his philosophy of nature. We can see this, for example, in a May 20, 1851, journal entry, in which Thoreau recasts several passages from Asa Gray's *Manual of the Botany of the Northern United States* (1848) to unfold what he calls the "perfect analogy between the life of the human being and that of the vegetable, both of the body and the mind"[18] Whereas Gray understands the organs of plants as divided between organs of growth and of reproduction, Thoreau seeks to understand his organs of physical, intellectual, and moral growth, and how his labor and his mind will bear fruit. Like Gray's plant, he asserts, the mind develops "upwards to expand in the light and air; and downwards avoiding the light to form the root," and thus there is "[f]or each new successive idea or bud, a new rootlet in the earth" (*J* II: 203). Or, again: "The most clear and ethereal ideas (Antaeus-like) readily ally themselves to the earth, to the primal womb of things. … No idea is so soaring but it will readily put forth roots" (J, II 204). Thoreau then refines the structural analogy: the stem, the "axis and original basis of the plant," becomes the "the rudiment of mind, already partially developed." Moreover, as Darwin will later, he pays special attention to the sensitivity of the radicle (even if he understands it here in relation to the human mind: "This organ of the mind's development, the *Root,* bears no organs but spongelets or absorbing points" (*J* II: 203). For, as Thoreau puns, a true "radicle" is one who "sends down a tap-root to the centre of things" (*J* II: 203). Insofar as this "schema" bears on the character of humans generally, he concludes, we can divide those whose minds are balanced and firmly planted from those whole loosely rooted arguments might be "overthrown by the first wind" (*J* II: 203). We can separate those whose minds are like parasitic plants, who have their roots in other plants: indeed, Thoreau rhetorically asks of his contemporaries, "most are not such?!"

In another journal entry from March 7, 1859, Thoreau similarly seeks a kinship between human and vegetal life, but here further unfolds it in terms of the "Transcendent use" of the life of plants as revealed by the poet:

> The mystery of this life of plants is kindred with that of our own lives, and the physiologist must not be in too much haste to explain their growth according to mechanical laws. … The ultimate expression or fruit of any created thing—is the fine effluence which only the most ingenuous worshipper perceives at a reverent distance from its surface even—The cause & the effect are equally evanescent & intangible—and the former must be investigated within the same spirit & with the same reverence with which the latter is perceived—Only that intellect makes any progress toward conceiving of the essence which at the same time perceives the effluence.
>
> (*J* XII: 23–24)

On the basis of the "fine effluence" of the plant, Thoreau rejects the physiological explanation of the phototropism of the potato vine:

> Accordingly I reject Carpenter's explanation of the fact that a potato vine in a cellar grows toward the light—When he says—"The reason obviously is, that, in consequence of the loss of fluid from the tissue of the stem, on the side on which the light falls, it is contracted, whilst that of the other side remains turgid with fluid. The stem makes a bend, therefore, until its growing point becomes opposite to the light, & then increases in that direction" (C's "Vegetable Physiology," page 174.). There is no ripeness which is not so to speak something ultimate in itself—& not merely a perfected means to a higher end—In order to be ripe it must serve a Transcendent use. The ripeness of a leaf—being perfected—leaves … the tree at that point & never returns to it. It has nothing to do with

any other fruit which the tree may bear—& only [the] genius [of the eye] of the poet can—pluck it. The fruit of a tree is neither in the seed or in the full grown tree (the timber)—but it is simply the highest use to which it can be put.

(*J* XII: 23–24)

Here, Thoreau's understanding of vegetal growth and developments is over-coded by how the poetic intellect, exemplified by what he calls elsewhere the "poetic perception of metamorphosis," sees the plant as a striving for a higher use, a "ripeness" of a fruit that goes beyond its temporary embodiment as seed or full-grown tree.

In this way, Thoreau's frequent analogies between the development of the human mind and the process of plant growth often serve as purposeful poetic conflations, and jolt complacent anthropocentric understandings of the mind. In *Walden*, to this end, he asks: "Shall I not have intelligence with the earth? Am I not partly leaves and vegetable mould myself?"[19] It is significant that Thoreau describes this intelligence (which Laura Dassow Walls reminds us comes from the Latin "to choose," "to gather," or "to perceive")[20] not as intelligence "about" the earth or "of" the earth, but as intelligence *with* the earth. This "with" does not imply a form of mastery or representation, but posits intelligence as a joint venture, or an essential hybridity: he is part vegetable matter himself. Like the neo-platonic figure of "Sympathy with Intelligence" he aspires to in "Walking," intelligence *with* the earth is an ongoing getting to know the living, nonhuman, and wild world. In a journal entry on September 9, 1854, Thoreau registers the maternal care the earth itself provides for turtle eggs as a vitalist earth intelligence:

I am affected by the thought that the earth nurses these eggs. ... It suggests a certain vitality and intelligence in the earth, which I had not realized. This mother is not merely inanimate and inorganic. ... The earth has some virtue in it; when seeds are put into it, they germinate; when turtles' eggs, they hatch in due time.

(*J* XIII: 28)

His notion of earth intelligence is in direct relation to his notion of "wildness" as both open an epistemological space in which humans participate in non-anthropocentric modes of thinking and being. His wild apothegms are well known: "Life consists with wildness. The most alive is the wildest:"[21] "We have a wild savage in us" (*E*, 213); "We need the tonic of wildness" (*W*, 317); "It is in vain to dream of a wilderness distant from ourselves. There is none such. It is the bog in our brains and bowels" (J, IX, 43). He celebrates "the uncivilized free and wild thinking" of the *Iliad* and *Hamlet*, but his "wild thinking" also is a becoming-wild of thinking in which epistemology verges on ethology, entomology, botany, ecology telmatology, or even meteorology (*E*, 207). He patiently observes the instinctual labors of squirrels and the "swift and beautiful" mallard-thought of wild ducks. The loon on Walden Pond becomes a model of inscrutable insouciant animal intelligence: it is cunning and surveys; it makes up its mind and reconnoiters. The loon thus thinks in ways that confound Thoreau's human-all-too-human "endeavor to calculate" his next move or "to divine his thought" in his own (*W*, 235).[22]

Amidst the transcriptions of natural phenomena in his journal, Thoreau finds manifold nonhuman figures for the human mind. He transforms insect eggs into a metaphor for the transmission of thought: "While I am abroad, the ovipositors plant their seed in me; I am fly-blown with thought and go home to hatch and brood over them" (*PJ* 2: 338–9). He wants to write a "meteorological journal of the mind" (*PJ* 3: 377), and conflates thinking-feeling with the weather: "Would you see your mind—look at the sky. Would you know your moods, be weather-wise" (*PJ* 4: 291). Thoreau's instances of wild thinking limn a poetic theory of the mind as superjected beyond its confines as a human, body-bound phenomenon. He thus prompts us toward a radical re-inscription of intimate, deliberate knowledge into the thinking of wildness and the wildness of thinking. He both anthropomorphizes human intelligence through his analogies with animals, plants, or the weather, and points to the "intimate alterity"[23] of the wild within the bog in our brains. But, as his writings invite us to join him in a process of encounter in which mind and nature enter a dynamic reciprocity, or a constant falling into the difference of the other, at the same time, he also registers the radical alterity of human and nonhuman animal, plant and earth intelligence. On Walden Pond, the loon's incalculable, demonical thinking remains resistant to human decipherment, and the wild thinking of wild plants might entail an altogether inhuman swamp or vegetal swarm intelligence.

In his journal, the inhuman alterity of plants Thoreau encounters in Concord's swamps inspires him both "to get to know" its plants as his strange neighbors and to lament that he is unable to fully and systematically know them all. Not without a note of resignation, that is, he reports,

I remember gazing with interest at the swamps about those days and wondering if I could ever attain to such familiarity with plants that I should know the species of every twig and leaf in them, that I should be acquainted with every plant (excepting grasses and cryptogamous ones), summer and winter, that I saw. Though I knew most of the flowers and there were not in any particular swamp more than half a dozen shrubs that I did not know, yet these made it seem like a maze to me of a thousand strange species, and I even thought of commencing at one end and looking it faithfully and laboriously through till I knew it all. I little thought that in a year or two I should have attained to that knowledge without all that labor. Still, I never studied botany and do not to day

systematically, the most natural system is still so artificial. I wanted to
know my neighbors, if possible,—to get a little nearer to them.

(*J* IX: 157)

Or, again, the following year: "I am interested in \ each contemporary plant
in my vicinity, and have attained to a certain acquaintance with the larger
ones. They are cohabitants with me of this part of the planet, and they bear
familiar names—Yet how essentially wild they are—as wild really as those
strange fossil plants whose impressions I see on my coal" (*J* IX: 406). What
does it mean to get to know his plant neighbors, or to get nearer to them?
These passages assuredly reveal the increasing method with which Thoreau
approached his botanical observations, culminating in his phenological
project of returning repeatedly to given plants, and recording their blooming
over the course of years. At the same time, it marks how Thoreau's non-
appropriative thinking works to cultivate an eco-ethics of approach toward
his "planetary cohabitants": not to have and to hold, but to let-be and to
behold them. His admiration and reverence toward wild, botanical life are
the timbre of his meditations.

But we should also note Thoreau's desire to integrate his human
intelligence within the collectivity of plant intelligences that comprise
the vital space of the swamp. To get to know the swamp's plants, that
is, is also to get to know the plants as themselves knowing, and thus to
resituate his human knowing within a heterogeneous multi-agent system of
knowing. Thoreau marks this as he follows his "genius," as if instinctually
or "unconsciously,"[24] to go "a-cranberrying" in the swamp. There, like the
cunning loon he stalks on the pond, he seeks "cunning little cranberries"
(*J* IX: 38) which either stay "high and dry" on top of the sphagnum, or lay
low among the mosses—in either case enacting their own means of evading
predation and optimizing the conditions of their environment. As Branka
Arsić notes, "swamps become workshops of life, sites in which all strange or
'cunning' mixtures are enacted" and "embod[y] the incessant continuity of
mutation."[25] Thoreau recognizes that it is not just animal intelligence that is
given to its "cunning" but plant intelligence insofar as it effects all manner
of beneficial symbiotic or parasitic relationships, or adjusts its behavior to
better its collective situation.

Although Thoreau does not claim to get to know the "cryptogamous"
plants (whose categorization Arsić deftly shows to stem from the Greek for
"hidden marriage"—*kryptos gameein*),[26] the method of nature is marked
by its dynamic hidden marriages of symbionts and parasites. In the name of
the lichen, in yet another journal passage, Thoreau celebrates this in terms
of the "value" of such "mutual intelligence."[27] As plants have their own type
of "low cunning," too,[28] their cunning is nonetheless put in relationship
to Thoreau's own genius. As is often the case in Thoreau, the relationship
between human and plant cohabitants is emphasized without privileging the

human. A desire to know without control, an ethics of approach without appropriation, and a reverence without anthropocentrism mark how Thoreau seeks to better "get to know" the plants in his local environment. It marks the manner in which he posits his genius as among them, even if this puts him at odds with the human-all-too-human practices of "systematic" botany, which Thoreau still takes to be "artificial."

To record the method of nature through such figures of mutual intelligence or intelligence with the earth, Thoreau develops his own experimental and multilayered writing method, which combines empirical observations about botanical and other phenomena, with narrations and reflections on his scientific and poetic practices. Thoreau outlines his project as the passage cited above continues:

> I soon found myself observing when plants first blossomed and leafed, and I followed it up early and late, far and near, several years in succession, running to different sides of the town and into the neighboring towns, often between twenty and thirty miles a day. I often visited a particular plant four or five miles distant, half a dozen times within a fortnight, that I might know exactly when it opened, beside attending to a great many others in different directions and some of them equally distant, at the same time.
>
> (*J* IX: 58)

Recent critics have compellingly analyzed Thoreau's developing scientific interest in phenology and the methods through which he rigorously transcribes "when exactly" a flower opens in the spring.[29] But, as he does so, he also marks plants' collective responses to meteorological and other physical variations. For plants to synchronize these responses, plant biologists argue that plants must have a mechanism for remembering variations such as the time since the last cold day, in order to know it is safe to flower. As Stefano Mancuso explains in *The Evolutionary Genius of Plants*, this occurs as a kind of biochemical memory:

> [Plants'] reproductive success and ability to generate progeny are based, above all else, on their ability to bloom at the right time. Many plants only bloom for only a set number of days at the end of the winter cold. They are therefore able to remember how much time has passed. This is clearly an epigenetic memory. ... Epigenetic modifications seem to play a greater role in plants than in animals. Prions [a type of protein abnormality given to harmful effects] in animals are not good news ... [i]n plants, however, they may provide an original form of biochemical memory. Contrary to what one might think, the importance of these studies goes beyond the purely botanical. ... In addition to solving the mystery of how plants remember, understanding the workings of memory in organisms without

brains will help lead to a better understanding of how human memory works: what mechanisms lead to its alterations or pathologies and how its distinctive forms can be situated outside the nervous system.[30]

Not only is the right timing of plants' blooming essential to their own survival, it is essential to the survival of the ecosystem as well, insofar as an early blooming or leafing would disrupt the life-cycles of a host of other organisms, such as the migratory animals that depend on spring flowers for nutrition. Although plant biochemical memory, understood through environmental epigenetics, is only now becoming an important area of biological research, Thoreau's phenological observations compiled in his Kalender already provide an extensive record of instances of the self-memory of plants. By marking when, over a course of years, that Concord plants bloom, he implicitly registers their internalization and self-awareness of intensive temperature differences, their own processes of vernalization, and of other environmental factors. "February 23, 1860. 3P.M. Thermometer 58° and snow almost gone, river rising. We have not had so warm a day since the beginning of December, which was unusually warm. I walk over the moist Nawshatuck hillside, and see the green radical leaves of the buttercup, shepherd's purse, sorrel, chickweed, cerastium, etc. revealed" (J XIII: 158–59). Often, such passages are records not only of an individual plant's blooming, but also of Thoreau's perception of that plant's blooming, and the "idea or image" of the plant that "occupies his thoughts" in the midst of his "botanical rambles."[31] Thoreau's own perceptual-memory system and the perceptual-memory system which his journals develop thus work in tandem with the memory systems of plants themselves.

In his "Natural History of Intellect," and in a way reminiscent of Thoreau's botanical meditations, Emerson asserts that "Man seems a higher plant."[32] But this is perhaps less true in the sense of an evolutionary superiority of humanity over plants, than in how a vegetal intelligence might provide an alternative format for understanding the bases of human intelligence: a memory that occurs otherwise than in a brain or a nervous system, and thus disaggregates a unified subject of phenomenological consciousness; a different type of collective perceptual system that operates at different temporalities. Whereas these possibilities were not yet legible to him, Thoreau's cunning cranberries and spring blossoms nonetheless offer a living archive of a nonanthropocentric intelligence with the earth, one in which his writing participates and seeks to perpetuate.

Forest Thinking

One of the challenges of understanding plant intelligence is the divergent timescale under which it operates. We are accustomed to thinking of intelligence in terms of the individual human animal as it negotiates the performative space of its *Umwelt*: as it perceives successive environmental affordances, more or less in sync with the timescales of its consciousness; as it interweaves activated memories with imagined adjacent-possible and longer-term scenarios. We can thus surmise "what [it] is like to be a bat."[33] However, plant intelligence is less relative to the momentary temporalities of individual stimuli and response, and as Trewavas notes, should instead be thought in terms of a long-duration processes involving a collectivity of agents (akin more to colony-building or swarm intelligence than to an individual subjectivity). Mainly sessile plants cannot flee or fight in the face of a predator, or evade adverse environmental circumstances, but need to develop alternative, attenuated tactics of survival. As such, the temporality of plant intelligence, as is the case with plant memory, happens at a slower pace than animal intelligence, even as its eventuation might depend on a set of animal agencies and temporalities. We can discern the method of Nature in the swamp, then, as a tangled space of bacterial, fungal, vegetal, and animal agencies, the dynamic symbioses and parasitisms among these, of chemical and mineral flows and meteorological changes, of nonlinear causalities and multi-temporalities—all constituting an integrated ecology of cognition.

In Thoreau's later writings, the forest, like the swamp, serves as another ecology of cognition, realized through collective agencies and dynamic symbioses. There, he posits vegetal intelligence not only in terms of plants' sessile existence, but also in terms of "succession" (or forest reproduction and endurance) and, relatedly, "the dispersion of seeds." He carefully charts the dispersion of seeds through plants' anemophily (oaks seeds borne on the wind), entomophily (insect dispersion), and zoophily (the red squirrel and birds that instinctually digest and disperse cherry seeds). In the "Succession of Forest Trees," Thoreau likens the process to a natural transportation system by which a "seed is transported from where it grows, to where it is planted":

This is done chiefly by the agency of the wind, water, and animals. The lighter seeds, as those of pines and maples, are transported chiefly by wind and water; the heavier, as acorns and nuts, by animals. In all the pines, a very thin membrane, in appearance much like an insect's wing, grows over and around the seed, and independent of it, while the latter is being developed within its base. Indeed this is often perfectly developed, though the seed is abortive; nature being, you would say, more sure to provide the means of transporting the seed, than to provide the seed to be transported. In other words, a beautiful thin sack is woven around the seed, with a handle to it such as the wind can take hold of, and it is then committed to the wind, expressly that it may transport the seed and extend the range of the species; and this it does, as effectually, as when seeds are sent by mail in a different kind of sack from the patent-office. There is a patent-office at the seat of government of the universe, whose managers are as much interested in the dispersion of seeds as anybody at Washington can be, and their operations are infinitely more extensive and regular.

(E, 167)

Thoreau indulges the metaphorical conceit of the patent office, pushing his saga of the wind's transporting the seed to the brink of the bureaucratic sublime. But at another level of abstraction (and following Jacques Monod's philosophical work in biochemistry), he implies that dispersion or succession relies on a co-evolutionary play of teleonomy and chance: on a self-directed, auto-poetic, and self-aware transportation, that is nonetheless given to the manifold vicissitudes of physical circumstance (the seeds are transported by the whims of the wind). In "Wild Apples," Thoreau details this co-evolution as a "natural alliance" between animals and apple trees: "The leaves and tender twigs are an agreeable food to many domestic animals, as the cow, horse, sheep, and goat; and the fruit is sought after by the first, as well as by the hog. Thus there appears to have existed a natural alliance between these animals and this tree from the first." Such natural alliances work across categorical and species distinctions and recast plants not as individuals but collectivities. For Thoreau's time, this served to disprove Agassiz's notion of special creation *in situ*; and for ours, it reminds us that the evolution of a particular species never takes place apart from its co-evolving ecology. Contra Agassiz, that is, he notes in "The Succession of Forest Trees":

> As for the heavy seeds and nuts which are not furnished with wings, the notion is still a very common one that, when the trees which bear these spring up where none of their kind were noticed before, they have come from seeds or other principles spontaneously generated there in an unusual manner, or which have lain dormant in the soil for centuries, or perhaps been called into activity by the heat of a burning. I do not believe these assertions, and I will state some of the ways in which, according to my observation, such forests are planted and raised. Everyone of these seeds, too, will be found to be winged or legged in another fashion. Surely it is not wonderful that cherry trees of all kinds are widely dispersed, since their fruit is well known to be the favorite food of various birds. ... Thus, though these seeds are not provided with vegetable wings, Nature has impelled the thrush tribe to take them into their bills and fly away with them; and they are winged in another sense, and more effectually than the seeds of pines, for these are carried even against the wind. The consequence is, that cherry trees grow not only here but there. The same is true of a great many other seeds.

(E, 169)

Some seeds, like pine seeds, travel in cones, while maple seeds have evolved an asymmetrical vane to fall slowly and be borne on the wind across great distances. Others, like cherries, learned to produce fruits delicious for animals to consume, which they later excrete and thus disperse; oaks produce heavy acorns which small mammals transport. Although cherries and acorns lack physical wings, for Thoreau, they thus gain wings or legs "in another fashion." (It is worth noting in this context that the evolutionary rise of mammals is coeval with the rise of trees, both around 300 million years ago.)

In his journal, Thoreau posits vegetal modes of self-organization, dispersion, and self-preservation as a form of wild thinking, albeit one that has a different temporality to human or animal thinking. Drawing on the work of Darwin, Gray, and Lyell, he describes the slow beginnings of philosophy in the forest:

> So botanically—the greatest changes in the landscape are produced more gradually than we expected. If nature has a pine or an oak wood to produce she manifests no haste about it. Thus we should say that oak forests are produced by a kind of accident i.e. by the failure of animals to reap the fruit of their labors—Yet who shall say that they have not a fair knowledge of the value of their labors—that the squirrel when it plants an acorn—or the jay when it lets one slip from under its foot has not a transient thought for its posterity? Possibly here, a thousand years hence, every oak will know the human hand that planted it.
>
> (J XIV: 212–13)

The possibility of "oak knowing" refers to the internal logic of the forest trees that mark their own slow formative processes, the accidental labors of squirrels and jays, and even the intervening hands of humans. Taken together the forest system's distributed cognitive ecology verges on a self-awareness of the co-construction of its future, even in the jay's "transient thought for its posterity." Thoreau again marks with close attention a multiplicity of micro-processes and creative involutions. Animal instinctual knowledge conspires with vegetative self-organization. A squirrel's instinct in plucking and stripping a pine cone becomes an event of mutual emergence with the pitch pine's "seed[ing] of new plantations." "How tenacious its purpose to spread and plant its race! By all methods nature secures this end, whether by the balloon, or parachute, or hook, or barbed spear like this, or mere lightness which the winds can waft" (J III: 65). Of course taking the forest as a collective intellective space which includes human actants (the hand that planted them) might also lead to adverse effects for the forest. He details on October 16, 1860, in an entry on White Pond and its neighborhood, how a human farmer negatively affected the forest ecology by over-foresting and irresponsible burning.

Anthropologist Eduardo Kohn, in his recent book *How Forests Think,* argues the forest itself might be thought of as a form of relational thinking: a nonhuman, non-linguistic semiotic system, a swarm intelligence. This semiotic system, however, is not limited to trees:

> Life-forms—human and nonhuman alike—because they are intrinsically semiotic, exhibit what Peirce calls a "scientific intelligence". By scientific he does not mean an intelligence that is human conscious, or even rational, but simply one that is "capable of learning by experience." ... Biological lineages also think. They too, over the generations, can grow to learn by experience about the world around them, and as such too demonstrate a "scientific intelligence." In sum, because life is semiotic and semiosis is alive, it makes sense to treat both lives and thoughts as "living thoughts."[34]

Here forest succession becomes a thoughtful biological lineage, an ongoing open-air archive, but one conceived through the common efforts of animals, plants, and other intelligences and agencies. Yet it is a lineage that takes a long time to bring to bear: forest temporality is slow and works at a timescale that makes it seem extrinsic to the momentariness of human consciousness. Nevertheless, in an October 13, 1860 journal entry, Thoreau praises the resilience and patience of oak and other trees: "They have learned to endure and bide their time. When you see an oak fully grown and of fair proportions, you little suspect what difficulties it may have encountered in its early your ... driven back into the earth again twenty times,—as often as it aspires to the heavens" (*J* XIV: 121). Succession appears, then, as a complex of temporalities and agencies: a "co-intellective" space;[35] in this context, we can understand one of the most detrimental effects of anthropogenic climate change to be how forest temporalities become out of sync with human and other living temporalities. As such we endanger the co-intellective spaces in which we dwell and might thrive.

The Soil's Summer Thought and How Wild Apples Grow

Forest thinking, "as also driven back into the earth," entails not only, as Richard Powers might call it, an "overstory," but also the dynamic and vast "understory" of subterranean communication in the soil medium, across the rhizosphere. Hayles, as we have seen, explores plant cognition in terms of their abilities to recognize chemical gradients in the soil and friendly and enemy roots. In turn, drawing on Darwin's *Movement of Plants*, Mancuso argues: "The entire root system guides the plant like a sort of collective brain or, better still, a distributed intelligence on a surface that can be huge."[36] For Mancuso, this is tantamount to "a decentralized system, consisting of many small 'agents,' explorers operating in parallel."[37] Trewavas, similarly, identifies the soil system as a dynamic heterogeneous network composed of biota, fungal symbionts, insects, annelids, and many other agents.[38] The rhizosphere is the underground counterpart of the branches and leaves which disperse their seeds and succeed: thus the forest emerges as a collective and communicative super-organism. If a tree wants to communicate across distances, it can take advantage not only of the disseminative patent and postal system, but also through subterranean routes. While Thoreau himself was not aware of such advances in plant biology, his notion of earth intelligence opens us, in vital material terms, to this possibility.

Thoreau's attention to the soil as medium for collective human, animal, plant, mineral and other agencies and communication networks becomes legible, if in a different way, in his discussion of agriculture. As he writes in his journal on March 2, 1852: "The farmer increases the extent of habitable earth. He makes soil. That is an honourable occupation" (J III: 329). The labor of the farmer, even though it may involve draining swamps or clearing oak trees, cultivating corn or cattle, is to co-operate with the earth; or, as Thoreau says on November 8, 1857, to "play with the natural forces" (J X: 170). As such, agriculture, a central interest for Thoreau, likewise emerges as a system of negotiating collective intelligences, one involving human knowledge (how to cultivate), animal instinctual knowledge (dispersing digested seeds, pollination), and collective forms of plant intelligences. Nowhere is this more evident than in his meditations on bean cultivation in *Walden*:

> Removing the weeds, putting fresh soil about the bean stems, and encouraging this weed which I had sown, making the yellow soil express its summer thought in bean leaves and blossoms rather than in wormwood and piper and millet grass, making the earth say beans instead of grass- this was my daily work. As I had little aid from horses or cattle, or hired men or boys, or improved implements of husbandry, I was much slower, and became much more intimate with my beans than usual. ... And, by the way, who estimates the value of the crop which nature yields in the still wilder fields unimproved by man? The crop of English hay is carefully weighed, the moisture calculated, the silicates and the potash; but in all dells and pond-holes in the woods and pastures and swamps grows a rich and various crop only unreaped by man. Mine was, as it were, the connecting link between wild and cultivated fields; as some states are civilized, and others half-civilized, and others savage or barbarous, so my field was, though not in a bad sense, a half-cultivated field. They were beans cheerfully returning to their wild and primitive state that I cultivated, and my hoe played the *Ranz des Vaches* for them.
> (W, 156–8)

Although Thoreau will often laud the farmer as a hero, to make the earth "say" beans is nonetheless dependent on processes in which human cognizers are not in a privileged position of stewardship. He rather sees himself as a "connecting link between wild and cultivated fields." In celebrating his beans as themselves half-wild, like the Walden cats who de-domesticate into wild cats once their owners are dead, and like the wild apples whose tastes he seeks, Thoreau's agriculture is oriented toward the wild, and in a crucial sense relies on the wild as a co-cultivator. The labor of agriculture becomes a shared act of co-creation or co-cultivation with the earth: it is an intelligence with the earth instantiated as a compositing of human and plant intelligences and natural agencies. As the connecting link between the wild and the cultivated, Thoreau posits himself in a chain of concatenated agencies in which human intelligence conspires with plant intelligence to form a collective soil-bean-human intelligence through which the soil can express its collective summer thought as bean leaves and blossoms.[39]

We could set in productive contrast to Thoreau's agricultural thought how he extends his notion of the "wild thinking" to wild apples, thus conflating the pomological and the epistemological. Similarly to his agricultural writings, he engages the long history of the wild apple from Pliny forward. Yet Thoreau's admiration for the wild apple stems not only from its biocultural history or even to its singularly sour taste, but from its wild growth. It is "not planted by man" and thus grows independent of human agency; it is free like humanity in its ability to "run wild" (E, 270). The apple tree is therefore an example of stubborn and clever survival. Although its tree shrub may be cut annually by a "browsing" ox, "it does not despair; but, putting forth two short twigs for every one cut off, it spreads out low along the ground in hollows" until it forms a "dense and impenetrable clump of bushes" which the cows cannot get past. As Thoreau surmises, "[s]uch are the tactics by which it finally defeats its bovine foes" and overcomes the "adverse circumstances" which affect it. The apple shrub, then seeking the higher light, "darts upward with joy" (E, 274) and "bears its own peculiar fruit in triumph" (E, 274). Later, although beyond the reach of hungry cows, the trees generously offer them shade and a taste of their fruit, "and so disperse the seed" (E, 274). Even if it is not planted by human hands, and eschews the browsing ox, its "tactics" provide a "lesson to man": it is an example of how "the most persistent and strongest genius defends itself and prevails, sends a tender scion upward at last, and drops its perfect fruit on the ungrateful earth" (E, 276). Like the pine forest or the cherry tree, the wild apple is part of a network of agencies and intelligences.

What is more, "Wild Apples" describes tasting apples as a connoisseurship by which apples come to be known by their wild flavors, if not their *seasonality*. But, as the cows who delight in the apples testify, taste is described not merely as an event of anthropocentric perception. Rather, what is at stake is a relational human-nonhuman epistemology of tasting wherein tasting is an event of mutual emergence or of communication between plant biochemical self-organization and animal instinct and sensation— and one that further aids the dispersion of seeds. Taste, as a mode of this non-linguistic, material, and nonhuman semiotics, is thus a form of mutual attraction that occurs down to the molecular level. As such, taste indicates a cooperative set of creative involutions of plant intelligences in terms of responses to light, chemical or molecular sensations, and self-organization of matter, and animal physiology and instinct.

Conclusion: Vegetal, All Too Vegetal?

Thoreau's "wild thinking" invites us to consider vegetal intelligence as dependent on a series of complex symbiotic and multi-agential relationships. His practice of phenology provides an archive of collective plant responses to environmental changes and cumulative biochemical self-memories. His thoughts on swamps, forest succession, and the dispersion of seeds give us a picture of a collective vegetal intelligence (swamp intelligence, "oak knowing," forest thinking, or agriculture) effectuated through plant-mammal-insect-wind-water natural agencies. He develops a human-nonhuman connoisseurship for the taste of wild apples, gesturing to how fruit has evolved to taste good to animals because they will digest it and disperse its seeds. Across these varied instances, his descriptions of animal, plant, or atmospheric intelligences thus provide a basis for asserting a set of interactions across different forms of nonhuman intelligence. In so doing, the wild is revealed as more than the "preservation of the world," but also Thoreau's name for a mode or style of thinking that seeks to understand the nonhuman agencies that conspire with or against human thinking. After Hayles, it might be another name for our planetary cognitive ecology of heterogeneous symbionts.

Yet Thoreau's attention to soil and the dynamics of taste, however, also points to what could be called the material being of the vegetal. As vegetal life operates at the level of the molecular or material interchange, that is, one could assuredly go further toward the molecular and material to understand its dynamics. Thoreau hints at this in *Walden*. When examining the vegetative forms of the furrows made by rivulets of melting ice make through a sand bank in the spring, he writes: "You find thus in the very sands an anticipation of the vegetable leaf. No wonder that the earth expresses itself outwardly in leaves, it so labors with the idea inwardly. The atoms have already learned this law, and are pregnant by it" (W, 306). Here, Thoreau reprises the idea that the beans and blossoms are the expression of the summer thought of the soil insofar as the sand's self-organization in so many rivulets or veins of liquid transmission express "leaf." Thoreau often understands both life and nonlife in vitalist, organicist terms. Indeed, Thoreau will proclaim at the end of *Walden* that there is "nothing inorganic": the earth's processes of self-organization, its self-writing in the sand, seem teleologically directed for him toward the "leaf" (W, 308).

But perhaps one might go in the opposite direction to stake out a theory of plant intelligence that is not based on the notion that everything is organic, but rather that begins to understand plants in terms of the inorganic materialities and elements through which they self-organize. Attention to vegetal life in terms of material flow might provide a different way of approaching the question of the relation between materiality and plant intelligence, if not between materiality and consciousness. Oliver Sacks, to this end, seeks to understand plant self-awareness as dependent on its calcium-ion channels, so to take material transfers across plant cellular membranes as informational or semiotic systems. For Sacks, this is also a question of a decelerated temporality: he discusses the slow transmission of impulses or action potentials through plants which if sped up in time lapse or other technologies would come to resemble animal relay speeds.[40]

Deleuze and Guattari, at the end of *What Is Philosophy?* (rather than taking everything as organic as might Thoreau), posit an inorganic life of things, an inorganic vitalism that takes plant sensation and what they call plant "contemplation" as its centerpiece. They write:

> Sensation is pure contemplation, for it is through contemplation that one contracts, contemplating oneself to the extent that one contemplates the elements from which one originates. ... The plant contemplates by contracting the elements from which it originates—light, carbon, and the salts—and it fills itself with colors and odors that in each case qualify its variety, its composition: it is sensation in itself. It is as if flowers smell themselves by smelling what composes them, first attempts of vision or of sense of smell, before being perceived or even smelled by an agent with a nervous system and a brain. Of course, plants and rocks do not possess a nervous system. But, if nerve connections and cerebral integrations presuppose a brain-force as faculty of feeling coexistent with the tissues, it is reasonable to suppose also a faculty of feeling that coexists with embryonic tissues and that appears in the Species as a collective brain; or with the vegetal tissues in the "small species." Chemical affinities and physical causalities themselves refer to primary force capable of preserving their long chains by contracting their elements and by making them resonate: no causality is intelligible without the subjective instance. Not every organism has a brain, and not all life is organic, but everywhere there are forces that constitute microbrains, or an inorganic life of things.[41]

By positing a "faculty of feeling" in plants, Deleuze and Guattari encourage us to think of a form of sensation that is not dependent on the perception of a second organism with a brain or nervous system. Rather, the flowers "smell themselves" in pure contemplation or self-sensation. To come to this, they are following Raymond Ruyer's notion of "primary consciousness," which relies on a notion of matter to "survey" itself.[42] Elizabeth Grosz explains:

> Far from being anthropomorphic, consciousness constitutes the conditions under which human life and human consciousness become possible, the dynamic forces of self-perpetuation that pre-exist life and make it possible and that each type of life develops in its own way … consciousness is not a separate organ added to life at a certain state of its growing complexity; rather, it is the condition for the dynamic unity of an organism, an organism's capacity to survive, to act in its environment, in short, to enjoy itself, to experience autoaffection, immediate self-enjoyment.[43]

But could we go yet another step to think of intelligence, or indeed consciousness, whether human, animal, plant, bacteria, or viral, in terms of materiality itself? This would be in the spirit of William James's assertion that we should not search for the dawn of consciousness as an "irruption into the universe of a new nature, non-existent until then,"[44] a notion of consciousness as always already *in* matter. That is, it is not that consciousness emerged or arose at some ancient neuro-evolutionary moment of origin, but that consciousness is always already implied in the structure of matter itself. Would such a material-consciousness need to rely on a separate agent with a brain or a nervous system to perceive it? Or could there be a material consciousness in itself, what Raymond Ruyer has called a "primary consciousness": that is, a self-sensation or pure contemplation? This would be to understand consciousness as "the unity and direction of the organism and its material conditions."[45] Deleuze and Guattari's notion of pure plant contemplation based on an inorganic life of things requires us to rethink our notions of materiality and consciousness quite literally from the ground up.

Assuredly this brings us past the scope of Thoreau's botanical meditations. Nonetheless, Thoreau prompts us to get to know our planet's cognizers as offering specific modes of wild thinking that occur through an assemblage of different of animal, plant, and material eventuations. It takes, as he says in his journal, a long time to get to know our neighbors: our brute neighbors, our plant neighbors, and all those nonhuman material neighbors in the wild bogs of our brains and our bowels. In this task, we have only begun to see the tip of the radicle.

6 ⚹

Green Fire: Thoreau's Forest Figuration

Monique Allewaert

[E]ach wind is self-registering.
THOREAU, *JOURNAL*, NOVEMBER 3, 1861 (LAST JOURNAL ENTRY)

Registering Nature

Henry David Thoreau's late, unfinished manuscript *Dispersion of Seeds* advances the theory of cross-species figuration and interpretation he slowly developed in his *Journal*. Thoreau's *Journal*, which a number of Thoreau's finest critics have argued was his primary work (Cameron; Walls; Arsić), is a massive compendium of natural historical events occurring in and near Concord from 1837 through 1861. While occasionally entries to the *Journal* offer philosophical and literary mediations that scholars have excerpted as parts of larger analyses, more than anything it chronicles details that can only seem mind-numbingly incidental and without any taxonomizing principle. The unfinished *Dispersion of Seeds*, which Thoreau primarily wrote in late 1860 and revised in the fall of 1861 and into early 1862, was to offer the theory for registering and interpreting this surfeit of natural historical detail that he recorded over the twenty-four years he actively wrote the *Journal*. Indeed, this close relation between the *Journal* and *Dispersion* might partially account for the gradual decline of his journaling across 1860.[1]

If, as Sharon Cameron argues, the *Journal* was an experiment in "writing nature," or in capturing "nature writing itself,"[2] *Dispersion* was the effort to develop a method of seeing, registering, and interpretation adequate to such writing. That Thoreau believed that natural historical events had an import beyond their mere occurrence is everywhere evident in the *Journal*. In 1856, for instance, Thoreau copied out at length Cotton Mather's description of a heavy snowstorm in Boston on December 10, 1717. Despite Mather's conclusion that such "odd accidents" had no "relation to philosophy," Thoreau concluded that this description of a snow storm 150 years past was among the most important of Mather's works and "would be worth all the philosophy [Mather] might dream of".[3] In the *Journal*, Thoreau does not articulate the philosophy that might follow on such descriptions of long-ago snowstorms. *Dispersion's* exploration of the relation of natural history to human history and writing elaborates this philosophy.

Following on Cameron's suggestion that Thoreau's aim was to forge a relation between natural inscription and human writing about nature, as well as Branka Arsić's proposal that Thoreau's *oeuvre* attempts "a new poetry ... and a new science," I propose that the *Dispersion* was to have served as a primer for the method of registering and reading nature that Thoreau slowly developed over the years he produced the *Journal*.[4] This mode of registering and reading forests anticipates what later critics have called biosemiosis in order to describe the signs given off by life forms and read by other life forms. However, more than the problem of meaning that is often the target of scholars focused on biosemiosis and that is sometimes Thoreau's focus as well, *Dispersion* attends to the problem of morphogenesis, which he conceives as a shape-making, figural process in which vegetable and animal beings together partake. This Thoreauvian figuration testifies to the transit of a formative impulse that precipitates relations but that has no meaning as such and certainly not the meaning of evolutionary vitality that theorists of biosemiosis propose.[5] *Dispersion* offers a forest geosemiosis whose site is not species but ecosystem and whose focal transmission is not the *will* to live but, first, a *way* to live that involves the conversion of energy into shape and beauty, and second, a *way to live together*, which is to say an ethics that follows on a semiotic community's conversion of forest shape and beauty into a set of shared obligations.[6]

To make this argument, I will first outline the main line of *Dispersion*: namely, the articulation of a method of reading that would teach human beings to see forest histories so as to live symbiotically with trees, instead of at "cross purposes" with them (part 2). Because Thoreau's primary interest in *Dispersion* is the arboreal figuration that he calls "forest geometry" in distinction from the exclusively human geometry usually practiced by the citizens of Concord, I separate out the problem of figuration from that of meaning with which figuration is often equated. Doing so foregrounds the extent to which Thoreau conceived figuration not simply as shape-making but as the transformation of solar and aeolian energies across diverse material substrates (part 3). Drawing on this account of figuration, I then take up the problem of the meanings of Thoreau's literary figurations. Here I propose that while Thoreauvian figuration does not preclude literary representation or meaning it is ultimately less interested in generating propositional or representational content than in the obligations that bind together trees, human beings, and other phenomena (part 4). Finally, drawing on Thoreau's interest in the obligation that binds together forest denizens, I elaborate how Thoreau's forest geography gives onto a forest chromography that is a tribute to and sign of these forest denizens' obligation to the light from whence they came.

Airborne

Dispersion's primary aim is to trace the antecedents of trees and other vegetable phenomena so as to counter the still-prevalent belief that vegetable life could arise by spontaneous generation.[7] In making this argument, Thoreau elaborates on but also diverges from the argument Darwin makes in *Origin of the Species*, which he had read with enthusiasm the January before he began *Dispersion*.[8] While the *Origin* focuses on populations to propose that the origin of "species" was a slow-acting evolution that operated via natural selection, Thoreau focuses on the origin of *forests*, that is to say, groupings of diverse tree populations. In the manuscript, Thoreau traces the relay of abiotic and biotic forces through which forests emerge and into which they pass and he attempts to develop a method of reading capable of apprehending this relay of earth forces. Thoreau argued that even if pine trees produced pine seeds, they also provided the ecological conditions necessary to oak, beech, and maple trees, and in this sense pines produced oaks and other trees. The antecedents of pine trees, then, were not only their own seeds but also the prevailing winds on which they lofted and that were themselves recorded in the shapes that pine forests took as well as the sunlight that pines converted into their own material bodies. With wind and light as antecedents, pine trees and forests come from the air.[9] Thoreau is not simply interested in the antecedence but also the "succession of forest trees," as he titled an 1860 lecture and article that drew on his work for *Dispersion*. The succession of trees that he describes by which oak forests follow on pine forests that serve as their nurseries carries a trace of and replays this aerial antecedence: oaks follow on and fill out shapes that winds and birds give the pine forest, and oak forests themselves are planted by birds and squirrels that continue the work of bringing the celestial to the terrestrial: thus aerial antecedence continually operates in succession.[10]

Thoreau's reversal of the ordinary sense that trees are earth formations partly derives from his proclivity for inverting the intuitive order of the celestial and the terrestrial so as to emphasize that terrestrial is a part of the heavenly and atmospheric. More importantly for our point here, his proposition that trees are aerial as much as terrestrial indicates his interest in the processes by which the energetic phenomena of light and wind could be turned into substantial forms.

As my précis of *Dispersion's* mainline argument suggests, it's not obvious that the manuscript offers an account of figuration or anything else remotely close to the literary. As Laura Dassow Walls notes, *Dispersion* has proven especially resistant to literary readings. Indeed, some of its keenest readers have been agroecologists and historians.[11] Literary critic Joan Burbrick, for instance, puzzles over Thoreau's seemingly inexplicable and rapid turn from the question of beauty that preoccupies him in other late writings he was producing at the same time, including the also posthumously published "Autumnal Tints," to what she sees as the utilitarian science of *Dispersion*.[12] Several recent literary critics have studied *Dispersion* and other late writings not so much for their literary import but for their scientific significance, a significance that these critics ultimately treat as distinct from the literary: for instance, the manuscript has been read as evidence of Thoreau's late work's affinity with an ascending Darwinian science and also to document the difference between the phrenological rhythms that Thoreau tracked and those of our own moment so as to track the emergence of the so-called Anthropocene.[13] Despite the fact that *Dispersion* has not struck its readers as a particularly literary text, the entire final third of the manuscript is a sort of grammar book that elaborates on the fact that morphology is common to language and plants to instruct human persons in the reading of arboreal shapes that might also be taken as signs.[14] The final pages of the manuscript present readers with two arboreal texts, each counterposing Thoreau's detailed narrative descriptions of the relation of trees in forests around Concord with simple hieroglyphic rendering of the spare shapes and sequences of the forests in question as seen from above, for instance, by a seed floating on the air (Figures 1 and 2).[15]

The first of these arboreal texts asks readers to consider an "oak woodlot some twenty years old with a dense, narrow edging of pitch pines about a rod and a half wide and twenty-five or thirty years old along its whole southern side, which is straight and thirty or forty rods long, and next to it ... an open field or pasture" (165). Thoreau's use of "rods" to designate size (the length and width of the pine edging) and years (the age of the pines composing this edging) indicates that spatial description is from the outset a history. Thoreau proceeds to offer an interpretation of the history of this woodlot, explaining that the straight edging of pitch pines is a relic of a pine forest that had stood in the place now occupied by oaks and that had acted as the oaks' nursery. The straight lines that separate the pine forest from the

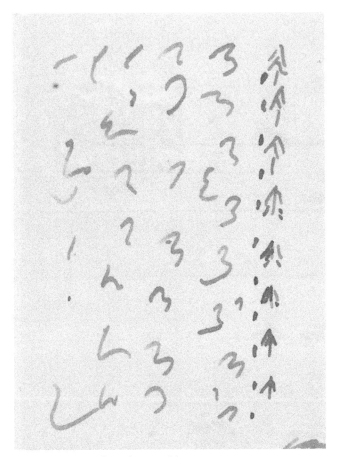

FIGURE 1 *Thoreau's visual rendering of forest geometry.*
Henry W. and Albert A. Berg Collection of English and American Literature, The
New York Public Library.

oak are aftereffects of human beings' property lines and testify to the whims
of the owners of property on one or the other side of a property line.[16] If
this forest's straight lines testify to human beings' enclosures as well as to
human beings' historically and (because he also notes traces of indigenous
arbiculture) culturally divergent valuations of forests, Thoreau continues
that this woodlot does not only tell a human history because it also registers
an arboreal history that Thoreau suggests will surpass the human histories
that play out in them since vegetable civilizations work through the night as
well as the day and since they also compel human beings to do their bidding,
whether by transporting seeds or providing structures for climbing.

On presenting readers with a second arboreal text, Thoreau asks them to
solve for where in this forest they would find a wall or property line, noting
that any reader who has followed the lessons of *Dispersion* closely would

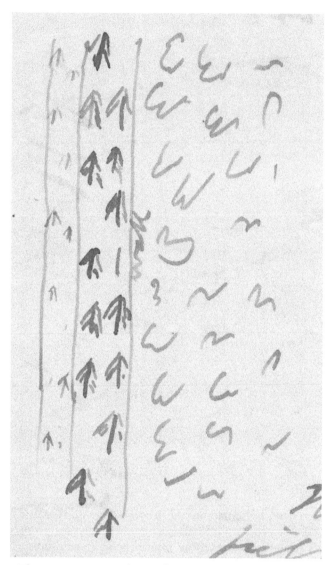

FIGURE 2 *Thoreau presents readers with an image from which they might read the intersection of arboreal and human history.*
Henry W. and Albert A. Berg Collection of English and American Literature, The New York Public Library.

need only "think a moment" to know precisely where to locate a wall (166). After confirming this most basic arboreal literacy of seeing from a distance how Algonquin and New England farmers, merchants, and surveyors have shaped the order of trees as well as trees' own re-inscription of this human shaping, Thoreau launches a lengthy interpretation of this forest text that reads each spare arboreal sign and the history of vegetable, avian, squirrel, bovine, and human shaping that it tells, spooling back in time over a hundred years (166–71).

That Thoreau closes *Dispersion* with a lesson for readers in interpreting "forest geometry," or the shapes that emerge from the coproductions of wind, light, and arboreal life, makes the manuscript something like an early version of what contemporary critics call *biosemiosis*, which Wendy Wheeler defines as the "study of those interweaving natural and cultural sign systems of the living."[17] Wheeler and other recent scholars of biosemiosis make three key claims: first, that semiosis and evolution are conjoined processes with semiosis driving (not following) evolutionary process; second, sign processes are therefore constitutive of all life forms; third, complex sign processes like human language or birdsong are elaborations on, and ultimately traceable back to, the biological and evolutionary semiosis from which they derive.[18] Semiosis by this account generally follows a loosely Peircean definition of the sign as something that means something to some one/thing. Clearly what *Dispersion* terms "forest geometry" is focused on building relays between of what seem to be distinctly natural signs (patterns of tree succession legible to other trees as well as to squirrels and birds that serve as planters of these trees) and distinctly cultural signs (human beings' reading of words in books so as to learn the patterns of tree succession legible to other life forms). Indeed, Thoreau's ultimate point is that it's not possible to divide natural from cultural signs since human as well as other beings produce conjoined natural and cultural signs: thus, he attends to the rectilinear plots into which human beings organize the landscape, which in the above examples shape and are also shaped by arboreal organizations of the terrain in the history of "cross purposes" that he laments.[19] And the explicit aim of his book is to suggest that on becoming capable of reading forest signs human beings might organize their homes, properties, bodies, and lives in ways that work with, instead of against, arboreal civilizations.

That Thoreau shows that pines and oaks produce non-linguistic signs that are legible to other life forms and that contribute to the evolution— or "succession"—of forests makes clear that he practices and instructs readers in something close to biosemiosis. Yet while Thoreau is interested in the shapes and signs of life, in *Dispersion* he is ultimately less focused on determining what arboreal shapes *mean* for the tree, rodent, avian, and human beings that encounter them than he is in processes of shape-making and shape-transmission in which these beings are not so much readers of signs as they are media through which shapes transmit and manifest. Tracing the shapes and, in the concomitant "Autumnal Tints," colors that trees generate, Thoreau is most interested in forest figurations and chromatics that precede meaning and need not have meaning (a significance for someone). In short, Thoreau's forest geometry is more interested in shapings and chromatics—which together I designate as *figuration* to describe a relational process of taking form and becoming apprehensible to other forces whose concatenation comprise a milieu—than he is in the meanings that might be assigned these figurations. For Thoreau meaning is a significant yet secondary problem that follows on the recognition and contemplation of figures.

By disarticulating figure from meaning, Thoreau lays the grounds for a more finely wrought account of figure and meaning than those offered by most contemporary theorists working on the relay between nonhuman and human figural and semiotic processes. For one, *Dispersion* and other late arboreally focused works like "Autumnal Tints" treat figuration as an organization of energetic and material forces in space and time—or more precisely because more situatedly, in the New England milieu, that *precedes and is the ground for* meaning. Second, Thoreau's belief that figuration precedes meaning does not collapse all figuration into meaning. In refusing to collapse figure into significance, he allows that certain marks and phenomena do not primarily serve—for their producers or those who apprehend them—a transitive, communicative function. This allowance opens the possibility of an investigation of an inter-species shape-making, which we might call an aesthetics in the sense that such shape-making makes phenomena sensually apprehensible. Here aesthetics is not a function or an ultimately ends-oriented process but the transformation of a relation into a shape. This aesthetics is the condition for communicability but does not resolve into an intention, a meaning, or an end. Finally, Thoreau's disarticulation of figuration from meaning allows us to produce a richer account of meaning than that generally offered by scholars working on biosemiosis. These scholars do not substantively treat what they presume "to mean" or "meaning" signify and thus allow "to mean/meaning" to be reduced to a simple vitalism whereby organisms that read biosemiotic signs always and only produce one meaning—the will to live that in turn drives evolution. The sort of meaning that follows from this sort of vitalism is both too general and too particular. Too general because meanings must be contestable and it is hard to call a biological will to life contestable even if the organisms possessing this will might be in competition with each other or compelled by a death drive. Too particular because if the meaning that each organism gives off signifies only its capacity to maintain its thisness or its existence, such meaning is so entirely intrinsic as to preclude any substantive communication of this meaning.

So, while Thoreau closes *Dispersion* with an exercise that asks that readers apprehend a meaning (namely, the tension between the ways that trees and human beings give shape and order to the landscape around Concord) from which they might derive a simple lesson (namely, that human beings need to learn to live with the movements of trees instead of building civilizations at cross-purposes with those of vegetable life), the bulk of the manuscript teaches human readers to recognize the shape-making of vegetable life, particularly pines. Indeed, *Dispersion* several times notes that the vast majority of vegetable seeds never germinate, suggesting that pitch pines and white pines extravagantly disperse their seed not only to ensure the survival of the species but also to fulfill a disposition for making conical shapes. As Thoreau puts it, "as the pines themselves, not to mention their fruit [pinecones], have a more regularly and solidly conical outline than deciduous trees, so with the groves they form" (164). That pine trees which are themselves conical, produce cones on smaller scales (fruit) and larger ones (the conical shape of the pine forest) might seem to suggest that pine trees practice an entirely isomorphic figuration, replicating the shape of their own bodies on every scale, as though pine-being were an endless repetition of its own shape and self onto all that it encountered. However, Thoreau makes clear that pine trees do not exist or produce this shape on their own: they derive this conical shape from their relation to the wind since it is the wind that produces the dryness that prepares the cones to open and disseminate seeds and it is the wind that, on blowing through existing pine forests in a prevailing direction, transmits pine seeds in an ovoid or conical outline that replicates the shape of the parent forest, the tree itself, and its fruit. If pine trees make conical shapes on various scales, then this is not the pines' own inscription but one that follows on their relation to the wind. The pine tree and cone, then, are figures for the wind. The cone is not simply the shape of the pine but the shape that follows on, and registers, its relation with prevailing winds that transport seeds in the same direction. In this sense, the forest shapes that Thoreau records in *Dispersion*, like the trees themselves, come from the air.

If pines really do create conical shapes on the land that they inhabit, the oak forests that Thoreau shows come in the wake of pine forests give density to the arcing and "flanking" shapes that pines trace, and in so doing change the shape of the forest into an irregular circle. The circular shapes that oaks produce with the help of pines loosely mimic oaks' own shapes as seen from above. Yet the oak's irregular circle, like the circles of its acorn fruit and the forests they produce, is not simply their own shape. Rather, these shapes derive from oaks' relation to pines, wind, and also squirrels, birds, and human beings who sow their plantations by eating their fruits. The shape of the oak tree is not the effect of a Buffonian internal mould but an effect and expression of an interspecies confabulation.[20]

Trees replicate not only their own shapes (shapes that are themselves reinscriptions of the material-energetic and interspecies coproductions through which they emerge) but also the shapes of other life forms in their milieu. Thoreau attends to the fact that birch scales bear the shape of "fleur de luce" (*fleur de lys*) which Thoreau notes "hav[e] the exact form of stately birds with outspread wings, especially of hawks sailing steadily over the fields" (42). Inside of these scales that look like flowers (*fleur de luce/lys* or lilies) that look like birds are forms that "are practically far more bird-like and are wafted much further by the wind" (42). The birch scale/flower/bird's still smaller bird-like seeds might also "pass for tiny brown butterflies" (42).

What are we to make of the bird and butterfly host that Thoreau finds in the seeds of birches and maples? At the close of *Walden*, Thoreau mused that leaf-like shapes emerged in the sand of streams. Contemplating this "sand foliage" Thoreau concludes that "[y]ou find thus in the very sands an anticipation of the vegetable leaf. No wonder that the earth expresses itself outwardly in leaves, it so labors with the idea inwardly."[21] Elaborating on Johann Goethe's proposal that the plant is an endless accumulation and metamorphosis of the shape of the leaf, here at the close of *Walden* Thoreau proposes that not only the plant but the earth itself emerges through metamorphoses of leaf-shapes or, more precisely, through the accumulation and transmission of the waving reliefs that water sketches on land and that are later replayed by vegetable civilizations as leaves. Indeed, here the shape of the leaf is first an earth formation that then follows on the movement of water, sand, and wind on sediment and that is replayed in the leaves that also come from water, sand, and wind, as well as from sunlight. Biology here follows on physics and geometry.[22] Drawing on *Walden's* closing suggestion that the leaf is itself a repetition of a protean elemental earth shape, we might understand *Dispersion's* account of the bird and butterfly shapes enclosed in the seeds of birches and maples as variations on leaves: a bird as two leaves joined by a central stem-body, and a butterfly as four leaves on a central stem-body. Here leaf shapes are the antecedents of birds and butterflies. By this reading, leaves and the trees that follow on them are metamorphoses of the shapes drawn by elemental forces and hold within themselves a trace of later evolutionary metamorphosis: not just of the leaf into the various parts of the plant (as Goethe suggested) but the plant and tree into the forms of animal life that followed on vegetable life. By this account, the birds and flies that emerge later in evolutionary history are themselves but further metamorphoses of leaves.

There is another way to understand the avian and insect shapes that Thoreau notes are enclosed in arboreal seeds. Birch and maple scales and seeds loft on the wind as do birds and flying insects. The winged shape that each of these life forms takes might suggest, for Thoreau, a convergent evolution by which various species separately take the same form suited to traveling on the wind. Here the similar shapes of some tree seeds, birds, and butterflies would be evidence of living forms' adoption of the shapes advantageous to navigating the milieu that sustained them. These two logics by which we might understand Thoreau's vegetable birds and butterflies might seem entirely antipodal. The first is of a sort of primal shape: the whorling shapes of water on sediment that is endlessly metamorphized to eventually give rise to cones and ovals that become leaves and then other living forms. The second is an evolution of shape that follows on organisms' relations to their generating milieu. Yet these apparently antipodal logics might also be variations on the same logic, with the ovoid or conical shape of the leaf and the tree indicating the shape particular to the first living beings that emerged from the play of elemental forces and the repetition and duplication of these ovoid forms in seeds, birds, and flies—evidence of the compound forms that follow on living beings' responses to divergent milieu.

Thoreau's discussion of the shape of oak leaves in "Autumnal Tints," which was written at about the same time as *Dispersion*, speaks to his belief that the arboreal shapes he tracks in *Dispersion* are expressions of their milieu. Meditating on the elaborate shape of the oak leaf, Thoreau notes that "if you connected all the points of the [oak] leaf" it would amount to "a simple oval" that recalls the conical shape of pines.[23] Yet the oak's "scollop[ed]" leaves offer a shape "much richer" than simple ovals: in still weather, the oak's leaves ornament "forest windows" (a phrase that suggests that human structures mimic arboreal ones, not vice versa). In the wind, oak leaves "dance arm in arm with the light,—tripping on it fantastic": the leaves blowing in the wind are "so intimately mingled" with light that it's difficult "to tell at last what in the dance is leaf and what is light."[24] If the oak leaf's ornate variation on the ovoid form of vegetable life makes possible this arboreal dancing, Thoreau cannot decide if this leaf shape evidences the cheapness of the materials from which leaves are made (i.e. the cheapness of sunlight, wind, water, and soil), the tree's "lavish expense" of resources in the production of beautiful forms, or a natural economy in which the materials of vegetable life are not cheap at all but carefully economized and at the same time oriented toward extravagant beauty. Whatever resolution we give this conundrum, "Autumnal Tints'" encomium to the shape of oak leaves is ultimately not focused on the economy of vegetable life or on the principles of its making but on the ways that the shapes of oak leaves divulge the beauty of their generating milieu. Ultimately oak leaves' beauty is not attributable to their substantial forms but to these forms' capacity to move with the wind so as to seem to pass back into the light from which they came.

Thoreau proposes that animal life produces an art that elaborates on the forms produced by vegetable life. Thus, he notes that squirrels whittle pine cones into perfect flowers on which human sculptors and tools could not improve (31). And human beings, too, unconsciously and consciously repeat vegetable forms and movements. Although the straight lines that farmers' and land owners' geometry draws all over the landscape indicate an attempt to cover over and reject their own vegetable origin, the proliferate metaphors of human speech reveal that human forms and actions are repetitions of vegetable forms and actions. On this point, Thoreau also proposes that human balloonists unconsciously mimic the action of seeds on the atmosphere and that fishermen's casting of nets unconsciously replicates vegetable life's entrapment of animal life (87, 96). We might also consider Thoreau's above-discussed claim that oak leaves blown by wind in the autumn "trip the light fantastic." Thoreau's metaphor does not use a human action to describe a vegetable movement but, to the contrary, suggests that human dancing and the metaphor used to describe it—tripping the light fantastic—are unconscious translations of the movement of leaves, wind, and light. When a human being moves with improbable grace, the metaphor used to describe such movement (tripping the light fantastic) reveals a germinal understanding that in their highest art human beings, like leaves, express themselves most fully by moving with and passing into the air and light from which they, too, came. Aesthetics, here, involves the apprehension and replaying of elemental force in organic shape.[25] If most of the time human action, including speech, only unconsciously reveals human beings' half-awareness of their relation to vegetable life, in "Autumnal Tints" Thoreau suggests that human beings who can join forest geometry with forest chromography might cultivate a way of seeing that participates in arboreal expression. He writes: "Looking across this woodland valley, a quarter of a mile wide, how rich those Scarlet Oaks, embosomed in Pines, their bright red branches intimately intermingled with them! They have their fullest effect there. The Pine-boughs are the green calyx to their red petals."[26] The human forest geometer-cum-chromographer partakes in a natural aesthetic impulse when, on seeing the arcing whorls of green pines and red oaks, he apprehends a flower emerge from the autumn atmosphere. The pine and oak together form extensive, cross-species flowers. These autumn flowers are the effect of an abstraction of vision by which human beings learn to stop seeing trees as individuals or species to instead recognize forest collectivity, in so doing finally perceiving not an abstraction but the real existence of the forest. The real existence of the forest is not a reproductive compulsion that produces self-sameness, as Darwin would have it. Rather, it is an extravagant and decadent beauty only apprehensible on giving up on the idea of evolution as biological (re)productivity and instead imagining evolution as the repetition and transformation of elemental shapes. The real existence of the forest is not as thing but as a fleeting experience of this unfolding of elemental shape that catches light to give color.

Aeolian Registry: Figuration as Energetic Transit

The relation between wind and trees—or between water, dirt, and wind in *Walden's* discussion of earth shapes as the antecedent for vegetable shapes— does not only give shape to phenomena like forests: it is and it transits formative energy. In other words, Thoreauvian figure is not only an effect of the confabulation of energetic and material phenomena (light, wind, and trees) through which forms emerge, but that figure retains a trace of its energetic origin and for this figure branches out, each ramification not only a flat transformation of its antecedent but also a redirection of the energetic impulses expressed by antecedent forms. In this sense, Thoreau's figures are not simply shapes but a registering, a carrying across, or *metaphorizing* (from *pherein* "carry" and *meta* "across" or "over"), of an energetic impulse (transited by light and wind) across phenomena in ways that re-express it. Shape, then, is a metaphor of energy.[27] Thus, the whorling lines in stream beds, the leaves of pines and oaks, and the shapes of human beings dancing do not only transform an elemental shape across different phenomena— they also transit something of the formative energy that they express.

To follow out Thoreau's interest in how energetic phenomena give onto shapes that also transit formative energy consider his claim in *Dispersion* that "In some unremembered gale the winged seeds of the white pine are gently wafted to their resting places, and a few years afterward we began to see the landscape dotted there with their cheerful green fires and are pleased to wind our way around them" (171). Here the young pines dotting the terrain and slowly becoming a forest shape are an effect of a long-forgotten storm that passed through Concord. This pine stand that follows on aeolian and solar forces doesn't only materialize and substantialize these forces (as photosynthesis turns light into mass or the direction of seed-bearing winds gives shape to the coming forest) but also transits these forces into different expressions: the sun's fire and light becoming the pines' "cheerful green fires" and the turbulence of the gale registers in the haphazard relation between the trees, which departs from the usual flanking arcs sketched by pines. This forest figure traced by an "unremembered" storm in turn precipitates movements that themselves re-express and transform the force through which it was generated, whether human beings' unknowing replaying of this force in the winding shape of their walking, the shape these walkers trace on the earth in so walking as they produce an inadvertent landscape art, or the affects that follow on so walking.

Thoreau again suggests that energetic transfer and dissipation are central to the wind's cascading figural processes in his last *Journal* entry, which describes the marks left by "an easterly storm" on the "surface of the railroad causeway composed of gravel." Thoreau continues:

These lines as it were of stratification are perfectly parallel & straight as a ruler diagonally across the flat surface of the causeway for its whole length—Behind each little pebble, as a protecting boulder −1/8 or 1/10 of an inch or more in diameter extends NW a ridge of sand which it has protected from being washed away—while the heavy drops driven almost horizontally have washed out a furrow on each side—& on all sides are these ridges—half an inch apart & perfectly parallel.[28]

He concludes that "each wind is self-registering."[29] Thoreau's focus on the wind's figural power is likely linked to his long-time interest in the Aeolian Harp, here the wind's force producing not (only) sounds but shapes and inscriptions.[30] The storm winds that Thoreau documents in this final *Journal* entry "self-registe[rs]" in lines in the gravel that Thoreau meticulously measures and then records in the lines of the *Journal*, lines which are at once a translation of aeolian force and figure into human measure and writing, and a means of turning himself and the journal into a vessel for conducting the expressions of winds.

What does it mean to claim that a wind self-registers? Does such self-registering promise that each event, regardless of how seemingly minor, is a sort of self that is not only preserved but gives onto corresponding phenomena that transmit it and even serve as its equivalents, such that a wind becomes lines on gravel becomes lines in a dying man's journal? Are earth processes simply a massive set of correspondences, each one registering and memorializing previous ones? Is such self-registering a promise that although all passes nothing is lost? To engage these questions, note that the wind is not a self in any of the ways that that term usually means. After all, this wind is not identical to itself since it is not the expression of an essence but, quite to the contrary, an expression of shifting intersecting factors particular to a milieu, including air pressure, heat, and humidity, that together produce a force. Moreover, although Thoreau grants this wind a sort of reflexivity (it registers itself after all), this reflexivity is not an introspective feat that redounds to a self that is confirmed by this reflection. Instead, the reflexivity that Thoreau evokes consists in the wind's transmission of something of the power it gleans from its milieu to another phenomenon—the gravel in a causeway. This is, then, a thoroughly mediate reflexivity that coincides with the diminishment of the force of the "self" so registered. Just as importantly, the phenomena through which the wind self-registers—the gravel of the causeway, Thoreau himself, Thoreau's journal—are not determinate substances through which the wind mechanically acts. The gravel of the causeway, Thoreau, and the journal are all phenomena with tendencies, energetic processes, potentials, reserves, and histories, and these tendencies, energies, and histories inflect the ways that they express the wind, in so doing re-expressing (and changing) themselves. To self-register, then, consists in a phenomenon's passing something of its power to other phenomena so as to be mediated, transformed, and dissipated. To self-register is to disperse. Something registers, to be sure, but this registering is not a repetition of the wind or the reproduction of the force of the wind—rather it is its metamorphosis into inscriptive phenomena that bear no resemblance even if they correspond.

This account of wind as enacting and motivating a figural force that dissipates across a range of grounds makes clear the strange nonhuman theory of figuration by which Thoreau imagined that "all science, all nature" might become "a poem for many."[31] Sharon Cameron's brilliant exegesis of that status of writing and figuration in Thoreau, *Writing Nature*, verges on elaborating this account of figure as something closer to energetic transfer than the production of meaning.[32] She probes what seems to be a key equivocation in *Walden* and the *Journal*: was Thoreau's aim to write *about* nature? Or was his aim to practice a sort of inscriptive conduction whereby he might serve as the intermediary by which nature might write itself, making his writing but one set of shapes through which nature self-registers? These aims seem incommensurate since the first presumes a representational logic according to which Thoreau's thinking and writing are essentially separate from the nonhuman processes that they would describe; the second presumes a nonrepresentational logic by which Thoreau's thinking and writing express nonhuman natural processes as though human bodies and books were but one of many integuments that indicate and transmit, even if they also congeal, nonhuman as well as human processes. Does Thoreau, on writing of a connection between the labor of raking cranberries and that of thinking about such labor, pose raking cranberries as a metaphor about human thinking? If this is the case, his figurations would ultimately demonstrate the deconstructionist claim prevailing when Cameron wrote that human writing is always at an impossible distance from nature or any of the things it describes and for this is always and only about (human) writing itself. Or, Cameron muses, are these Thoreauvian meditations posing a connection between labor that directly engages and transforms nonhuman nature (raking cranberries) and the labor of writing about this sort of labor, both revealing that the labor of the farmer and the labor of the philosopher and writer manifest, and also express, the fact that human labor of all sorts is imbricated in nonhuman processes that are not simply material but also energetic and that they transmit? If this is the case, his writing claims and demonstrates that figuration transits nonhuman figural processes into human writing and for this is always a transmission of something inhuman into a human form (itself always incipiently alien and more than human). The latter would seem to be the conclusion toward which Thoreau's *Journal* presses. Yet, Cameron muses, does this conclusion render the proliferate and intricate conventional figurations through which Thoreau describes the connection of human and nonhuman as "gratuitous" since "the mind and pond [nonhuman nature] need not be connected" by figures of any sort given that "they are already presumed to be part of one another."[33]

Attending to *Dispersion* and the late *Journal* demonstrates that Thoreau did indeed propose this strange, incipiently self-cancelling theory of figure that Cameron adumbrates. If such a theory of figure is not mechanistic (since energy doesn't simply transit across determinate phenomena in predictable ways but is changed by the energies, tendencies, and histories of these phenomena),[34] and if it offers a complex account of correspondence that doesn't make linked phenomena equivalent to each other, does such a theory of figure require us to dismiss the problems of meaning and representation which we generally attach to figure, and in so doing rendering our usual understanding of figure gratuitous?

On Meaning

In the previous sections, I elaborated Thoreau's interest in figures that have no meanings as such since they are diverse actualizations of energetic phenomena across mediating substrates. Yet that *Dispersion* offers a moral that is communicated through representational language makes clear that meaning and representative language are not irrelevant to Thoreau's project. In this section, I will explore how this energetic transfer that drives cascading figural processes can give rise to meanings. I will also demonstrate that these meanings move beyond the evolutionary vitalism that is presumed by most theorists of biosemiosis.

To engage the problem of meaning, it's necessary to distinguish two separate yet linked processes that Thoreau explores in his late writing. First, figuration or the emergence of shape that expresses and also transits a formative impulse. Second, what I'll follow Thoreau in calling tropology, which he casts as the turning of a figure or shape to some end that allows it to mean something to someone. We might call these two processes figuration (the transmission of a formative impulse that gives onto shape and testifies to a transspecies aesthetic impulse) and tropology (the turning of a figure to some end that makes it _about_ something, and in so doing endowing it with meaning, or informational content). The first process is intransitive (non ends-oriented) and as such presemiotic and, while the latter is transitive (endowed with some end) by some interpretant, or community of interpretants, and for this semiotic.[35]

On February 18, 1860, in the midst of a set of *Journal* entries that challenge John Ruskin's theories of language and aesthetics, Thoreau proposes that the "best and most harmless animal names are those which are an imitation of the voice or note of an animal."[36] Thoreau's other writing suggests that the names necessary to representative language as it is usually conceived pose three sorts of harm to that which is named: a name cancels out the singularity of the named by making it something general; a name shifts attention away from the formative relations through which a given material phenomenon emerges and through which it persists and for this allows the phenomenon to seem isolate and fixed; a name makes it possible to speak about a phenomenon and for this makes the phenomenon secondary, not primary, which in turn permits the phenomenon to be more easily instrumentalized. Of course, Thoreau is not against names and representational processes and here he suggests that a good name might mitigate (but not eliminate) these harms by repeating the voice of the animal in human language. He is clearly talking about intentional human language that carries meaning to those who participate in this semiotic community (which need not only be human beings even if they are primarily human beings). In this preferable sort of naming, the unintentional figural processes that need not carry any meaning are turned so as to achieve some end, namely that of designating the being whose sound is repeated. Thus, this is a semiotic process.[37] This is not a naïve Romantic theory of language that presumes no distance between signifier (sound image) and signified (concept).[38] Rather, it attempts to keep a trace of propulsive figural energies in representative language via onomatopoeia. Such language recalls the thing evoked and the cross-species relation through which it emerges as a trace within representational language.

A few *Journal* entries previous to the one discussed above, Thoreau quite explicitly thinks about the role of tropes in representational language. He writes that "when natural objects are described, it is an advantage if words derived originally from nature, it is true, but which have been turned (*tropes*) from their primary signification to a moral sense are used, i.e. if the object is personified."[39] Here, words are taken "from nature," likely much in the way that he thinks a good animal name iconically represents the sound it makes. This is what Thoreau calls a "primary signification," and one that carries the shape of animal being (in this case something of its voice) into a human representational field. Here the shape of the animal is carried into language where it becomes what is heard as habitual to that animal and thus serves as its name. This hardening of something of animal shape (sound) into a recognizable and repeated shape (a name) comes from nonhuman nature but also makes it possible for human beings to refer to nonhuman nature. This figure is then turned to produce what Thoreau suggests is a secondary, moral signification. Thoreau proposes that this process of turning a primary representational signification to some moral significance, which Thoreau also calls "personification," is necessary to good description. Here "moral" signifies in the conventional sense of good action that should become a conventional mode of action (*mores*). Good description, then, is not precisely a description that mimics or is in some other way close to the thing described but description that provokes moral action from those using representational language. For Thoreau, language turned to this sort of moral end is personification. Personification, here, is the process by which a human person takes shape via tropological power borrowed from elemental energies. This second-order troping shapes human beings and conduct rather like the way that wind disperses seeds that pines in turn "pinefy" by producing their distinctive, replicated shapes. Both the first and the second turnings are ways through which wind self-registers, but the second is able to stand apart from the energetic force from which it descends as a replicable shape.[40]

In this same entry, Thoreau continues to track how tropology produces this moral orientation, arguing that to speak about something well, a writer should "love and understand" what he describes.[41] Thoreau's explanation of how the figural transit he traces in *Dispersion* can become semiosis, or a process of producing and transmitting meaning, suggests that the morality that interests him is essentially affective or, more precisely in this nineteenth-century

context, sentimental. He links this affective dimension of good description
to a gendering of that which is described and moralized, noting that a writer
capable of good, moral-bearing, description "incline[s] to personal pronouns"
that abjure "neuter gender" and that make their "words ... doubly tropes."[42]
The love and understanding that Thoreau imagines are provoked by such
tropology transits outside of purely symbolic semiotic exchange and back
to the thing described. This turn back to the thing described is, according
to Thoreau, the doubling of the trope, a doubling whereby the trope turns
human sentiment to a nonhuman end. In short, for Thoreau, good description
provokes an affective relation that passes "love" from the representational
field into a broader physis.

In this exegesis, Thoreau stumbles on the problem that dogs all theories
of "natural" language: the naturalization of convention. To be sure,
Thoreau calls this a doubling of the trope such that the gendering that
structured bourgeois Anglo-European conventions might be turned from
that particular human civilization to nonhuman phenomena not structured
by these conventions. This suggests that what Thoreau describes is less a
naturalization of convention than the redirecting of what Thoreau supposes
is good about such conventions onto a field of pulsations and desires that
is *not* itself naturally gendered. That Thoreau's own mode of sentimental
bachelorhood would not neatly fit within the gendering he would project
outside of the human fold is one reason among many that Thoreau alone
is insufficient to elaborating any theory of more than human semiosis. Still,
despite this pressing limit of Thoreau's theorization that I do not mean to
put to the side, what I'd like to emphasize here is that Thoreau casts semiosis
as an ends-oriented tropological process, one that layers morals and affects
onto representational language. These morals and affects operate in two
directions: on the one hand, they are central to what Thoreau sees as the
ends at stake in representational processes: namely that representation is
not simply the transfer of information or meaning but the transfer of an
affect and obligation that shape the propositional content of representation.
On the other hand, the affects and obligations that this representation
demands from those engaged in it pass outside of it, both to beings that
might not participate in that representational fold and also as part of an
impulsive, non-meaningful figural residuum. The obligations that follow on
Thoreauvian figuration operate within and across species, and are a way of
recognizing and binding together an engendering ecology.

The sort of semiosis that Thoreau describes in *Dispersion* and in the
late *Journal* clearly operates outside of exclusively human representational
languages. After all, even if *Dispersion* was to have been a printed book, its
aim was to make human readers attentive to vegetable shapes and signs,
which he calls "hints" that he suggests are generally unheeded by human
beings, so as to spur these readers' love for and obligation to trees (82;
87; 167; 184). Recognizing such obligations is the tropological function

of the text: one that Thoreau suggests requires recognizing the ways that other forest creatures—notably birds and squirrels—are motivated by "a dim recognition" that the "value of their labor" is not simply that of sustaining themselves but of sustaining and giving homage to the forest and the elements from which they too came (130). Trees as well as squirrels and birds can also engage in the ends-oriented tropology that Thoreau associates with semiosis and it is also possible for one life form to learn to read the signs of other life forms, as when human readers learn to read the "hints" given off by trees or squirrels and birds glimmeringly understand an obligation to sustain the forests on which they follow. Although the semiosis that follows on Thoreau's attention to forest geometry aims to produce an affective and ethical charge that is both transitive (love and obligation toward something) and that also carries a vestige of an intransitive and asemiotic impulses (feelings and obligations only glimmeringly realized if at all), this semiology can also transmit a variety of propositional contents.

On this last point, it's worth turning to one of the several instances in *Dispersion* where Thoreau quite explicitly considers the meaning of conventional human metaphors. "We often say that a person's clothes are old and seedy," Thoreau notes (97). But what exactly does this phrase mean? What are its antecedents? And what affects and obligations does it entail? He moves through two possible meanings and touches on the antecedents, affects, and obligations associated with each meaning. The phrase might designate clothes "that ... are far gone and dilapidated like a plant that is gone to seed—or, possibly, that they are made untidy by many seeds adhering to them" (97).[43] If the metaphor means to designate clothing that falls into pieces as a seed pod does, then the antecedent to this meaning is an analogical relation between plant and human beings. Is the figure, then, not only a way of describing dilapidated clothes but also a trace of the essentially iconographic relation between life forms? And if so, does the metaphor not only transmit the meaning of clothes falling to pieces but also human beings' protean recognition of a latent interspecies semiosis by which they endlessly replicate plant-being on other scales and to different ends? Or is the metaphor suggesting that animal beings are made untidy by their work of carrying out the work of plants? Indeed, is the metaphor suggesting that human beings are not entirely separate from vegetable beings since they are in a sense external plant organs that carry out the work of vegetable sex, dispersing their own coats into the air as they do so? In this second case, the seedy coat is not obsolescent but, to the contrary, fulfilling its office of serving vegetable being. Here the antecedent to the metaphor is not an analogical relation between separate life forms but an intersectional relation between conjoined life forms that each, in their own way, dissipate into their milieu.

Thoreau does not determine which of these meanings is borne by the metaphor that casts human clothes as *seedy*. That this metaphor could mean clothes that reveal that human beings sometimes look like plants or that human clothes serve vegetable ends indicates two different propositional contents. Moreover, these propositional contents transmit two different accounts of the relation of animal to vegetable life: first, that vegetables and animals exist in an analogical relation; second, that plants and animals exist in an intersectional relation. The "meanings" of these tropes are not so much a representational content or even a concept but a call to action and an incitement to consider the mode of relation that might inform such action. Thoreau argues that representational languages should incite affects that give onto moral action but, since it is not clear what relation is presaged by metaphors that follow on the "hints" given by vegetable life, the affects and obligations that this metaphor would require are contestable and not determined in advance.

Finally, that human metaphors have antecedents in nonhuman phenomena, and that these antecedents suggest two different logics (analogy, intersection) that plants and human beings might both attempt to read and act upon (are human beings like plants, or are they extensions of plants?) suggests a sort of transspecies semiosis, one in which trees give off signs (going to seed) that human beings take up and reroute into intrahuman semiosis (metaphors about clothes dispersing into the air, a dispersion that can mean at least two different things) and one in which human beings give off signs (coats) that plants recognize as bearing significance. Here semiosis does not simply and endlessly designate life or its evolution as it does for Wheeler and most other recent theorists of biosemiosis. Instead, it can evince divergent propositional contents that would give rise to different actions and ethics. Moreover, the semiosis that Thoreau sketches here allows that one life form might read and evolve in relation to another, but this reading and evolution do not only serve life (although they might if one takes human beings to be plant genitalia). After all, for Thoreau it serves the project of expressing the affects and obligations that bind together expressions of the formative impulses of light and wind in their earthly transit.

Vegetable Stars

If Thoreau's work on arboreal figuration gives onto a literary tropology from which we can glean meanings, the most highly valued process of his forest geometry is not semiotic and not even ultimately figural but an ethic that follows on the sorts of obligations discussed in the previous section. But how does this ethic extend to the light and wind that generate the life forms Thoreau joins in ties of mutual obligation? To address this question, it's necessary to follow out the relationship between the forest geometry that Thoreau takes as his explicit problem in *Dispersion* and the forest

chromography he takes as a problem in the concomitantly written "Autumnal
Tints." While Thoreau sometimes speaks of color in *Dispersion* and of forest
shapes in "Autumnal Tints," that he separates out these problems suggests
that he sees a fundamental difference between forest shape and color. If
shape follows on the self-registering of light, wind, and other energies as
when wind takes the more static shape of pine forests that then fills into
the roundness of oaks forests, then color is the visible dissipation of shape
back into energy. The figural force of light and wind that manifest in forest
geometry and the chromatic force these forests give off are asymmetrical:
the former strong impulsive forces, and the latter weak, reactive powers.
This asymmetry between two different sorts of forces is the ground from
which Thoreau spins out the ethic that binds forest forces to the celestial
forces from which they come.

In "Autumnal Tints" Thoreau claims that before a deciduous tree loses
its leaves it "require[s] less nourishment from any source, and that ... from
the sun and air."[44] Drawing their energy from the sun and the air, the tree's
leaves glow into obsolescence giving color back to the sky on which it feeds.
Describing the Scarlet Oak, Thoreau writes that

> every such tree becomes a nucleus of red, as it were, where, with the
> declining sun, that color grows and glows. It is partly borrowed fire,
> gathering strength from the sun on its way to your eye. It has only some
> comparatively dull red leaves for a rallying-point, or kindling-stuff, to
> start it, and it becomes an intense scarlet or red mist, or fire, which finds
> fuel for itself in the very atmosphere.[45]

A "nucleus of red" that evokes nineteenth-century senses of *nucleus* as
seed and celestial body (OED), the New England oak's autumn seeding does
not give off shapes but a "partly borrowed" chromatic light that makes it
into a celestial being, a minor star. The light is triply borrowed: first, it is an
energy that transits through the oak and that for this is not its own; second,
the redness that the oak gives off gains its intensity from the particular
expression of the light of the sun on an autumn day in 1859; third, the oak's
chromatic light gains something of its expression by virtue of its passage
through the medium of the atmosphere that itself follows on biotic and
abiotic forces gathered together to constitute the milieu. In this New England
autumn ritual, trees borrow from the sun and their surroundings to wane
into astral being before dropping their leaves to the ground where these
leaves turn into earth that retains a trace of their astral transit.[46] Thoreau
does not suggest that this set of transformations—of the tree into a celestial
force and then into terrestrial substance that retains a trace of its double
astral heritage—can be reduced to an account of the cycling of chemicals
through living bodies, the thermodynamic postulate that energy can never
be created or destroyed but only change form, or any other promise of the

endless effervescence of the physical world as energy transits, informs, and transforms across a series of media. Unlike the sun, the chromatic light of vegetable stars produces no heat and it cannot be used to power anything other than their own transitory misting and coloring. Instead of the eternity of light, power, and the cyclings of energy and matter, this vegetable starlight is but a fleeting expression of light as color that cannot be cycled, stored, and for this it offers no promise of endless renewal or any other eternity.

Trees in Concord come from sunlight and pass into chromatic starlight. The astral force of their origin and that which they give off in their annual ritual of departure are not equivalent qualities or quantities. One is a radiant, cycling energy that unspools on intervals that dwarf even the longest durée environmental histories; the other a vanishing energy whose frequencies are only perceptible at a particular crepuscular interval in a phenological rhythm that itself plays out in a delimited historical moment because the New England forests Thoreau experiences didn't exist before or afterward on the scale they did then.[47] This spectacle reveals only what its viewers experience: namely, the forest collectivity that includes the relation between pines, oaks, birds, squirrels, and human beings and the chromatic starlight that they collectively make visible if only for the duration of a sundown. If life forms are integuments of starlight, and if Thoreau here has them give off a light that recalls this solar origin, vegetable stars are not stars since the quality and quantity of their power are different as are the timescales on which they phosphoresce.

That trees, squirrels, birds, and human denizens of Concord live on and give off a borrowed light suggests that they possess this power transiently and that, on so possessing, they accumulate a debt. That there is a debt recalls the ethic of obligation that Thoreau suggests binds together the beings that compose the forest flowering. However, here the ground of obligation shifts from the obligation that they owe each other (an obligation that on being realized, even if only incipiently, constitutes an ecology) to the obligation that they together owe the light from which they came. This obligation cannot be repaid in kind. Moreover, the celestial forces to which this debt is owed cannot perceive or take in the tribute they are offered. The ethic we might derive from the long-durée transaction of starlight into a short durée chromatic spectacle requires recognizing an obligation that demands repayment yet can never be repaid: it is a sign of and promissory note for an unpayable debt.

7

The Riddle of Forest Succession

Mark Noble

*Here you can dig, not gold, but the value which gold merely
represents; and there is no Signor Blitz about it. Yet farmers' sons
will stare by the hour to see a juggler draw ribbons from his throat,
though he tells them it is all deception. Surely, men love darkness
rather than light.*

THOREAU, "THE SUCCESSION OF FOREST TREES"

It had been raining most of a September morning when Thoreau took the
stage in the Concord Town Hall to present what would become, while he
lived, his most widely read work. The storm depressed turnout at the 1860
Middlesex County Agricultural Fair, but it packed the hall in the afternoon.
So Thoreau encountered a room full of neighbors, probably damp, with
nowhere to turn for festival entertainment but to a lecture on trees. By all
accounts, he saved what remained of the day.

"The Succession of Forest Trees," which appeared in the *New York Weekly
Tribune* the following month, has generally been regarded as a signal moment
in which Thoreau's eremitic labor as a woodland surveyor earns a measure
of public recognition. In this case, the scientific achievement on display was
decades ahead of its formal theorization by botanists and ecologists at the
turn of the century. For its introduction of the phrase "I have great faith in
seed," the address has often been celebrated for its popular advertisement of
the spiritually inflected vitalism animating Thoreau's late work.

But the lecture also has a dark side. Thoreau begins with an invitation
to see woodland ecosystems in vivid detail, but then ends with a morbid

condemnation of our limited capacity for such wonder. What looks at first like a genial demonstration of empirical solutions to a practical puzzle becomes, in the final lines comprising the epigraph above, a forlorn concession to a much deeper riddle. Stranger still, the turn reflects a tension found throughout the address: Thoreau remembers to play to the room while hinting at much harder questions he elsewhere explores in more radical terms. While keeping the tone appropriately light (at least until the end), the lecture also wonders whether a scientific paper can illustrate the mostly blind roles *we* play in ecological transformations without demolishing credulity in the practical wisdom science advertises.

The following reading of "Succession" introduces three claims about its importance to Thoreau's naturalism. First, the rhetorical gestures meant to charm his audience are more than incidental features of a text ostensibly focused on describing empirical findings. Thoreau's jokes and digressions, including the melancholy note on which he ends, help contextualize a larger question about what exactly links science and stewardship of the woods. Second, the answer to that question unfolds most powerfully, if provisionally, in Thoreau's *Journal*, which both delights and despairs in efforts to dissolve the epistemic boundaries on which public science depends. Third, reading these texts together highlights Thoreau's prescience not just as an ecologist ahead of his time but as an early philosopher of modern science raising questions about its conceptual boundaries and public function with which we continue to grapple.

I

In spite of his reputation as a Transcendentalist crank, Thoreau was invited to speak because he promised to solve a land-management puzzle that frequently confounded landowners whose woodlots he surveyed. Back in April of the same year, a meeting of the Concord Farmer's Club raised a question none of its participants could fully answer: why do pine groves so often succeed oak groves, and vice versa, whenever either is felled for timber?[1] After breaking the ice and listing his credentials as a wanderer in the woods, Thoreau set to work explaining the mechanics of forest succession, which he had meticulously traced in *Journal* entries spanning the preceding decade. His solution describes an elaborate tangle of material agents: pine seeds travel by wind to remote oak groves; birds and squirrels deposit acorns amid the pines; saplings emerge from transported seeds but do not mature in the shade of their rivals; clear-cutting then allows the invading trees to dominate; and so on.

Thoreau wasn't the only naturalist of his generation to document the interlaced phenomena comprising ecological succession, but his first hand accounts offer a lucid picture of the forest in motion more than forty years before Henry Chandler Cowles theorized the "sere"—an iterative sequence of changes specific to a community of species—at the University of Chicago in 1899.[2] Records from the afternoon of the Agricultural Fair suggest Thoreau's neighbors appreciated the lucidity. An official report composed by a representative of the Massachusetts Board of Agriculture described "large numbers" of fairgoers attending with "apparent interest and satisfaction to an excellent address" that captured the "great vitality of seeds" and the dynamism of natural systems.[3] The Middlesex Agricultural Society president lauded the presentation as "plain and practical"—which is to say, not-so-Transcendentalist-as-we-had-reason-to-fear.[4] After Horace Greeley published it in his *Weekly Tribune*, subsequent reprintings followed in periodicals and agricultural journals across the country, and the cattle-show lecture quickly became the piece that circulated most widely during Thoreau's lifetime.

It also remains a prominent moment for readers of Thoreau's late writing and his career as a surveyor. Reading "Succession" today reminds of its connection to at least two major threads in the scholarship. On one hand, the lecture offers candid proof of Thoreau's talents as a proto-modern ecologist, offering an explicit instance of that "plain and practical" gift for illustrating motions of woodland ecosystems. The practical dimension helps coordinate his idiosyncratic role in a story about emerging scientific disciplines and in policy debates about land management—a story outlined in Robert Thorson's study of Thoreau's maps and models of fluvial morphology, for instance, or Laura Walls's account of his anticipation and interpretation of Darwin.[5] At the same time, the lecture's speculative gestures link it to interest in Thoreau's materialist vitalism and faith-in-a-seed pantheism, resounding with work ranging from Alan Hodder's account of "ecstatic witness" to Branka Arsić's readings of Thoreau's theory of mourning.[6] For scholars, the "Succession" lecture offers one among several points of contact between these lines of thought. It models what Walls calls "a nonmodern science" that finds its own methods of description and reflection, no less than the elements comprising woodland ecosystems, "caught mutually in a web of relations."[7]

But assessing what makes Thoreau's lecture compelling, whether to its initial audience in Concord or its subsequent readers and eventual scholars, also means exploring its unusual sequence of rhetorical moves meant to work the room, win a few laughs, and then close on a darkly melancholy note. From the beginning, "Succession" assumes that a shared joke intimates a shared connection in a broader sense. Thoreau opens, for instance, with a self-effacing quip that quickly widens to a caricature of the assembled body:

Every man is entitled to come to Cattle-show, even a transcendentalist; and for my part I am more interested in the men than in the cattle. I wish to see once more those old familiar faces, whose names I do not know, which for me represent the Middlesex country, and come as near being indigenous to the soil as a white man can; the men who are not above their business, whose coats are not too black, whose shoes do not shine very much, who never wear gloves to conceal their hands. It is true, there are some queer specimens of humanity attracted to our festival, but all are welcome.[8]

The gesture links the eccentricity of the speaker to the inclusivity of the gathering by positing a related correlation between immediacy and nativity—between dirt under farmers' nails and a claim to proximate indigeneity. As a rhetorical ploy, the appropriative idiom transfers the symbolic currency of aboriginal attachment to an account of shared regional and class bonds. That the Nipmuc, Massachusetts, and Wampanoag descendants at once memorialized and displaced by such a move were largely invisible to landowners in Middlesex County by 1860 only served Thoreau's point: authenticity flows from environmental intimacy.[9] While the official topic for the afternoon was the relation between pines and oaks, these men with familiar faces and unknown names, and in whose hands the fates of Thoreau's forests largely reside, become the lecture's real interest.

The bulk of "Succession" nevertheless details the transmigration of seeds, observed and recorded by one of those "queer specimens" who spend uncounted hours watching squirrels and birds. Explaining the mobility of arborescent species requires both vivid imagery and strategic analogies to human and nonhuman forms. The "beautiful thin" membrane "woven around the [pine] seed" looks, for instance, "much like an insect's wing" and has been employed so ingeniously it competes with modern techniques for dispersing ideas. "There is a patent-office at the seat of government of the universe," Thoreau quips, "whose managers are as much interested in the dispersion of seeds as anybody at Washington can be, and their operations are infinitely more extensive and regular."[10] Throughout the lecture, as in much of his late writing, analogic illustrations posit a family resemblance between human and natural agencies. Accounting for seeds that do not fly on their own, later in the lecture, presses that resemblance into an elaborate trans-species tangle of bodies:

If you ever ate a cherry, and did not make two bites of it, you must have perceived it—right in the centre of the luscious morsel, a large earthy residuum left on the tongue. We thus take into our mouths cherry stones as big as peas, a dozen at once, for Nature can persuade us to do almost anything when she would compass her ends. Some wild men and children instinctively swallow these, as the birds do when in a hurry, it being the shortest way to get rid of them. Thus, though these seeds are not provided with vegetable wings, Nature has impelled the thrush tribe to take them into their bills and fly away with them; and they are winged in another sense, and more effectually than the seeds of pines, for these are carried even against the wind.[11]

Bringing to mind the taste of cherries in late September, a move Emily Dickinson called a "sacrament of summer days" in 1859,[12] initiates a striking sequence of transformations: persons become as birds, birds become as the membranes around pine seeds, and the good news delivered by the guts of either species becomes, in a sense, what shapes our winged appetites.

The mission of Thoreau's lecture depends in no small part on these digressions, especially where they tacitly ensnare his listeners in the complex of agencies comprising the succession drama. Again, the stated purpose of the event was to advance public knowledge of arboreal mechanics with an empirical picture of trees on the move—a view of the woods made possible by the objective clarity only scrupulous observation achieves. But any full answer to a question born of uncertainty about the sequence of timber crops includes *our* appetites for harvesting trees among its several players. Thoreau locates his audience right alongside, not ontologically distinct from, the patterns of wind, the talents of squirrels, and the composition of soil. In a twist that became familiar to ecologists in subsequent decades, the scientific insight that prompted so many 1860s reprintings of "Succession" also troubles the objective distance presumed to authorize such knowledge in the first place. And yet precisely that epistemological frame prevails among the men who presume to own the woods. The lecture's comedic gestures and rhetorical flourishes thus pave the way, cautiously, to the suggestion that proprietors who see trees as commodities and squirrels as vermin come round to a richer understanding of the intricate performativity of their woodlots—a picture that necessarily includes, even as it instructs, the humans who fell the trees.

That his lightly funny approach frames most of the lecture makes Thoreau's dolorous conclusion all the more striking. Having finished the blow-by-blow account of the connection linking squirrels and saplings, he pivots to an anecdote about the thrilling vitality of his own garden seeds, presumably to help dispel assumptions that forest trees, like cultivated orchards, reproduce asexually.[13] One 1857 seed, remembered in the spirit of the festival, generated 310 pounds of yellow squash—"Convince me that you have a seed there, and I am prepared to expect wonders."[14] But then his ardor abruptly gives way to a final statement that takes an ornery turn:

You have but little more to do, than throw up your cap for entertainment these American days. Perfect alchemists I keep, who can transmute substances without end; and thus the corner of my garden is an inexhaustible treasure-chest. Here you can dig, not gold, but the value which gold merely represents; and there is no Signor Blitz about it. Yet farmers' sons will stare by the hour to see a juggler draw ribbons from his throat, though he tells them it is all deception. Surely, men love darkness rather than light.[15]

Perhaps this was merely one more rhetorical flourish, calculated to win knowing laughter or nodding approval by citing scripture to farmers perennially struggling to extract labor from their children.[16] Or maybe Thoreau hoped for an awkward silence before applause, in which the shock of his misanthropy would register more powerfully by undercutting nostalgia for cherries and genial boasting about squash. In any case, whether he means it ironically or earnestly, "Succession" ends with a dropped-mic disavowal of the communitarian good faith with which Thoreau opened and which presumably sponsored the event in the first place.

Signor Blitz, his metonym for every species of popular culture diminishing the souls of American youth, was the stage name used by Antonio van Zandt, who emigrated from England in 1834 and rose to fame as a comedian and magician known for catching bullets, spinning plates, and compelling canaries to sing. Van Zandt, who published an autobiography in 1871, also relied on carefully managed rhetoric and strategic self-deprecation to inspire belief in invisible phenomena.[17] That such a show shared a genre with the presentation Thoreau had just given—another public wizard briefly drawing occult knowledge into view—might have inspired the antipathy. Blitz does not appear in the *Journal* or in Thoreau's published writing. By impugning the magician, Thoreau resumes the role of learned curmudgeon satirized in his opening: *kids these days* neglect the authentic magic of nature and dote instead on so many virtual, or Blitzian, deceptions. The ending takes parting shots at both popular simulacra of natural wonders and the function of capital in the succession model: the magic garden reproaches the magic trick while also subtly rebuking the trick of commodification ("gold merely represents") that compels Thoreau's audience to harvest trees in the first place.

But does the churlish twist at the end help clarify the lecture's larger insight about the material roles we play in ecological succession? The abruptness of the turn makes it difficult to discern whether remarking on our perennial indifference to what elevates nature's magic above mere carnival tricks also instructs about our role in the dispersion of seeds. After all, the forest drama Thoreau unfolds includes natural phenomena discernible only in concert with landowners' hapless cutting, complicating the lines thought to separate the agencies of seeds and their planters. Are the men finally different from the squirrels? Perhaps men *do* love darkness rather than light, like infant trees standing for a time in the shade, insofar as that preference characterizes their role in an arboreal situation. But what would *that* insight mean for the lecture's efforts to instruct Middlesex landowners about the science behind forest succession? What would it mean for the woods if we loved the light?

Or, to put the question another way, how does the instruction to distinguish one kind of magic from another correspond to the lecture's implicit argument—that we should be informed stewards of forest systems—if that same lecture also reveals the distinctions we make are largely internal to, rather than observant of, an arboreal situation? Oddly enough, the tension between the statement's rhetorical posturing (the youth prefer deception) and its objective sense ("men prefer darkness") looks at once like an unacknowledged discrepancy and, in a way, like its most provocative feature. Many of the lecture's most salient insights locate persons on the same plane as squirrels—reducing subjects to objects in hopes of illustrating their tangle of relations. But then the grouchy gardener in those final lines seems to expect so much more of us. The querulous concluding statement hints at Thoreau's long held belief that only the eremitic discipline that earned him his queer reputation could bring things like the mechanics of forest succession into view. And yet that vantage too assumes the sort of objective distance the lecture elsewhere troubles.

While his succession model won praise for its lucidity, at least one aspect of Thoreau's advice to the Agricultural Society audience is neither plain nor practical. When he implies that in this woodland gospel "men love darkness" refers not simply to original sin but to a material situation linking persons and plants, Thoreau closes the address with a more difficult riddle: not the one about how species of trees come to succeed one another, which he solves easily enough; but the one about what connects forest phenomena to the observer, whether scientist or farmer, who traces their patterns of becoming. As generations of his readers have noticed, encounters with this harder riddle preoccupy dozens of *Journal* entries in which Thoreau painstakingly watches it slip into and out of focus. In those volumes, repeated efforts to map the magic garden collide with the recognition that such work could only be legitimated by a privilege in which the speaker also disbelieves.

Is it even possible, the cattle-show lecture asks, to make such a problem legible in the light of a public gathering? In Thoreau's *Journal*, any scientific finding worth bringing into such light flows from a radical intimacy that blurs the lines said to distinguish the mind from the world it surveys. Some of those findings include the recognition that we do, perhaps axiomatically, love our darkness. So perhaps taking the competing aims of "Succession" seriously requires reading the layered significance of a statement like "Surely men love darkness rather than light" not simply as cryptic grousing, nor simply as rhetoric for provoking Middlesex county, but as the speaker of the *Journal* might have read it.

II

From its earliest pages, the *Journal* sees the dance performed by pines and oaks as an invitation to correlate human experience with natural forms. In just the second entry in his first of forty-seven manuscript volumes, recorded three months after his twentieth birthday, Thoreau proposes that the decomposition of trees fuels his own development:

> The oak dies down to the ground, leaving within its rind a rich virgin mould, which will impart a vigorous life to an infant forest. The pine leaves a sandy and sterile soil, the harder woods a strong and fruitful mould.
>
> So this constant abrasion and decay makes the soil of my future growth. As I live now so shall I reap. If I grow pines and birches, my virgin mould will not sustain the oak; but pines and birches, or, perchance, weeds and brambles, will constitute my second growth.[18]

The analogy is elegant but oblique. Dying trees generate the humus responsible for nurturing subsequent generations, modeling a theory of personal growth that incorporates death as life. Rather than presume disintegration must be antithetical to development, the *Journal* begins by aligning its own trajectory with woodland cycles of decomposition and fruition. But the entry makes no effort to define "this constant abrasion and decay" of its speaker, neither illustrating the importance of "second growth" nor introducing features of that "strong and fruitful" personal substrate.

Read in light of experiments to follow, however, that obliquity also makes this an intriguing passage. As a preliminary sketch, it introduces Thoreau's decades-long effort to limn the correspondence between the twists and turns of human experience and the rhythms of natural systems. Considered alongside the 1860 lecture, for instance, the early moment is also striking because it appears to get the mechanics of forest succession exactly wrong. The assertion that one's "virgin mould" generates a facsimile of earlier growth—"If I grow pines" then I "will not sustain the oak"— assumes the fusion of dying to living breeds continuity, even homogeneity, between generations of trees and thus between periods of a life. While later observations of pines and oaks would overturn that presumption by linking soil and growth in more complex assemblages, and facets of experience in more nuanced arrangements, the effort to coordinate personal and arboreal ontogenies becomes one of the *Journal*'s most consistently beguiling preoccupations. As in later instances, Thoreau's method is analogical while the larger statement he hopes his prose might witness is necessarily ontological.

Reading Asa Gray's *Manual of the Botany of the Northern United States* in May of 1851, for instance, Thoreau finds that cutting-edge documentation of vegetal morphology confirms his "perfect analogy between the life of the human being and that of the vegetable, both of body and mind."[19]

Citing Gray's description of the embryonic tissue, or radicle, that emerges first from a seed, Thoreau concludes unhesitatingly that such stem cells are in fact "the rudiment of the mind ... slumbering coiled up, packed away in the seed."[20] When Gray tracks the growth of root and stem on two axes, one descending and one ascending, Thoreau turns to his pines and oaks for corroboration:

> So the mind develops from the first in two opposite directions: upwards to expand in the light and air; and downwards avoiding the light to form the root. One half is aerial, the other subterranean. The mind is not well balanced and firmly planted, like the oak, which has not as much root as branch, whose roots like those of the white pine are slight and near the surface. ... The mere logician, the mere reasoner, who weaves his arguments as a tree its branches in the sky,—nothing equally developed in the roots, —is overthrown by the first wind.[21]

If minds grow as plants grow, then the so-called depth of our thinking refers no less to an underground network that loves the darkness than to profundity enjoyed in the open air. Importantly, tracking this congruence between intellectual and vegetal growth means materializing not just minds but thoughts along within them, so that mental phenomena too develop unseen foundations: "The thought that comes to light, that pierces the empyrean on the other side, is wombed and rooted in darkness."[22] Such *Journal* moments compel interest for many of the same reasons they strain credulity. Later in the entry, still energized by Gray's manual, he again proposes blurring distinctions between thoughts and things—"No thought but is connected as strictly as a flower, to the earth"—only to then further radicalize the analogy by confounding the properties thought to distinguish both ideas and objects: "A cloud is uplifted to sustain its roots."[23]

While such moments can be captivating, it bears repeating that the *Journal*'s alignments of subjective and objective phenomena are so intriguing because they are so often provisional—at times even dubious. The analogy between trees and minds, for instance, frequently dovetails with a related effort to link seasons and moods. Entries that span the 1850s, years in which Thoreau also uncovered the logic of forest succession, variously capture an uncompensated longing for the sorts of congruence the prose labors to simulate. In August of 1851, to cite an early example, reflecting on the passage of summer means discovering a mind in nature that provokes human feeling:

> This coolness comes to condense the dews and clear the atmosphere. The stillness seems more deep and significant. Each sound seems to come from out a greater thoughtfulness in nature, as if nature had acquired some character and mind. The cricket, the gurgling stream, the rushing wind amid the trees, all speak to me soberly yet encouragingly of the steady onward progress of the universe. My heart leaps into my mouth at the sound of the wind in the woods.[24]

Attributing thoughtfulness to early autumn displaces the engine of the human affect from self to world, suggesting that what makes the heart leap must be the effects of a "character and mind" not our own. But the joy these sentences take in captivation by the sounds of August makes it all the more startling when a fully self-conscious speaker resumes control of the entry just a few lines later:

> Ah! if I could so live that there should be no desultory moment in all my life! that in the trivial season, when small fruits are ripe, my fruits might be ripe also! that I could match nature always with my moods! that in each season when some part of nature especially flourishes, then a corresponding part of me may not fail to flourish![25]

The turn implies that recording those moments in which nature coordinates feeling—in which a mind out there in the world governs the "small fruits" of experience—has the perverse consequence of reintroducing the disjunction between persons and seasons emblematized by the transience of our moods. The lamentation reminds not only that any efforts to live with "no desultory moment" remain a perpetual struggle, but also that language meant to capture those exquisite glimpses of a life subordinated to natural rhythms cannot, by definition, discharge the point of view that organizes the reflection. The tantalizing irony is that Thoreau's effort to "match nature always with my moods" generates just the sort of desultory insight he hopes to relinquish—or, as Sharon Cameron puts it in her reading of the same passage, "the description of the constancy solicited calls its fact into question."[26]

Contending with such frustration in 1851 does not mean Thoreau gives up inventing techniques for tacking the commensurability between minds and trees. In fact, the *Journal* displays increasing confidence in experiments that locate human affects in vegetal time. Once again charmed by an August remission of summer, now in 1854, Thoreau finds his mental fruits ripening exactly on time:

Do you not feel the fruit of your spring and summer beginning to ripen, to harden its seed within you? Do not your thoughts begin to acquire consistency as well as flavor and ripeness? How can we expect a harvest of thought who have not had a seed-time of character? Already some of my small thoughts—fruit of my spring life—are ripe, like the berries which feed the first broods of birds; and other some are prematurely ripe and bright, like the lower leaves of the herbs which have felt the summer's drought.[27]

Maintaining the analogy between thoughts and fruits, as between trees and minds, once again means both subordinating the mind's temporality to the passage of the seasons while objectifying the mental phenomena responsible for the distinction objectivity implies. When he succeeds, Thoreau argues, the ardent listener hears "strains of his thought far surpassing any oratorio."[28] But that achievement also courts a version of the paradox that haunts the "Succession" lecture: disavowing the writerly prerogative that is the *Journal*'s métier nevertheless means *writing* one's way into those "[s]easons when our mind is like the strings of a harp which is swept, and we stand and listen."[29]

Whether a given passage finds our moods in sync with seasonal transitions or incurably stuck to selfhood, what animates Thoreau's several efforts to externalize experience includes his presumption that such alignments must be more than nonliteral resemblances. Never content with figurative connections linking disparate categories—say, thoughts and things— the *Journal* persists in its effort to witness an ontological kinship toward which the most ingenious analogy merely gestures. The resulting assertions thus tend to transgress against common-sense boundaries necessary for understanding things like causality, object permanence, identity, and temporality. "The seasons and their changes are in me," he claims in 1857, "I believe the Concord would not rise and overflow its banks again, were I not here."[30] In 1858, even the "humblest plant, or weed, as we call it, stands there to express some thought or mood of ours, and yet how long it stands in vain!"[31] In early 1859, a nuthatch witnessed "giving vent to the spring within it" demonstrates "that we, in our anticipations and sympathies, include in succession the moods and expressions of all creatures."[32] In the fall of the same year, time spent recording those anticipations and sympathies enables one to "know when in the year to expect certain thoughts and moods, as the sportsman knows when to look for plover."[33] In the "crystalline winter" of 1860, every meteorological nuance, from the clearness in the sky to the exposure of ice to air, comes freighted with affects we share without owning, "so entirely do we sympathize with the moods of nature."[34]

On the one hand, a phrase like "moods of nature" signals the *Journal*'s investment in figurative devices for making the forms and motions of woodland ecosystems resound with psychological phenomena typically understood to share neither the materiality nor the temporality of pines and oaks. On the other hand, such efforts often result in language that pushes past metaphor, confounding distinctions thought to separate qualia from the qualities of objects by transposing mental and material elements. Consider, for instance, the following moment from the summer of 1857, in which trees' performance of a seasonal transition illustrates a theory of change that transforms the theorist:

> This is June, the month of grass and leaves. The deciduous trees are investing the evergreens and revealing how dark they are. Already the aspens are trembling again, and a new summer is offered me. I feel a little fluttered in my thoughts, as if I might be too late. Each season is but an infinitesimal point. It no sooner comes than it is gone. It has no duration. It simply gives a tone and hue to my thought. Each annual phenomenon is a reminiscence and prompting. Our thoughts and sentiments answer to the revolutions of the seasons, as two cog-wheels fit into each other. We are conversant with only one point of contact at a time, from which we receive a prompting and impulse and instantly pass to a new season or point of contact. A year is made up of a certain series and number of sensations and thoughts which have their language in nature. Now I am ice, now I am sorrel.[35]

The convolutions in this passage can be dizzying. Beginning with an observation about entangled species of trees, in which deciduous arrivals reveal by contrast the darkness of evergreens, would seem to focus the entry on the mechanics of observation. But then the "trembling" of aspen leaves transfers to "fluttered" thoughts, which in turn generate a feeling of belatedness—as if the onset of summer were too rapid and replete with detail for a speaker who would claim just a few months later that "seasons and their changes are in me."[36] That feeling of arriving too late to the aspens then triggers a bewildering sequence of assertions: (1) seasons have no duration because (2) they are only discernible as tones and hues of thought, implying (3) natural phenomena are subordinated to the mind's temporality. But describing seasons as occasions for "reminiscence and prompting" also leads, conversely, to the recognition that (4) *we* are the ones bound to nature's transformations. It is rather (5) our "thoughts and sensations" that become the infinitesimal points and (6) transform constantly as the wheel turns, implying (7) the mind is subordinated to world's temporality.

At the start of the entry, we own the vantage that both keeps time and compares foliage; only a few sentences later, we are the fugitive traces of natural events—now ice, now herbs. Despite our pretensions, correlating seasons and affects reduces experience to mere points of contact linking the rhythms of nature to the rhythms of a life. To objectify thought, or locate its "language in nature," here means to inhabit a mind that knows only its occasional state—summer *or* winter, never both, never neither. In such moments, Thoreau depicts the point of view from which a person sees (reminisces, anticipates, documents) as both perilously open to unforeseen depths of feeling and weirdly ephemeral thanks to nature's determinism. Many of the most provocative entries filling the last decade of the *Journal* witness this transfer of power, in which finding that persons become as trees, for instance, dispossesses the mind of its own thoughts. Or, to put the problem a different way, the congruence Thoreau longs to simulate— between lives and trees, or between moods and seasons—obviates the human exceptionalism that might make such insight useful, verifiable, or (as subsequent generations would put it) valid science.

III

Three months later, in September of 1857, Thoreau recorded several of the observations he would repurpose for the cattle-show lecture. As in similar descriptions of his succession model found in surrounding entries, the discovery relies on a precise, prosaic account of plants on the ground:

> P. M.—I walked to that very dense and handsome white pine grove east of Beck Stow's Swamp. It is about fifteen rods square, the trees large, ten to twenty inches in diameter. It is separated by a wall from another pine wood with a few oaks in it on the southeast, and about thirty rods north and west are other pine and oak woods. Standing on the edge of the wood and looking through it,—for it is quite level and free from underwood, mostly bare, red-carpeted ground,—you would have said that there was not a hardwood tree in it, young or old, though I afterward found on one edge a middling-sized sassafras, a birch, a small tupelo, and two little scarlet oaks, but, what was more interesting, I found, on looking closely over its floor, that, alternating with thin ferns and small blueberry bushes, there was, as often as every five feet, a little oak, three to twelve inches high, and in one place I found a green acorn dropped by the base of a tree. I was surprised, I confess, to find my own theory so perfectly proved.[37]

Noticing the oaks, and finding that lucky acorn, depends on movement from the edge to the interior of the pine grove. The discovery boasts intimate familiarity with the scene, but without relinquishing the objective gaze capable of revealing that what appeared "mostly bare" is in fact replete with ferns and blueberries. Such observation corroborates important conclusions about forest succession drawn the year before—namely, that "[s]carcely enough allowance has been made for the agency of squirrels in dispersing seeds" and that clearcutting for timber must be what gives those infant oaks their chance to thrive.[38] Excised from the *Journal's* effort to "stand and listen" while the world plays the mind like an instrument, these are the sorts of findings that make "plain and practical" sense in a public address.

The unresolved tension between such untroubled objectivity and the more radical dispossessions cited above may hold the key to understanding the tragic turn at the end of "The Succession of Forest Trees." For the most part, the rhetorical comportment of the 1860 lecture reflects an educated guess that festival audiences had little interest in analogies binding minds to plants and little patience for a meteorological theory of affect. Even today's readers, often eager for a dose of trans-species vitalism, tend to find presumptive homologies between seed dispersal and the roots of the mind far-fetched. But Thoreau cannot leave the stage without reminding about the moral and epistemological consequences of his finding. So how then to emphasize the material significance of the human agents whose role in the succession story betrays a grasp of the system no wiser than the squirrel's? His parting shot—"surely men love darkness rather than light"—refers the ecological question to an idiomatic formula for our inveterate moral limits. In the verses to which the lecture alludes, the gospel-writer has Jesus explain that punitive judgments reflect our indifference to what has been illuminated. Perhaps Thoreau hoped the consequent soteriological paradox would be as familiar as the scriptural idiom: the juridical model implies knowledge of the light; the "love," on the other hand, is hopelessly congenital.

This is not to say that "Succession" amounts straightforwardly to a parable of ecological perdition. Read alongside the decade of *Journal* entries from which most of the lecture is drawn, the decision to close by indicting our limited grasp of precisely the sort of environmental science just exhibited refers to an unspoken challenge found in both texts: how to instruct about managing the woods while recognizing the manager as merely a component in the thing managed? Does the parting insult recommend remodeling our attachments to natural objects or merely describing our role in vanishing ecologies? That sequence of entries linking mental and vegetal properties, for instance, invites at least two competing readings of a phrase like "men love darkness"—a figurative reading that impugns the audience in hopes of changing its mind, and a literal reading born of so many attempts to describe the roots of the mind. In one case, we are taken to task for neglecting the authentic magic on display in the woods; in the other case, we are mere functions and features of that display. Stranger still, these options are linked in a terribly disorienting chiasmus: the figurative reading posits scientific inquiry as a means to moral redemption; the literal reading dispenses with redemption while actually positing a scientific insight.

Perhaps that explains why both contemporary reviewers and generations of critics have tended to overlook the quip at the end, emphasizing either the lecture's cheerful accessibility or its idiosyncratic place in the history of emerging scientific disciplines. The lecture intimates what the *Journal* dares to explore: the sort of attention capable of bringing natural systems into focus also courts its own objectification, even at the cost of undermining the conceit of practical veracity that led to several reprintings of the 1860 lecture. Retuning to "The Succession of Forest Trees" with the *Journal*'s full range of experiments in mind positions Thoreau as an important early historian of such tangles in modern thinking about ecology and environmental literacy. That he offers no determinate solution to this larger riddle of forest succession, and only deepens its resonance in forty-seven volumes of *Journal* experimentation, reminds that our understanding of what links science and stewardship remains perilously fraught. In lieu of redemption from our dark role in the shape of arboreal transformations, Thoreau generates thrilling, if disorienting, formulae for finding oneself among the trees—as in a strangely prescient *Journal* entry from 1840:

> It would be well if we saw ourselves as in perspective always, impressed with distinct outline on the sky, side by side with the shrubs on the river's brim. So let our life stand to heaven as some fair, sunlit tree against the western horizon, and by sunrise be planted on some eastern hill to glisten in the first rays of the dawn.[39]

"Succession" resembles one such effort to illustrate the perspective with which we see ourselves both as and alongside some sunlit tree—one cast in the terms of an exoteric model of what animates the woods in which we walk. The *Journal* describes a related effort grounded in an esoteric willingness to remodel relations between persons and plants. Whether such prose amounts to a magic garden or a magic trick, Thoreau's writing both introduces and advances ongoing struggles to grasp what it means that even such glistening things cannot but love the darkness.

8

Low-Tech Thoreau; or, Remediations of the Human in *The Dispersion of Seeds*

Jason Gladstone

However diverse recent posthumanist and ecocritical projects have been, those focused on the imbrication of humans and nature have generally been organized as recognitions or disclosures of the integration of the human with the nonhuman as an always, already, abiding condition. Insofar as this is the case, these projects are essentially continuous with the major literary critical accounts of Henry David Thoreau's canonical works (from R. W. B. Lewis through Sharon Cameron, Lawrence Buell, and Branka Arsić) that configure the Thoreauvian problematic of naturalizing the human in terms of recognizing, disclosing, or otherwise actualizing an extant continuity of the human with nature.[1] The argument of this essay, however, is that Thoreau's unfinished manuscript *The Dispersion of Seeds* features a naturalization of the human that does not resolve into a realization of such continuity.[2] From the outset of the manuscript, it is apparent that the task of "show[ing] how the seed is transported from where it grows to where it is planted" entails an overhauling of the observer: in order to document and display

Reprinted from Gladstone, Jason. "Low-Tech Thoreau; or, Remediations of the Human in *The Dispersion of Seeds*," *Criticism* 57, no. 3 (2015): 349–76. Copyright © 2015 Wayne State University Press, with the permission of Wayne State University Press. The essay has been updated and revised for inclusion in this volume.

the modes, means, and mechanisms of seed dispersal, the observer needs to be calibrated to the spatial and temporal intervals that separate a seed's growth from its planting (D, 24). As the manuscript proceeds, it becomes clear that, for Thoreau, this overhauling of the observer does not constitute an actualization of the potential naturalness or inhumanity of the human; nor does it constitute a nonactualization, materialization, or iteration of such a potentiality.[3] Rather, what this overhauling of the observer resolves into is *a modification of the human that makes it natural:* a conversion of the human-writing into nature's recording function.

This late manuscript of Thoreau's, then, features a sustained engagement with the vegetal, specifically, with seeds and their transport. Here, the vegetal is not so much thought through as a category as it is the site of a focused investigation—that is, how seeds are transported from where they grow to where they are planted—that underwrites a sustained consideration of the relationship between humanity, technology, and nature. As will become clear in the pages that follow, in *The Dispersion of Seeds* the vegetal is less vibrant than it is operational. It is not creaturely, and it does not think. It operates. And in doing so the vegetal emerges as an aspect of a nature that both coopts human actions and serves as the unacknowledged basis of the bulk of human technologies. Nevertheless, for Thoreau this coextension of the vegetal and the technological is not enough to make the human natural. Rather, for that state to be achieved the human-writing must undergo extensive modification. Accordingly, this essay has two main tasks. The first is to elucidate the specific remediation of writing featured in *The Dispersion of Seeds.* As Jay David Bolter and Richard Grusin define it, *remediation* is the process by which new and old media constitute and reconstitute themselves by "appropriat[ing] the techniques, forms, and social significances" of other, competing, media.[4] In *The Dispersion of Seeds* the overhauling of the observer—the conversion of the human-writing into nature's recording function—entails a remediation of writing whereby writing adapts a central aspect of the emerging media of photography. In so doing, writing reconfigures itself as a medium that is capable of capturing the too-slow-to-be-perceived motions of a nature that works "systematically" (D, 151), at "a geologic pace," and "over the greatest distances" (D, 36).[5] As is explained in the pages that follow, this remediation of writing appears as a refunctioning of photographic *automaticity* that converts the human-writing into an apparatus that can produce desubjective representations of nature. In the now-standard critical optic installed by Jonathan Crary's and Friedrich Kittler's poststructuralist accounts of nineteenth-century media culture, such a conjunction of writing and technological media can be understood as an aspect of the general supplantation of agency that coincided with the advent of modernity.[6] However, insofar as Thoreau's remediation of writing derives from an intentional reorganization of action, the particular conjunction of writing and technological media in *The Dispersion of Seeds* resolves into an *instantiation* of modern literary agency.

The other main task of this essay is to detail how *The Dispersion of Seeds* presents this remediation of writing as a thoroughly technological mode of naturalizing the human. *The Dispersion of Seeds* thereby reconfigures a problematic that has recently emerged as an important feature of both ecocriticism and posthumanism and has long been central to Thoreau criticism. At least since R. W. B Lewis's *The American Adam* (1955), critics have registered Thoreau's interest in integrating the human into nature; at least since Leo Marx's *The Machine in the Garden* (1964), critics have routinely noted that, for Thoreau, the development of modern technology threatens—and thereby makes more urgent—the possibility of effecting the sort of "total immersion in nature" that would "bring into being the natural man."[7] Contemporary Thoreau criticism most often considers the ways in which Thoreau presents literary modes of representing nature as vehicles for naturalizing the human. Paradigmatically, in *Writing Nature*, Sharon Cameron argues that, in Thoreau's *Journal*, "[t]he self ... is to be converted to nature" through the reading and writing of a nature that is "disassociated from human significance."[8] In *The Environmental Imagination*, Lawrence Buell then identifies this particular literary endeavor as one of the "environmental projects" that characterize *Walden* (1845–7)—a set of projects that also include literary modes that personify, allegorize, or otherwise appropriate nature—and he argues that these compiled projects locate Thoreau's work as the founding instance of an "aesthetics of relinquishment" based on the effort "to forgo the illusion of mental and even bodily apartness from one's environment."[9] As Timothy Sweet has recently noted, the publication of *The Environmental Imagination* facilitated "the consolidation of ecocriticism in the 1990s," thereby installing Thoreau "as the progenitor of the modern 'environmental imagination.'"[10] Consequently, Buell's configuration of the Thoreauvian problematic of integrating the human into nature was instituted as a core commitment of this version of ecocriticism.[11]

A version of this problematic has also emerged as a defining feature of the strain of posthumanism that concerns itself with the relationship of humans to animals, and rocks, and stones, and trees. Following on Jacques Derrida's late writings on "animality" and "the animal," studies such as Cary Wolfe's *Animal Rites* and David Wills's *Dorsality* work to disclose the constitutive inhumanity of the human by imbricating the human with the nonhuman through divers retro-extensions of non-self-identicality into "nature."[12] And, as W. J. T. Mitchell notes in his foreword to *Animal Rites,* "The Rights of Things," the implied trajectory of this strain of posthumanism is the recalibration of nonsentient things as subjects and, therefore, as "subject[s] of rights."[13] Mitchell writes that once "the rights of plants and animals have all been worked out in new forms of bioethics and biopolitics, there will still be work to do. At that point it will be time to take up the rights of *things,* of inanimate objects."[14] Of course, in her now canonical study, *Vibrant Matter*, Jane Bennett both extends and modifies precisely this trajectory by enlisting Thoreau, Bruno Latour, and Gilles Deleuze and Félix Guattari (among others) in a theory of "material vibrancy" that recalibrates the agencies of humans and nonhumans as degrees of "effectivity" so as to bracket subjectivity and imply "an ontological field without any unequivocal demarcations between human, animal, vegetable, or mineral."[15] More recently, Branka Arsić's *Bird Relics* has fully integrated Thoreau into this strain of posthumanism by arguing that he is committed to a "radically materialistic brand of vitalism" in which "all matter is treated as contemplative, alive, and thoughtful."[16]

However diverse these literary-critical, ecocritical, and posthumanist projects are, all of them configure the naturalization of the human as a matter of recognizing, realizing, or otherwise actualizing an always-already established continuity of the human with the nonhuman. For most of these projects, this actualization then takes the form of a reconception of the human. As is discussed later in this essay, a number of Thoreau's works undoubtedly feature many such attempts to reconceive the human so as to be able to understand it as an aspect of nature. However, in *The Dispersion of Seeds,* the Thoreauvian problematic of integrating the human into nature is configured differently—it is configured as a project that requires not the rethinking of the human but its modification. That is, in this late unfinished manuscript of Thoreau's, the naturalization of the human is presented as a technical project rather than a philosophical one. What necessitates such a technical configuration of this problematic is that Thoreau here maintains ontological demarcations between humans and the continuum of nature.

Most pertinently, *The Dispersion of Seeds* identifies humans as rational subjects whose capacity to perform intentional or purposeful actions categorically differentiates human agency from "the agency of the wind, water, and animals" (*D,* 24). Thoreau designates such an "activity" (*D,* 151) or, more regularly, such "operations" (*D,* 36) as actions that fulfill functions (such as seed transport) and that neither require nor imply a state of intentionality, purposefulness, consciousness, or subjectivity. Nevertheless— in what amounts not to a critique but to a specification and repurposing of the Cartesian relegation of animals to the status of "automatic responders"— in *The Dispersion of Seeds* the animal's capacity to automatically know how to perform particular tasks and functions (a capacity Thoreau specifies as a knowing not based in thinking) identifies animals as the model for integrating the human with nature.[17] It is this capacity of the animal to operate that serves as the basis for Thoreau's efforts to make the human capable of operating as nature's recording function—to adapt photographic automaticity in order to make the human-writing capable of producing desubjective representations of nature.

As will become clear in the pages that follow, the conversion of the human-writing into nature's recording function does not actualize a potential continuity of the human with nature. Rather, Thoreau specifies the occasional but iterable integration of the human with nature featured in *The Dispersion of Seeds* as a state of continuity that is both generated by and emerges from the reorganization of actions as operations entailed by this particular remediation of writing. The remediation of the human-writing thus produces an alignment or, better, an adjacency of the human and nature that is also a consolidation. As such, the state achieved as and through the naturalization of the human described in Thoreau's manuscript is perhaps best characterized by Deleuze's (and Deleuze and Guattari's) term for such an "intensive continuity," a "consistency."[18] The human-writing as nature's recording function: an assemblage, a "distribution of inequalities."[19] But, crucially, this assemblage is Cartesian rather than Spinozian. It is not a distribution whose "formula" is "ontologically one, formally diverse" (as for Spinoza, Deleuze, and Bennett) but, rather, ontologically diverse, formally one.[20] In *The Dispersion of Seeds*, the ontological demarcations between human subjects and natural agents require the naturalness of the human to be identified as a state of nature that can be achieved only through technological means—through the engineering of a consistency of the human with nature.

I

In the provisionally accepted introduction to *The Dispersion of Seeds*, Thoreau suggests that the need for perceptual equipment is proportional to an observer's Americanness. Whereas "[t]he planters of Europe ... know that forest trees spring from seeds" and do so because they have inhabited their territories long enough and in such a way as to have halted the "regular succession" of their forests, the continuing succession of America's forests has made it so that American observers "hardly associate seeds with trees," know only "that [trees] come out of the earth when [they] cut them down" (*D*, 23), and believe that new forests are "sudden new creation[s]" (*D*, 36) that "sprang ... from nothing" (*D*, 24). For *The Dispersion of Seeds*, then, a major aspect of North America around 1860 is that it features an instituted organization of perception in which the dissemination of seeds is invisible—an organization of perception that is backed by a conception of nature in which new forests "regularly" spring from nothing (*D*, 23). After establishing this, Thoreau asserts that the common sense that new forest trees and plants are regularly "spontaneously generated" is a "vulgar prejudice" (*D*, 36). Accordingly, after Thoreau declares that such trees and plants always come from seeds—"[w]hen, hereabouts, a forest springs up naturally where none of its kind grew before, I do not hesitate to say that it came from seeds"—he sets the main task of *The Dispersion of Seeds* as that of making the dissemination of seeds generally apprehensible (*D*, 24).[21]

For *The Dispersion of Seeds,* the common sense that new forest trees and plants can be "spontaneously generated" is a "vulgar prejudice" not only because it displays an ignorance of the "geologic pace" at which nature works but also because it supports the belief that nature is maintained by the interventions of an extra-natural agency. Against this sense that new forests are manifestations of "the Creator's controlling hand,"[22] Thoreau asserts that "[t]here is no mystery about the … propagation" (D, 86) of forest trees and plants: they invariably "came from seeds—that is, are the result of causes still in operation, though we may not be aware that they are operating" (D, 36). Thoreau's grounding of the generation of new forests in a set of occulted natural operations thus locates their growths as obdurately natural events.

Thoreau's insistence that new forests invariably "came from seeds," then, necessarily amounts to an expurgation of divine agency from the contemporary natural world. Yet, Thoreau does not thereby divest nature of illimitability. Rather, in this manuscript the illimitability usually ascribed to the sacred backing of natural phenomenon is located as an aspect of the naturalness of such phenomenon:

> Perhaps one whose down is particularly spreading and open rises steadily from your hand, freighted with its seed, till it is several hundred feet high and then passes out of sight eastward. … Astronomers can calculate the orbit of that thistledown called the comet, conveying its nucleus, which may not be so solid as a thistle seed, somewhither; but what astronomer can calculate the orbit of your thistle-down and tell where it will deposit its precious freight at last? It may still be traveling when you are sleeping.
>
> (D, 87)

As Bradley P. Dean notes, sightings of the comet that Thoreau is referencing (which "appeared in the northwestern New England sky each evening during late September and early October of 1858") prompted myriad newspaper articles and letters debating what the appearance of this comet "might portend" (D, editor's notes, 241). By here referring to the comet as "thistledown," Thoreau refuses such an extra-natural axis of speculation and, instead, grounds the extraterrestrial circulations of this comet in the natural systems that govern the transit of terrestrial seeds. Thoreau's referring to the comet as a thistledown is a declaration that American observers' interest is doubly misplaced: not only is their mode of apprehending the comet mistaken but so too is their choice of it above the thistledown, for it is not the comet but the thistledown whose destination and orbit are incalculable.

Whereas the orbit of a comet can be calculated by an astronomer equipped with a telescope, there is no commensurate combination of human and equipment to observe and calculate the flight paths of the thistledown. In part, this is because the need for such an apparatus is not recognizable in an

America where the dispersion of seeds does not register as a phenomenon. And, in part, there is no such apparatus because a seed may be "traveling when you are sleeping." That is, Thoreau here cites some discrepancies between humans and seeds—that, unlike seeds, humans occupy such states as waking and sleeping; and that humans' bodies preclude them from achieving the modes of airborneness which seeds' bodies allow them to attain—and identifies them as factors that limit the capacity of humans to observe the flight paths of seeds. However, what Thoreau mainly means to indicate by stating that there is no "astronomer [who] can calculate the orbit" and destination of the thistledown is that the innumerable variations of the interactions between the "solid" seed and the features of the air through which it rises and then travels (temperature, weather conditions, wind strength, and so on) render the trajectories of seeds as both irregular and singular.

Thus, *The Dispersion of Seeds* identifies the flight paths of seeds as empirically incalculable. And Thoreau here locates the dispersion of seeds as the instantiation of a literal illimitability grounded in the operations of nature itself. Thoreau, that is, specifies the limitations on calculating a seed's flight path as both spatial ("what astronomer can ... tell *where* it will deposit its precious freight at last" [emphasis added]) and temporal ("it may still be traveling *when* you are sleeping" [emphasis added]) and indicates that these limitations are practically insurmountable (*D*, 87). At the same time, Thoreau thereby establishes "the dispersion of seeds" as a natural phenomenon. By identifying the dispersion of seeds as the "still operating" material "cause" of new forests, Thoreau works to mitigate against the identification of the growths of new forests as the "visible" manifestation of an extra-natural, "intelligent, controlling power."[23] He also mitigates against understanding the growths of new forests as evidence that nature is, itself, endowed with a consciousness: those who regard the surface of the earth "as the cuticle of one great living creature" inappropriately ossify nature by mistaking its reticulations for the circulations of a being (*D*, 151).

That is, for *The Dispersion of Seeds,* those who think that nature is maintained by or endowed with a mind hold a mistaken account of the fact that "almost every part of the earth's surface is filled with seeds or vivacious roots of seedlings of various kinds"—a fact that Thoreau asserts is a consequence of the "activity of the animals and of the elements in transporting seeds" (*D*, 151). Even as the manuscript continues to employ certain conventional personifications of nature, Thoreau here mitigates against conceiving of nature as an entity whose material and immaterial aspects correspond to those of an embodied consciousness. Accordingly, when Thoreau details how seeds are "transported ... by the agency of wind, water, and animals," he implies that such "agency" does not correspond to that of a conscious entity (*D*, 24):

See how artfully the seed of the cherry is placed in order that a bird may be compelled to transport it—in the very midst of a tempting pericarp, so that the creature that would devour this must commonly take the stone also into its mouth or bill. ...

Thus, though these seeds are not provided with vegetable wings, Nature has impelled the thrush tribe to take them into their bills and fly away with them; and they are winged in another sense, and more effectually than the seeds of pines, for these are carried even against the wind. The consequence is that cherry trees grow not only here but there. The same is true of a great many other seeds.

(D, 68)

When Thoreau here writes that seeds such as the cherry's are "not provided with vegetable wings" but are, instead, "winged in another sense," the difference that he acknowledges between winged seeds (such as the pine) and those seeds that rely on animal wings (such as the cherry) is a quantitative one: cherries are "more effectually" winged than pine seeds because the nonvegetable wings of cherries can carry them "against the wind," which is to say that the cherry seed is as continuous with the thrush's wings as the pine seed is with its "vegetable wings." The thrush's being "compelled" to pick up the cherry seed is as much a component of the cherry seed's means of dispersion as the "pericarp" that "impels" the thrush to pick it up. The driving of the thrush (its being compelled) and the driving of the cherry (its being what impels) are thereby identified as commensurate aspects of cherry seed's dissemination.

More generally, in *The Dispersion of Seeds*, the "animals [that] systematically seek the fruit of trees" (D, 151) are integrated into the systems of natural operations that compose "the dispersion of seeds" (D, 50). In the manuscript, animals are identified as being continuous with nature through the systematicity of their actions: the animal's automatic performance of actions (seeking fruit, stripping pinecones, and so on) is based on the fact that the animal "does not have to think what he knows" (D, 32). The actions of animals are here identified as actions without subjectivity: they are identified not as the outcomes of intentions but as automatic implementations of a knowledge not based in thinking and sourced not in a consciousness but a system. In other words, in *The Dispersion of Seeds*, the actions of animals are identified not as actions but as *operations,* and it is on this basis that the animal is located as an agent motively independent of the forces of nature (it can move with, against, or without wind, water, and so on) and, nevertheless, continuous with them. Insofar as animal agency is delimited by a capacity to operate, the actions of animals are here identified as one of the agencies that (along with wind and water) compose the continuum of natural agencies by which seeds are transported.

II

In *The Dispersion of Seeds,* then, there is no mind of nature, and there are no minds in nature. Rather, nature is composed of systems of operations that include agents (animals) whose capacity to operate locates them as both independent of and continuous with these systems. And the default relationship of humans to nature is one in which humans unknowingly and belatedly haunt apparatuses and techniques made available to them by nature: humans are represented as being habitually unaware that their actions are either sourced in nature or are means to natural ends:

> [T]he thistle seed would oftener remain attached to its receptacle till it decayed with moisture or fell directly to the ground beneath it if [the goldfinch] did not come like a midwife to release it—to launch it in the atmosphere. ...
>
> All children are inspired by a similar instinct and, judging from the results, probably for a similar purpose. They can hardly keep their hands off the opening thistle-head.
>
> (D, 84)

At moments such as this, or those like Thoreau's description of the *Adherents* such as the *Bidens* or *Desmodium* that, by dint of their "barbed spears, or hooks" (D, 95), anticipate "the coming of the traveler, brute or human, that will transport their seeds on his coat" (D, 96), the shape of the human (if not the human itself) seems to be included in nature's operations. However, it is important to note that, while Thoreau depicts humans and animals as being equally capable of filling such functions as "midwife" or "traveler," the human is not thereby rendered natural. In the case of the *Adherents,* Thoreau cites how the coats that humans sometimes wear can function as an occasional means of transport. In the case of the thistle, that it draws human and avian touch is an indication of the effectiveness of the plant's functioning as a handsome lure that operates as effectively as the cherry that compels both humans and animals to take "cherry stones" into their mouths (D, 68).

Here and elsewhere in the manuscript, then, Thoreau's use of the language of "instinct" to describe humans' relation to nature is meant to testify not to a naturalness of the human but to an efficiency of nature's operations. Accordingly, *The Dispersion of Seeds* most regularly represents humans as unknowingly registering and acting on nature's "hints." There are explicit moments: for example, when Thoreau locates the production of dandelions—"the first of that class of downy or fuzzy seeds" to appear in the fall—as constituting the "first of the many hints we get to be about our own tasks" (D, 82); and when he claims that the lofting abilities of light-winged seeds such as the milkweeds and thistles gave "a hint to balloonists" (D, 87). There are other moments in the manuscript when this relationship of the hint informs without being mentioned: for example, when Thoreau describes the postal system's approximation of the wind-transported maple seeds by stating that the wind delivers the seeds at least "as effectually as when seeds are sent by mail in a different kind of sack from the Patent Office" (D, 50); or when he argues that the English method for using pines as nurseries for raising oaks is an unknowing adoption of a "method of Nature" and is thus "at most only the rediscovery of a lost art" (D, 124–5).

Each of these hints names a somewhat different relationship: in the case of the dandelion, nature can be said to signal humans; in the case of the balloonists, the thistle and milkweed instantiate the achievement of a particular function—staying airborne; in the case of the post and the maple seeds, delivery mechanisms are compared in terms of efficacy; and in the case of the nurseries, natural processes and human processes are ordered in terms of precedence. However, all of these instances belong to the set "hint" insofar as they are all situations in which nature is the unacknowledged or unknown basis for human apparatuses or techniques that are less advanced than the natural processes they approximate. Thoreau repeatedly describes operations of nature through the figures of the human technologies they gave rise to and does so in such a way that underscores both the technologies' indebtedness to nature and their inadequacy in comparison to the natural processes from which they derive. The maple seed's delivery by the wind and natural agents is described as being governed by "operations [that] are infinitely more extensive and regular" than the delivery of seeds effected by the "Patent office" in "Washington can be" (D, 50). And the human balloonists are less capable than the winged seeds they owe their apparatus to in that these natural balloonists can convert whatever wilderness they arrive at into a home: "Here is a wise balloonist for you, crossing its Atlantic—perhaps going to plant a thistle seed on the other side; and if it comes down in a wilderness, it will be at home there" (D, 85).

The result of such relations of debt and inefficiency is that the default mode of human presence in the natural world is one in which, "step by step," human endeavor follows in the path of a "method of nature without knowing" (D, 123). The characteristics of such a state of belated habitation are perhaps most explicitly indicated in Thoreau's treatment of some recommendations that British botanist John Loudon offers regarding the proper method of storing nuts for future planting. After describing at some length his coming upon a stash of walnuts, in the Concord woods, that were kept well preserved by a bunch of "wet and moldy leaves" that fell on them, Thoreau quotes a passage from Loudon's *Arboretum et Fruticetum Britannicum; or, The Trees and Shrubs of Britain* (1844) in which Loudon advises that "when the nut is to be preserved through the winter for the purpose of planting it the following spring, it should be laid in a rot heap as soon as gathered, with the husk on" (*D*, 134). Thoreau comments that this is yet another instance of man "stealing Nature's thunder" and goes on to ask, "How can a poor mortal do otherwise?—for it is she that finds fingers to steal with and the treasure to be stolen. In the planting of the seeds of most trees, the best gardeners do no more than follow Nature, though they may not know it" (*D*, 134). As is the case with the cherry, the thistle, the dandelion, and so on, nature's capturing of the functioning of the human hand is again identified as a natural manipulation of the human that, as such, instantiates the way in which humans are ghosted by the natural operations their actions are sourced in and facilitate.

Given this mode of belated occupation, it is perhaps not surprising that in *The Dispersion of Seeds* the form that human action most often takes is that of a briefly registering "interference" (*D*, 59, 170). If it were not for "our plows and spades and scythes," Thoreau writes, there would be "nothing to prevent [pines] springing up all over the village" (*D*, 36). Similarly, the degree to which the birch's seeds are "scattered over the country like a fine grain" suggests "how surely and soon the forest would prevail here again if the village were deserted" (*D*, 45). In *The Dispersion of Seeds*, that is, human interferences are constantly minimized by a nature always in the process of reclaiming its territories by erasing the structures and markings that human actions leave on the landscape: "cow paths," "bare space[s]," "woodlot[s]," and so on (*D*, 155, 151, 170). Moreover, nature regularly repurposes, rather than simply effaces, human incursions into its territory: even the more substantially mechanical and industrial artifacts of human manufacture are presented as being co-optable by nature. Thoreau writes that factories that use such plants as teasel are in turn used by nature as they "may distribute its seeds from one [place] to another by means of the streams which turn their machinery" (*D*, 81). Regarding the locomotive, he relates that when one lays down tracks and thus "run(s) a barrier ... through" a planting of willows, "in a short time it will be lined with them; for it both collects the seeds and defends the plants against man himself," and in this way nature can be observed "taking advantage even of the railroad, which elsewhere invades and disturbs the domains of trees" (*D*, 60–1).

III

In *The Dispersion of Seeds*, nature is conceived of as organized combinations of related sets of operations. Accordingly, the default relationship of nature, humanity, and technology in this manuscript differs markedly from the relationship usually associated with Thoreau's published works, in which technological development represents either an insurmountable or surmountable threat to nature and to the integration of the human into nature. *The Dispersion of Seeds* is not a critique of pastoral ideology of the sort Leo Marx first identified, nor is it a regressive effort to incorporate the development of modern technology into the pastoral ideal that such technology renders obsolete: Thoreau does not here identify technological development as a force that either disrupts or facilitates the production of a cultivated wilderness. Neither is *The Dispersion of Seeds* an ecocentric renovation of pastoral ideology of the type Lawrence Buell describes: Thoreau does not identify technological development as a force that only negligibly disrupts, if not facilitates, humans' capacity to relinquish the illusion of their discontinuity with nature.

Rather, in this manuscript, nature repurposes machines, effaces human alterations of the landscape, and is identified as the basis for various human apparatuses and techniques. This set of representations makes clear that in the manuscript's conception of a nature where the dispersion of seeds composes the material connections between generations of forest trees and plants—a conception of nature that works "systematically," at "a geologic pace," and "over the greatest distances"—both industrial and nonindustrial technologies are rendered continuous with nature to the extent that they are either sourced in or adapted from natural operations. Yet, while humans are thereby represented as inhabiting a culture that is largely tricked out with devices, methods, and structures that are either advertent or inadvertent extensions of nature, throughout the manuscript Thoreau makes it clear that such a situation is not a sufficient condition for the human to be considered natural. For *The Dispersion of Seeds,* the naturalness of the human is not a given but a state that has to be achieved. And the naturalization of the human is presented as a project that entails not, or not only, a revision of instituted perceptual habits but a thoroughgoing reorganization of action that is modeled on the operational capacities of animals—but is not a matter of taking on any particular animal's attributes or functions:

> I can easily manage small trees, fifteen or twenty feet high, climbing till I can reach the dangling green pickle-like fruit with my right hand, while I hold to the main stem with my left; but I am in a pickle when I get one. The cones are now all flowing with pitch, and my hands are soon so covered with it that I cannot easily cast down my booty when I would, it sticks to my fingers so; and when I get down at last and have picked them up, I cannot touch my basket with such hands but carry it on my arm, nor can I pick up my coat which I have taken off unless with my teeth—or else I kick it up and catch it on my arm.

(D, 39)

Coming just a few pages after the description of the squirrel's ability to effortlessly acquire and strip a pinecone, the comedy of this hapless effort to play the squirrel is both intentional and pointed: it derives from the discrepancy between the squirrel and the human, and it serves to both isolate and inflect this lack of fit. It is precisely the human features of Thoreau's embodiment (his size, his arms and legs, his use of clothing and implements, and so on) that disable him from operating as a gatherer and distributor of pinecones, and this emphasizes the inherent, irresolvable mismatch between the features of Thoreau's embodiment and those of the animal that is actually suited to the task he here attempts.

Thoreau's effort to merge with nature thus resolves into a confrontation with the way in which it is not the *fact* of human embodiment but the *features* of human embodiment that preclude such a merger. Accordingly, this episode from *The Dispersion of Seeds* can be identified as an instance of a type of episode that recurs in Thoreau's works: an encounter with a natural body (a pond, an aggregation of rocks, an animal, and so on) that is staged as an effort to incorporate the human into nature. These episodes are, for the most part, configured as attempts to realize—to recognize and thereby actualize—an extant continuity of the human with nature. And insofar as these attempts are delimited by the conditions of embodiment, these episodes regularly develop into either a revelation that the fact of human embodiment facilitates the incorporation of the human into nature or a resignation to the way in which the features of human embodiment preclude such an incorporation. There are, for instance, episodes like the sandbank passage in *Walden* (1854) that, as Buell notes, culminates in "a vision of the coextensiveness of the human body with the inanimate earth."[24] And there are episodes like the "burnt lands" passage in "Ktaadn" (1848)—a passage that begins with Thoreau's recognition that the inhuman materiality of his own body makes it coextensive with the rocks that surround him, and that ends with Thoreau's resignation to the way in which such recognitions are, themselves, sourced in an immaterial aspect of his humanity radically discontinuous with the materiality instantiated by human and lithic bodies.

However, while the aforementioned episode from *The Dispersion of Seeds* does resolve into an encounter with both the fact and the features of human embodiment, it is not affectively charged as either a revelation or an impasse. To be more specific, while this episode culminates in Thoreau's recognition that the features of his embodiment preclude him from incorporating himself into nature by occupying the functions of the squirrel, the entire episode is affectively charged as a comedy. This affect indicates that such incorporations are not, in fact, a concern of this manuscript. By framing this entire episode as a comedy, if not a farce, Thoreau implies a certain distance from efforts to realize or actualize a human continuity with nature. Rather, in the logics of this manuscript, Thoreau's failed attempt to imitate a squirrel registers how animal agency offers a model for naturalizing the human even as the integration of the human into nature is not a matter of inhabiting the functions of any particular animal. As already discussed, animals in *The Dispersion of Seeds* are described as not having "to think what they know," as entities that, while incompletely incorporated into nature (insofar as they are motively independent of natural forces), are nevertheless continuous with it (insofar as their agency is delimited as a capacity to operate and their desubjective actions are then located as the iterations of a natural system). In what is less a critique than a retooling of the Cartesian account of animals as "mere animated machines" (according to Thoreau) capable of manifesting only "natural movements" (according to René Descartes), Thoreau's unsuccessful attempt to become animal indicates that—as the agencies of animals automatically correspond to the features of their embodiments—the naturalization of the human entails engineering a mode of agency modeled on the operational capacities of animals but fitted to the features of human embodiment.[25]

One of the main tasks of the manuscript is thus to isolate a set of human actions that can be operationalized to effect natural ends, as Thoreau does when he declares that "I do not always state the facts exactly in the order in which they were observed, but select out of my numerous observations extended over a series of years the most important ones, and describe them in a natural order" (*D,* 104). Most narrowly, Thoreau here delineates the manipulation of recordings of natural phenomenon so that their sequence corresponds to their "natural order" rather than to the order in which "they were observed." More generally, Thoreau implies that recording phenomenon "in the order in which they were observed" preserves a subjective ordering that is in no way identical to a natural order; reciprocally, such a natural order can be produced only if these observations are disassociated from the subjectivity (the "I") of the human who recorded them. Having earlier indicated that observations of certain natural processes are inherently incompletable—insofar as seeds "pass out of sight" and "may still be traveling when you are sleeping" (*D,* 87)—Thoreau indicates that, for *The Dispersion of Seeds,* it is precisely by producing desubjectivized *recordings* of such observations that the human can achieve naturalization.

Accordingly, when Thoreau represents himself capturing and thereby making apprehensible the modes, means, and mechanisms of seed dispersal and transport, he consistently registers himself as a minimized "I," an interchangeable component that links such observing and recording functions as "I notice," "I counted," "I heard," "I see," "I have observed," "I measure," and "I examined" (*D,* 27, 28, 33, 49, 54, 55, 78). In these passages, Thoreau's presence is identical to and delimited by the functions he performs; he depicts himself, that is, as a thoroughly operationalized "I." But, crucially, the pronoun here precedes the verb: Thoreau's operational standing is situated as the result of a successful engineering on his own part rather than as an instituted effect of automation or mechanization. This operationalization of the human is generated in conjunction with the project of "[l]ooking again more carefully" at a particular set of natural processes so as to be better able to record them (D, 115):

> On June 19th, 1860, we had half a dozen distinct summer showers, from black clouds suddenly wafted up from the west and northeast, and also some thunder and large hail. Standing on the Mill Dam in the afternoon, just after one of these showers, I noticed the air as high as the roofs full of some kind of down, which at first I mistook for feathers or lint from some chamber. It rose and fell just like a flight of ephemerae, or like huge white dancing motes, from time to time coming to the earth. Next, I supposed it to be some gauzy, light-winged insect. It was driven by a slight current of air between and over the buildings and went flying in a stream all along the street, and it was very distinct in the moist air, seen against the dark clouds still lingering in the west.
>
> The shopkeepers stood in their doorways wondering what it could be. This was white-willow down which the rain had loosened. ... I traced it to its source in a large wil-low twenty rods distant and a dozen rods from the street, behind the blacksmith's shop.
>
> (D, 56–7)

Having accepted the empirical impossibility of completely tracking even a single seed to its eventual destination, Thoreau here performs something of the available inverse by tracing a phenomenon to its source where it resolves into willow down. Only rendered present through the operations he performs—"standing," "I noticed," "I at first mistook," "I supposed," "I traced it"—Thoreau transcribes a coordinated series of maneuvers in which he progressively improves his focus and then supplements this ocular activity by physically tracking the shower of down to its cause: "a large willow twenty rods distant." While the shopkeepers only wonder after the down, Thoreau represents himself as pursuing it through a series of transformations—from "lint" to "dancing motes" to a "light-winged insect"—that achieves resolution when, having traversed the short distance to its terrestrial source, he identifies it as "white-willow down."

As critics since Perry Miller have recognized, reading the natural world has been part of American culture's relationship to nature at least since the Puritans endeavored to read "sermons in brooks and morals in stones."[26] And both Thoreau's published works and his unpublished *Journal* feature innumerable scenes where nature is either read or interpreted. However, in *The Dispersion of Seeds,* Thoreau represents himself as a close observer of the natural world who is involved in an active effort to not-read nature:

> I brought them all home in order to ascertain what seeds they were, and how they came there. Examining the chest-nuts carefully in the evening,

and wondering if so small a bird as a chickadee could transport one, I observed near the larger end of one some very fine scratches, which it seemed to me might have been made by the teeth of a very small animal while carrying it—certainly not by the bill of a bird, since they had pricked sharply into the shell, sucking it up one way. I then looked to see where the teeth of the other jaw had scratched it, but could discover no marks and was therefore still somewhat in doubt about it.

But an hour afterward I examined these scratches with a microscope, and then I saw plainly that they had been made by some fine and sharp cutting instrument like a pin, which was a little concave and had plowed under the surface of the shell a little, toward the larger end of the nut, raising it up. And, looking further, I now discovered on the same end at least two corresponding marks made by the lower incisors, plowing toward the first and about a quarter of an inch distant. These were scarcely obvious to the human eye, but quite plain through the glass. I now had no doubt that they were made by the incisors of a mouse, and comparing them with the incisors of the common wild or deer mouse (*Mus leucopus*, whose skeleton I chanced to have), I found that one or two of the marks were exactly the middle of its two incisors combined, or about a twentieth of an inch, and that the others, though finer, might have been made by them; and the natural gape of the jaws corresponded. On one side at least it had taken fresh hold once or twice. I have but little doubt that these seeds were placed there by a deer mouse, our most common wood mouse.

The other chestnut, which had no marks on it, I suppose was carried by the stem end, which was now gone from both. There was no chestnut tree within twenty rods.

(*D*, 147–8)

Thoreau here performs a way in which looking closely at a marked natural object does not grant one access to an order of natural significance. Rather, examining the "very fine scratches" and "marks" on the chestnut under the microscope produces more of the same: another set of marks. These marks, like their more easily discernible compliments on the other surface of the chestnut, are not understood to be anything but marks or scratches; they are not, that is, imagined to be either signs or symbols. This feature is further instantiated by Thoreau's declining to compare the sets of marks to either written artifacts or to any other humanly manufactured object or structure. Instead, he literally compares them with another component of nature: the mouse skeleton. Nature is here used to study … nature. The end of Thoreau's examination of the nuts and the skeleton is the determination of the natural origins of the marks on the chestnut's surface (a mouse's teeth) and what such marks tell one about how the seed was transported (by a mouse carrying it in his jaws). They have no significance beyond that. What Thoreau performs, in other words, is a mode of observing nature that entails not-reading it: the purpose of observing nature is not to make it either symbolically or literally available for human purposes. Rather, the end of observing nature is to observe and record nature.

In passages such as this examination of the marks and scratches on a chestnut, Thoreau models a relation to nature through which the human can be made consistent with a natural world that persistently resists and repurposes human manipulations: by not-reading nature—by producing desubjective representations of nature—the human-writing can be transformed into nature's recording function. At the same time, passages such as this one suggest that the manuscript's commitment to not-reading nature is based on a conviction that nature cannot be read. In the foregoing passage, Thoreau is scrupulous about not presenting the natural marks he examines as interchangeable with the features of a text. In these regards, Thoreau's encounter with the chestnut is not only illustrative but paradigmatic: at all stages of his not-reading of the marks and scratches on the nut's surfaces, Thoreau refuses to employ a rubric of textual significance—even at maximum magnification, the marks and scratches do not resolve into signs.

Thoreau's commitment to not describing nature as a text is perhaps most evident at the moment where he seems to depart from the rigors of this commitment by describing a "woodlot" as a "written" artifact:

> A few days later I examined more carefully the young oak wood east of the wall, and I found not only the stumps of the pines which were cut when it sprang up some fifteen years ago and which were then about forty years old, as appeared plainly from their annual rings—but, to my surprise, the stumps in great numbers, now much decayed, of an old oak wood which stood there and was cut between fifty and sixty years ago. Thus I distinguished three successions of trees, and, I may say, five generations. ...
>
> I frequently find in numbers in our forests the stumps of oaks which were cut at the very beginning of this century or the end of the last, while a forest the third in succession, including them, waves over them. No doubt we may thus in many cases behold the stumps, at least, of trees which stood here before the white man came, and in this case we have one advantage over the geologist, for we can not only detect the *order* of events but often the time during which they elapsed by counting the rings on the stumps.
>
> Thus you can unroll the rotten papyrus on which the history of the Concord forest is written.
>
> (D, 169)

In *The Dispersion of Seeds*, the term *woodlot* designates an area where nature has been altered (but not necessarily cultivated) by human action, and this moment features Thoreau's efforts to not-read such an area and the actions that produced it: the construction of a wall and the occasional cutting down of trees. After describing the successions and generations of forest trees that can be "distinguished" by examining the extant "stumps"—which are less natural objects than artifacts of human action— he then extols the advantages he has over the geologist: whereas the geologist can ascertain "the order of events" by studying the earth, Thoreau can ascertain "the time during which [events] elapsed" by studying the stumps of trees. Both geologic strata and tree rings are the outcomes of the interactions of matter with the environment over long spans of time; in both cases, the activity designated as "detect[ion]" is the studying of such natural formations to ascertain temporal information about events (their order, when they occurred, their duration, and so on).

After working through the relations among these cases, Thoreau attempts to concentrate this episode into a single sentence: "Thus you can unroll the rotten papyrus on which the history of the Concord forest is written." In an endnote to the 1993 edition of the manuscript, Bradley P. Dean notes that the final four words of this line—"Concord forest is written"—are not present in the manuscript and have been "recovered from the journal source of this entry" (D, editor's notes, 262). Dean then also notes, "Thoreau drew a single line through these two paragraphs, which indicates that at one time he planned to delete them, but later he apparently erased the line" (D, editor's notes, 261). Thus, the moment in the manuscript where Thoreau comes closest to identifying nature as a text is also the moment where his hesitancy to do so is most graphically registered. Not only does the foregoing passage end with a sentence fragment that does not include the final four words from the *Journal* entry that it is ostensibly based on—the four words that would decisively designate the Concord forest as written—but the entire passage is marked as a contested site by the conflicting gestures of a drawn line indicating a planned deletion and the subsequent partial erasure of that line (Figure 1). Most narrowly, this registers that, in the logic of the manuscript, natural formations such as tree rings and geologic strata are legible but are not, therefore, versions of writing. More generally, this anxious drama of circumscription, hesitation, omission, erasure, and restoration registers the difficulty that attends Thoreau's efforts to represent nature as legible without implying that this legibility is a version of textuality or that the materiality that here characterizes nature is an aspect of writing.

IV

In *The Dispersion of Seeds,* the project of not-reading nature is grounded in the fact that there are no natural texts—that texts are not natural and that there are no texts in nature. What is crucial about this disarticulation of writing from natural materiality is that it locates writing as a human technique that (unlike planting, the balloon, the postal system, the

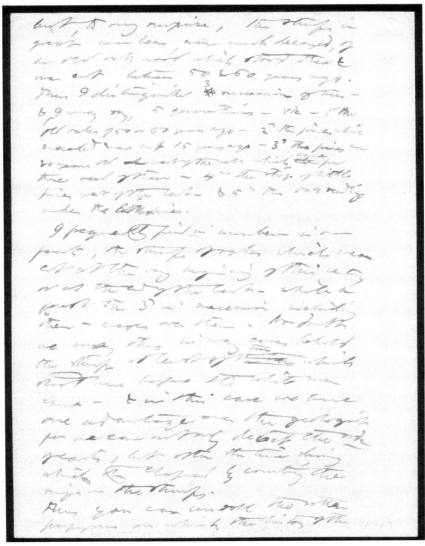

FIGURE 1 *Henry David Thoreau,* The Dispersion of Seeds *(msp. 390). Courtesy of the Henry W. and Albert A. Berg Collection of English and American Literature, the New York Public Library, Astor, Lenox, and Tilden Foundations. The manuscript text is in ink. The note at the bottom middle of the page, the note at the bottom right of the page, and the line drawn through the final two paragraphs of the page are in pencil. The final paragraph of the page reads: "Thus you can unroll the rotten papyrus on which the history of the" (ending as an incomplete sentence). The note at the bottom of the page reads, "Insert more here by and by—but first go on to 199–&200" (as in the original); and the note at the bottom right of the page reads, "VD 203" (ending as in the original).*

barometer, and so on) is not adapted from or otherwise sourced in nature's operations. Writing, that is, is here isolated as a technology that is not an extension of nature and that, as such, specifies the nonnaturalness of the human. While the manuscript does not furnish anything like a theorization of writing to explain the basis for this isolation (a lack that is, perhaps, registered by the conflict that attends the aforementioned nondesignation of the Concord forest as written), Thoreau's commitment to identifying writing as a human technique that is not sourced in nature makes it clear that one of the core projects of *The Dispersion of Seeds* is to articulate a thoroughly technological mode of naturalizing the human.

Insofar as the manuscript's featured mode of integrating the human with nature entails the production of desubjectivized representations of nature, it can be identified as an implementation of what Sharon Cameron isolates as the project of Thoreau's *Journal* and what Buell then characterizes as one of *Walden*'s environmental projects: the "record[ing of] impressions of nature" that are "dislocate[d] from the person who has generated [them]" such that they locate their author as "nature writing itself."[27] For Cameron, this project is configured as the development of a potential continuity of the human with nature through an extremity of action. In the *Journal*, Cameron argues, the speculation "that nature is a text" enables humans to produce natural texts—"to write sentences which lie 'like boulders on the page'"—and thereby to produce a work that (according to Thoreau) can be regarded "*as* it were at a structure on the plain" and that, as such, transforms the author into "the scribe of all nature."[28] For Buell, this project is configured as the recognition of an already established continuity of the human with nature. According to Buell, this project is a component of Thoreau's "aesthetics of relinquishment" in which one "give[s] up individual autonomy" by becoming "receptive, to the feeling of being constituted ... by the forms of nature."[29] Although Cameron and Buell configure this project differently, then, they both identify it as an actualization of an extant continuity of the human with nature. In *The Dispersion of Seeds*, however, the disarticulation of textuality from natural materiality isolates writing as nonnatural such that the manuscript's proposed conversion of the human-writing into nature's recording function cannot be identified as a mode of recognizing, developing, or otherwise actualizing the human's continuity with nature. Rather, *The Dispersion of Seeds* identifies writing as a properly technological medium (as a technique that is not adapted from or otherwise sourced in nature). It further implies that only through an overhauling of this medium can a consistency of the human with nature be engineered.

Insofar as this refunctioning of writing entails the intentional operationalization of a set of actions (those that compose the medium of writing), it can be characterized as a repurposing of a central aspect of mechanization: here, the dehumanization that attends the systematic diminution of actions into operations is redirected toward natural ends. More specifically, this operationalization of action is directed toward the conversion of the human-writing into an apparatus that is capable of producing desubjective representations of nature such that the conversion can be identified as an adaptation of the central *mechanical* aspect of a particular media technology—namely, the *automaticity* of photography. As Allen Trachtenberg notes, in a *Journal* entry of February 2, 1841, Thoreau writes that "Nature is readily made to repeat herself in a thousand forms, and in the daguerreotype her own light is amanuensis."[30] As Trachtenberg then elucidates, by using such terms to describe the daguerreotype "Thoreau alludes to the most commonplace idea of photography, that by its mediation nature becomes her own 'amanuensis,' her own scribe" insofar as the camera is understood to be "capable of producing a picture automatically, in disregard of its operator."[31] As Walter Benn Michaels explains, this conception of photography disconnects the operator of the camera ("as a particular person") from the photograph itself ("as a particular picture") insofar as "the actual making of the picture is, on this account, not so much an action as an event, and the picture itself is best understood as the outcome of a series of mechanical interactions between the camera and nature."[32] As Irene Tucker explains, this understanding of photography identifies it as a technology that "circumvents mediating perceptual agency" by enabling "the representation of a perception without the mediation of a human agent."[33] In this conception of photography, then, the medium is defined by its capacity to produce representations automatically that are desubjective insofar as they are neither expressions of the intentional states of particular persons nor manifestations of the sensoria of human agents.

It is precisely this automaticity that gets isolated as the definitive feature of photography both in the *Journal* entry that Trachtenberg cites and, more substantially, in "Walking" (1862) when Thoreau compares surveying and photography: "[T]hese farms which I have myself surveyed, these bounds which I have set up, appear dimly still as through a mist; but they have no chemistry to fix them; they fade from the surface of the glass."[34] Here photography and surveying are specified as marking processes that can be compared in terms of their permanence. The implied basis for this comparison is that whereas the lines of a survey have to be "set up" by the actions of a surveyor, the lines of a photograph are automatically "fix[ed]" by the "chemistry" of the photographic process. In entries and passages such as these, Thoreau sources photography's capacity to produce desubjective representations in the way that it bypasses human agency by producing images that are the automatic outcomes of a set of agentless processes and interactions.[35] However, as we have seen, in *The Dispersion of Seeds* the production of desubjective representations is isolated as the outcome of a set of intentional states and actions. Paradigmatically, in the foregoing passage where Thoreau demonstrates his ability to not-read nature while examining the "marks" and "scratches" on a chestnut, he performs a series of operations on these traces—measurement under a microscope, comparison to a mouse skeleton, and so on—in order to *fix* an image of the deer mouse that produced them (*D*, 147–8). Moreover, while Thoreau notes in the *Journal* that stillness is a requirement for the production of a photograph and the *instant* is the basic temporal unit of photography—"that an impression may be taken, perfect stillness, though but for an instant, is necessary" (February 2, 1841)[36]—as already detailed, the manuscript renders capturing the dispersion of seeds as a process that requires both movement and delay. That is, the natural motions of seed dispersal and transport are invisible not because of their instantaneity but because of their spatial extension and temporal duration. Accordingly, the recording apparatus required to capture the dispersion of seeds must be calibrated such that there are built-in delays between impression and recording. This apparatus must also be capable of performing a series of separate but coordinated movements (tracking propagations, growths, and so on). Rather than an automatic machine capable of rapid exposures, the documentation of seed dispersal and transport requires a recording apparatus that is mobile, that is capable of making and storing observations, and that can perform a series of analytic and synthetic operations on these observations (compression, sorting, sequencing, comparison, selection, and so on) in order to transform them into desubjective representations of nature.[37]

In *The Dispersion of Seeds,* then, Thoreau's effort to convert the human into nature's recording function is neither a reactionary effort to reinstate an obsolete model of perception (as it would be for Crary) nor an unconscious registration of the media effects of an emergent discourse network (as it would be for Kittler).[38] Rather, in *The Dispersion of Seeds,* media occur as sets of processes, equipment, capacities, techniques, and problematics, and Thoreau's conversion of the human into nature's recording function is then specified as the conversion of writing into a medium that—unlike photography—can capture the too-slow-to-be-perceived processes of a nature that operates at a "geologic pace" and "over the greatest distances" (*D*, 36). Thoreau's adaptation and refunctioning of photography's automaticity should therefore be understood as an instantiation of literary agency—as part of a distributed effort to constitute writing as a technological medium with its own specific areas of competence. Insofar as this agency is, here, directed toward naturalizing the human, the naturalness of the human emerges as a condition that can be achieved only through a thoroughgoing modification of the human: in order to be made consistent with a nature that consists of combinations of related sets of operations, the human has to be remade into something other than what it is. Rather than describing the core project of *The Dispersion of Seeds* as the naturalization of the human, then, it is perhaps more accurate to describe it as the *naturization* of the human.[39] For, in *The Dispersion of Seeds,* only through technological means can the human be made natural. Thoreau thereby begins to make available a *technics* that is neither supported nor constrained by an instituted disjunction of technology from nature.

9

On Thoreau's Ecoerotics

Cristin Ellis

At the end of a particularly damp April in 1851, Thoreau's thoughts turned to love—and then, almost immediately, to chastity. In his journal, he wonders:

> Does not the history of chivalry and Knight-errantry suggest or point to another relation to woman than leads to marriage ... perchance transcending marriage? ... I am sure that the design of my maker—when he has brought me nearest to woman—was not the propagation of the species—but perchance the development of the affections—and something akin to the maturation of the species.[1]

To most modern readers, there's something suspect about this 33-year-old bachelor's privately confessed desire for a strictly sexless union with an impersonal "woman." It's hard not to sense something compensatory in the gallantry he ascribes to himself here, hard not to catch the whiff of an alibi for the absence of normative heterosexual desire to which he seems, in this moment, to be testifying.

It is therefore perhaps not surprising that over the past few decades, scholars have increasingly come to gloss Thoreau's celebrations of chastity and his apparently lifelong celibacy as indications of repressed or latent homosexuality. Along these lines, Walter Harding and Henry Abelove propose that Thoreau's exaltation of "absolute chastity" stems from the fact that he felt only "abhorrence and disgust" at the prospect of heterosexual sex.[2] Readers from Perry Miller to Michael Warner add further dimension to this case by highlighting Thoreau's equally exacting insistence upon chastity in his intercourse with male friends.[3] Thus, for instance, when Thoreau claims that to "enjoy the most intimate society" with friends he must "not only be silent, but commonly so far apart bodily that we cannot possibly hear each other's voice in any case," his bizarre contortion of intimacy into physical distance seems to register an anxiety that, for Warner, is typical of Thoreau's "difficult expressions of desire" for prohibited erotic community with other men.[4] "Thoreau's writings circle around conspicuously unsatisfied desires," Warner observes, and it would be "a mistake to sanitize such passages by thinking that they refer only to homosocial friendship."[5] As a refusal of erotic attachment to both men and women, then, Thoreau's idealization of chastity emerges, on these readings, as a screen for non-normative desires: on the one hand, his commitment to chastity furnishes him with a self-congratulatory excuse for his lack of erotic attraction to women; on the other, this commitment suggests an ambivalent repression of his erotic attraction to men.

Without wishing to supplant this entirely plausible account of Thoreau's homosexuality, I propose here to read Thoreau's relationship to chastity somewhat differently: as a practice through which he understood himself to be expressing, rather than simply suppressing, his sexuality. What my reading shares with the queer readings sketched above is the sense that Thoreau's commitment to chastity should not simply be read as an expunging of sex. But from the perspective of the analysis I'll offer here, those queer readings remain too attached to the repressive hypothesis—to the idea that Thoreau's praise for celibacy is the transmuted articulation of a homosexual desire he was unable to name—to offer much insight into Thoreau's own sense of his erotic orientation as he attempts to describe and define this for himself in his writings. Examining his essay "Chastity & Sensuality," the "Higher Laws" chapter of *Walden*, and entries scattered across the *Journal*, I'll be suggesting that Thoreau conceives of chastity as a discipline not of self-mastery but of sensuous self-surrender, a practice that involves attending to subtle inclinations of the body which can only arise when we are alone in nature and which urge us—through tugs of attraction, threads of affection, and bursts of sensual exhilaration—toward the gratifying expression of a libidinal economy Thoreau identifies with vegetal sexuality.

My reading of Thoreauvian chastity thus opens onto a broader and perhaps more estranging account of how Thoreau conceives of his sexuality via the vegetal. At stake in this account is a set of historical questions about how Thoreau interpreted his own erotic experience, and how (and to what extent) he drew upon discourses of vegetal sexuality in fashioning that self-understanding. At the same time, as I'll ultimately suggest, Thoreau's effort to re-theorize sexuality starting from plants rather than humans raises questions about the assumptions that organize our normative and critical discourses of sexuality today and speaks, more particularly, to recent efforts to map the intersections between queer theory and the nonhuman.

Although the features of vegetal sexuality may not be familiar to us, as I'll discuss in my first two sections below it was a topic of sustained concern in the eighteenth and nineteenth centuries and particularly to Romantic thinkers like Thoreau. Key to vegetal sexuality's Romantic fascination was its dependence upon radical metamorphosis: whereas animals (including humans) retain the same physiological form from birth to sexual maturation, reproducing offspring in the stereotyped image of that same fixed form, plants undergo a process of wholesale transformation on the way to sexual maturity, morphing, in dynamic response to their changeful environments, from seed to seedling to flower to fruit. Thus, when Thoreau, in the quotation I began with, distinguishes between sexual "propagation" on the one hand, and "development" or "maturation" on the other, he's citing a distinction that was central to the Romantic era's understanding of vegetal sexuality's distinctiveness—its transformative rather than merely reproductive nature. In expressing his desire for maturation, Thoreau echoes a common Romantic tendency to valorize metamorphosis as life's highest aim; indeed as we'll see, Romantic thinkers often viewed the vegetal drive toward metamorphosis as evidence of an instinct for development that is foundational to the human and all other forms of animate life. At the same time, as sections 3 and 4 below will elaborate, what distinguishes Thoreau's treatment of vegetal sexuality even from other Romantic thought is the emphasis he places upon development as an organic *alternative* to heterosexual reproductivity. In Thoreau, as we'll see, plants exemplify a sexuality that is oriented toward self-transformation and the fructification of thought rather than toward heterosexual coupling and the propagation of offspring. But if vegetal sexuality is thus explicitly non-heterosexual for Thoreau, it remains for him at the same time wholly natural and universal—a foundational drive that is inherent within all humans as it is, indeed, within all organisms.

What follows here, then, is an attempt to expand the available frames through which we might view Thoreau's libidinal life. I was launched in this effort by my persistent sense that, with their emphasis on frustration and repression, our readings of Thoreau's chaste life in nature require us to discount myriad instances of intense sensual pleasure and even erotic fulfilment that Thoreau's writings about nature relate in often quite vivid detail. Indeed, it seemed clear to me that, alongside the rather pinched, body-phobic, and frustrated virgin who emerges from many of our biographical accounts of Thoreau (and who, let me acknowledge, does emerge regularly enough on Thoreau's page), there is also another Thoreau who ardently details his ostensibly chaste life in nature as one that is, in fact, rich with sensual pleasures and erotically satisfying encounters. Flip through the *Journal* and you're as likely to find him in the throes of some new ecstasy as you are to find him austere or disappointed. "My body is all sentient," he trills one December day. "As I go here or there I am tickled by this or that I come in contact with—as if I touched the wires of a battery" (*J* VIII: 44).

Indeed, on page after page of his writings, we find him acutely alive to his body and committed to heightening his pleasure by conscientiously attending to its minutest sensory thrills. "This is a delicious evening," he reports from Walden, "when the whole body is one sense, and imbibes delight through every pore" (W 129). Although these scenes of exhilaration are solitary (in the conventional sense that Thoreau is the only human present at them), Thoreau tends to frame them in terms that insist on their erotic significance. He confesses his "strong attraction ... to nature" (PJ 4: 186) in language ("for joy I could embrace the earth"; (PJ 4: 368), "I could ... stroke and kiss the very sward" (J XII: 97); "all nature is my bride" (J XII: 97)) that freights his relationship to nature with all the sensual, emotional, and even biological significance his culture reserved for heterosexual coupling.[6] Indeed, he leaves these encounters with nature expectant, emphasizing their (re)productive consequence: "It is the marriage of the soul with nature that makes the intellect fruitful—that gives birth to imagination. ... [S]ome grains of fertilizing pollen floating in the air fall on us—& suddenly the sky is all one rainbow. ... [T]he poet is a fertile & perfect flower" (PJ 4: 4).

For all its merits as a diagnosis of his possible sexual orientation, then, the reading of Thoreau's closeted homosexuality falls short, for me, as a description of his erotic life. What to make of these episodes which are neither hetero- nor homo- but, for lack of a ready term, ecoerotic, and how are we to square all this quivering pleasure with the asceticism Thoreau also endorses? If homosexuality is our only explanatory key, then our options are to ignore these experiences as irrelevant to the analysis of Thoreau's libidinal life (as most readers do), or (as Harding suggests) to view them as symptoms of sexual "sublimation," thereby discounting them as secondary deformations of Thoreau's true (i.e., homosexual) sexuality.[7] Yet both of these approaches presume that we are in a position to produce a more authoritative account of Thoreau's libidinal life than his own writings do. Hence it seems worthwhile to stop and ask ourselves: What might we lose when we displace Thoreau's accounts of erotic satisfaction with our own?

In its basic form, clearly, this question confronts us with the methodological difficulties that attend any effort to inquire into the sexuality of figures from the past. Over three decades of queer theoretical work has by now astutely and extensively mapped the hazards inherent to sexual historiography. One obvious and frequently observed problem is that the ways we discuss and define sexuality change over time. Thus for instance, we might note that the terms we use to gloss Thoreau's erotic life today ("homosexuality" from the homo/hetero binary formally codified in late nineteenth-century sexology, "sublimation" from late nineteenth-century Freudian psychology) are unlikely to capture his own perception of his sexuality since these terms belong to discourses that were unavailable to Thoreau during his lifetime.[8] But terminological anachronism is only one of the challenges we're up against. As David Halperin has argued, the trouble is not only that the ways we talk about sexuality evolve over time, but that sexuality itself changes. That is, sexuality is not "a timeless and ahistorical dimension of human experience"; instead the shape of our desires, the textures and intensities of our physical sensations, and the very ways in which we inhabit and experience our bodies are subject to historical change.[9] The upshot of this is that applying modern terms to historical sexualities may not simply misrepresent a historical figure's perception of their sexuality but may, instead, misrepresent their sexuality as such. Put in the simplest possible terms: if we go searching the past for evidence of sexuality as we now know it, we're liable to be looking for erotic economies that aren't there while we grope blindly past those that are.

It's under this thought that we can see why simply calling Thoreau closeted might in fact be a conservative move. For even though repression allows us to understand his sexuality in terms that are usefully familiar to us now, it also insulates our contemporary sexual categories from the challenges and provocations that history's sexual alterity might pose to them.[10] It is this possibility that animates Peter Coviello's recent and powerfully generative suggestion that "much of what looks like sex to [Thoreau] has, over time, dropped out from our commonsense understanding of where the perimeters of the sexual actually lie."[11]

In the readings to follow, then, I seek to highlight how consistently Thoreau deploys vegetal sexuality as a model for imagining his own, non-heteronormative erotic life. In the sexually alien yet indisputably familiar figure of the flower, Thoreau finds a logic for rethinking chastity as the practice of an alternative libidinal economy oriented, like the plant's, toward transformative development. And yet if vegetal sexuality resists conscription to the regimes of heteronormative and biopolitical reproductivity, it also remains stubbornly incompatible with contemporary discourses of sexuality. As a principle of continual metamorphosis, vegetal sexuality cannot ground a stable sense of identity, and thus resists the taxonomizing tendencies that continue to organize contemporary discourses of sexual identity (e.g., of hetero-, homo-, bi-, pan-, asexuality) and the political projects which flow from them. In this way, Thoreau's deployment of vegetal sexuality challenges us to critically reexamine some of the tensions (e.g., between anti-foundationalism and identity politics) and assumptions (including anthropocentrism) that structure our studies of sexuality today.

The *Vert* in Pervert

As hard as it is to imagine today that plant sex might have any meaningful relevance to our own sex lives, the decoupling of vegetal from human sexuality is in fact a comparatively recent development in Western thought.

For centuries, Western philosophic and scientific discourse framed vegetal sexuality through the lens of human sexuality.[12] More specifically, vegetal sexuality was understood to be troublingly divergent from human sexual norms: plants were the original sexual deviants. Indeed, before "sexual inversion" came to describe same-sex erotic preference in late nineteenth-century sexological discourse, the term was first widely applied to the morphology of plants. In an extensive tradition of botanical thought stretching from Plato through Linnaeus, plants were portrayed as "inverted animals," with their "heads" (the site where they take in nourishment) rooted in the ground and their sexual organs (the stamens and pistils contained in the flower) waving brazenly in the open air.[13]

In Platonic philosophy, for instance, the plant's inverted morphology indicates the moral inferiority of vegetal being. As Michael Marder reminds us, Plato presents the wantonness of plant morphology as an outward expression of the base sensuousness of the vegetable soul. That soul, Plato maintains, is merely appetitive, sharing "not at all in opinions and reasoning and mind but in sensation, pleasant and painful, together with desires."[14] However, rather than measuring the absolute difference between plant and human being as we might expect, this unreflectively desiring vegetable soul instead links plants and humans in Plato's thought, insofar as he understands the vegetable soul to form the rudimentary foundation of all organic life. On this view—which was further elaborated by Plato's most famous student, Aristotle—humans, as the most highly developed form of life, are inspirited by a tripartite soul in what we might think of as a geologically tiered system of animation: with vegetable soul (representing alimentation, growth, reproduction, and senescence) at the foundation, animal soul (representing perception, sensation, and locomotion) above that, and crowned with the noblest soul of all, the rational or human soul (representing thought, intellect, and reflection). In order to give expression to their rational souls and thus come into their full humanity, Plato taught that humans first have to learn to master the sensuous appetites of their vegetative souls. It is only by overriding the vegetable instinct within them that human subjects transition "from the immature reliance on the senses to a life illuminated by Ideas."[15] By contrast, plants (and those who fail to rise above their planty natures) only ever think, as it were, with their *other* heads.

The idea that plants have sexuality (that they reproduce via sexual organs in the flower) fell out of favor sometime after Plato, languishing for centuries until it was revived in the seventeenth century and then widely—and controversially—popularized in the eighteenth century by Carl Linnaeus.[16] With the publication of his *Systema Naturae* in 1735, Linnaeus introduced a revolutionary new system of binomial nomenclature which ordered the plant kingdom according to the number and arrangements of the sexual organs (pistils and stamens) within the flower. What was revolutionary in Linnaean botany, then, was not only its important new system of naming, but also that system's predication on vegetal sexuality: Linnaeus made the visible sexual morphology of flowers the basis of his botanical taxonomy.

Moreover, like Plato, Linnaeus reads plant sex through the lens of human sexuality. In designating the parts of the flower, he refers to pistils and stamens as *maritii et uxores* ("husbands and wives") and dubs the floral base, sepals, and petals that surround these reproductive organs the *thalamus* (bed chamber), *calyx* (concealing curtain), and *corolla* (wedding garland). Linnaeus thus constructs an extended metaphor that depicts flowers as, in his words, "Bridal beds that the great Creator has so gloriously provided, adorned with many delightful fragrances, where the bridegroom and his bride may celebrate their Nuptials with so much greater solemnity."[17] Whether out of a sense of personal modesty (he was, after all, the son of a Lutheran curate), or in an attempt to preempt moral outrage at the exposed floral genitals he was reintroducing to the world, Linnaeus throws a rhetorical veil over the plant's visible sex. With this elaborately extended marital metaphor, he works to rehabilitate Plato's promiscuously inverted plants by enclosing plant sex within the consecrated "flower" of marriage.

And yet, if it succeeds in domesticating the flower's sexual inversion, Linnaeus's nuptial metaphor has the opposite effect at the level of his overarching taxonomic system, where it reveals that floral sexuality in the plant kingdom is radically more diverse and floral "marriage" more permissive than human laws allow. Indeed, a first glance over the Linnaean table immediately divulges that heterosexual monogamy is exceedingly rare among plants: of the twenty-four total classes of plants Linnaeus identifies, only one class, the *Monandria*, features exactly one "husband" and one "wife" sharing a conjugal "bed." The rest of the plants appear to engage in "marriages" that scandalized Linnaeus' critics: polygamous marriages (involving from two up to twenty or more "husbands"); mixed-rank marriages (featuring "some males above the other"); incestuous marriages (in which the "husbands, like brothers, arise from one base"); marriages with "husbands" homoerotically "joined together at the top"; and a whole category of apparently unhappy marriages including those in which "husbands live with their wives in the same house, but have different beds" (i.e., a plant bears separate male and female flowers), "husbands and wives have different houses" (i.e., individual plants of the species bear either only male or only female flowers), or "husbands live with wives and concubines" (i.e., a plant bears some female flowers and others with both pistils and stamens).

Moreover, despite the gender binarism and heterosexuality implied by his nuptial metaphor, Linnaeus acknowledged that there are not two but three sexes within the plant kingdom, and that the vast majority of plants are, in fact, hermaphrodites which reproduce asexually.[18] His taxonomy makes clear that only a small fraction of plant species produce single-gendered individuals (i.e., bearing either only male or only female flowers) and that the remaining majority of species are therefore hermaphroditic in one form or another (i.e., bear flowers with both stamens and pistils, or bear both male and female flowers on a single individual, or some combination of single-gendered and hermaphroditic flowers). Linnaeus thus also indicated that reproduction in plants is not, for the most part, heterosexual. Of course, in a broad sense, all plant reproduction could be considered "heterosexual" insofar it involves the fertilization of a pistil by a stamen. Observed at the level of the organism, however, what Linnaeus' nuptial metaphor casts as a heterosexually reproductive "marriage" resolves, in the case of most flowers, into an instance of hermaphroditic self-fertilization. Indeed, self-fertilization is the norm among plants; reproduction involving two separate hermaphroditic individuals is slightly less common, while reproduction between two separate *and* differently-sexed individuals—the closest plants come to "heterosexual" sex—is comparatively rare.

Like Plato, then, Linnaeus frames plant sex through the lens of human morphology and sexual mores, and in so doing, highlights the radical unlikeness of vegetal sexuality to sanctioned human practices and norms. Given the sheer alterity of gender and sexual arrangements that Linnaeus' new map of the plant kingdom exposed, it is perhaps not surprising that his sexual system of botany often met with outraged resistance as it gradually spread across Europe. "What man will ever believe that God Almighty should have introduced such confusion, or rather such shameful whoredom, for the propagation of the reign of plants," the Prussian botanist, Johann Siegesbeck, protested. "Who will instruct young students in such a voluptuous system without scandal?"[19] While not all of Linnaeus's detractors found his system sacrilegious, most at least shared Siegesbeck's concern that his sexual system of classification made the study of botany morally compromising. The British botanist Charles Alston warned that parts of Linnaeus's book were entirely "too smutty for British ears," and his contemporary, Richard Polwhele, cautioned in particular about its effects upon "female modesty." As Polwhele observed, "botany has lately become a fashionable amusement with the ladies"; should the Linnaean system be adopted, he envisioned a dangerously "unsex'd" near future in which well-born young women "point to the prostitution of a plant; / Dissect its organ of unhallow'd lust, / And fondly gaze the titillating dust."[20] As some historians have noted, Alston's and Polwhele's concerns may well have been exacerbated by the fact that Linnaeus's sexual system arrived in England at a time when botanically themed pornographic satire was already popular ("The TREE OF LIFE, another name / For p-n-s, but in sense the same / Is a rich plant of balmy juice / And own'd to be of sovereign use").[21] In any case, efforts were made to shield the populace from his licentious plants: in addition to those botanists who continued to deny plant sexuality (an opposition that carried forward well into the nineteenth century), others, like William Withering, set to work bowdlerizing Linnaean terminology to produce versions of his botany more suitable for female study.[22]

As in Plato's day, then, in the wake of Linnaeus the sexuality of plants again seemed to represent a threatening inversion of human sexual norms. This sense of the plant kingdom's perversion arises from the habit of reading vegetal sexuality through the lens of human sex: as a consequence, any sign of the plant's alterity (for instance, that its sexual organs appear at its topmost point, or that a single individual may feature both female and male organs) will always appear as a kind of sexual deviance. But what happens if we reverse the direction of this reading habit? As we'll see below, when Thoreau invokes plant sex in his writings on chastity, he invites us to reimagine human sexuality through the lens of vegetality.

Inverting Chastity and Sensuality

Against then still powerful currents of Platonic moral philosophy and anti-Linnaean moral panic, Thoreau, in his essay on "Chastity & Sensuality" (1852), champions the sexually inverted plant as a paragon of virtue designed for human emulation. Thoreau presented this essay, with characteristic social tact, by way of an engagement gift to his good friend Harrison Blake before Blake's wedding.[23] Blake had written to Thoreau and Bronson Alcott asking for advice on how to keep his romance fresh: "How shall we treat each other, with what reserve, with what Holy Reverence so that the Mystery, the Poetry, & Beauty which hang about the dawning of love, may not be changed by too close an intercourse, by sharing, in common, the cares of daily life?"[24] Of course, in inquiring after ways to preserve the intensity of new love, Blake was not, in all likelihood, looking for a lecture on abstinence. And yet, as stodgy as Thoreau's responding essay on chastity seems today—or, as some would suggest, as symptomatic of his visceral revulsion towards heterosexual sex—I would like to suggest here that "Chastity & Sensuality" does not, ultimately, recommend replacing sex with no sex. It is not, in other words, chastity *per se* that this essay champions. Instead, weaving threads from Linnaeus and Plato into a fundamentally Romantic philosophy of vegetal growth, Thoreau urges us to remake human sex as plant sex.

"Chastity & Sensuality" argues that, far from advertising vegetal licentiousness, flowers are "intended for a symbol of the open and unsuspected beauty of all true marriage." Thoreau elaborates this claim by quoting at length the Linnaean botanist, Isaac J. Biberg, who observes:

[T]he organs of generation which in the animal kingdom are for the most part concealed by nature as if they were to be ashamed of, in the vegetable kingdom are exposed to the eyes of all; and when the nuptials of plants are celebrated, it is wonderful what delight they afford to the beholder, refreshing the senses with the most agreeable color and the sweetest odor, and at the same time bees and other insects, not to mention the humming bird, extract honey from their nectaries, and gather wax from their effete pollen.[25]

Thoreau thus invokes Linnaeus's marital metaphor to turn the shamelessness of the plant's sexual inversion (its genitals "exposed to all") into a sign of its innocence, holding the flower up as an example of wholesome intercourse. Indeed, here the virtue of floral sex appears to be that it is not only innocently public but that it is also publicly minded, producing not just fruit and seed but beauty, scent, nectar, and wax. Yet Thoreau's aim in this essay is not to embolden human lovers to embrace sex more freely or engage in it more communally. Rather, if the flower symbolizes "true marriage" for Thoreau, this is not because flowers represent sex without shame but because vegetal sexuality is akin to chastity. After all, as Linnaeus acknowledges, the "conjugal" scene within the flower is also, properly speaking, an instance of hermaphroditic self-fertilization. Under this description, the intercourse that unfolds in the floral chamber—that is, the fertilization of a pistil by a stamen contained within the same flower—no longer looks like an instance of heterosexual reproduction, but instead instantiates a form of asexual reproduction—of self- rather than cross-fertilization. And thus the "marriage" that the hermaphroditic, self-pollinating flower celebrates is also, technically, celibate. Indeed, in the lines leading up to this quote, Thoreau explicitly links flowers to celibacy, asserting that "[v]irginity ... is a budding flower" and "[w]hoever loves flowers, loves virgins and chastity" (*EEM* 276).

Ultimately, however, we find that it is not sexual abstinence that Thoreau means to advocate here. It is, rather, what chastity *yields*, not what it suppresses or withholds, that excites him. As the essay's conclusion makes plain, Thoreau understands plant sexuality to model an alternative mode of generativity which humans may emulate—one that, unlike heterosexual reproduction, entails individual development and social transformation, and results in "fruits" not of the loin but of the mind. In the essay's final movement, Thoreau equates floral sex with inspiration, defining true marriage as an act whose highest aim is not the production of children but the fructification of thought. A few lines below the quotation from Biberg, he offers the following observations:

The intercourse of the sexes, I have dreamed, is incredibly beautiful, too fair to be remembered. I have had thoughts about it, but they are among the most fleeting and irrecoverable in my experience. It is strange that men will talk of miracles, revelation, inspiration, and the like, as things past, while love remains. A true marriage will differ in no wise from illumination. In all perception of truth there is a divine ecstasy, an inexpressible delirium of joy, as when a youth embraces his betrothed virgin. The ultimate delights of a true marriage are one with this.

(*EEM* 277)

Through a curious interpretive metonymy, Thoreau here translates the flower, his symbol of true marriage, into a dream of "the intercourse of the sexes" which, like the flower that symbolizes it, is at once "incredibly beautiful" and "fleeting." In his next breath, the ravishing evanescence of this intuition about sex proves to be exemplary of the fruits of the ideal intercourse he has in mind, for Thoreau now pronounces that true marriage is equivalent to "revelation," "inspiration," and "illumination." This impression is accompanied by "a divine ecstasy" akin to the pleasure of the youth who "embraces his betrothed virgin," with the exception that illumination's orgasm results not in conception but in "a perception of truth." Thoreau's examination of "the subject of sex" concludes, then, by arguing that "the delights of a true marriage," while comparable to orgasm and sexual reproduction, are engaged in the service of an alternative economy of production whose highest aim is not the propagation of children but the generation of new thoughts, dreams, and revelations.

Reversing Plato's equation of vegetality with unenlightened sensuality, and repurposing Linnaeus' marital metaphor, "Chastity & Sensuality" thus presents the sexually inverted flower as the model of a libidinal life devoted (as Plato himself had urged) to the blossoming of the mind. In presenting chastity as an asexual mode of reproduction, Thoreau frames it not as an alternative *to* sexuality so much as an alternative form *of* sexuality. Indeed, his larger argument here will be that we have understood human growth all wrong by imagining that men and women come into their maturity by marrying and becoming sexually reproductive. To this end, he closes the essay with a diatribe against sexual reproduction that is not strictly anti-sex. "The only excuse for reproduction is improvement," he proclaims. "Nature abhors repetition. Beasts merely propagate their kind, but the offspring of noble men & women will be superior to themselves, as their aspirations are. By their fruits ye shall know them" (*EEM* 278). Thoreau here provocatively insists that humans are inherently equipped with not one but two ways to reproduce: a "beastly" way that yields repetitious offspring and a more natural and "noble" way that yields singular offspring—offspring which, like our highest "aspirations" and other best "fruits" of our minds, foster a transformed future. Thoreau's closing statement thus clarifies that the target of this essay's critique of sensuality is not, in fact, the baseness of sex but rather his culture's blanket valorization of the reproductive marriage as the sign of achieved manhood or womanhood. For Thoreau, this narrative drastically underestimates humanity's potential for growth: simply propagating children is no substitute for the transformative labor of self-cultivation. In the end, then, this essay would not have us replace sex with no sex, or subdue our sensuous appetites with the dour discipline of renunciation for the sake of asceticism merely. Rather, Thoreau's critique looks beyond sex (yea or nay) to argue that the true path to maturity—that is, the most admirable and ennobling channel for our desires—is the pursuit of development.

In differentiating here between a form of reproduction that is merely repetitive and one that is developmentally progressive, Thoreau invokes a distinction at the heart of the Romantic era's understanding of the difference between animal and plant sexuality. For Romantic philosophers like Goethe and Hölderlin, as Elaine Miller has shown, the chief distinction between plants and animals is that, whereas animals retain the same physiological form from birth to sexual maturation (merely expanding in size until they are ready to begin reproducing offspring in the image of that fixed form), plants undergo a series of radical physiological transformations as they grow toward sexual maturity.[26] In the process of developing from seed to seedling to flower to fruit, the plant unfolds out of itself a series of new morphological structures (stem, leaf, calyx, corolla, etc.), thus continually transcending its prior forms. Put simply, whereas beasts merely propagate more of the same, plants metamorphose over the course of their life. Aspiring toward blossom, seedlings undertake a wholesale transformation into flowers before they are ready to bear fruit.

For Romantic thinkers like Goethe and Hölderlin, the mutability demonstrated in the plant's process of sexual maturation illuminates a fundamental biological principle—namely, the essentially metamorphic nature of all being. In other words, although the self-transcending movement of plant sexuality is known by its marked contrast to the reiteration of fixed forms modeled in animal reproduction, Romantic thought embraced the plant as illustrative of an instinctive mutability—an inborn drive toward self-transformation—that is inherent to all forms of life. Thus, Goethe concludes that all organic "form is a moving, a becoming, a passing thing. The doctrine of forms is the doctrine of transformation. The doctrine of metamorphosis is the key to all signs of nature."[27] And for Goethe, it is in the morphology of plants that the universal truth of becoming is most perfectly demonstrated: "All is leaf," he proclaims. Or as Thoreau would later paraphrase this thought: "Vegetation is the type of all growth," a concrete testament to the larger truth that "the very globe continually transcends and translates itself" (W 306).[28]

As in Plato, then, vegetality for the romantics forms a ground-note of organic life. And yet whereas Plato's sexually inverted vegetable soul represents the most abjectly appetitive and unenlightened dimensions of human life, the romantics' sexually metamorphic plant exemplifies human life's noblest aim: moral development, self-transcendence, *bildung*. In this sense, the Romantic era proposed a wholesale reevaluation of vegetal sexuality. No longer denigrated as the lowliest mode of embodied life which humans must overcome in order to reach full maturity, the vegetal now stands for our highest capacities for individual growth and collective transformation.

In referring us back to our vegetal natures, then, Thoreau is challenging us to take a more capacious view of humanity's procreative potential. He is concerned that his culture's valorization of reproductive heterosexuality, just like its enthusiasm for industrialized production (both forming part of the deadening "machinery of modern society" (*J* IV:185) that he laments), has condemned us to a meaningless cycle of "beastly" propagation. Can we really be satisfied by this endlessly reiterative reproduction—of more children, more goods, more profits? Thoreau insists that we are capable of far more valuable kinds of growth than such simple numerical increase. As he explains, reverting to an all-vegetal metaphor, if "[t]he common man is the Baldwin," an apple cultivar that is "propagated by mere offshoots or repetitions of the parent stock," then "the genius is a seedling"—not a clone but a novel thing in the world (*PJ* 4: 361). In other words, we are capable, both individually and speciologically, of a form of production that does not just perpetuate but advances us; we can, if we try, create new and socially transformative forms of life. But in order to do this, we must ourselves become self-transcending. We must resist our animal instinct to "propagate" endless clones of the past. Instead, like plants, we must cultivate our organic drive toward metamorphosis, fruition.

Development as Sexuality: The Higher Laws of Vegetal Life

To follow Thoreau in thinking of chastity not as an alternative to sexuality but as an alternative (vegetal) form of sexual expression, we must first unlearn our habit of reading vegetality back through human sex. Thoreau's floralization of sex—with its preference for development over copulation and for the fruition of ideas over children—will continue to seem like a vote for de-sexualization so long as we remain committed to the anthropocentric (or more broadly animal-centric) assumption that growth is not an aspect of sexual life. Indeed, as I will elaborate in this section, the sheer alterity of vegetal sexuality to our present ways of thinking about sex consistently threatens to obscure Thoreau's efforts to articulate chastity's relation to erotic life. Yet, as I will argue, he is, himself, consistent in presenting chastity as a form of sexuality. Turning to the "Higher Laws" chapter of *Walden*—which contains Thoreau's longest meditation on the bodily economy of chastity—we can begin to understand how Thoreau conceives of chastity's sexuality by identifying the desire for development as a drive which is felt in the innate urges and inclinations of the body.

As in "Chastity & Sensuality," as well as in the quotation which opens this chapter, "Higher Laws" presents us with a choice between propagation and development, between repetitive reproduction and transformative fruition. Once again, though, Thoreau stymies our expectations in refusing to paint chastity as involving the repression of our bodily appetites. Instead he explains: "The generative energy, which, when we are loose, dissipates and makes us unclean, when we are continent invigorates and inspires us." Against our modern tendency to imagine that our sexual orientation is fixed in us from birth, Thoreau here posits a libido ("the generative energy") which has no predetermined orientation. As "Higher Laws" lays out for us, this energy may be expended in what he characterizes as "animal" sensuality (reiterative pleasures like eating, having sex, masturbating, etc.), or it may be husbanded toward invigoration and growth, toward new thoughts and inspirations. Crucially, though, *both* options—both fucking and thinking, both beastly sensuality and fructifying chastity—qualify for Thoreau as expressions of the same generative energy, which is to say neither option entails repressing the body's libidinal drive. This drama of sexual choice thus runs counter to post-Protestant (not to mention Platonic) forms of asceticism which imagine chastity as the suppression of sensuality. Instead, Thoreau here defines chastity as sensuality's transformation: it is the husbanding of our libidinal energies, plant-like, toward development. As he describes it, this vegetal orientation is one instinctive form of libidinal life which may be cultivated over other potential orientations (e.g., animal sexuality, reiterative reproduction) in the body.[29]

But if vegetality or development constitutes a form of sexuality for Thoreau, it is one that challenges many of our entrenched notions about how sexuality operates, and this misalignment of vision makes it hard to hold onto his sense that the desire for development is an organic libidinal drive. As we've just seen, for instance, Thoreau's theory of vegetal sexuality requires us to imagine that sexual orientation is a matter of choice: that we are endowed with a generative energy but that this energy does not come with a predetermined set of ends toward which it inclines us (e.g., toward sex with women, sex with men, or not sex but development). Indeed, in one of its most difficult passages of thought, "Higher Laws" suggests that animal and vegetal sexuality are ultimately not alternative and mutually competitive orientations—binary sexual options—so much as they are coextensive and sequential. "I found in myself, and still find," Thoreau tells us, "an instinct toward a higher, or, as it is named, spiritual life, as do most men, and another toward a primitive rank and savage one, and I reverence them both. I love the wild not less than the good" (W 210).[30] Thoreau's stark juxtapositions (higher/lower, spiritual/primitive) seem to array moral development against sensuous embodiment here, tempting us to read this passage as a call for moderation between opposites (to let your goodness be tempered with wildness, and vice versa). However, Thoreau proceeds to clarify that the instinct toward wildness is, in fact, an engine of moral development: when closely attended to, the body's "savage" appetites, it turns out, drive us toward spiritual metamorphosis. Hence, Thoreau recommends hunting and fishing—"primitive" pastimes in his book—because he believes that within these predatory urges an instinct toward development is also expressing itself.

> Such is oftenest the young man's introduction to the forest, and the most original part of himself. He goes thither at first as a hunter and fisher, until at last, if he has the seeds of a better life in him, he distinguishes his proper objects, as a poet or naturalist it may be, and leaves the gun and fish-pole behind. ... [He] might go [to the pond] a thousand times before the sediment of fishing would sink to the bottom and leave [his] purpose pure; but no doubt such a clarifying process would be going on all the time.
>
> (W 213)

Wildness functions here as a stage of moral development, not strictly development's competitor. Within the noise of our animal appetites the signal of our vegetal desire for development resonates. Chastity, on this view, is a discipline not of suppression but of finer attunement: a "clarifying process" by which we come to discern the true "purpose" toward which our more basic bodily appetites have, we discover, been pointing all along. Thus may the "seeds" of our higher life germinate.

This portrait of development as a subtle instinct—an appetite on a lower, if more powerful frequency—in turn raises a third difficulty for our modern understanding of sexuality and thus, too, for our ability to perceive the sexuality of development. For Thoreau imagines that our desire for growth is, if embodied and instinctual, nonetheless also curiously faint and objectless. As the foregoing metaphor of sedimentation and clarification indicates, we may only belatedly realize what it is that this instinct has been impelling us toward. In this sense, the vegetal drive seems hardly sexual, since today we are more accustomed to thinking of our erotic appetites as strongly directional and object-driven, even fetishistic: seizing on specific bodies and body parts, demanding satisfaction in this particular act, smell, or texture. This expectation makes it difficult to discern anything quite like eroticism in an appetite for development that Thoreau invariably describes as vague in both force and orientation: "a faint intimation" (W 214), "the faintest but constant suggestions of [our] genius" (W 216).

Yet in another sense, it's precisely this drive's delicacy that links it to the erotic, since discerning its subtle promptings requires a heightened sensual responsivity. Thus, Thoreau narrates his own transformation from youthful hunter-fisherman to adult vegetarian as the result not of moral enlightenment but of an incremental process led by slight bodily intuitions and disinclinations to which he responded with no particular purpose in mind. "When I had caught and cleaned and cooked and eaten my fish, they seemed not to have fed me essentially," he recalls, detailing his slight but growing "repugnance to animal food" and describing this indefinite aversion as "not the effect of experience, but ... an instinct" (W 214). Although following this instinct leads Thoreau to make a series of renunciations (he gives up meat, fish, coffee, tea, condiments), he characterizes these not as depriving his appetite but, in true voluptuary fashion, refining it, so that his new diet feeds "the imagination" as well as "the body" (W 215). "Who has not sometimes derived an inexpressible satisfaction from his food in which appetite had no share?" (W 218) he wonders, voicing a question that sounds more like a gourmand's than an ascetic's. As a bodily economy, the orientation toward development urges austerity toward some senses (e.g., "gross taste") so that his appetite for other, more intricate pleasures may be heightened and gratified. "The laws of the universe are ... forever on the side of the most sensitive" (W 219), he tells us: development is a discipline of acknowledging and enhancing, not overruling sensation. It is thus no coincidence that a key example Thoreau turns to in this chapter is the butterfly—insects which, he informs us, "in their perfect state, though furnished with organs of feeding, make no use of them" but rather "content themselves with a drop or two of honey" (W 215). As presumably un-deliberative, instinct-governed organisms, butterflies can hardly be thought of as principled, body-phobic ascetics. What they are is quintessentially metamorphic and wondrously beautiful. And here their abstemiousness in mature form confirms for Thoreau that, although it may entail certain sensual renunciations, the drive toward development stems from the body and leads toward transformation that is gratifying to that same body's senses. By training us to become "most sensitive" to its elusive prompting within us, the instinct for development distills our "animal" hunger into an aesthetic sensuality that erupts in beauty and other "inexpressible satisfaction[s]."

Practicing Fructification

"Chastity & Sensuality" and "Higher Laws" offer valuable insight into how Thoreau conceived of this vegetal instinct toward development. If the first essay helps us to recognize Thoreau's re-theorization of chastity as a commitment to development, the latter chapter clarifies how he could understand development as an expression (rather than simply a repression or sublimation) of the body's libidinal energies. Across these writings, then, we can trace the development Thoreau's theorization of vegetal sexuality. But vegetal sexuality was not strictly a matter of philosophical speculation for Thoreau; it is also the erotic orientation that he claims for himself, forming the lens through which he identifies and interprets his own erotic experience. In this section, then, I turn to Thoreau's *Journal* as the site in which he testifies to his first-hand experience with the libidinal urge toward development and documents its sensuous satisfactions. Examining his journal entries can help us to see how pursuing this curiously faint and objectless drive toward development felt, to Thoreau at least, like surrendering to a sexual economy. Moreover, as I shall suggest, the dispossession entailed by this surrender to metamorphosis led Thoreau to reflect on vegetal sexuality's hostility to taxonomy, or indeed any attempt to assert or secure a stable sense of identity.

In passages scattered throughout the *Journal*, Thoreau describes himself coming sensuously, tinglingly, teemingly to life in his encounters with nature. He is frequently ravished by his life outdoors: "My heart leaps into my mouth at the sound of the wind in the woods. ... For joy I could embrace the earth" (*PJ* 3: 368). Indeed, while he acknowledges that most of his contemporaries view his life as perversely isolated and indolent, he does not experience his solitude as lonely, nor his rambles as profitless. "I see that my neighbors look with compassion on me, that they think it is a mean and unfortunate destiny which makes me to walk in these fields and woods so much and sail on this river alone," he admits. Yet he explains, "I find here the only real elysium"; in roaming and contemplating and writing about nature, "the depth and intensity of the life [is] excited" (*J* IX: 121). Indeed, it is no doubt Thoreau's peculiar capacity for arousal in nature—for being pitched to elation by the squelch of sphagnum between his toes— that makes his sprawling *Journal* such a surprisingly compelling read. Excitement courses through the lines of his prose, galvanizing long-dead landscapes to life. "Standing at the right angle we are dazzled by the colors of the rainbow in colorless ice. ... It is a wonderful fact that I should be affected—& thus deeply & powerfully—more than by aught else in all my experience—that this fruit should be borne in me" (*J* XIII: 45). In passages like these, Thoreau's propensity to be "deeply & powerfully" affected by encounters in nature begets our own heightened responsivity. At their best, his ecstasies raise the hair on our own flesh. Which is to say that our bodies may acknowledge what our studies have not: that we are capable of receiving an erotic charge from nature, or perhaps more specifically, that the sensuousness of ostensibly aesthetic appreciations of nature may not, after all, be so neatly differentiable from the sensual stimulation we distinguish as sexual. As Thoreau testifies before a particularly scarlet sunset, "this red vision excites me, stirs my blood—makes my thoughts flow—& I have new & indescribable fancies" (*PJ* 4: 222).

But beyond finding these sensuous encounters arousing, Thoreau understands them to be reproductive in a vegetal sense: they draw him toward fruition. "There is no doubt a perfect analogy between the life of the human being and that of the vegetable—both of the body & the mind,"

he observes. "I am concerned first to come to my *Growth* intellectually &
morally; (and physically, of course, as a means to this, for the body is the
symbol of the soul) and, then to bear my *Fruit*—do my *Work*—*Propagate*
my kind, not only physically but *morally*—not only in body but in
mind" (*PJ* 3: 224–5). Though childless, Thoreau does not see himself as
un-reproductive, nor does he understand his production of work to be a
surrogate for the sexual reproduction of children. By "a perfect analogy"
(which is perhaps to say, something more like a tautology) vegetality defines,
for Thoreau, his sexual reproductivity which, like the plant's, consists of a
process of fructification—in his case, of thought. "The fruit a thinker bears
is *sentences*" (*J* XIII: 238).

This sexualization of thought in Thoreau's work produces a number of
estranging features in his erotics. For instance, as we've already seen above,
in his description of being brought to fruition by the beauty of ice, Thoreau
often casts as *erotic* experiences we might otherwise tend to describe as
aesthetic or even intellectual. Indeed, a defining characteristic of his
ecoerotics is this refusal to distinguish sensuous from sensory stimulation,
or erogenous from intellectual excitement. "I am like a bee searching the
livelong day for the sweets of nature," he explains. "Do I not impregnate &
intermix the flowers, produce rare & finer varieties by transferring my eyes
from one to another? ... With what honied thought any experience yields
me I take a bee line to my cell. It is with flowers I would deal" (*PJ* 4: 53).
Identifying himself both as a promiscuous inseminator of flowers and as a
bee become gravid with their honey, Thoreau insists on the erotic quality of
the aesthetic pleasures he finds in nature and the flush of inspiration they
afford him. In this way, his ecoerotics remaps the terrain of sexual pleasure,
eliding the difference between things that affect us and things that arouse us,
between our life and our loves.

Moreover, because the vegetal model subtending this ecoerotics identifies
sexual expression (or the fructification of thought) with development,
sexuality emerges, in Thoreau, as a drive which precludes the formation of
any stable identity. For Thoreau, the metamorphic nature of plant growth
provides a template for thinking of sexuality as something that one does
not possess as a defining feature of identity (as Linnaean taxonomy and
late-nineteenth-century sexology both suppose) but as something that is,
on the contrary, dispossessive and transformative—a force that oversees
one's perpetual self-transcendence. Sexual expression is thus not, on this
view, a form of self-expression. On the contrary, the metamorphic ontology
Thoreau invokes via vegetality renders selves ultimately un-representable.
For, as he notes in his *Journal*, a fundamentally protean or developmentally
oriented self is one who is not adequately reflected in any of its temporal
instantiations. "Some men's lives are but an aspiration—a yearning toward
a higher state," he observes, concluding, "we cannot pronounce upon
a man's intellectual & moral state until we foresee what metamorphosis

it is preparing him for" (*J* 4: 145–6). If the essence of life is becoming, then identities are inessential—necessarily transient, provisional, merely preparatory.

In associating vegetality with a metamorphic ontology that resists classificatory schema, Thoreau echoes a refrain that was common within Romantic thought about plants. As Theresa Kelley observes, "Romantic writing about botany was repeatedly drawn to the way that plant differences give systematic protocols the slip."[31] Thus, even as this period saw the expansion of efforts to comprehensively map the plant kingdom, the Romantic era was also home to "a strong suspicion that plants might 'confound' any system devised to accomplish this goal."[32] Indeed for Goethe, Elaine Miller elaborates, acknowledging the metamorphic nature of plant growth ultimately led him "to reject the possibility of any real natural individual, that is, of a natural entity that is clearly demarcated and can be designated as a unity." Abandoning Linnaeus' botanical taxonomy as fundamentally mistaken, Goethe moved toward an understanding of nature "as a collection of vital forces that mutually transform one another."[33] Thoreau, as it happens, was also skeptical of Linnaeaus's "artificial" system and preferred alternatives which acknowledged the "*quaua*versal affinity of plants"—that is, the essential relationality of plant life and thus, too, the impossibility of dividing it into stably differentiated types (*J* 4: 335). Extending this principle to human identity, Thoreau further concluded: "Just as true is this of man.— even of an individual man. He is not to be referred to or classed with any company. He is truly singular—and so far as systems are concerned, in a sense, ab-normal ever" (*J* 4: 335).[34] Thus, inspired by the way the plant's protean growth unsettles the urge to classify, Thoreau's vegetal theory of human sexuality constructs sexuality as a process of becoming which, as such, is not susceptible to taxonomization.

Vegetally conceived, then, sexuality no longer serves as a ground of identity, and the consequent dissociation of sexual expression from self-expression shows up in what I have already noted is the curious (to us) aimlessness of Thoreau's ecoerotic inclinations. Indeed, although he attests to feeling compulsively attracted to his work in nature, Thoreau also describes being unable to specify what ends (or even what objects) his desires point towards:

My Journal should be the record of my love. I would write in it only of the things I love. My affection for any aspect of the world. What I love to think of. I have no more distinctness or pointedness in my yearnings than an expanding bud—which does indeed point to flower & fruit to summer & autumn—but is aware of the warm sun & spring influence only. I feel ripe for something yet do nothing—cant discover what that thing is. I feel fertile merely.

(*PJ* 3: 143–4)

If "Higher Laws" suggests that our desire for development is faint by comparison to our animal appetites, Thoreau's account of his personal experience of this desire suggests that its indistinctness is in fact programmatic. For unlike copulation, development is not a predetermined end toward which one can purposively aim but is instead an open-ended process to which one can at best submit. Like the seedling that leans toward the congenially "warm sun and spring influence," Thoreau's erotic agency consists here in surrendering to his affections without knowing in advance how they will transform him, what fruits they will draw out of him. His love, in this sense, is not an expression of the self but a letting go of it. And here Thoreau suggests that the *Journal* might serve as the instrument of that self-surrender, a means not of mastering nature by deliberate study, but of becoming-vegetal by undeliberateness, by writing down what he loves despite not knowing what that love, or its record, might amount to.

Disentangling Queer and Green

In the readings above, I've tried to indicate some of the ways that vegetal sexuality, as Thoreau conceives of it, unsettles the norms of obligatory heterosexuality and biological reproductivity. In this final section, I want to broach the question of how Thoreau's vegetal anti-normativity might be thought in relation to queer theory. I'll begin by suggesting how attending to Thoreau's identifications with vegetal sexuality might extend queer readings of his work by Michael Warner and Peter Coviello, before turning to consider, on the other hand, what we risk losing by equating vegetal sexuality with the queer.

   In proposing that Thoreau challenges contemporary notions of sexuality, I am preceded and inspired by two important readings of his erotics. Across a pair of essays each, Michael Warner and Peter Coviello have argued that, even more than the signs of his attraction to men, what makes Thoreau's writings queer are the ways in which his solitary erotics unsettle both antebellum and twenty-first-century regimes of sexuality. As Warner observes, the vivid yet non-reproductive pleasures Thoreau enjoys mark his resistance to both heteronormative and capitalist systems of production, as well as to the liberal model of sexuality which underwrites them. Instead, in Thoreau's sensuously satisfying solitude, we learn that "not all erotic desires must have their source in self/other relations. ... Like many other intense pleasures that Thoreau describes, his ecstasy over musical sounds reminds us that an increasingly official liberal sexuality, with its self/other logic of 'love,' does not exhaust the possibilities of the erotic."[35] Warner ultimately suggests that Thoreau's "turn away from both production and reproductive sex" dreams of a redeemed economy, "at once erotic and economic," which would "recuperate waste, luxuriate in surplus," and bypass the self/other logic of difference that presumptively grounds liberal heterosexuality.[36] Reiterating and extending this analysis, Coviello further notes how Thoreau's solitary erotics blurs the boundary between self and world. Seizing upon Thoreau's experiences of "carnal ravishment" in response to sounds and landscapes, Coviello notes,

> If we are right in calling these sex scenes, then sexuality for Thoreau is not something isolated in persons, not something apprehensible in the self alone, but is instead the name for what inheres between selves and the objects around them, for the current that connects and momentarily confounds them, and in doing so suggests back to the self nothing short of a revised template for being.[37]

Thus both Warner and Coviello suggest that, in his preference for solitary sensuous encounters, Thoreau is not "foreswearing the realm of the intimate as much as seeking relief from the terms and logic in which intimacy is available to him."[38] Rather than simply signaling his sexual repression, Thoreau's chastity expresses his longing for a more radically reimagined erotic economy—one not conscripted to biocapitalist imperatives, nor reducible to "another of the liberal self's secured properties."[39]

The queer Thoreau who emerges from these accounts is thus more than a closet story. Yet Warner and Coviello also find Thoreau's erotics largely proleptic—on their reading, his work describes a non-instrumentalized, non-possessive, and sensuously self-relating sexuality which Thoreau himself can but dimly conceive. Thus Warner concludes that Thoreau's alternative erotics remains "utopian in the rather strict sense that Thoreau cannot concretely imagine [its] realization."[40] Similarly, Coviello dubs this an "untimely" erotics of "expectancy": "Thoreau refuses what he thinks of as the instrumentalization of sex in reproduction in favor of something other, some mode of relation he can only qualify with references to the antique past and the unwritten future."[41] For Warner and Coviello, then, Thoreau's desire remains hazily speculative, not so much lived as imagined. In this respect, their readings echo the more literal queer readings which precede them in deeming Thoreau's erotic life unfulfilled—marked by longings he could not imagine satisfying—and in thus discounting his ecoerotic ecstasies as shadows of a more fulsome pleasure he could not attain in life.

It should be clear that the account of vegetal sexuality I've been outlining reaffirms the conclusions Warner and Coviello arrive at, including Thoreau's resistance to biocapitalist (re)productivity and his de-emphasized sense of identity. I want to close, however, by arguing for the importance of recognizing the vegetal as the lens through which Thoreau conceptualizes his unorthodox erotics. As I've been emphasizing throughout, Thoreau does not simply deploy vegetal metaphors as a way of describing non-normative desires he cannot otherwise name; rather, his theory of sexuality is vegetal from the ground up. At least three consequences flow from taking the vegetal in Thoreau's erotics seriously.

The first of these pertains to our approach to Thoreau's work more generally. As we've seen, in identifying development with sexuality (via vegetality), Thoreau radically expands the domain of the erotic. In the wake of this shift, whole tracts of his thought we have not read as sexual now appear differently. A whole range of nonhuman encounters, sensory experiences, aesthetic transports, and even minor moments of non-ecstatic contemplation emerge now as instances in Thoreau's development and, as such, expressions of his sexuality. All of a sudden the erotic, in Thoreau, is everywhere.

The second consequence pertains to our understanding of the temporal—which is also to say the political—dimensions that we attach to Thoreau's alternative erotics. For both Warner and Coviello, the transformed libido Thoreau envisions is purely speculative—a hazy hope for a future Thoreau can't quite imagine. But to recognize vegetal sexuality as the basis from which Thoreau works is to suggest that the change he calls for is not, to his mind at least, so utopian. In the metamorphic, flowering world around him, Thoreau saw not just the glimmering possibility but the concrete demonstration of a redeemed economy of production whose highest aim is not biocapitalist reproduction but transformative development. Moreover, Thoreau understood this libidinal economy to be already extant within humans—an embodied instinct that only awaits our submission. The revolution Thoreau's erotics demands, on this view, is not contingent upon an unprecedented break from the past into an all-but-unimaginable "revised template of being." Rather it means returning to an uncannily familiar template; it means re-naturalizing—re-vegetalizing—the human.

Finally, and most consequentially, to recognize the vegetal as Thoreau's sexual template is to locate an ontology of metamorphosis—an ontology Thoreau associates with vegetal growth—at the center of his non-normative erotics, and it is this third consequence that, I think, raises questions about the extent to which this erotics can be folded into our sense of the queer. There are, on the face of things, many good reasons to read Thoreau's vegetal sexuality alongside queer theory. If, as Elizabeth Freeman suggests, queerness envisions "ways of living aslant to dominant forms of object-choice, coupledom, family, marriage, sociability, and self-presentation," then Thoreau's ostensibly chaste, solitary, non-reproductive, aimless, and unprofitable erotic orientation toward development is unarguably queer.[42] Moreover, in identifying this libidinal drive with vegetal nature, Thoreau could be said to anticipate queer ecology's arguments against the de facto "naturalness" of heteronormativity and "aberrance" of queer desire.[43] Thoreau's vegetal sexuality affirms a natural world of proliferating sexual possibilities in which sex is non-dyadic, humans reproduce both heterosexually and hermaphroditically (via the self-fertilization of fructification), and eroticism organically permeates all kinds of encounters (genital and non-genital; social and solitary; hetero-, homo-, interspecies, and nonhuman). Moreover, this world's metamorphic processualism and resistance to taxonomization resonate with queer theory's overarching commitment to queering, or unsettling, regimes of normalization wherever they congeal. As David Eng, Judith Halberstam, and José Muñoz define it, queer critique undertakes a "continuous deconstruction of the tenets of positivism at the heart of identity politics," a deconstruction which extends "to a continuing critique of its privileged assumptions" about its own subject—about what queerness signifies, or whom it describes, in the first place.[44] Insofar as queer theory understands itself as a process of ongoing (self-)critique, it bears a strong family (or queer kin) resemblance to Thoreau's vision of a world whose highest truth is its own ongoing transformation.

Yet it is also precisely this metamorphic ontology at the heart of Thoreau's vegetal sexuality which renders its alignment with queer theory problematic. As the mission statements above make clear, queer theory has tended to understand itself as an inherently oppositional project—articulating possibilities that run aslant prescribed norms, destabilizing that which is fixed, and clearing space for desires otherwise ruled out by hegemonies of power and discourse. This oppositional positioning reflects the more basic fact that "queerness" is, itself, an artifact of exclusion: it is only through the operation of normalizing regimes that the figure of "the queer" emerges as that which lies outside of the normal. There is, by contrast, no inside or outside of Thoreau's vegetal ontology. As I've argued, this metamorphic ontology is anathema to systems of classification and the normalizing forces they exert. Absent these engines of distinction, there is neither queerness to recover nor discipline to oppose. Jordy Rosenberg makes a version of this point when he argues that queer ecological appeals to the "aleatory nature" of material nature produce a "despecification of the queer object" which obscures the historical forces—including, for instance, racism and settler colonialism—from whose normalizing regimes "the queer" originates. Thus he concludes, "when queerness comes to indicate an ontological or essential form of resistance, we can lose sight of the conditions that make queerness as such legible in the first place."[45] If the most imminent concern here is that ontologizing queerness is dehistoricizing (turning our attentions from forms of oppression still at work), the more basic point is that, in an ontology of "*sheer* queerness," "the queer" therefore ceases to exist.[46] In this sense there is, strictly speaking, nothing queer about Thoreau's vegetal sexuality. The ongoing metamorphosis his vegetal sexuality expresses is immune to systems of categorization and normalization, and as such incapable of seeing queerness to begin with. Or as Thoreau puts this point somewhat differently, as processual beings we are each "truly singular ... in a sense, ab-normal ever." That is, in its lush proliferation of self-difference, Thoreau's vegetal ontology makes everyone—which is also to say, no one— queer.

10

Chance Encounters: Thoreau's Pomontology

Vesna Kuiken

"A Chance Wild Fruit"

In the fall of 1850, Thoreau began amassing in his journal various insights about feral fruits and plants, insights that gradually organized themselves around the question of vegetal reproduction. These observations became the foundation for one of the last of Thoreau's lectures—"Wild Apples," the final piece he revised for publication.[1] Those botanical investigations were also the primary source for three of Thoreau's large unfinished projects: *Wild Fruits*, *Dispersal of Seeds*, and the Kalendar. At the time he began systematically to examine wildlife on his daily walks through the New England woods, Thoreau also began to lecture on all things wild that reside in local forests, delivering for the first time in April 1851 and then many times again a lecture that soon became his favorite: "The Wild."[2] The talk later grew into another, broke off from it, and was finally merged with, another lecture that subsequently became an essay—"Walking," a piece Thoreau held in such high esteem as to regard it "as a sort of introduction to all I may write hereafter."[3]

"Walking" and "Wild Apples" share more than the time when the journal entries they emerged from had been recorded. Their connection is conceptual: both define walking or running-wild as journeying *away from* the familiar ("Walking") or the familial ("Wild Apples"), and both unfold this kind of movement as an ethical model for how one ought to live. In "Walking" the invitation to walk—"to leave father and mother and brother and sister, and wife and child and friends, and never see them again"—turns into an injunction to abandon the truths that define our world by "losing ourselves for half an hour in the woods."[4] This unfamiliar environment, Thoreau believes, is conducive to physical disorientation that dismantles the recognizable conceptual structures—he calls them our "master," certainly not without a slavery-related valence (W 286)—that subtend our relation to the world, our convictions, and our attitudes. When we are lost, we are forced to create our worldview anew, and it is this condition of being lost to the self we know that Thoreau calls Wildness or the Wild (W 273).

As walking is to physical bafflement and conceptual defamiliarization, running-wild is to taxonomic dismantling. In "Wild Apples" Thoreau takes the act of walking and losing oneself to a quasi-biological level by focusing on the wild apple's disorderly reproductive procedure. "A chance wild fruit, planted by a cow or a bird on some remote and rocky hill side" (WA 83), the apple reproduces by cross-pollination, which means that it needs wind, insects, or animal pollinators who will distribute pollen grains to female gametes and disperse its seeds as widely as possible in order to increase the number of future fertilization opportunities. Because of the random middleman (wind, animals, insects, water), the pollen from one apple variety *by rule* crosses with a number of other varieties of the same apple species, resulting in its potentially endless genetic variability. However, unlike the cultivated kind, *Malus domestica*, where grafting procedures determine in advance which desired varieties are to be produced and exactly what properties they will have, the wild apple involves a chance encounter between a number of factors—the trees' reproductive organs, pollinators, the season, environmental conditions, and so on—whose diversity brings about "new and undescribed varieties" (WA 82). Hence when Thoreau urges us to "consider how the apple tree has spread over the country, through the agency of cows and other quadrupeds, making almost impenetrable thickets in many places and yielding many new and superior varieties for the orchard,"[5] it is not for a stylistic flair that he describes wild apples as having been "set out by [the owner] in a somnambulistic state" (WA 78). Unless the plant has been subjected to the precision of grafting and to related protocols of cultivation, neither apple farmers nor apple trees themselves can control the boundless proliferation of this "chance wild fruit" and its "new and undescribed varieties" (WA 83, 82).

Furthermore, in contrast to other wild fruits such as pears, cherries, and berries, the wild apple of which Thoreau speaks should not be confused with the originally wild apple—"the native and aboriginal crab apple, *Malus coronaria*, whose nature has not yet been modified by cultivation" (WA 79). Thoreau's wild apple runs wild from its cultivated parental lineage and becomes what he calls "a wilding" (WA 85)—albeit a wilding that is nonetheless "the noblest of fruits."[6] The wild apple's paradoxical nobility arises, therefore, not from its diverse cultivars and variants but from its having reversed the standard trajectory of cultivation. Instead of having its once wild but now cultivated nature subjected to further grafting and to the production of marketable varieties, the apple had "migrated to this New World" fully cultivated only to eventually "run wild":

> Here on this rugged and woody hill-side has grown an apple-tree, not planted by man, no relic of a former orchard, but a natural growth, like the pines and oaks. ... Corn and grain, potatoes, peaches, melons, etc., depend altogether on our planting; but the apple emulates man's independence and enterprise. It is not simply carried but, like him, to some extent, it has migrated to this New World, and is even, here and there, making its way amid the aboriginal trees, just as the ox and dog and horse sometimes run wild and maintain themselves. Even the sourest and crabbedest apple, growing in the most unfavorable position, suggests such thoughts as these, it is so noble a fruit.
>
> (WA 78–9)

Thoreau's brief outline revises the official botanical history according to which today's cultivated apple was derived from its feral ancestor *Malus sieversii*. Two thousand years ago the latter traveled to Europe from its birthplace in Kazakhstan's Thien Shan mountains through the ancient routes of the Silk Road where its seeds crossed with local varieties of the "sourest and crabbedest" European wild apple, *Malus sylvestris* ("apple of the forest"). Interbreeding with the softer wild apple from Asia had likely sweetened and readied its European counterpart for cultivation. In the sixteenth century, colonists brought the fully cultivated *Mauls domestica* to the Americas,[7] a point at which most histories turn to recording the apple's various cultivars.

Thoreau's genealogy poses a botanical conundrum: taxonomically, the wild apple of which he speaks falls somewhere between the originally wild and the cultivated, yet historically it emerges in the aftermath of the fruit's cultivation. Scholars have attempted to resolve this classificatory complication by yoking Thoreau's research into the wild apple with his scientific interest in evolution, wherein the apple's wildling comes to figure as one of its many varieties alongside the Macintosh, the Empire, the "Porter and the Baldwin" (WA 83), and other familiar cultivars. To corroborate the link, critics point out that Thoreau's botanical explorations in seed dispersal and species variability coincided with his reading, in January 1860, of Darwin's *The Origin of Species*[8] which defines variability as "descent with modification" and identifies it with a species' primary survival mechanism— natural selection. While it is true that Thoreau and Darwin derived similar inferences concerning seed dispersal and variation,[9] Thoreau had articulated his own as early as 1856, three years before the publication of *The Origin of Species*.[10] However, the taxonomic conundrum of Thoreau's pomaceous wilding goes beyond the question of historical precedence: neither cultivated nor wild, apple wilding is for Thoreau a fugitive not only from its cultivated lineage but from the classificatory coordinates that frame Darwin's project as a whole: "I am not in search of stocks," Thoreau clarifies in "Wild Apples," "but of the wild fruit itself, whose fierce gust has suffered no inteneration" (WA 83).

In contrast to cultivated ("intenerated") apples which are grown under closely monitored conditions to yield a uniform look and taste, wild apples "have hung in the wind and frost and rain till they have absorbed the qualities of the weather or season, and thus are highly *seasoned*" (WA 85–6). Every wild apple absorbs and in turn reflects—Thoreau says "commemorates"— its own environmental arrangement: the weather, the strength of the wind and its direction, the position of the sun, the closeness of the tree's branch to the ground, the individual apple's accessibility to birds, squirrels, cows, and people. As he explains:

> It is rare that the summer lets an apple go without streaking or spotting it on some part of its sphere. It will have some red stains, commemorating the mornings and evenings it has witnessed; some dark and rusty blotches, in memory of the clouds and foggy, mildewy days that have passed over it. ... Painted by the frosts, some are uniform clear bright yellow, or red, or crimson, as if their spheres had regularly revolved, and enjoyed the influence of the sun on all sides alike,—some with the faintest pink blush imaginable,—some brindled with deep red streaks like a cow, or with hundreds of fine blood-red rays running regularly from the stem-dimple to the blossom-end ... some touched with a greenish rust, like a fine lichen, here and there, with crimson blotches or eyes more or less confluent and fiery when wet; and others gnarly, and freckled or peppered all over on the stem side with fine crimson spots on a white ground. ... Others, again, are sometimes red inside, perfused with a beautiful blush.
>
> (WA 87–8)

Because of the environment's discreteness and the wild apple's reproductive "chanciness," the new apples are inherently "volatile" (WA 74). For, unlike the wildest ("crabbedest") apples which are always "sour enough to set a squirrel's teeth on edge and make a jay scream," and unlike the grafted kinds which are "very tame and forgettable" (WA 85), wild apples yield an abundance of gustatory combinatorics. Some of them, Thoreau observes, "produce fruit of opposite qualities, part of the same apple being frequently sour and the other sweet; also some all sour and others all sweet, and this diversity on all parts of the tree" (WA 86). Hence, *something* of the disavowed parent's cultivated sweetness *may* (but doesn't have to) linger in *some* (though not all) individual apples, and *sometimes* (not always) in only one part of a single apple. The singularity of flavor, fragrance, and look of each wild apple—the effect of the wilding's "volatile" and "fugacious ethereal qualities" (WA 74, 76)—renders redundant any taxonomizing structure. Thoreau's pomology, only superficially biological and scientific, is in fact ecological and ontological in that it focuses on the absolutely unique—the "irreducibly specific" and the "peculiar."[11] The consequences of this injunction are dramatic: while an apple may share some traits with another apple, it may also share some traits, and the circumstances under which it was generated, with other living forms—plants, animals, or humans. In Thoreau's view, then, a network of mutual properties that cut across definable taxa precedes any group identity of a phylum, order, family, genus, or species. By eschewing taxology and by insisting on the radical singularity of each individual creation, the Thoreauvian wild apple dismantles the classificatory categories that give rise to and maintain the scientifically inflected hierarchy of life which in turn authorizes the logic of normative domination, "stewardship," and mastery—mastery of the humans over the non-human world; of some humans over some other "lesser" humans; of the male over the female, etc. If constitutive elements of every individual body are singularly arranged and generated, while at the same time being constitutive of *other* taxonomically disparate bodies, then the matter of classification and hierarchical order as well as of the superiority of some over others (and let's not forget that Thoreau is writing in the pre-Civil War America) is rendered obsolete. Thus by dismantling the possibility of classificatory distribution, Thoreau takes to its extreme consequences Emerson's already radical proclamation that human affairs—Emerson uses the term "politics"—are by no means "exceptional, but subject to the same laws with trees, earths, and acids."[12]

Environmental Minds, Chance Selves

On May 12, 1851, ten days before he wrote down in his journal the reflections that would eventually become the core of "Wild Apples," Thoreau had all of his teeth pulled out and replaced by a new set. The painful dental procedure required the use of nitrous oxide, known also as the ether or "laughing gas," an analgesic with side-effects akin to euphoria,[13] which Thoreau experienced fully:

> By taking the ether the other day I was convinced how far asunder a man could be separated from his senses. You are told that it will make you unconscious, but no one can imagine what it is to be unconscious—how far removed from the state of consciousness and all that we call "this world"—until he has experienced it. The value of the experiment is that it does give you experience of an interval as between one life

and another,—a greater space than you ever travelled. *You are a sane mind without organs,—groping for organs,—which if it did not soon recover its old senses would get new ones.* You expand like a seed in the ground. *You exist in your roots,* like a tree in the winter. If you have an inclination to travel, take the ether; you go beyond the furthest star. It is not necessary for them to take ether who in their sane and waking hours are ever translated by a thought.

(*J* II: 194, emphasis added)

If the disembodied "sane mind without organs" is to be read here as a replication of Emerson's "transparent eyeball"—pure thinking in need of no body—Thoreau's identification of the mind with the root ("you are a sane mind … you exist in your roots") gets a bit confusing. Ten days after his oral surgery, in a series of lengthy observations, he attempted a way out of this contradiction by claiming "a perfect analogy" between the protocols of vegetal life—growth and reproduction—and thinking:

There is, no doubt, a perfect analogy between the life of the human being and that of the vegetable, both of the body and the mind. … The mind is not well balanced and firmly planted, like the oak. … For each successive new idea or bud, a new rootlet [grows] in the earth. … As with the roots of the plant, so with the roots of the mind, the branches and branchlets of the root are mere repetitions for the purpose of multiplying the absorbing points, which are chiefly the growing or newly formed extremities, sometimes termed *spongelets*. It bears no other organs. … This organ of the mind's development, the Root, *bears no organs but spongelets or absorbing points*.

(*J* II: 201–3 and *passim*; emphasis added)

What might have appeared as the celebration of the mind's ideal disembodiment is soon undermined by Thoreau's equation of the mind with the root, and of the mind's groping movement with the expansive movement of the root's branchlets and spongelets. As Branka Arsić explains in the introductory essay to this volume when commenting on this very passage, for Thoreau, in contradistinction to Plato and the idealist tradition, the mind must be "rooted in the body and pass through it" to be operational.[14] Just as the nutrients pass through the root to sustain the life of the plant and allow it to flower and fruit (for Thoreau, flowering and fruiting are the equivalents of ideas), so bodily sensations provide the material that the mind converts into ideas and thoughts. According to this procedure, the mind's thinking occurs *in the aftermath* of the body's response to the sensations received from the environment, the mind being generated, and so counterintuitively mastered, by the environment. Crafted by what is neither internal nor entirely proper to it, a master neither of itself nor of its environment, the self born out of this protocol is indeed vegetal, or more precisely—environmental. This is why the experience of ecstasy, occasioned by the laughing gas, was so disconcerting for Thoreau: it demonstrated to him that thinking is, in fact, a corporeal rather than a spiritual affair, for unless the mind is grounded in the body ("groping for organs,—which if it did not soon recover its old senses would get new ones"), it remains suspended in a form of non-living, a state akin to death (in "an interval as between one life and another").

The next day, May 21, still on alert from these inferences induced by his ecstatic experience, Thoreau fumbled through a book of dentistry in search of some clarification of the centuries-old dilemma regarding precisely the nature of the mind/body dualism:

> I think that the existence of man in nature is the divinest and most startling of all facts. ... "We live / We of this mortal mixture, in the same law / As the pure colorless intelligence / Which dwells in Heaven, and the dead Hadean shades." ... Looking into a book on dentistry the other day, I observed a list of authors who had written on this subject.
>
> (*J* II: 208)

As one might expect, the medical book didn't provide much in the way of clarification. Yet, as if charting the manner in which the mind chances upon ideas, Thoreau's physical contact with the book advanced one of his most famous meditations—later incorporated verbatim into the definition of wildness in "Walking"—on names and the practice of naming. The closing segment of that journal entry ponders the names of the dentistry book's authors—"Ran and Tan and Yungerman"—which prompt Thoreau to conclude briskly that "there is nothing in the name," and to argue that personal names should be abolished altogether because they annul, rather than reveal, personal idiosyncrasies:

> It was as if they [the dentistry book authors "Ran and Tan and Yungerman"] had been named by the child's rigmarole, *Iery [wiery] ichery van, tittle-tol-tan*, etc. I saw in my mind a herd of wild creatures swarming over the earth, and to each one of its herdsman had affixed some barbarous name in his own dialect. ... We seem to be distinct ourselves, never repeated, and yet we bear no names which express a proportionate distinctness; they are quite accidental. ... A familiar name cannot make a man less strange to me.
>
> (*J* II: 208–10)

Unlike nicknames, Thoreau will add in "Walking," which are "our only true names" (W 280) because they are created anew for every person to fit their peculiarity and idiosyncrasy, proper names are reductive. They fail to "express the proportionate distinctness" of each and every one of us, confining us instead to characteristics imposed on us by familial lineage: "We have but few patronymics, but few Christian names, in proportion to the number of us. ... It is interesting to see how the names of famous men are repeated,—even of great poets and philosophers. ... The boor names his boy Homer, and so succumbs unknowingly to the bard's victorious fame" (*J* II: 209–10).

The entry on names (May 21), which develops from Thoreau's identification of man with plant via ecstasy (May 20), concludes with a note about wildness: "You have a wild savage in you, and a savage name is perchance somewhere recorded as yours" (*J* II: 210). The conclusion seamlessly carries over to the next journal entry of May 23—"And wilder still there grows elsewhere, I hear, a native and aboriginal crab-apple" (*J* II: 211)—as if the new entry figures as a continuation of the thought about the wild man that closes the previous one. This new entry, which starts with "the native and aboriginal crab-apple," unfolds into a lengthy meditation on the proliferation of cultivated apple varieties and their names only to culminate, unsurprisingly, in the celebration of the wild apples' freedom from the confines of taxonomical nomenclature. Thoreau later incorporated the whole May 23 entry into "Wild Apples":

> In 1836 there were in the garden of the London Horticultural Society more than fourteen hundred distinct sorts. But here are species which they have not in their catalogue. ... There is, first of all, the Wood-Apple (*Malus sylvatica*); the Blue-Jay Apple; the Apple which grows in Dells in the Woods (*sylvestrivallis*), also in Hollows in Pastures (*campestrivallis*); the Apple that grows in an old Cellar-Hole (*Malus cellaris*); the Meadow-Apple; the Partridge-Apple; the Truant's Apple (*Cessatoris*), which no boy will ever go by without knocking off some, however late it may be; the Saunterer's Apple,—you must lose yourself before you can find the way to that; the Beauty of the Air (*Decks Aeris*); December-Eating; the Frozen-Thawed (*gelato-soluta*), good only in that state; the Concord Apple, possibly the same with the *Musketa-quidensis*; the Assabet Apple; the Brindled Apple; Wine of New England; the Chickaree Apple; the Green Apple (*Malus viridis*);—this has many synonyms; in an imperfect state, it is the *Cholera morbifera aut dysenterifera, puerulis dilectissima*;—the Apple which Atalanta stopped to pick up; the Hedge-Apple (*Malus Sepium*); the Slug-Apple (*limacea*); the Railroad-Apple, which perhaps came from a core thrown out of the cars; the Apple whose Fruit we tasted in our Youth; our Particular Apple, not to be found in any catalogue,—*Pedestrium Solatium* ... and a great many more I have on my list, too numerous to mention,—all of them good.
>
> (WA 88–9)

In the journal entries of May 23 and 29, 1851, which contain both the germ and the gist of the essay "Wild Apples," Thoreau adds forty-nine other similarly peculiar names. Robert Richardson understands this compendium simply as Thoreau's contribution to the nineteenth-century pomological fashion of proliferating apple varieties and their names, dismissing the list, as most scholars do, as playfully benign.[15] Similarly, David Robinson reads the new "mock-fancy"[16] names as Thoreau's attempt to celebrate the sites where he had found his apples—the names thus memorializing Thoreau's life rather than the apples'.[17]

Yet, the new names sound inconsequential only because they fail to designate the apples' collective homology and classifiable identity (or variety). For, as Michael Marder explains, "names are meant to capture the essence of the plant by assigning to it an exact place in a dead, albeit highly differentiated, system that swallows up the [plant's] singularity and uniqueness."[18] The failure of Thoreau's names to capture the essence is intentional, though, since labels such as December-Eating, Railroad-Apple, or the Frozen-Thawed aim to demonstrate that *each* apple's discrete disposition is reflective of minute differences that are themselves the outcome of an extraordinarily contingent and transitory arrangement of elements—environmental or otherwise—elements that aren't, strictly speaking, proper to any individual apple, much as the thoughts that produce the mind aren't the property of the mind and yet constitute it. Hence, to be a "godfather at the christening of the wild apples," one would have to

> exhaust the Latin and Greek languages, if they were used, and make the *lingua vernacula* flag. We should have to call in the sunrise and the sunset, the rainbow and the autumn woods and the wild flowers, and the woodpecker and the purple finch, and the squirrel and the jay and the butterfly, the November traveller and the truant boy, to our aid.
>
> (WA 88)

As with human names, of which there is a shortage ("We have but few patronymics, but few Christian names, in proportion to the number of us," *J* II: 209), so with the scientific naming of apples. The time of the day, perhaps even the very hour, the seasons, the rainbow, the random members of the geographically and seasonally particular flora and fauna—*all* of that, and then some, would have to be "called in" to aid the naming of each and every wild apple. Nor is Thoreau's emphasis on ecological conditions reducible to the doctrine of environmental determinism, for Thoreau doesn't conceive of habitat in the singular. Each apple emerges from *its own* idiosyncratic ecological abode crafted by nuanced labors of the myriad different agents and their singularly complex arrangements—all of which are irretrievably lost when a taxonomy pulls a vast number of apples into what Thoreau disparagingly calls "the selected lists of pomological gentlemen" (WA 84).

In the same gesture, though, Thoreau alerts us to the fact that scientific taxology is far less credible than is commonly believed since it derives botanical names by a wrong kind of accident, attaching them as it does to whoever was first in the position to name a plant. Black huckleberry, for example, is called "*Gaylussacia resinosa* after the celebrated French chemist," Joseph Louis Gay-Lussac, who "doesn't appear to have ever seen one" (WF 37). Huckleberries are equally unreasonably

> classed by botanists with the cranberries, snowberry, bearberry, mayflower, checkerberry [etc.]; ... and they are called all together the Heath Family, they being in many respects similar to and occupying similar ground with the heath of the Old World, which we have not. If the first botanists had been American this might have been called the Huckleberry Family, including the heaths.
>
> (WF 40)

In other words, while claiming objectivity and universality, scientific taxology remains as accidental as Thoreau's nomenclature, the difference between the two being that Thoreau's names commemorate the singular specificity of each piece of fruit by at least attempting to memorialize its specific biography, while scientific classification assigns such specificities to oblivion.

This is why Thoreau's renaming of the wild apples is not meant to exhaust the London Horticultural Society's inventory but to critique the very practice of cultivating, cataloging, and classifying. A nod to the wild apples' breaking free from the classificatory stability imposed on them by familial lineage and botanical variety, it is also Thoreau's attempt to recover the unique elements and complexity of contingent relations that have created each and every one of them and in which they, once created, further partake by becoming an environment that invites, facilitates, and hosts generation of other entities and environments, human as well as nonhuman: "Not only the Indian, but many indigenous insects, birds, and quadrupeds, welcomed the apple-tree to these shores," like the tent-caterpillar who "saddled her eggs on the very first twig that was formed," and the canker-worm who had "abandoned the elm to feed on it"; "the bluebird, robin, cherry-bird, king-bird, and many more" nested in it "and so became orchard-birds"; the woodpecker "perforated it in a ring quite round the tree before he left it,—a thing which he had never done before, to my knowledge"; and the rabbit, the squirrel, the musquash "greedily devoured it," as did the crow and the jay, while "the owl crept into the first apple-tree that became hollow, and fairly hooted with delight, finding it just the place for him; so, settling down into it, he has remained there ever since" (WA 246–7).

If this enumeration appears to align with Darwin's theory that yokes evolutionary modification with environmental changes, Thoreau's interest lies elsewhere. Born out of complex chance encounters, wild apples themselves become the physical and narrative contexts that can literally change lives. The story Thoreau invokes at the end of *Walden* is a case in point:

> Every one has heard the story which has gone the rounds of New England, of a strong and beautiful bug which came out of the dry leaf of an old table of apple-tree wood, which had stood in a farmer's kitchen for sixty years, first in Connecticut, and afterward in Massachusetts,—from an egg deposited in the living tree many years earlier still, as appeared by counting the annual layers beyond it; which was heard gnawing out for several weeks, hatched perchance by the heat of an urn.[19]

The apple tree, believed dead for sixty years, has been alive all along in at least two ways: by exerting power on the farmer's family in pulling it together within its dining environment, and by serving as a body that gestates and gives birth first to a bug and then to the story that "has gone the rounds of New England," which Thoreau lifted from Chester Dewey's 1829 *History of the County of Berkshire, Massachusetts* and which in turn inspired his concluding meditation on natural and social regeneration in *Walden*. And as Thoreau's theory of ecstatic (re-)generation would have it, this story about "a strong and beautiful bug [hatched from an egg 'deposited in the wood seventy-three years before'] that ate out of a table made from an apple-tree, which grew on the farm of Maj. Gen. Putnam, in Brooklyn, Conn,. and which was brought to Williamstown when his son, Mr. P. S. Putnam, removed to that town,"[20] was also picked up by Melville in the early 1850s to serve as the core of his short story "The Apple-Tree Table." Although both Melville and Thoreau had read Dewey's *History*, Frank Davidson argues that, in fact, "there is reason to believe that, before writing, Melville saw and was influenced by a version of the apple-tree story as told in the closing paragraph of Thoreau's *Walden*."[21] And so while every apple recovers the conditions of its own becoming, it also generates the conditions for other becomings—physical and not.

The nature of Thoreauvian recovery is, thus, inherently narratival and aesthetic. The wild apple commemorates the conditions of its making in the same way that "the stream keeps a faithful and a true *journal* of every event in its experience," its "natural history thus written on [its] banks" (*J* IV: 187). In the *Journal*, the seed of all of his published works and lectures, Thoreau formally adopts the ontological protocol of the stream, of the wild apple, and of the mind—all of which he understands to be crafted from "improper," external elements from without—by obsessively recording the minutest occurrences in his surrounding in an attempt to recover and retain (or "commemorate," to use his word) the unique circumstances of their ecstatic generation. And even if in the published works the minute journal observations often get transformed into an allegorical illustration of human affairs—such as when Thoreau says in "Wild Apples" that "our wild apple is wild only like myself" (WA 79) or when in *Walden* the story of the apple-tree table allegorizes social rebirth—the meticulous elaboration of, and his frenzied focus on, the wild apple's escape from classifiable variety unsettles the expected primacy of the human in the nature/human correspondence. As Barbara Johnson argues, "although Thoreau draws on many centuries of analogical writing, there is a subtle difference in his rhetorical use of nature. ... What begins as a fairly routine analogy tends, in the course of its elaboration, to get wildly out of hand. The fascination with the vehicle as an object of attention in its own right totally eclipses the anthropomorphic tenor."[22] Put differently, rather than anthropomorphize the wild apple, which is how many critics understand it, Thoreau's "Wild Apples" *pomologizes the human*, wresting it away from the predication of its biological class and cultural determinants, and embedding the singularity of each and every one of us in a complex network of our generative idiosyncrasies.

It is not for nothing, then, that Laura Dassow Walls labels "Wild Apples"—rather than, say, *Walden* or "Civil Disobedience"—Thoreau's "only autobiography."[23] If Thoreau argues that "our wild apple is wild only like myself, perchance, who belong not to the aboriginal race here, but have strayed into the woods from the cultivated stock" (WA 79), it is because the ontology and history of the human are wild in the same sense as the wild apple. It is for the sake of this ontological wildness that in all of his works—from botanical to political—Thoreau obsessively calls for resistance to familial bondage, conventional relations, and received truths. They pre-determine our lives in ways that are far more dangerous than the chance encounters that stir us to existence. True, self-determination and free will seem alarmingly absent from both of these paradigms: according to the former, we are preconditioned by the scientific categories, by tradition, and by culture (what in "Walking" Thoreau calls "the master," W 286); according to the latter, living beings are the product of environmental accidents. Yet, for Thoreau, the difference between the two is critical in that the operation of chance applies democratically to all forms of life, while the former is a paradigm of coercive regulation that all too often results in hierarchization and the logic of mastery.

It might be worth clarifying that Thoreau's peculiar take on environmentalism, which emphasizes the conservation ("commemoration") of chanciness rather than the conservation of natural resources, doesn't negate the cultural specificities and historical legacies that participate in the crafting of all identities. The conceptual proximity, which I mention at the beginning of this essay, of "Wild Apples" (a text, strictly speaking, about plants) and "Walking" (a treatise on ethics), is a case in point: in rendering both ontology and ethics ecological, he asks that all bodies be viewed as embedded in a larger context of chance encounters, in which humans accidentally share traits with apples, worms, and jays.

It is with this distinction in mind—between coercion and chance—that in "Walking" Thoreau famously exclaims: "In Wildness is the preservation of the world" (W 273). Here "Wildness"—not wilderness!—is to be understood, again, not as a conservationist effort toward preserving the species and the forests from environmental destruction, but as a radical leveling of the ontological field. At the same time, the "World" should be understood as the sphere of difference and irreducible singularity of all life. That world, which is all we have and which we ought to preserve through our own wildness, will be destroyed lest we conceive of the circumstances of our own coming into being as taking place on the same ontological plane as the circumstances about which the wild apple autobiographically narrates. The rapid physical destruction of the planet cannot be divorced from the master logic to which Thoreau had so prophetically alerted us 150 years ago. The rage of the Anthropocene will only ever be mitigated if Thoreauvian wildness, the nexus of *pomo-ontological* chance encounters, were taken seriously and as a serious political project.

Chance Operations

In *Lecture on the Weather*, a composition commissioned to mark the bicentennial of the American Revolution, John Cage explains why Thoreau's work so readily lends itself to the protocol of chance operations:

> It may seem to some that through the use of chance operations I run counter to the spirit of Thoreau (and '76, and revolution for that matter). The fifth paragraph of *Walden* speaks against blind obedience to a blundering oracle. However, chance operations are not mysterious sources of "the right answers." They are a means of locating a single one among a multiplicity of answers, and, at the same time, of freeing the ego from its taste and memory, its concerns for profit and power, of silencing the ego so that the rest of the world has a chance to enter into the ego's own experience, whether that be outside or inside.[24]

Lecture on the Weather consists of two movements: the "Preface," a prelude read aloud by a single voice; and the "Lecture," an unconducted segment during which "12 speaker vocalists (or instrumentalists), preferably American men who have become Canadian citizens, each using his own sound system given an equalization distinguishing it from the others," read from Thoreau's *Journal*, *Walden*, and "On Civil Disobedience."[25] Each score in the second movement is accompanied by sounds of an approaching storm and by nature drawings randomly chosen from Thoreau's *Journal* that briefly flash before the audience as lightning.

It is not surprising that Cage should give Thoreau the lectern in a work that expounds fierce criticism of the United States' profit-driven interventionism and destruction of the planet: "Our leaders are concerned with the energy crisis," the "Preface" charges:

> They assure us they will find new sources of oil. Not only will earth's reservoir of fossil fuels soon be exhausted: their continued use continues the ruin of the environment. ... I have wanted in this work to give another opportunity for us, whether of one nation or another, to examine again, as Thoreau continually did, ourselves, both as individuals and as members of society, and the world in which we live. ... The desire for the best and the most effective in connection with the highest profits and the greatest power led to the fall of nations before us: Rome, Britain, Hitler's Germany. Those were not chance operations. We would do well to give up the notion that we alone can keep the world in line, that only we can solve its problems. ... I dedicate this work to the U.S.A., that it become just another part of the world, no more, no less.[26]

It appears, though, that Thoreau's centrality to the *Lecture* stems less from his persistent lecturing about the United States' environmentally catastrophic projects than from his insistence that such projects never unfold by chance. They emerge, rather, from what Thoreau calls "the master" (W 286) or "predication" (*J* I: 182), akin to the pomological grafting practices, which Cage translates in the first quote above as "the mysterious source of 'the right answers'": a pre-given normative framework that determines the answer in advance, before a question has been asked, leaving no other "opportunity for us."

It is Thoreau's lifelong obsession with the Wild, which he understood as the negation of all things predetermined, that drew Cage to Thoreau. In an effort to enact the possibility of "another opportunity for us," the *Lecture* assembles excerpts from Thoreau's works by way of chance operations, a compositional protocol Cage had devised from *I Ching,* or the *Book of Changes*, an ancient Chinese divinatory system. He converted this complex Taoist method into a procedure for generating incidental, mutually unrelated numbers, each of which, once randomly chanced upon, translates into a formal artistic property: tonality, silences, tempo, or duration in music; brush strokes, color, size, or arrangement of objects in etchings and drawings. In Cage's rendition, the *I Ching* frees the artist from making a choice about the artwork's final form—it makes that choice *for* him—and so turns the artwork into "a framework within which chance could operate."[27] The artist's role in the process is largely philosophical: he postulates the problem that the work of art works through.

To that effect, the second movement in Cage's *Lecture*, titled "The Lecture," is composed of a cacophonous auditory overlay of twelve voices reading simultaneously from Thoreau's works. The audience hears and sees only bits of already truncated texts and images, each member in the audience picking up a different fragment depending on where they sit in relation to any of the twelve vocalists and the projection screens.[28] The form or meaning (the "answer") of the artwork—Cage's as well as Thoreau's— is thus dissipated in the complex play of chance encounters between sound, image, ear, light, eye, voice, and text, its formal and semantic unity undermined by the noise that no longer constructs intelligible patterns. "The Lecture's" chance confluence of various media and its refusal to compartmentalize meaning into clearly audible paragraphs, sentences, or even whole words force the audience to abandon that "mysterious source of 'the right answers'"—namely, their own individual "egos," as Cage puts it in the "Preface," which inevitably determine, and so predicate, the meaning of the artwork. Cage's chance operations thus compel both the artist and the audience to muffle their egos' epistemological structure (the "mysterious source") which predicates its "taste and memory, its concerns for profit and power," to contingent influences from the outside world ("freeing his ego from taste and memory ... so that the rest of the world has a chance to enter into the ego's own experience"). With the surrender of the ego's source of knowledge, the audience's normal comprehension is thrown into disarray and prevented from being stabilized by formulaic, predicated, and predictable truth patterns.

The goal here is not confusion for confusion's sake but a possibility, if only for a moment, of what Cage credits Thoreau with providing us with— namely, "another opportunity for us." For what comes to replace this "mysterious source of the right answers" is not some other truth-structure but *an* answer ("a single one among a multiplicity of answers") which by virtue of its being multiple attunes the audience, Cage hopes, to foreign truths and unknown worlds: "We need communion with everyone," the *Lecture's* "Preface" concludes. "Struggles for power have nothing to do with communion. Communion extends beyond borders: it is with one's enemies also."[29] *Lecture on the Weather* urges us, as Thoreau does throughout his own work, to attune ourselves to another way of perceiving the world and its relations because truths, beliefs, bodies, and identities arise not from set patterns and forms that predicate them by way of a pre-arranged universality but like wild apples—from pomontological chance encounters.

11

"Wild Only Like Myself": Thoreau at Home with Plants

Mary Kuhn

Thoreau and the Botanical Marketplace

In his memorial to Thoreau, published in the *Atlantic Monthly* in 1862, Emerson characterizes his friend as "the attorney of the indigenous plants" who even preferred weeds to plants that had been imported.[1] Thoreau's passion for indigenous plants is visible across his lifetime, in the pages of his journal and in his late writings. Armed with his makeshift hat-qua-botany box, Thoreau would roam the Concord woods for hours a day, desiring to know the name and nature of every plant he encountered. He relished plants that grew tucked away in places that seemed to bear little trace of human cultivation, and he praised above all the profusion of wild plants that he observed anew daily on his walks.

Yet despite Emerson's assertion, Thoreau was also deeply knowledgeable about changes in the land due to plant imports, and across his life he participated in a robust conversation about the implications of global plant circulation. Plant introductions, both intentional and unintentional, impacted the way that nineteenth-century New Englanders understood their local environments, and particularly how they approached concepts like nativity, wildness, naturalization, and indigeneity—in the plant realm and beyond. For Emerson, the plants Thoreau studied in the woods around Walden were entirely set apart from the cultivated plants entering the ports at Salem and Boston. For Thoreau the division was not so neat. A burgeoning botanical marketplace was rapidly increasing biotic transfer across continents, and Thoreau recognized that these exchanges raised new questions about how plants and humans claimed land.

Thoreau and Emerson were part of a generation that experienced a massive influx of new plants into New England from abroad. With the eighteenth-century acceleration of imperial bioprospecting, government-sanctioned searches for new and valuable plants, plants moved around the world through human channels at a rate never before seen. Improvements in horticultural and steam technology and the rise of commercial nurseries suddenly put foreign plants within reach of many middle-class consumers. Nursery catalogues made reference to the provenance of new plants, from places as far away as Australia, and the market for "exotics" took off. On top of this, the political economy of valuable crops informed new state-sponsored exploratory missions, from the Lewis and Clark expedition that began in 1804 to the so-called opening of Japan in 1853. These expeditions introduced new species into American ports, and by the early nineteenth century the distinction between local and foreign plants was on the minds of many in the United States.

The government invested in importing new plant species and adopted measures to manage and regulate this influx. The patent office, for instance, distributed newly acquired seeds from abroad to farmers across the country.[2] And against a backdrop of deforestation, as Philip Pauly has illustrated, nineteenth-century horticulturalists envisioned ways to repopulate woodlands with species from abroad.[3] While some argued for restoration of "primitive" forests,[4] and others for tree plantings that were emblematically "American," a third school of thought took a decidedly cosmopolitan approach. They advocated for whatever trees could be successfully naturalized from other parts of the globe, granting nurserymen the power to choose what they considered the most valuable. The woods might be replenished through the deliberate planting of choice specimens from abroad. And it was not just forests. Cosmopolitanism also featured in the changing makeup of the midwestern prairie. As Courtney Fullilove has recently shown, Mennonite farmers who immigrated to Kansas and other Plains states played a key role in the introduction of Turkey Red wheat, one of the most important staple crops.[5] Shifts in regional biotic composition often accorded with larger human population movements.

These literal connections to human circulation as well as the economic stakes of the trade made questions of plant provenance and movement profoundly political in the mid-nineteenth century. Thoreau was among a number of authors who invoked botanical migration to address questions of human settlement. For Thoreau's contemporary Nathaniel Hawthorne, the idea of transplantation provided an appealing metaphor for domestic life. When Hawthorne famously characterized the ideal family genealogy as marked by mobility, he did so using plants. In the Custom House Preface to *The Scarlet Letter* the narrator wryly observes how "transplantation is perhaps better for the stock" of "my countrymen." Later he observes how "Human nature will not flourish, any more than a potato, if it be planted and replanted, for too long a series of generations, in the same worn-out soil. My children have had other birthplaces, and, so far as their fortunes may be within my control, shall strike their roots into unaccustomed earth."[6] Hawthorne, whose novels obsessively engage New England's violent history, wrote at length about the ways in which familial intransigence might poison the land for future generations. Unaccustomed earth for him disrupts such a lineage, providing an alternative to intergenerational stagnation.[7] Mobility destabilizes the familial transfer of property, even as it invites the possibility of new claims to land elsewhere.

Thoreau's relationship to cultivated plants was more ambivalent. He often and enthusiastically praised wild fruit and wild methods of propagation, and his botanizing was often associated—not least by Emerson—with his celebration of the native species growing in and around Concord. Thoreau was an advocate of the local and the experiential, and often dismissive of the commodified plant caught up in a web of commerce that reduces it to little more than the "mere bark and rind."[8] His late writings expound on the delights of uncultivated plants growing in out of the way places. But Thoreau's writing also registers the ways in which the idea of the local biota was already changing in light of the massive circulation of people and plants.

Thoreau's interest in plant movement through such human as well as natural channels shaped the way that he conceptualized wildness and what it means to be at home in Concord. Thoreau's keen empirical observations about what grew in Concord vex the clean partition between fruits of the Americas and foreign imports. The blurriness of this distinction is not just an environmental observation for Thoreau, given the close affinity he sees between humans and plants, but one with implications for how he understands human history. For all that he is suspect of strict property boundaries and legal land claims, Thoreau sees in plant migration a way to make a wild home in New England, a way to naturalize himself on this land.[9]

Circulation

Thoreau felt an intimate affinity for the plants he studied, born out of a meticulous empiricism that is by this point well established. Scholars such as Laura Dassow Walls, Cristin Ellis, Kristen Case, and Branka Arsić have shown how his material engagements with the natural world aligned with philosophical and cultural beliefs that were once considered separately.[10] Thoreau's empirical observation was inseparable from his understanding of human culture and human experience, and this entanglement is particularly evident in the ways that he thought about plant mobility.

Thoreau praised experiential knowledge of plants in part because of the close relationship he saw between plants and humans. Toward the end of his encyclopedic and unfinished manuscript *Wild Fruits*, Thoreau foregrounds direct observation over book learning about the vegetable kingdom: "So many plants, the indigenous and the bewildering variety of exotics, you see in conservatories and nurserymen's catalogues, or read of in English books, and the Royal Society did not make one of them, and knows no more about them than you!"[11] *Wild Fruits* also begins with a dismissal of imported fruit. By his own account, "Famous fruits imported from the East or South and sold in our markets—as oranges, lemons, pineapples, and bananas—do not concern me so much as many an unnoticed wild berry whose beauty annually lends a new charm to some wild walk or which I have found to be palatable to an outdoor taste." His problem with an imported West Indian orange or pineapple, in other words, is not its importation *per se*, but the way that an imported object has been stripped of all experiential context, leaving only the "very coarsest part of a fruit." In contrast, "our own [fruits], whatever they may be, are far more important to us than any others can be. They educate us and fit us to live here."[12]

The majority of Thoreau's statements on local flora can be characterized in this vein: there is a direct, material connection between the plants of a region and the people. In particular, Thoreau praises native plants' unique ability to spur the imagination and serve as the basis of good health. That is, the people and plants of a region closely identify with each other, and the health of the former depends upon a healthy and intimate knowledge of the latter. As Conevery Bolton Valencius notes, the idea of a "geography of health" pervaded early-nineteenth-century America, tied to a belief that the human body was intimately connected to the healthfulness of the surrounding environment.[13] Thoreau too considers how bodily health might be linked to environment in his understanding of plants as potent medicine. Local plants might cure local diseases. In May 1851 he writes in his journal that "it is an interesting inquiry to seek for the medicines which will cure our ails in the plants which grow around us. At first we are not disposed to believe that man and plants are so intimately related." The relation, he continues, is manifest in the "countryman's familiarity" with the otherwise obscure plants in his surroundings.[14] Of course, this possessive claim begs the question of what counts as "our own" fruits in this context, and the extent to which "our" is geographically, politically, or historically inflected.

For all that, Thoreau disdained commercial plants; he was interested instead in their histories, and especially how the wild became the sown. Thoreau's observations of commercial plants uncovered surprising genealogies of wild ancestors. His discussion of various common crops in *Wild Fruits* includes details about their provenance. The potato, for instance, was commonly assumed to have originated in North America when in fact it can be traced back to a wild ancestor in South America; Thoreau observes that Darwin found potatoes growing wild in the Chonos Archipelago.[15]

The pumpkin, likewise, is another staple crop with a commercial and political history that Thoreau finds worthy of recitation. In *Wild Fruits* his entry on pumpkins includes a brief description taken from the 1854 Patent Office Report, which corrects the widespread idea that pumpkins originated in Asia rather than in the Americas. In fact, the seeds that Thoreau grows himself in the spring of 1857 are themselves from the Patent Office, whose label identifies them as "*Potiron Jaune Grosse*." Thoreau proudly notes that six seeds of this variety produced 310 pounds of pumpkin, recording that "[t]hese talismen had perchance sprung from America at first and returned to it with unabated force."[16] This genealogy provides an American provenance for the crop, but however much the pumpkins might have been grown from wild seeds, Thoreau was familiar with the commercial and governmental aspects of how those seeds were circulated.

The introduction of new species—both intentional and accidental—corresponded with rapid industrial and urban development across the middle decades of the nineteenth century, and the increase in imported plants helped shape an idea of "wild" plants as contrasting with those in deliberately cultured contexts. In this respect, wild was associated closely with an idea of wilderness spaces set apart from human culture. Laura Dassow Walls has compellingly shown how Thoreau's understanding of "wildness"—"a quality, something ineffable and strange and raw at the heart of the most common experience"—relied in part on the contemporaneous emergence of the idea of "wilderness."[17] "Wildness," she notes, is a pluralistic idea that stresses democratic inclusion and the possibility of finding the wild anywhere. "Wilderness," in contrast, relies upon the idea of a dualistic separation between humans and nature; its power lay in its complete separation from human will, which allowed for it to serve as a means to spiritual transcendence. Thoreau both believed in the inherent wildness to be found anywhere and in the importance of wilderness spaces set apart from the realm of human affairs.[18]

The productive tension between wildness and wilderness also influenced how Thoreau reconciled wildness with home. Domesticity, as many have noted, has often been aligned with cultivation and defined against wilderness spaces. While wild/domestic often functioned for his contemporaries as a neat binary, the latter term, as Barbara Nelson has argued, is no more stable in Thoreau's work than the former.[19] The plants that Thoreau encountered in his hometown woods prompted reflection on the idea of local nature and what it might mean for a plant to be at home in a particular environment. For Thoreau—and perhaps for a number of his peers—domesticity and the home itself could take on a biotic sense.[20] Home was not always simply synonymous with human cultivation, but could serve as an environmental idea stressing proto-Darwinian migration, adaptation, and ecological fitness.

In short, plants could be perfectly at home in wilderness, and Thoreau found inspiration and vitality in the process of species that migrated of their own doing into new environments.

Thoreau's understanding of wild fruits reflects an appreciation of wildness that is at once independent of human value and integral to the Concord home. Take the huckleberry. "Are they not the principal wild fruit?" he asks in his journal. This question comes at the end of a long description of the fruit in which Thoreau suggests the huckleberry may be globally ubiquitous at the same time that it affords a connection to place. They are "food for the gods and for aboriginal men. They are so abundant that they concern our race much ... I cannot imagine any country without this kind of berry. Berry of berries. On which men live like birds. Still covering our hills as when the red men lived here."[21] The berry's endurance through what Thoreau believed to be the disappearance of Indigenous groups in the region signals their ability to thrive without human intervention. Yet the passage closes with an appreciation for the huckleberry's culinary pride of place, emphasizing the cultural significance of this wild fruit in a domestic context. He observes that "Huckleberry puddings and pies, and huckleberries and milk, are regular and important dishes."[22] The berry's wild abundance and longevity are what make it so central to the Euro-American kitchen, making the wild fruit significant in the domestic sphere.

Plant introductions could likewise blur the distinction between human purposiveness and a plant's own autonomy. In his journal for 1861, he comments that he knows "of one foreign species which introduced itself into Concord as [a] withe used to tie up a bundle of trees. A gardener stuck it in the ground, and it lived, and has its descendants." While the gardener plants the twig binding and assists it in taking root, Thoreau credits the "foreign species" with "introduc[ing] itself into Concord."[23] This transplantation subsequently proliferates, as the single twig produces multiple descendants.

In the middle decades of the nineteenth century, Thoreau was just one of many fascinated by plants that moved on their own. Articles propounded the circulatory reach and adaptability of plants. One from *Putnam's* in 1855 entitled "Nature in Motion" claims that "plants have ever travelled most and furthest of all children of this earth."[24] Naturalists were intrigued by the ways that plants used water, wind, and animals to disperse their seeds far and wide. Seeds might be propelled by a stream or ocean current, drift through the air, or get carried by a bird or animal miles—or thousands of miles—from their point of origin. Early in his journal Thoreau delights when "Nature condescends to make use of me without my knowledge, as when I help scatter her seeds in my walk, or carry burs and cockles on my clothes from field to field."[25] He praises weeds for their ambition to forge new homes for themselves.

Thoreau likewise thought deeply about the place of introduced species on Massachusetts' shoreline, engaging the language of cosmopolitanism to refer to plants that had migrated to the United States from other continents and adapted to this new environment. Jimsonweed (also known as Datura) growing on the eastern shore of Massachusetts prompts Thoreau to imagine its global ambitions:

> On the beach at Hull, and afterwards all along the shore to Plymouth, I saw the Datura ... I felt as if I was on the highway of the world, at sight of this cosmopolite and veteran traveler. It told of commerce and sailors' yarns without end. It grows luxuriantly in sand and gravel. This Captain Cook among plants, this Norseman or sea pirate, Viking or king of the bays, the beaches. It is not an innocent plant; it suggests commerce, with its attendant vices.[26]

The weed here, like an entrepreneurial captain, is an opportunist good at taking root and spreading in new environments.

At the same time, Thoreau is drawn to the plant precisely as a weed, for its behavior not as a captain but as a stowaway. Weeds, as Michael Pollan reminds us, are plants out of place, ones that have failed to fit within the parameters of human desire, acting of their own accord in propagating unexpectedly, taking stubborn root, or hitching a ride across great expanses of water or land unawares.[27] Emerson's eulogy elaborated on Thoreau's love of weeds, specifying that Thoreau praised their tenacity and vigor despite the hoeing of "a million farmers all spring and summer." According to Emerson, Thoreau spoke of the way "We have insulted [these weeds] with low names ... as Pigweed, Wormwood, Chickweed, Shad-Blossom" when "They have brave names, too,–Ambrosia, Stellaria, Amelanchia, Amaranth, etc."[28] Thus, Thoreau quotes an unnamed naturalist on the jimsonweed's ability to "emigrat[e] with great facility, ... often spring[ing] up in the ballast of ships, and in earth carried from one country to another." He adds the fact that "it secretes itself in the holds of vessels and migrates. It is a sort of cosmopolitan weed, a roving weed. What adventures! What historian knows when it first came into a country."[29] By the time Thoreau observes the weed growing along the Massachusetts shoreline, it has already robustly propagated itself in this new climate. But it did so at the expense of other plants, and so the adventures of weeds raised the more general questions of how certain plants managed to succeed others.

Naturalization and Succession

Thoreau's understanding of identity—personal, communal, and national—depends upon his understanding of the relationship between people and place. And plants served as a key proxy for the meaning of a place. If plants could migrate from a domestic setting into a wild one, or make themselves "at home" in the woods without human intervention, they might easily become naturalized. For Thoreau human affinity to these plants suggested that plants might serve as a model for humans, an idea that held significance for the way that he imagined European settlement as cultural succession.

Scholars over the years have persuasively illustrated that Thoreau's cultural, political, and environmental philosophies overlapped, and his understanding of plant transplantation and succession is no exception. As Lance Newman, James Finley, and others have argued, the environmental and the political were not separate realms in Thoreau's work, but subjects that dovetailed frequently in his writing. In terms of slavery, Finley argues, Thoreau worked toward "ecologically oriented social reform."[30] But if environmental observations provided a foundation for his anti-slavery writings and engagement with the Free Soil movement, Thoreau's ecological attitudes about transplantation and plant circulation illustrate a more disturbing position when it comes to the rights—and even the contemporaneous visibility—of Native Americans. In short, plant circulation could lead Thoreau toward an idea of human succession that naturalized colonization.

Thoreau's understanding of plant succession is probably most associated with the essays in which he took up the subject explicitly. Thoreau participated in the debate about seed dispersal, culminating in his well-known late essay "The Succession of Forest Trees" (1860) and the unpublished late manuscript *The Dispersion of Seeds*. Forest succession, Thoreau sought to show, occurred through the migration of seeds, which could largely be attributed to the wind, water, and animals that played a vital role in their distribution. Plants, for their part, displayed remarkable resilience and creativity in their means of dispersal. Nodding to the extensive role of the patent office in distributing seeds to American farmers, Thoreau imagines "a patent-office at the seat of government of the universe, whose managers are as much interested in the dispersion of seeds as anybody at Washington can be, and their operations are infinitely more extensive and regular."[31] To stress the regularity of nature's operations, Thoreau turns to the most bureaucratic and political of metaphors: the nation's capital. In one of his late journal entries, Thoreau conveys his fascination with the opportunistic nature of seeds, like all organisms, in "contending for the possession of the planet," noting that each "suggests an immense and wonderful greediness and tenacity of life."[32]

Near the end of *Wild Fruits* Thoreau reflects on the question of naturalization, and rather than continuing to draw a sharp line between indigenous and introduced plants, he celebrates plants that have adapted to new climates. "All [are] truly indigenous and wild on this earth," he notes.[33] Indigeneity takes on a planetary scale here, and is more a matter of mobility out of the garden or cultivated plot than a matter of origins or of being bound to one particular area on the globe.

This is nowhere more apparent than in his discussion of wild apples in *Wild Fruits*. After praising the indigenous crab apple, Thoreau turns to the cultivated apple that has spread beyond the confines of civilization and naturalized itself to the local environment. In a well-known passage he admits, "*Our* wild apple is wild only like myself, perchance, who belong not to the aboriginal race here, but have strayed into the woods from the cultivated stock."[34] This wild apple is not native to North America as the crab apple may be, but Thoreau celebrates it equally, if not more. He explains that while the crab apple is "indigenous, like the Indians, I doubt whether they are any hardier than those backwoodsmen among the apple trees, which, though descended from cultivated stocks, plant themselves in distant fields and forests, where the soil is favorable to them."[35] The apple that has strayed from the cultivated path is the celebrated fruit, the real focus of his admiration. Naturalization, on Thoreau's view, can be conceived as a process of finding a home in the wild. In a later entry on the European cranberry, he reflects that "I know of no mark that betrays an introduced plant, as none but the gardener can tell what flower has strayed from its parterre; but where the seed will germinate and the plant spring and grow, there it is at home."[36] An introduced plant can establish itself "at home" by straying from its parterre.

Home in this context for Thoreau is a process of habituation and adaptation, not a fixed coordinate. It admits colonization as a "natural" strategy. And it is expansive: anywhere on the globe where a plant might take root and establish itself constitutes it being at home. In this way, Thoreau champions not simply the indigenous plant but the naturalized plant as well, and because he sees such a close affinity between plants and people, this becomes a way to assert the process of human wilding—or rewilding, rather, after an experience of cultivation within society.

Thoreau's material identification with these fruits provides an organic logic for justifying his own naturalization and provides a way to claim a primary relationship to the land, one that evidently surpasses or supplants that of the Native American population. Scholars have been divided about Thoreau's view of Native peoples. Some point to his extensive writings on Native Americans and his Indian Books, an unpublished collection of excerpts and commentary on Native Americans that runs upward of 3,000 pages, as a sign of Thoreau's interest in and engagement with issues of Native sovereignty. Others, like Joshua Bellin, argue that his writings "reveal Thoreau to have been unable or unwilling to liberate himself from the dominant mid-century complex of beliefs concerning American Indians, their relationship to Euro-American civilization, and their ultimate fate."[37] Thoreau's temporal sense of human succession seems as matter of fact as his sense of forest succession. The language of naturalization provides him with an organic understanding of displacement. If plants colonize new soil, so too might Thoreau establish a wild home in New England.

At Home with Thoreau's Plants

Emerson's "attorney of indigenous plants" appears in a different light when we consider how the movement of plants in the nineteenth century was unsettling categories of place. Thoreau's botanic understanding of naturalization helps us see how the relationship between plants and indigeneity was not straightforward in the nineteenth century, and how thinking about plants in this context shaped his thinking about human culture.

During his eulogy Emerson also spoke to Thoreau's "fancy for referring everything to the meridian of Concord." Scholarship has largely followed suit, noting that while Thoreau might have been cosmopolitan in his reading, he was limited in his physical travel. Yet New England nature was not materially static in the mid-nineteenth century and Concord's biotic composition reflected broader patterns in circulation. The movement of plants, the rise of horticultural experiments, and increasing debates over the means of botanical dispersal all shaped Thoreau's understanding of the local environment. If Thoreau coordinates his observations through the local flora and fauna he regularly encounters, he acknowledges that what constitutes the local at any moment is a matter of historical processes, and that what it means to be at "home" in nature is a matter of adaptation and circulation. Concord was not a fixed coordinate against which global biotic change might be measured, but an environment that was in itself very much in flux.

Today home ranges for plants are again making the news as global weather dramatically reshapes growing climates, and Concord has again surfaced as a symbol of these changes. As fluctuating seasonal weather patterns and increased temperatures shift bioregions, plant species are migrating, adapting, or going extinct at an unprecedented rate. Because Thoreau kept meticulous records of plants encountered, leaf-out dates, daily temperatures, and ice-out dates on Walden Pond, his journal and unpublished Kalendar have been invaluable to contemporary scientists trying to illustrate the pervasive effects of climate change. Richard Primack, an evolutionary biologist at Boston University, used Thoreau's journals as a benchmark for studying the contemporary climate at Walden Pond. Primack's study, which he described in his 2014 book *Walden Warming*, partially involved looking in present-day Concord for plants that Thoreau recorded, and noting the differences between their bloom-out dates in the nineteenth- and twenty-first centuries.[38] The Thoreau who emerges in his work is a dedicated patron of local flora and a quintessentially New England figure whose temporary home on Walden's shore has become an American cultural icon. Primack believes this facet of Thoreau's legacy could help Americans pay attention to the realities of climate change.[39]

Indeed Primack's own project is shaped by a sense of the importance of the concept of home—both personal and national. Primack spent most of his career studying the rainforest in Borneo, but decided to pursue work in Massachusetts because in order to shape environmental policy in the United States, he felt he needed evidence collected within the nation: "People might not know or care much about proboscis monkeys and pitcher plants on the other side of the world, but they would not be able to ignore the evidence from places closer to home and species they know and care about." On this view, care correlates with cultural and geographic proximity. For the audience Primack hopes to reach, it is a question of what is happening in "our own backyard."[40] Primack returns to Concord in frustration at a parochial American politics that cares only about the nature it literally claims to possess—one vision of a backyard. But Thoreau understood that plants make and move their homes around the globe, and that the backyard humanity should care for is equally global in scope.

12

Plant Life and Poetics of Transtemporality

Gillian Osborne

In the spring and summer of 1836, teenager Fanny Elizabeth Appleton journeyed from Massachusetts to Europe. On the other side of the Atlantic, she traveled widely, hitting up literary landmarks along the way: from the tombs of poets (Virgil) and the imagined resting places of their creations (Petrarch's Laura and Shakespeare's Juliet), to the residences of Romantic authors (the villas of Madame de Stael and Byron in Switzerland), to sites synonymous with Romantic poems (Burns's Aberfeldy waterfalls and Wordsworth's Tintern Abbey). At every site, she gathered a plant: a vine, a leaf, a flower.[1]

Appleton was not unusual among nineteenth-century travelers in her collection of plants, either gathered in language or dried and pressed for an herbarium, as a means of literary tourism. In his journal of just a few years later, Ralph Waldo Emerson documented plants he encountered while loping about England, setting these in relation to species he had observed around Concord and Cambridge.[2] Two decades later, the central Massachusetts poet Frederick Goddard Tuckerman made two European tours similar to Appleton's, collecting flowers from locations of literary importance in Scotland and England during a summer visit in 1851, with additional specimen gathered in Switzerland and Italy during a later European tour in 1854–55: mallow from Stratford on Avon; *Epilobium* from "The Cataract of Lodore," a waterfall made memorable by Southey in an exhaustingly sonic poem whose gerunds mimic the craggy cascading of water. On his second European trip, Tuckerman plucked flowers from the Italian graves of Shelley and Keats.[3]

For these voyagers, gathering plants from the location of a famous author's home or final resting place, or from some other location where literature was believed to *have happened* was a means of connecting materially with the past, not unlike gathering rocks from the Parthenon or Coliseum. The difference, however, was that plants, unlike stones, are alive; as biological entities, participants in life at both an individual and species level, plants intersect materially with human history in ways that are different from the deep geologies of stone. Furthermore, in the examples I consider here, a poem, or a poet, rather than an entire civilization, or epoch in history, provides the primary impetus for a visitation to a place, a ghostly closeness to the past facilitated through the particular trans-temporal nature of slowly evolving living things. To touch a daffodil in Windermere is to connect, materially, to daffodils Wordsworth saw while wandering lonely as a cloud.[4] So, for poetic-botanical tourists like Appleton and Tuckerman, attending to poetry and plants as co-referents for one another was a means of entering into an ongoing life of poetry. Unsurprisingly, then, neither of these travelers limited their attentions solely to poets of the past. On that same trip where she communed with the seductive ghost of Byron through a flower, Fanny Appleton also met her future husband, the poet Henry Wadsworth Longfellow. And on the same trip during which he visited with a long-gone Shakespeare through the open visage of a mallow, Tuckerman exchanged poems with Alfred Tennyson, then at the beginning of his tenure as England's poet laureate.

In seeking to connect with poetry as a living archive, different plants, with their variant characteristics, and especially the different scale of their lifespans, offer alternate experiences. While many of the plants gathered by Appleton and Tuckerman, or transcribed to lists by Emerson, are ephemeral—flowers that arrive and recede within a season—other plants persist longer as individuals, presenting occasions to commune not only with the life of a species, or a particular cultivar, but with a single living being whose experience of time extends beyond the limit of any human life. In Cambridge, England, for example, Tuckerman pressed two leaves, labeling them through their relation to literature: "Milton's Mulberry," a tree said to have been planted in 1608, the year that Milton was born, and that still grows in the Fellows Garden at Christ's College today. The leaves take up the upper half of one page of Tuckerman's collection, their ragged heart-shaped edges gently askew. Later, he gathered a sprig from the grove of yews at Borrowdale, which Wordsworth had described in a poem. On one side of the evergreen spray, Tuckerman copies parts of Wordsworth's poem from memory, with accordant aberrations in lineation, wording, and even a missing line. On the other side he parenthetically notes: "(The tree from which this spray was broken is said to be more than a thousand years old)."[5]

Wordsworth died four years before Tuckerman's visit to the trees he had commemorated in a poem. Both poets are drawn to the yews by the

material portal they provide into a thickening human past. In the opening
lines of his poem, in a segment earlier than the one cited by Tuckerman,
Wordsworth describes the trees persisting through particular battles of the
Norman invasion. In a journal, he speculates that one of the trees may be
"as old as the Christian era" and relates how a local guide "used gravely to
tell strangers that there could be no doubt of its having been in existence
before the flood."[6] Part of Wordsworth's project was uncovering human
history intertwined with natural history, through a poetic excavation of
the region in which he lived. But the way Wordsworth gets at that history,
through trees, and through a poem, is not a straightforward account. In the
passage of the poem copied by Tuckerman into his herbarium, Wordsworth
combines accurate description ("each particular trunk a growth / Of
intertwisted fibres serpentine" and hard but fragrant "unrejoicing berries,"
all above a "grassless floor of red brown hue" that the "sheddings from the
pining umbrage tinged / Perennially"), with "fantasy" of "ghostly shapes"
and allegory: the grove a spot where "Fear and Trembling Hope, / And
Death the Skeleton, and Time the Shadow" mingle amid the yew's spooky
shade. The natural world is already a haunted place for Wordsworth, and by
the time Tuckerman visits Borrowdale, an earlier poet's lines rattling around
in his memory, that haunting is compounded: a pilgrimage toward the
entanglements of human, literary, and environmental history. Wordsworth
revered how trees growing close to his home indexed an earlier human era;
but Tuckerman has crossed an ocean and traveled to this particular enclave
of ancient arboreal limbs to commune with a poet through the living record
of vegetal life forms that inspired a particular poem.

Relying on plants as a connection to a poem, or a poet, wasn't only
something nineteenth-century Americans did when visiting Europe.
Similarly, talismanic exchanges took place on this side of the Atlantic as well.
Tuckerman kept a more explicitly scientific herbarium of plants gathered in
the vicinity of his home in Greenfield, Massachusetts in the 1850s. And while
many of these pages stick to the standard protocol of identifying species
by Latin nomenclature, along with the time and location of their sighting,
Tuckerman occasionally embellishes his herbarium with descriptive notes,
or poems. Of *Epigenea repens*, or mayflowers, one of the earliest spring
flowers in Massachusetts, a pale white-pink flower with a low-lying leaf
that nestles in the snow, celebrated by poets from Whittier to Dickinson,
Tuckerman notes: "Flowers sometimes as large as an English sovereign: with
pale green red-ribbed leaves." Elsewhere, besides a specimen of *Agrimonia
euratoria*, he pens two lines from a poem, this time Emerson's "Humblebee":
"Columbine with horn of honey, / Scented fern and agrimony."[7] Meanwhile,
Fanny Appleton's eventual husband, Longfellow, received a variety of plant
specimens in the 1870s and 1880s from his readers: moss gathered from
a waterfall in Minnesota named for Minnehaha, Hiawatha's love interest
in Longfellow's long poem; chestnuts gathered from a tree Longfellow

described in "The Village Blacksmith," and even a chair (paid for by local Cambridge school children and families) made from the same tree.[8]

What do these examples have in common? In addition to quaint testament to a seemingly more botanically, and poetically, enthused material culture of the past, they evince a series of implicit claims about what such writers, readers, and visitors to places defined by poems believed poetry *to be*. Those claims were:

1. Poetry has a context that is not confined to the space of the poem.

2. Poetry responds to materials and has an afterlife that is accessible to readers: not only intellectually, aesthetically, or emotionally, but also *materially*.

3. Because of its material pre- and after-lives, poetry is *trans-temporal* rather than *historical*. It seeds itself through time.

4. In its unique relationship to place and time, poetry is plant-like; therefore, understanding what a plant is, in material terms, and how plant lives intersect with human lives, gives insight into how poetry persists through time.

While these claims are implicit in the nineteenth-century examples I provided above, similar claims have been made more directly by poets of the twentieth and twenty-first-centuries. Consider, for example, this prompt and resulting poem composed by C. A. Conrad, a gender-queer poet presently living in Philadelphia. Conrad is well known in contemporary poetry circles for the "(soma)tic rituals" they have devised to precede and activate the production of poems. Conrad explains that the term "(soma)tic" draws together an Indo-Persian word for the spirit and the Greek word for the body. The poet has been quite explicit about the first claim above: "Every poem written is filtered through the circumstances of the poet, through the diet of the poet," they have written; a poem is found through the process of "FIND[ing a] BODY to FIND [a] PLANET," and both poem and poet are "an extension" of that place-finding: "garbage, shit, pesticides, bombed and smoldering cities, microchips, cyber, astral and biological pollution, BUT ALSO the beauty of a patch of unspoiled sand, all that croaks from the mud, talons on the cliff." Just as all plants, not only ones strapped to vineyard trellises, incorporate the "terroir" of a region, so a poem is a living record of the circumstances that nurtured it. Reading poems, like drinking wine, is a way for a reader to connect with another time and place through the transmigrations of language/vines.

In the first (soma)tic prompt in Conrad's 2012 collection *A Beautiful Marsupial Afternoon*, for example, the author invites a reader to "[v]isit the home of a deceased poet you admire and bring some natural thing back with you." For Conrad, that poet is Emily Dickinson, and the "natural thing" they gather is "dirt from the foot of huge trees in the backyard," trees which elsewhere Conrad describes as "very large, very old" and "alive when Dickinson was alive" so that "she touched them, leaned on them, was part of their lives and they were part of Her life." After returning home, Conrad waits three days, then completes the ritual like this:

> I didn't shower for three days, then rubbed Emily's dirt all over my body, kneaded her rich Massachusetts soil deeply into my flesh, then put on my clothes and went out into the world. Every once in a while I stuck my nose inside the neck of my shirt to inhale her delicious, sweet earth covering me. I felt revirginized through the ceremony of my senses, I could feel her power tell me these are the ways to walk and speak and shift each glance into total concentration for maximum usage of our little allotment of time on a planet.

In the poem resulting from this procedure, "Emily Dickinson Came to Earth and Then She Left," Conrad visits with this long-dead poet through a torrent of steeply enjambed, syntactically multivalent phrases. Both poets occupy the "fun" and present pleasure of a "sweaty party dress" or a too-brief "tomato" season, set within a longer history of the Earth, in which "dinosaurs ruled Massachu- / setts," Homo sapiens are "winning" and "not needing / to dream is like not needing to see the world / awaken to itself indestructible epiphanies / consume the path." The indestructibly epiphanic roiling against a deep ecological history that humans are only a small, though spectacularly destructive footnote to, is at the heart of Conrad's poetics. (In another ongoing project, the poet lies down in different locations and feels the vibrations of all extinct species who used to occupy the same location.)

Reflecting on the constraints of this particular ritual, Conrad notes that it arose from a disagreement about what constitutes the life of a plant. Responding to a man claiming "No one's alive now who knew Dickinson," Conrad retorts: "'That's not TRUE, there are those ENORMOUS trees in the backyard!' He said, 'You know I mean PEOPLE!' AND I SAID, 'YOU KNOW I ALSO mean PEOPLE!'"[9] Like Conrad, Dickinson routinely referred to plants as people.[10] By expanding the typical definition of "people," both poets assert that the essential definition of a person may not have anything to do with all those features we routinely ascribe to humans; rather, what binds Dickinson and the oaks, or the towering blue spruce that still makes a "Sea— with a Stem" outside her window, is that each occupied a place, and time, as living things, whose timescales intersect without being fully commensurate.[11] The trees that knew Emily Dickinson, and that she knew, outlive her, just as her poems have done and will continue to do long after those trees have receded, like the poet, into "Grass — / Whom none but Daisies, know."[12]

In what follows, I will focus on the theory, writing, aesthetic practice, and legacy of a contemporary of Dickinson's. Henry David Thoreau remains one of the most important theorists of what I will call, "poetry in the common sense": a poetics defined by the claims outlined in this introduction. More than any other writer I know, Thoreau illuminates the material intersections of plants and people, the complicated trans-temporality of these exchanges, and how such encounters are mediated by an expansive, and yet infinitely available, conception of poetry. Following Branka Arsić, and her notion of "affirmative reading," I take Thoreau's claims about what poetry is literally, rather than metaphorically.[13] Reading him in this way, as a theorist as well as a practitioner of poetry, sheds light on the long cast of Thoreau's influence, both overt and covert on contemporary eco-poets writing today, which in turn reinforces his understanding of poems as deep-rooted, self-seeding, things.

So, what was poetry to Thoreau? Thoreau variously describes himself, Concord, and a season, as a "poem."[14] In suggesting that poetry is so capacious that it can encompass the entirety of a self or place, or all the material transmigrations of spring-time, Thoreau asserts that poetry is like living: buffered by the cyclical refrains of seasonal time, dependent upon particular geographies, and as undocumentable as any single human life. As such, poetry demands everything of a would-be poet—"Whatever things I perceive with my entire man—those let me record—and it will be poetry," Thoreau writes in his journal[15]—and is characterized by the inevitable let-down of all impossible tasks:

My life has been the poem I would have writ,
But I could not both live and utter it.[16]

This couplet is from Thoreau's first published book, *A Week on the Concord and Merrimack Rivers* (1849); the sentiments succinctly framed in these two lines—and more extensively throughout that volume, which, in addition to being a travel record, and an elegy for his brother John, includes Thoreau's fullest development of his poetic theory—are echoed by other American writers of the same period. But Thoreau's claims for the material and experiential foundations of poetry in particular are consistently more radical than those of his contemporaries.

"The true poem is not that which the public read," Thoreau writes on the same page of *A Week* in which this couplet appears. "There is always a poem not printed on paper, coincident with the production of this, stereotyped in the poet's life." A poem "is what he has become through his work."[17] In his novel *Pierre*, published three years later, Herman Melville riffs: "Two books are being writ; of which the world shall only see one, and that the bungled one. The larger book, and the infinitely better, is for Pierre's own private self. That it is, whose unfathomable cravings drink his blood; the other only demands his ink."[18] In Melville's version of this claim—that literature and life feed on one another—there is no outside to authorship. Whether in blood or ink, what defines Pierre is the fact that he is writing. But Thoreau's claim goes further, and is more specifically indexed to poetry: printed literature is not only in service to, and therefore a dull excrement in comparison with, the rabid imaginations of a writer; but poetry is still *happening*, even when nothing gets copied down at all.

"My life has been the poem I would have writ, / But I could not both live and utter it." The couplet is deceptively simple, vexed by the conflicting tenses of its verbs. The verbs Thoreau chooses here are those of being—"has been," "would have," and "could not ... live"—and two verbs about the uses of language, writing and speaking, that clang against one another at the lines' ends: "writ" and "utter it." Living extends from the past into the present; speaking has been ongoing; the only action that has not already happened is writing, cast off into a speculative subjunctive. Furthermore, while at first it may seem that what Thoreau is claiming is non-equivalence between life and poetry, he is actually claiming life *for* poetry, if not for language. In the regular iambic pentameter of the couplet, two words—"poem" and "live"— receive a special and corresponding emphasis as the third stressed syllable in each line, a lynch-pin of equivalence meditating between the beginning and end of each line, and between the two lines. Writing may be an unachievable outlier. But life has already *been* an untranslatable poem. Although in *A Week* he equates poetry with a life, the full extent of what a poem might involve is a topic he continues to revisit. "How to make the getting of our living poetic—!" Thoreau writes a few years later in his journal.[19]

Later in the same year as that journal entry, Thoreau looked back on his efforts in *A Week* and identified a particular quality of that book. At the end of June 1851, wedged between records of flowering plants (dogwood, potatoes) that began to more regularly infuse his journal entries at the beginning of that decade, he notes: "I thought that one peculiarity of my 'Week' was its *hypaethral* character." It is, he elaborates before the blossoming potatoes, an "unroofed book—lying open under the *ether*–& permeated by it. Open to all weathers—not easy to be kept on a shelf."[20] Here we see Thoreau extending his conception of a poem—as rooted in place, as subject to seasons—to a book that combined poetry and prose. A poem is a permeable, open thing. Thoreau enacts this stance in several of the lineated poems in *A Week*, including one beginning "My books I'd fain cast off, I cannot read, / 'Twixt every page my thoughts go stray at large / Down in the meadow, where is richer feed." While in the couplet we just considered, Thoreau claims the impossibility of writing poetry down, since poetry is too entirely taken up with life, here he claims a largeness for literacy that makes the idea that reading might require a book seem paltry. Although the book is open, the reader's thoughts don't belong to it; scampering toward the meadow, they fix together words and a material world the reader is eager to discover, and be nourished by, through a conception of reading as environmentally grounded. By the poem's end, the speaker *seems* to have fully eluded the constraints of language—"A clover tuft is pillow for my

head," he writes, "And violets quite overtop my shoes." But though there
is no sign of a book here, there is, of course, the book *we* are reading, the
poem that shapes Thoreau's, and our, ideas about how a poem might be
something more than lines on a page.[21] Expressing a similar sentiment—
also in verse—Emily Dickinson claimed a comparable openness, seasonality,
and irresolvable interpenetration between the material and the linguistically
fleeting: "To see the summers sky / Is poetry," Dickinson writes, "though
never in a book it lie / True poems flee."[22]

A poem for Thoreau was the living, rather than the record, of a life; and
even when a poem was written down, a book, at its best, remained open
to the material conditions supporting its production and reception. Despite
Thoreau's repeated claims for the interpenetration of poetry and materials,
this can begin to sound like heady, abstract stuff. But Thoreau claimed that
poetry was in fact the commonest of practices. In this, his ideas again echo
those of his contemporaries. Four decades later, looking back on his career,
Walt Whitman summarized the purpose of poetry in similar terms: "to give
ultimate vivification to facts, to science, and to common lives."[23] But Thoreau's
take on the commonness of poetry has more to do with materials. "It is the
simplest relation of phenomena, and describes the commonest sensations,"
Thoreau defines poetry in *A Week*. Writing against Wordsworth's Romantic
vision of poetry as the "overflow of powerful feelings," or the triumphal
power play of Shelley's "poetry in the general sense," Thoreau calls poetry
"not the overflowing of life but of its subsidence rather ... drawn from under
the feet of the poet."[24] To find poetry, we needn't look into ourselves, or project
our imagination upon what is; we need only "open our Narrow Hands," as
Dickinson does elsewhere, "to gather" what already exists. "A true account
of the actual is the rarest poetry," Thoreau again writes in *A Week*.[25] Poetry's
job, he asserts, isn't only to respond to or document common life. Poetry *is*
that underlying commonness undergirding life.

Thoreau's understanding of poetry in these terms was thus inextricable
from his growing attention to plants. Well-known descriptions of intellectual
and literary growth as vegetal in *Walden*—"I grew like corn in the night"—
are best understood in relation to his earlier work in *A Week*, written as
Thoreau was actively shifting his attention from one conception of poetry to
another.[26] In the decade between his graduation from Harvard in 1837 and
his publication of *A Week*, Thoreau felt his way toward this new poetics—
first the study and then the practice of it. In the late fall of 1841 into early
1842, he undertook a systematic study of English and Scottish verse—
from Chaucer and the ballads of Robin Hood to anthologies covering the
Metaphysical poets and the Romantics. In the midst of that study, he began
to draft what would become his first published essay, "On the Natural
History of Massachusetts," printed in *The Dial* in the summer of 1842, an
essay that seems to tack decidedly toward science, beginning by reading
John James Audubon and proceeding to review a collection of volumes

providing the first systematic overview of the natural resources of the state, overseen by the geologist Edward Hitchcock.[27] But the move from studying anthologies of verse to studying natural history evidenced in Thoreau's reading and writing during this period can also be understood as a shift closer to a theorization of poetry in the common sense that Thoreau would carry onward into his future work.

Writing in his journal that November, Thoreau compares "the commonest nature" visible "from the library window," to the "dry and dusty volumes" of poetry gathered in "one alcove" within, bemoaning the futility of his task: "Poetry cannot breath in the scholar's atmosphere," he writes. Berating himself for taking the trouble of coming to Cambridge "after poetry," he concludes: "I think it would not be a shorter way to a complete volume—to step at once into the field or wood." Developing his idea further, Thoreau continues to formulate his vision of poetry as the commonest of phenomena: "Good poetry seems so simple and natural a thing, that when we meet it we wonder that all men are not always poets," and continues a few lines down "The best lines perhaps only suggest to me that that man simply saw or heard or felt, what seems the commonest fact in my experience." Between these two claims, Thoreau responds to Shelley's terminology of "poetry in the general sense" and poets as the "unacknowledged legislators of the world." Introducing a crucial framework of "nature" into these formulations, Thoreau revises: "The speech of the poet goes to the heart of things—yet he is that one especially who speaks civilly to nature as a second person—and in some sense is the patron of the world. Though more than any he stands in the midst of nature—yet more than any he can stand aloof from her." Waffling between comparative conjunctions, this passage in Thoreau's journal is evidence of a definition of a poet's labor as embedded in the processes of the natural world. Shelley's world is human and political, and Thoreau's is also these; but Thoreau understands human politics and poetry as foundationally material, embedded in nature. The awkwardness of syntax in this journal entry reveals how he is still thinking his way toward this belief: of a poet as both nature's observer, and of nature.[28]

By the time he writes *A Week*, and in the years following, Thoreau begins to resolve this conundrum by turning increasingly toward plant-life as a framework. Poetry, he theorizes in *A Week*, "is a natural fruit. As naturally as the oak bears an acorn, and the vine a gourd, man bears a poem, either spoken or done." As with the couplet considered above, a poem is not a written thing: it is voiced, and acted, rather than recorded. Because poetry vegetates, it is a symptom of health, which Thoreau understands as receptivity to material impulse. A poet "needs such stimulus to sing only as plants to put forth leaves and blossoms," he writes, and a poet "should be as vigorous as a sugar maple, with sap enough to maintain his own verdure, beside what runs into the troughs." Like a fat plum, a "poem is one undivided unimpeded expression fallen ripe into literature," he concludes.[29]

Thoreau's affiliation of poetry and plant-life was not new—the sixteenth-century slippage of "poesy" as both an imaginative collection of words and a bouquet illustrates this long-standing allegiance nicely—and the rise of popular botany during the Romantic period reimagined poetry's vegetative qualities in increasingly material terms. Erasmus Darwin's *Botanic Garden* (1791), for example, mingled cutting-edge discoveries of plant sexual anatomy, heroic neoclassical verse, and footnoted confessional asides. In his "Preface to Shakespeare" of 1765, Samuel Johnson had framed the poet's work as "a forest" of "oaks" and "pines," in which "weeds and branches ... sometimes giv[e] shelter to myrtles and to roses." And in his lectures on Shakespeare in 1811–19, Samuel Taylor Coleridge pushed the analogy further, claiming that "meter, and measured sounds" themselves are like "a fellow-growth ... even as the bark is to the tree." Perhaps the most suggestive example of what M. H. Abrams called the valuation of a "vegetable genius" in this period is in John Keats's letter of 1818, in which the poet announced: "If Poetry comes not as naturally as the Leaves to a tree it had better not come at all."[30]

Thoreau's claims for poetry as plant-like often sound like Coleridge or Keats. But Thoreau differs from these Romantic predecessors in his acute attention to the material particulars of plant anatomy. In Keats's memorable quip, a leaf stands in—much as the leaf in Goethe's studies of plant physiology does—for vegetative behavior in general. But in Thoreau's formulations, different aspects of plant composition—not only fruits and flowers, but also the particular functions of leaves, and especially the fixity of roots and the potential of seeds—deepen the affiliation between poetry and plants, incorporating features that extend beyond the vegetative inspiration of an author or the ornamental flourishes of any aesthetic object. In the passages from *A Week* cited above, Thoreau's imagery is mainly of fruiting; elsewhere he distinguishes between the "flowers" and the "leaves of thought," and though he worries that "most of our thoughts are merely leaves," he couches his complaint in a key feature of leaf structure. Thoreau wonders how to make language "vascular," so that the writer becomes a conduit of his environment, not only translating materials into words, but becoming continuous with them.[31]

In books of plant physiology owned by Thoreau, such as Loring Dudley Chapin's *Vegetable Kingdom* (1843), William Carpenter's *Vegetable Physiology and Systematic Botany* (1858), or Harland Coultas's *What Can Be Learned from a Tree* (1860), there are descriptions of plants as made of the same stuff as the inorganic matter they ingest, so that "there is no element entering into the composition of organized bodies, which is not also found in the world around," as Carpenter writes. While this is true in some sense of all biological life, this translation of surrounding material conditions into new matter is especially pronounced in plants, whose metabolic organs are found along their edges. Carpenter describes the "lungs" of a plant as the stoma on the bottoms of leaves; they absorb nutrients directly through chlorophyll-filled epidermal cells and roots.[32] Coultas calls leaves and roots "absorbents beautifully adapted to the media in which they develop." Shifting circumstances leave "an indelible impression in the solid parts of its fabric. All the bright and stormy days of its life, every wind that has shaken its foliage, and every rain-drop that has wetted its roots, have helped to mould its physical organization." This receptivity makes plant bodies "easily impressible."[33] As living records of atmospheric, seasonal, or other circumstantial occasions, plants record the effects of climate change in the differences of bloom times between Thoreau's time and our own, and recall Conrad's contemporary observation that a poem, like a plant, "is filtered through the circumstances of the poet."[34] Thoreau's version is in the same journal passage in which he wonders how to make "speech" "vascular": "a man writing is the scribe of all nature, he is the corn & the grass & the atmosphere writing."[35] He writes, in other words, as a plant vegetates and breathes.

The receptivity of plants and the simplicity of their needs—soil, light, moisture, air—makes them more contiguous with their environment than animals are. "This mass of vegetable matter is only earth and air which has undergone transmutation!" Coultas exclaims. "The material alike of wandering zephyrs and rushing storms, of gently descending night-dews and angry thunder-showers, has been *here, on this spot*, metamorphosed!"[36] Coultas's emphasis of "*here*," "*on this spot*," draws attention to another defining feature of plants that was especially important to Thoreau: their roots.

In "Walking," Thoreau expands his terminology of flowering and fruiting—of a poet "whose words were so true and fresh and natural that they would appear to expand like the buds at the approach of spring, though they lay half-smothered between two musty leaves in a library,—ay, to bloom and bear fruit there"—to the centrality of roots. Thoreau imagines a poet that might "transplant [words] to his page with earth adhering to their roots."[37] Not coincidentally, Thomas Wentworth Higginson, an avid admirer of Thoreau, drew from just this terminology when introducing Emily Dickinson to the world in the first edition of her poems which he edited almost a half-century later: "In many cases these verses will seem to the reader like poetry torn up by the roots, with rain and dew and earth still clinging to them," Higginson wrote, claiming Dickinson as the poet of materials theorized by Thoreau.[38] Thoreau's interest in the rootedness of plants sheds light on his monumental efforts to document the particular biological phenomena of his home, as well as his understanding of such efforts as poetry. If a poem is a rooted thing, particular to its place, than Concord—and every other location where humans affix themselves—is also a poem.

Thoreau was equally drawn to the pent-up potential of seeds. In his journal in the winter of 1850, he described the feeling of "seeds beginning to expand in me, which propitious circumstance may bring to the light &

to perfection."[39] In a long journal passage the following spring, taking notes on Asa Gray's *Manual of Botany*, Thoreau knits back and forth between leaves, roots, and seeds, tracing the analogy that each suggests to human intellectual growth. Of seeds, he addresses the potential of intellectual expansion as "slumbering coiled up—packed away in the seed—unfolded (consider the still pale-rudimentary infantine radicle-like thoughts of some students, which who knows what they might expand to if they should ever come to the light & air.—if they do not become rancid & perish in the seed)." He concludes this meditation with an observation about a seed's possible persistence through time: "It is not every seed that will survive a thousand years."[40]

Although he expresses the idea negatively here, his observation clarifies how the potential Thoreau valued in seeds was not only in their ability to germinate, producing leaves, flowers, fruits, or sending down a tap-root affixing these to the nourishments of a particular location—but also a seed's ability to out-wait human time-scales, to lie in darkness in the tombs of the pyramids of Giza (as Melville also meditates on in a letter to Nathaniel Hawthorne), or to erupt in a swath of brilliant, wild poppy red amid the rubble of a bombed-out city (which happened in London after the blitz).[41]

Later in his journal, Thoreau connects the temporal potentials of seeds more overtly to poetry: "Facts collected by a poet are set down at last as winged seeds of truth—samarae," like the whirly-gigs of maple seeds that make such excellent nose adornments if you are a child. "O may my words be verdurous & sempiternal as the hills!" Thoreau continues, concluding: "Facts fall from the poetic observer as ripe seeds."[42] Seeds are both gathered and reseeded, and between those two actions are language and the particular timescales of geography: perennially green in the appropriate season, and everlasting (or at least as old as the geologic timescale of a hill). In 1851, theorizing the timescales of poetry—and its resemblance to the seed qualities in particular—Thoreau distinguishes between the scientific efforts of "close observation" in figures like "Humboldt" or "Darwin" and "Poetry" which "puts an interval between the impression & the expression—waits till the seed germinates naturally."[43] Seeds are both remarkable for their long duration, and for their gradual intervals: expose them to light and water and it will still be some time before they begin to unfurl in green. In both instances of these seemingly incommensurate timescales of a seed, Thoreau fixates on the gaps and silences that become inherent to germination. A seed is also a record of all the intervening time in which it did not begin to grow. A scientist is bent on translating observations into findings. But a poet does the same common thing, over and over again, across time. "The science of Humboldt is one thing," Thoreau writes in "Walking," "poetry is another thing. The poet to-day, notwithstanding all the discoveries of science, and the accumulated learning of mankind, enjoys no advantage over Homer."[44]

Thoreau develops a theory of poetry as plant-like across a *Week* in both the prose and the verse of that volume. The timeliness of plants, and of poetry, Thoreau suggests, is both outwardly and internally determined: responsive to seasons, but unfolding according to species-specific dictates as well: the particular requirements of a root and a seed. Situating the present in direct relation to "three thousand years ago" in one poem, Thoreau points to plants—"Behold these flowers"—and frames his theory in lines of verse: "Where is the spirit of that time but in / This present day, perchance this present line?"[45] Plants, and poems, carry history, and timescales alternate to those of humans—in their very bodies, so that "[n]one can say deliberately that he inhabits the same sphere, or is contemporary with, the flower which his hands have plucked," Thoreau writes. Although "his feet may seem to crush" a plant, in fact "inconceivable spaces and ages separate them, and perchance there is no danger that he will hurt it."[46] The relationship between humans and plants, then—a relationship of need, of admiration, and of possible damage—is intensified by the temporal disconnect between the times of plants and the time of humans. Thoreau's work helps us to see how plant-time is also the time of a poem.

In addition to his many contributions to ecological thinking and writing outside of poetic theory, it is hardly surprising that, given these insights, Thoreau remains such an important figure for contemporary ecopoets. For the remainder of this essay, I want to consider some examples from a writer whose work exemplifies—directly and indirectly—Thoreau's plant-oriented poetry in the common sense introduced above.

Earlier, I referred to the work of C. A. Conrad, whose (soma)tic poetry is explicitly targeted at engaging "the everyday," uncovering a contemporary poetry in a common sense. Conrad is fond of quoting Alice Notley who in her poem "C. '81" from the *Mysteries of Small Houses* writes: "Poetry's so common hardly anyone can find it," a sentiment that mirrors many of Thoreau's observations I cited earlier.[47] Now I'll turn to the "plein aire poetics" of Brian Teare, a poet whose work is intensely, though not always overtly, comparable to Thoreau's beliefs about the context, practice, trans-temporality—and vegetal nature—of poetry that I've just explored. In a recent essay about the balance of theory and praxis informing his work, Teare is explicitly ecological about his methods: the "informed fieldwork" he undertakes through multiple walks, and study of, a particular location as part of plein-aire poetics, "allows the poem to register the intertwining of ecosystems and anthropogenic change at a local level, a small-scale instance of the catastrophic intertwining ... at the biospheric level."[48] The attention to harm may seem distinctive to our contemporary setting; but it is a sentiment also characteristic of Thoreau, who recorded fluctuations, and even extinctions, within his local environs, and who scoured the landscape, and archives, for records of natural and human history—particularly of the indigenous peoples of the north-eastern lands of North America.[49]

For both Conrad and Teare, the clearest legacy of Thoreau's influence is on the value each poet attributes to walking. Before developing his (soma)tic rituals, Conrad co-composed a book with poet Frank Sherlock, *The City Real & Imagined*, that grew directly out of these two writers' "investigat[ion of] the city together, on foot, to deeply scrutinize the details." Conrad cites Thoreau as an explicit influence in this project—along with the Situationalists, and Charles Olson, who used to make his students at Black Mountain College "RUN across an open field to write their poems where the natural light was better. Olson told them the field and sun would be in the poem."[50] Not that the poem should describe a field, or sun, but that it should get into a poem, much as Thoreau thought a quicker approach to a "complete volume" of poems would be to escape from a library into a field. Meanwhile, almost all of Teare's poems grow from a practice of walking, a practice he comments on within the space of many of the resulting poems: "to think I have to / walk around looking," he writes, for example, in "Headlands Quadrant," composed during a residency on the coast of Marin County in California; or, walking around Philadelphia in "Toxics Release Inventory (*Essay on Man*)," he returns repeatedly to the "notebook open as I walk, / stride inflecting script // with wobble & slant, / blots & warps made by sweat, all the raw errata // of the transcribing body."[51] Teare attributes his interest in walking to A.R. Ammons, and his essay "A Poem is a Walk," rather than to Thoreau's essay "Walking"; but that may be because by the time he wrote "Walking," late in his life, Thoreau had ceased to actively theorize poetry in the way we saw him doing early in his career in *A Week*. Walking, Thoreau was simply practicing poetry as he understood it.

Teare's place-based poetics is most pronounced in his most recent volume, *Doomstead Days* (2019), though a preoccupation with location, and mapping, characterizes early work as well. His volume most directly concerned with plant-life is *Companion Grasses* (2013). In that collection, several poems use a particular plant species as a conduit for deeper engagement with place. "Tall Flatsedge Notebook," for example, begins by naming a species of grass, *Cyperus eragrostis*, and concludes by noting the location where the grass had been visited, and the poem found; in this case, Point Reyes National Seashore, on the northern California coast. In that poem, Teare posits "context" as a necessary, if unachievable, requisite of poetry: he wonders how "to risk authoring /// context as part of the lyric / only to fail at both."[52] The use of a plant as a way into context, and therefore, into poetry, is, as we've seen, a Thoreauvian strategy. The move from plant to place—and an interpenetration of theory and practice, verse and exegesis—that most resembles Thoreau's approach in *A Week* is in another poem from *Companion Grasses*: "Quakingrass" or *Briza maxima*.

Teare finds these grasses further down the California coast, among the dramatic inlets and misty precipices of Big Sur. In the poem, Teare draws together a plant-species and its location, as well as a series of meditations on the relationship between photography and poetry, as both arts strive to "frame" their contexts. The thoughts on photography arise from Teare's walking partner, another "companion" whose relationship to the author is erotically charged, an eros that infiltrates the landscape, and the poem, so that along with the "terrible weight" of attempting, as an artist, to do justice to "context," extends also to a meditation on "the privacy" of penetration, "of being entered": the way a thought enters a landscape, or a landscape enters a poem, or one body makes way for another. Teare unsettles the direction of these motions, so that an "image" of "a raptor over / coastal fields—" is "pierced by the ear" rather than piercing *to* the ear, or the eye; the body moves outward toward the horizon.

At this point in the poem, Teare interjects a question—"what is 'lyric'"— that mediates between the image of a raptor entering the ear, the "Santa Lucia Mountains behind us" and a frame for both the image and the question: "hawk, we thought." Naming the image, the companions also give a possible name to what a poem can be: a bird, knitting together earth and sky. As Teare continues to pursue this definition, another book enters the space of the poem:

Crow-sized, a harsh loud scream—

    the little book fell open, broken-spined—

    Sharp-shinned
    Cooper's
    Red-shouldered
    Broad-winged
    Swainson's
    Zone-tailed
    Red-tailed
    Rough-legged
    Ferruginous—

For a moment, a poem becomes a list of hawks; the landscape, through the possible identifications of its particulars, enters the poem. While Teare lingers here on birds, the way they enter and soar out of a frame, he is working his way toward a life form that is more fixed, toward the quaking-grass of the poem's end, when he will pose his question—what is "lyric" again—and provide a different answer.

    I gathered the grass from his hand—
        how "panicle" trembles
        (*panus*, "thread wound on a bobbin")—

Sweetly its crown to my face—
    (*penos,* "web")—
    pedicel, spikelet, glume & lemma—

Little grammar of attraction—
    inflorescence—
    (What is "lyric")—

The book fell open on its broken spine
    (*florere,* "to flower")—
    "It's quakinggrass," I said—

In both of these examples, Teare interrupts and breaks his lines so that the identification of a species blends into the definition of a poem. In this final answer, the questions about framing, intimacy, and penetration that the poem worked through earlier become focused around the particular forms of a plant body, and the common suggestiveness of touch between any two bodies: human and human, or animal and plant. The encounter is slight, but its effects—gathering, trembling, quaking—quietly dissolve the boundaries of the poem's—the encounter's—frame.[53]

The way Teare elides the "book" that "fell open on its broken spine" and the poem that he is writing recalls the poem by Thoreau we looked at earlier, in which the poet imagines "cast[ing] off books," lying in clover and burying his feet in violets, even as he imagines this totally "hypathereal" book inside the space of a lineated poem. In both instances, the poet's goal is to make the space of writing diaphanous, so that grass, or flowering, can get in. There are other moments in Thoreau's journal when lineation makes a surprising appearance, further blurring distinctions between common observation and encounter, and the work of making a poem. In this passage from August 1850, for example, we find Thoreau also concerned with grass, and flowers, before he shifts from prose into verse:

It was well grassed and delicate flowers grew in the middle of the
road—I
I saw a delicate flower had grown up 2 feet high
Between the horse's path & the wheel track
Which Dakin's & Maynards wagons had
Passed over many a time.[54]

In this passage, the common observation of the plant life along a road, and the interjection of a lyric speaker in relation to that space, prompts a turn toward poetry. There is very little in the "poem" itself that seems to rise to the status of polished verse—except for the fact that Thoreau has capitalized each beginning of a "line," set these mundane observations apart from the ones that proceed or follow them, and that the first line scans metrically as iambic, though with a six-beat duration, extending beyond a more expected common tetrameter or pentameter line. The steep enjambment of the third line—around "had"—fully dissolves the momentum of the first two lines. And yet, the alliteration between the first and third, second and fourth, end-words of each line does gesture toward the alternating rhymes of common meter in a way that makes Dickinson's slant advances to that form seem downright typical.[55]

If the parallels between Teare and Thoreau's poetics which I have been considering here have seemed mostly indirect, there are other moments when Teare evokes Thoreau more directly, as in another plein-aire poem from *Doomstead Days*, "Convince Me You Have a Seed There," written in Ripton, Vermont, in which Teare quotes Thoreau in the title and again, later in the body of the poem. In this poem, Teare invokes Thoreau's "faith in a seed," and his fascination with processes of forest succession, as he narrates an encounter with a genetically modified "SuperTree™" "bioengineerd by ArborGen®" to be "disease resistant" and "fast growing." While Thoreau marveled at the collective life of plants in a forest setting, how one species proceeds and alters the conditions of an ecosystem, ceding the way to another, Teare worries about the isolation of this particular tree within its larger context, "how farmers // can't contain / cross-pollination // between spliced / & wild species / & how hybrid trees // will intertwine // with the hungers / of the red squirrel." Thoreau becomes a naïve predecessor in this poem—admirable, but not required to confront the particular complexities of our current environmental challenges—but one that Teare wants to believe in. Earlier in the poem, he invokes Plato's "vision" of "the human" as "a heavenly plant," and offers a counter-proposal, of being "rooted in the two / worlds," a world of "soil" and ideas, participant in "the ensoiled soul // we're rooted in."[56] Nothing could be more Thoreauvian.

Except perhaps for one final way that Teare's work operates within the realm of poetry in the common sense theorized by Thoreau that I have tried to provide an outline of here. In his "Clear Water Renga" in *Doomstead Days*, Teare invokes the trans-temporality of plants through the timeline of North Californian "long / fraught occupation flowers /// non-native clover / & rye." These plants become an entry point into the deep human, and natural, history of the landscape, which extends from plant to animal and human, the intersecting of lives patterned by "seasonal," "cyclical" experiences of time:

> everywhere we live
> we destroy life:: I could walk
> due north all my years

& never not stand the way
I stand on land Coast Miwok

once camped on to fish
    peak salmon runs:: seasonal,
        cyclical, the tribe

            for centuries walked to shore
                then walked back inland to hunt

Teare writes of how European settlers "uncalendared that walking,"
drawing on terms that were both crucial for Thoreau, who reimagined
cyclical rhythms in his charts of "General Phenomena" for different seasons,
drawing on over a decade of seasonal events documented in his journals,
who may or may not have imagined compiling these observations, and those
of his *Indian Notebooks*, for another book, a "Kalendar" of Concord, and
who made walking the foundation of his poetic practice. While animals
and humans are a crucial feature of both Teare's and Thoreau's landscapes,
plants retain a privileged status, the material medium through which we
enter this living history. "[It] challenges the white mind," Teare writes, "to
look at this coast / & think *this is a ruin*:: / yellow bush lupine / grows so
thick I have to push / through it toward the Pacific." In his essay on "plein-
aire poetics," Teare describes his "commitment" to get to know "the layers
of empirical knowledge that get laid down by Western culture on top of the
land."[57] This was Thoreau's project, too; and when he called "Concord" a
poem, it was this deep written history of the landscape, accessible through
the timescales of plant-life that he was remembering.

"It's ALL Collaboration," C. A. Conrad says of (soma)tic poetry, and I
will conclude by suggesting of the definition of poetry in the common sense
I've begun to develop here.[58] Just as a plant incorporates the body of the
world around it into its own body, so a poem feeds on context, natural
and human. Reading a poem, like touching a plant, is an entry point to
other timescales than those we brush against via other modes of memory.
Frederick Jameson called history an "absent cause,"[59] an occurrence we
could never get at, and so required cultural forms to report on, to mediate
our encounters. But a plant can be more than that: the site of a material
encounter with something, or things, humans or other life-scales, that are
still living. The writers I've considered here see poetry in these terms, too: as
a portal into living, and being with, ongoing loss, rather than a final record.

NOTES

Introduction

1 Ralph Waldo Emerson, *Nature, Essays and Poems*, New York: Library of America, 1996, p. 11.

2 Henry David Thoreau, *The Writings of Henry David Thoreau: Journal*, 8 vols. to date, editor-in-chief, Elizabeth Witherell, Princeton: Princeton University Press, 1991–2002, p. 3:224. Hereafter abbreviated as *PJ*, followed by the volume and page number.

3 Thoreau's conclusion is probably fusion of two remarks by Gray; the one, quoted, and the other one, related to Gray's discussion of the plant "embryo," stating that in the embryo the first part of the plant that is developed is radicle, "preexistent" form of the stem (*PJ* 3: 225).

4 Thoreau repeats this claim on several occasions in the *Journal*. For instance, "the most clear & etherial ideas (Antaeus like) readily ally themselves to the earth-to the primal womb of things. … They put forth roots as soon as branches"; or: "For each successive new idea or bud—a new rootlet in the earth. The growing man penetrates yet deeper by his roots into the womb of things" (*PJ* 3: 226).

5 It isn't quite clear how Thoreau arrived at the claim that the flower is of all plant organs, most closely related to the earth. He draws such a conclusion on the basis of the following quotation from Gray: "Roots not only spring from the root-end of the primary stem in germination, but also from any subsequent part of the stem under favorable circumstances, that is to say, in darkness & moisture, as when covered by the soil or resting on its surface." That there is no mention of flowers here suggests only that promotion of the flower into the central organ of the plant that roots it is Thoreau's original theory.

6 Thoreau doesn't explain why his discussion of flowers all of a sudden moves to "buds."

7 G. W. F. Hegel, *Philosophy of Nature*, Part 2 of the Encyclopedia of the Philosophical Science, trans. A. V. Miller, Oxford: Oxford University Press, 2004, p. 304.

8 Ibid., p. 352.

9 Ibid.

10 Ibid., p. 351.

11 Ibid., p. 352.

12 Ibid., p. 304.

13 Ibid.

14 Ibid., p. 351.

15 Emerson, "The Method of Nature", *Essays and Poems*, pp. 121, 120.
16 Henry David Thoreau, *Thoreau's Wild Flowers*, ed. Geoff Wisner, New Haven: Yale University Press, 2016, p. 21.
17 Ibid., p. 16.
18 Ibid., p. 21.
19 Gillian Beer, *Darwin's Plots: Evolutionary Narrative in Darwin, George Eliot and Nineteenth-Century Fiction*, Cambridge: Cambridge University Press, 2000, p. 74.
20 Mary B. Hesse, *Models and Analogies in Science*, Notre Dame: University of Notre Dame Press, 1966, pp. 82–3. As Hesse explains, Cuvier's "structural homologies" try to isolate what is "common," and then idealize it into an essence shared by what appears to be irreducibly different: "The logical argument rests on the presumption that if AB is connected with D in the model, then there is some possibility that B is connected with D, and that this connection will tend to make D occur with BC in the explicandum" (p. 85).
21 Thoreau, *Thoreau's Wild Flowers*, p. 26.
22 Ibid., p. 14.
23 Ibid., p. 26.
24 Ibid., p. 45.
25 Philippe Descola, *Beyond Nature and Culture*, trans. Janet Lloyd, Chicago: The University of Chicago Press, 2013, p. 205.
26 Ibid., p. 202.
27 Ibid., p. 203.
28 Beer, *Darwin's Plots*, p. 74.
29 Hesse, *Models and Analogies in Science*, p. 78.
30 Henry David Thoreau, *A Week on the Concord and the Merrimack Rivers*, Princeton: Princeton University Press, 1980, p. 30.
31 Beer, *Darwin's Plots*, p. 78.
32 Henry David Thoreau, *Collected Essays & Poems*. ed. Elizabeth Hall Witherell. Library of America, 2000, p. 210.
33 Laura Dassow Walls, *Seeing New Worlds: Henry David Thoreau and Nineteenth-Century Natural Science*, Madison: Wisconsin University Press, 1995, p. 40.
34 Emerson, *Nature*, *Essays and Poems*, p. 11.

Chapter 1

1 H. A. Page, *Thoreau: His Life and Aims*, Boston: James R. Osgood & Co., 1877, p. 110, emphasis added.
2 Henry David Thoreau, *The Writings of Henry David Thoreau: Journals*, 14 vols, ed. Bradford Torrey, Boston: Houghton Mifflin, 1906, p. III: 427. Hereafter abbreviated as *J*, followed by the volume and page number.
3 Henry David Thoreau, "Civil Disobedience."
4 Henry David Thoreau, *The Writings of Henry David Thoreau: Journal*, 8 vols. to date, editor-in-chief, Elizabeth Witherell, Princeton: Princeton University Press, 1991–2002, 7: 15. Hereafter abbreviated as *PJ*, followed by the volume and page number.

5   *PJ* 4: 435, emphasis added. The next line reads: "It appears to be a law that you cannot have a deep sympathy with both man and nature. Those qualities which bring you near to the one estrange you from the other."
6   Walt Whitman, "Song of Myself," line 670–1.
7   Whitman, "Song of Myself," line 670–1, Henry David Thoreau, *Walden and Civil Disobedience*, ed. Owen Thomas, Norton Critical edition, W. W. Norton, 1966, p. 93.
8   Henry David Thoreau, *Walden and Resistance to Civil Government,* Norton Critical edition, ed. William Rossi, W. W. Norton, 1966, p. 93.
9   Jane Bennett, *Thoreau's Nature*, Rowman and Littlefield, 2000, p. 22. For more recent discussion of the wild, see Jos Smith, *The New Nature Writing: Rethinking the Literature of Place*, chapter 3 on "The Wild," London: Bloomsbury Press, 2017 and Jack Halberstam, "Wildness, Loss, Death," *Social Text* 121, 32, no. 4 (2014): 137–48.
10 Henry David Thoreau, *A Week on the Concord and Merrimack Rivers*, ed. C. F. Novde, Princeton: Princeton University Press, 1980, p. 339. Thoreau also invokes "winged thoughts" in "Walking": "We are accustomed to say in New England that few and fewer pigeons visit us every year. Our forests furnish no mast for them. So, it would seem, few and fewer thoughts visit each growing man from year to year, for the grove in our minds is laid waste ... and there is scarcely a twig left for them to perch on. ... Our winged thoughts are turned to poultry" (Thoreau, "Walking," in *Excursions*, ed. Joseph Moldenhauer, Princeton: Princeton University Press, 2007, p. 202).
11 People seek out the Wild, but so do other living things: "Every tree sends forth its fibers in search of the Wild. The cities import it at any price. Men plow and sail for it. From the forest and wilderness come the tonics and barks which brace mankind" Henry David Thoreau, "Walking," in *Excursions*, ed. Joseph Moldenhauer, Princeton: Princeton University Press, 2007, p. 202.
12 Thoreau, *Walden,* ed. Rossi, p. 211.
13 Henry David Thoreau, "A Yankee in Canada," in *The Writings of Henry David Thoreau: Excursions*, ed. Joseph J. Moldenhauer, Princeton: Princeton University Press, 2007, pp. 152–3, emphasis added.
14 *J* II: 9.
15 *J* II: 219.
16 Henry David Thoreau, *A Year in Thoreau's Journal: 1851*, ed. H. Daniel Peck, New York: Penguin Books, 1993, p. 126.
17 "But the moon is not to be judged alone by the quantity of light she sends us, but also by her influence on the earth. ... [The] astronomer admits that 'the notion of the moon's influence on terrestrial things was confirmed by her manifest effect upon the ocean,' but is not the poet who walks by night conscious of a tide in his thought which is to be refereed to lunar influence—in which the ocean within him overflows its shores and bathes the dry land." In a journal entry of September 21, 1851, Thoreau had described lunar influence upon men as "a tide" in thought wherein "the ocean within ... overflows its shores and bathes the dry land" (Thoreau, *A Year in Thoreau's Journal*, p. 229).
18 *PJ* 2: 212.
19 Henry David Thoreau, "A Natural History of Massachusetts," in *Excursions*, ed. Joseph Moldenhauer Princeton: Princeton University Press, 2007, p. 22.
20 Thoreau, *A Year in Thoreau's Journal*, p. 18.

21 *PJ* 4: 467–8.
22 Thoreau, *A Year in Thoreau's Journal*, p. 126. The journal entry is from July 23, 1851.
23 In this state, writes Branka Arsić, Thoreau "bypass[es] the human obsession with ideation and metaphorization" to become one of the "things and beings" that "generate meaning by affecting other beings, or, as Thoreau has it, by imprinting themselves on other beings, thus literally or materially altering them". Arsić explores this "semiosis of imprints" in *Bird Relics: Grief and Vitalism in Thoreau*, Cambridge, MA: Harvard University Press, 2016, p. 7.
24 Thoreau, *A Year in Thoreau's Journal*, p. 126.
25 Ibid., p. 188. The journal entry is from September 2, 1851.
26 Walt Whitman, "Morbid Adhesiveness—To Be Kept Down," unpublished manuscript found by William White, *Walt Whitman Quarterly Review* 4, no. 1 (1986): 49, https://ir.uiowa.edu/wwqr/.
27 Henry David Thoreau, *The Heart of Thoreau's Journal*, ed. Odell Shepard. New York: Dover, 1961. The journal entry is from August 23, 1853.
28 "When I see a fox run across the pond on the snow, with the carelessness of freedom, or at intervals trace his course in the sunshine along the ridge of a hill, I give up to him sun and earth as to their true proprietor. He does not go in the sun, but it seems to follow him, and there is a visible sympathy between him and it. ... When the ground is uneven, the [fox's] course is a series of graceful curves, conforming to the shape of the surface" (Thoreau, "A Natural History of Massachusetts," in *Excursions,* ed. Joseph Moldenhauer, Princeton: Princeton University Press, 2007, p. 16).
29 "The pond does not thunder every evening, and I cannot tell surely when to expect its thundering; but though I may perceive no difference in the weather, it does. Who would have suspected so large and cold and thick-skinned a thing to be so sensitive?" (Thoreau, *Walden*, ed. Thomas, p. 199)
30 "Water is so much more fine and sensitive an element than earth. A single boatman passing up or down unavoidably shakes the whole of a wide river, and disturbs its every reflection. The air is an element which our voices shake still further than our oars the water" (Thoreau, *Journal*, September 19, 1850).
31 Thoreau, *A Year in Thoreau's Journal*, p. 126. The journal entry is from July 23, 1851.
32 Thoreau, *Walden, Civil Disobedience and Other Writings*, ed. Rossi, p. 203. Thoreau also writes that "All material things are in some sense man's kindred. ... Even a taper is his relative—and burns ... only a certain number of his hours" (Thoreau, *Journal*, Fall 1846, at Walden Pond, cited in *Material Faith: Henry David Thoreau on Science*, ed. Laura Dassow Walls, New York: Mariner Books, 1999, p. 9). I am grateful to Rochelle Johnson for alerting me to this passage.
33 Thoreau, *Walden, Civil Disobedience and Other Writings*, ed. Rossi, p. 207. The claim appears in the "sand-foliage" passage of "Spring," which I discuss later in this chapter: "There is nothing inorganic. These foliaceous heaps lie along the bank like the slag of a furnace, showing that Nature is 'in full blast' within. The earth is not a mere fragment of dead history, stratum upon stratum like the leaves of a book, ... but living poetry like the leaves of a tree."

NOTES   239

34   Thoreau invokes the phrase in *Walden* ("Higher Laws"). The "atmospheric" influences affecting Thoreau on that July day are themselves subject to or affected by emanations coming *from* Thoreau.

35   Henry David Thoreau, *Walden and Resistance to Civil Government*, ed. Rossi, p. 87.

36   Ibid.

37   Also relevant here is the *sound of the fluttering leaves*. As Rochelle Johnson notes, Thoreau "indicates his own unsound state when he fails to heed sound: that is, his own soundness, like that of nature, depends on sound" (Rochelle Johnson, "'This Enchantment Is No Delusion': Henry David Thoreau, the New Materialisms, and Ineffable Materiality," *ISLE: Interdisciplinary Studies in Literature and Environment* 21, no. 3 (2014): 606–35).

38   Thoreau, *Walden and Resistance to Civil Government*, ed. Rossi, p. 87.

39   Ibid., p. 89.

40   As Milette Shamir notes, the kind of sympathy characteristic of the social reformer has for Thoreau "dyspeptic connotations." It is a "loosening of the emotional 'gates'" (Milette Shamir, "Manliest Relations," in *Boys Don't Cry?: Rethinking Narrative of Masculinity and Emotion in the U.S.*, ed. Milette Shamir and Jennifer Travis, New York: Columbia University Press, 2002, p. 73). The "Solitude" chapter of *Walden* affirms a better kind of sociality, one that is *inter-species*: "I am no more lonely than a single mullein or dandelion in a pasture" (Thoreau, *Walden and Civil Disobedience*, ed. Thomas, 1966, p. 92). Thoreau "admired plants and trees: truly, he loved them" (William Ellery Channing, *Thoreau: Poet-Naturalist*, Boston: Roberts Brothers, 1873, p. 202).

41   Thoreau, *Walden,* ed. Thomas, p. 210. Thoreau's call to make compassion "expeditious" overlaps somewhat with Nietzsche's claim for the virtue of "brief habits" in *The Gay Science*: "*Brief habits.*—I love brief habits and consider them an inestimable means for getting to know *many* things and states, down to the bottom of their sweetness and bitternesses; my nature is designed entirely for brief habits. ... *Enduring* habits I hate, and I feel as if a tyrant had come near me and as if the air I breathe had thickened when events take such a turn that it appears that they will inevitably give rise to enduring habits; for example, owing to an official position, constant association with the same people, a permanent domicile, or unique good health. Yes, at the very bottom of my soul I feel grateful to all my misery and bouts of sickness and everything about me that is imperfect, because this sort of thing leaves me with a hundred backdoors through which I can escape from enduring habits. Most intolerable, to be sure, and the terrible par excellence would be for me a life entirely devoid of habits, a life that would demand perpetual improvisation. That would be my exile and my Siberia" (Friedrich Nietzsche, *The Gay Science*, trans. Walter Kaufmann, New York: Vintage Books, 1974, p. 295).

42   Thoreau, *Walden*, ed. Thomas, p. 141.

43   Linda Ross Meyer speaks of a "being-with outside ourselves" that is "prior to any particular emotional experience of sympathy" Linda Ross Meyer, *The Justice of Mercy*, Ann Arbor: University of Michigan Press, 2010, p. 33.

44   Branka Arsić, "Letting Be: Thoreau and Cavell on Thinking after the *Bhagavat Gita*," *Belgrade Journal for Media and Communications* no. 7 (2015), p. 21.

45 Thoreau, *Walden*, ed. Rossi, p. 90.
46 Ibid., p. 93.
47 *PJ* 4: 55. See also Thoreau's description of these as manifestations of "infinite beauty," in *PJ* 4: 52.
48 Thoreau, *Walden*, ed. Rossi, p. 89.
49 *PJ* 4: 223. Journal entry from December 25, 1851.
50 Thoreau, *Walden*, ed. Thomas, p. 93.
51 In "Walking," Thoreau notes that bodies take on the odors of the materials they eat: "the skin of the Eland, as well as that of most other antelopes just killed, emits the most delicious perfume of trees and grass," just as "the trapper's coat emits the odor of musquash" (Thoreau, "Walking," in *Excursions*, ed. Joseph Moldenhauer. Princeton, NJ: Princeton University Press, 2007), p. 203.
52 G.W.F. Hegel, *Phenomenology of Spirit*, trans. A.V. Miller, New York: Oxford University Press, 1977, paragraphs 178–90.
53 *PJ* 2: 282–3.
54 Cited in David Skrbina, *Panpsychism in the West*, Cambridge, MA: MIT Press, 2005, p. 224.
55 Thoreau might now wonder whether he himself underestimated vegetal agency when, in *Walden*, he reduced his beans to the status of the raw material for writing: I hoed beans not in order to eat them "but, perchance, ... only for the sake of tropes and expression, to serve a parable-maker one day" (Thoreau, *Walden*, ed. Rossi, p. 109). Sean Ross Meehan has argued that such passages present us not with a set of stable entities engaged in relations with each other—pine needles, the wind, the man Thoreau—but instead different phases of a shared process of natural influences undergoing metamorphosis. For Meehan, because no descriptor can avoid being "literary in medium" (p. 301) it is best to choose a literary trope—metonymy—to name that peculiarly earthy quality of Thoreau's writing. "Metonymy ... is without metaphor, but not without figure. ... Metonymy speaks to the literal instead of the metaphorical sense of words, but the literal sense, of course, is still a matter of words" (p. 312). Meehan is primarily concerned to defend Emerson from the charge of having an overly metaphorical and spiritualized approach to Nature, and to close the gap between Thoreau-the-empiricist vs. Emerson-the-transcendental-idealist (Sean Ross Meehan, "Ecology and Imagination: Emerson, Thoreau, and the Nature of Metonymy," *Criticism* 55, no. 2 (2013): 299–329).
56 Michael Ziser, *Environmental Practice and Early American Literature*, Cambridge, MA: Cambridge University Press, 2013, pp. 2–8.
57 *PJ* 4: 53.
58 *PJ* 4: 219.
59 Was Thoreau influenced by Emerson's warning not to be too quick to project friendliness into Nature? In the 1836 version of his essay "Nature," Emerson says this: "The greatest delight which the fields and woods minister, is the suggestion of an occult relation between man and the vegetable. I am not alone and unacknowledged. They nod to me, and I to them. ... Yet it is certain that the power to produce this delight, does not reside in nature, but in man, or in a harmony of both" (Ralph Waldo Emerson, *The Collected Writings of Ralph Waldo Emerson*, vol. 1: *Nature, Addresses and Lectures*, Cambridge, MA: Harvard University Press, 1970, p. 10).

60 Mary Elkins Moller, *Thoreau and the Human Community*, Boston: University of Massachusetts Press, 1980, p. 79.

61 Emphasis added. Here is the whole passage, from Thoreau's Journal, May 12, 1851:

> If I had got false teeth, I trust that I have not got a false conscience. It is safer to employ the dentist than the priest to repair the deficiencies of nature. By taking the ether the other day I was convinced how far asunder a man could be separated from his senses. You are told that it will make you unconscious, but no one can imagine what it is to be unconscious— how far removed from the state of consciousness and all that we call 'this world'—until he has experienced it. The value of the experiment is that it does give you experience of an interval as between one life and another,—a greater space than you ever travelled. You are a sane mind without organs,—groping for organs,—which if it did not soon recover its old sense would get new ones. You expand like a seed in the ground. You exist in your roots, like a tree in winter. If you have an inclination to travel, take the ether; you go beyond the furthest star (Thoreau, *A Year in Thoreau's Journal*: 1851, p. 39).

62 Richard Doyle, *Darwin's Pharmacy: Sex, Plants, and the Evolution of the Noosphere*, Seattle: University of Washington Press, 2011, p. 21.

63 *PJ* 4: 50–52.

64 Henry David Thoreau, *Cape Cod*, Orleans, MA: Parnassus Imprints, 1984, p. 16.

65 Henry David Thoreau, *Cape Cod*, https://www.gutenberg.org/files/34392/34392-h/34392-h.htm

66 *J* XII: 85. The journal entry is from March 27, 1859.

67 Thoreau, *The Heart of Thoreau's Journal*, p. 85. The journal entry is from April 16, 1852. H. A. Page said in 1877 that Thoreau felt "a dim but real brotherhood" with nonhuman animals (H. A. Page, *Thoreau: His Life and Aims*, p. 62).

68 Thoreau, *Walden*, ed. Thomas, p. 92.

69 Thoreau, *Walden*, ed. Rossi, p. 203.

70 Ibid., p. 205.

71 Ibid.

72 Ibid., p. 204.

73 Ziser, *Environmental Practice*, p. 172.

74 Thoreau, *Walden*, ed. Rossi, p. 204.

75 Dietrich Diederichsen, "Animation, Dereification, and the New Charm of the Inanimate," *e-flux Journal* 36, July 2012.

76 The drop is, one could say, the last (or first) moment in a cosmic process of individuation-deformation. The drop is a "fall" back into a well of indetermination, but it is also a fall out of the protean sky into a world of actual things. My thanks to Jeff Dolven for this point.

77 Leo Bersani, "Sociability and Cruising," in *Is the Rectum a Grave? and Other Essays*, Chicago: University of Chicago Press, 2009, p. 55. Relevant also is Deleuze and Guattari's "refrain" in *A Thousand Plateaus: Capitalism and Schizophrenia*. trans. Brian Massumi. Minneapolis: University of Minnesota Press, 2003, p. 322.

78 Thoreau, *Walden*, ed. Rossi, pp. 203–5.

Chapter 2

1 Henry David Thoreau, *Walden,* Princeton: Princeton University Press, 1971, p. 17. Cited hereafter as *Walden.*

2 Raymond Williams, *Keywords: A Vocabulary of Culture and Society*, revised edition, New York: Oxford University Press, 1983, pp. 197–201, 197; René Descartes, *Discourse on Method*, in *The Philosophical Writings of Descartes*, vol. 1, Cambridge: Cambridge University Press, 1985, pp. 109–51, 141.

3 Cited from *The American Heritage Dictionary*, third edition, in which these two quotations are given as definitional, Boston: Houghton Mifflin, 1992, p. 1109 ["material"]; 1111 ["matter"].

4 Jane Bennett, *Vibrant Matter: A Political Ecology of Things,* Durham: Duke University Press, 2010, p. 121. For a useful summary of recent work on "the liveliness of matter" in the nineteenth century, see Joan Steigerwald, *Experimenting at the Boundaries of Life: Organic Vitality in Germany around 1800,* Pittsburgh: University of Pittsburgh Press, 2019, pp. 22–5.

5 Henry David Thoreau, *The Journal of Henry D. Thoreau*, 8 vols. to date, editor-in-chief Elizabeth Witherell, Princeton: Princeton University Press, 1981–2002, pp. 4: 420–1 (hereafter cited as *PJ* and followed by the volume and page number). Henry David Thoreau, *A Week on the Concord and Merrimack Rivers,* Princeton: Princeton University Press, 1980, p. 363.

6 Laura Dassow Walls, *Material Faith: Thoreau on Science,* Boston: Houghton Mifflin, 1999; Catherine L. Albanese, *Reconsidering Nature Religion,* Harrisburg, PA: Trinity Press, 2002, pp. 9–11.

7 Laura Dassow Walls, *Seeing New Worlds: Henry David Thoreau and Nineteenth-Century Natural Science,* Madison: Wisconsin University Press, 1995, pp. 84–93. My contrasting term, "rational holism," designated the (Cartesian) universe as a divine or transcendent unity breathed into being by the power of Divine Reason and so fully comprehensible only through *a priori* thought; see *Seeing New Worlds*, pp. 60–70. My study of rational holism is *Emerson's Life in Science: The Culture of Truth,* Ithaca: Cornell University Press, 2003; of empirical holism, *The Passage to Cosmos: Alexander von Humboldt and the Shaping of America,* Chicago: University Press of Chicago, 2009.

8 For more on this, see my essay "Earth" in *Cambridge Companion to Literature and the Anthropocene*, ed. John Parham, Cambridge: Cambridge University Press, 2021, pp. 37–53.

9 See Kathryn Yusoff, *A Billion Black Anthropocenes or None,* Minneapolis: University of Minnesota Press, 2018.

10 Hans Jonas, *The Phenomenon of Life: Toward a Philosophical Biology,* Evanston: Illinois University Press, 2001, p. 16.

11 Bruno Latour, *Down to Earth: Politics in the New Climatic Regime,* Cambridge: Polity, 2018, pp. 82, 88.

12 *Walden*, p. 283.

13 Thomas Kuhn, the philosopher of science who coined the concept of paradigms, attributed the origin of paradigm shifts to the build-up of anomalies, or observations unaccountable in the terms of the prevailing

paradigm, which are ignored until they build into mountains of counter-evidence whose pressure forces an innovative new conceptual model, a new paradigm. Those draw to the new paradigm will, in effect, not just see the world anew but will quite literally see a new and different world, one that remains unseen by those too insensible to the anomalies, or to their world-changing import, to agree that a new paradigm is justified. He literature on this foundational concept is immense. See Thomas Kuhn, *The Structure of Scientific Revolutions*, Chicago: University of Chicago Press, 1962; fourth edition, 2012.

14 Alexander von Humboldt, *Cosmos*, vol. 1, New York: Harper & Brothers, 1859, p. 84.

15 It bears remembering that the category of "human" being defended has traditionally excluded the plurality of the world's non-white peoples, an exclusion still incompletely healed.

16 Lorraine Daston, *Against Nature,* Cambridge, MA: MIT Press, 2019, pp. 7–12.

17 As Thoreau wrote in March 1853, in response to a membership invitation issued by the American Association for the Advancement of Science (he remained a member through 1853), "I am an observer of nature generally, and the character of my observations, so far as they are scientific, may be inferred from the fact that I am especially attracted by such books of science as Whites [*sic*] Selborne and Humboldt's 'Aspects of Nature'." See *Correspondence, vol. 2: 1849–1856,* ed. Robert N. Hudspeth, et al., Princeton: Princeton University Press, 2018, p. 151. For the powerful influence of Humboldt on the formative thinking of Charles Darwin, particularly on life and consciousness as properties emerging from the immanent constructive activities of nature itself, see Phillip R. Sloan, "'The Sense of Sublimity': Darwin on Nature and Divinity," *Osiris,* 16 (2001): 251–69.

18 Daston, *Against Nature,* pp. 16–17; Latour, *Down to Earth,* pp. 78–82. On Humboldt and critical zones, see my essay "Recalling Humboldt's Planet," in *Critical Zones: The Science and Politics of Landing on Earth*, ed. Bruno Latour and Peter Weibel, Cambridge, MA: MIT Press, 2020, pp. 212–22.

19 Daston, *Against Nature,* pp. 23–31.

20 Ibid., p. 31; Emerson, *Essays and Lectures,* New York: Library of America, 1983, pp. 47, 48–9 (cited hereafter as *E&L*).

21 *Walden*, p. 8; Emerson, "The American Scholar," in *E&L*, pp. 51–71, 67.

22 *Walden*, p. 236.

23 Laura Dassow Walls, *Henry David Thoreau: A Life,* Chicago: University of Chicago Press, 2017, pp. 228–30.

24 *Walden*, pp. 11–13.

25 Ibid., pp. 113, 132, 138.

26 *PJ* 3: 52–4, 108–9, 115–16.

27 This was the title on the book's spine; Charles Darwin's full title was *Journal of researches into the natural history and geology of the countries visited during the voyage of H.M.S. Beagle round the world, under the command of Capt. Ritz Roy, R.N.* 2 vols, New York: Harper & Brothers, 1846.

28 *PJ* 3: 219–20, 225–6, 253–9.

29 *PJ* 3: 350, 382.

30 *PJ* 4: 45–6, 28.
31 *PJ* 5: 174; 4:307.
32 *PJ* 4: 274.
33 Emerson, *Essays and Lectures,* pp. 967–8.
34 *PJ* p. 4: 223 (emphasis in original).
35 *PJ* 4: 468; cf. *Walden,* p. 225, which suppresses the original association with plant life.
36 Kristen Case argues these charts are the culmination of Thoreau's response to loss by recomposing his daily life, finding "community with his non-human neighbors" and existence "in a more-than-human world"; see her essay "Phenology," *Henry David Thoreau in Context,* ed. James Finley, Cambridge: Cambridge University Press, 2017, p. 261.
37 Walls, *Emerson's Life,* pp. 68–126; also Walls, "The Anatomy of Truth: Emerson's Poetic Science," *Configurations* 5 (1997): 425–67.
38 Daston, *Against Nature,* pp. 23, 31.
39 Joan Steigerwald, *Experimenting at the Boundaries of Life: Organic Vitality in Germany around 1800,* Pittsburgh: University of Pittsburgh Press, 2019, p. 39. As Humboldt wrote, "The history of organisms … is so intimately connected with geology, with the order of succession of the superimposed terrestrial strata, and with the chronometrical annals of the upheaval of continents and mountains, that [I will] … avoid establishing the natural division of organic and inorganic terrestrial life as the main element of classification" (*Cosmos,* vol. 5 p. 14).
40 Alexander von Humboldt, *Cosmos,* 2 vols, trans. Elise Otté, New York: Harper and Brothers, 1850, 1858; Baltimore: Johns Hopkins, 1997, 1:288; Alexander von Humboldt, *Views of Nature,* trans. Mark M. Person, Chicago: University of Chicago Press, 2014, p. 206.
41 Numerous translations and editions were published in the United States in the early 1840s, including an 1841 edition by James Munroe, who in 1849 would publish Thoreau's *A Week on the Concord and Merrimack Rivers.*
42 Humboldt, *Cosmos,* 5:11.
43 Humboldt, *Views,* pp. 129–30 (Thoreau annotated this essay).
44 Henry David Thoreau, *The Maine Woods,* Princeton: Princeton University Press, 1971, p. 71.
45 *PJ* 2: 143, 354.
46 Didier Debaise, *Nature as Event: The Lure of the Possible,* Durham: Duke University Press, 2017, p. 9.
47 *PJ* 4: 96.
48 See Henry D. Thoreau, *Faith in a Seed,* ed. Bradley P. Dean, Washington, DC: Island Press, 1993.
49 As Cristin Ellis argues in Chapter 9 of this volume, plant-thinking also queered Thoreau's sexuality. Or vice versa.
50 *The Writings of Henry D. Thoreau,* Princeton Edition Journal transcript, vol. 24, pp. 609–11 (November 5, 1857); cf. Thoreau, *Maine Woods,* pp. 164–6. The 1906 editors of Thoreau's *Journal,* by deleting *Maine Woods* material, deleted the social context of Thoreau's most cogent critique of scientific objectivity. Thoreau is alluding to the sinking of the SS *Central America* in a hurricane, which sent 400 souls and 30,000 pounds of California gold, worth

half a billion dollars today, to the bottom of the ocean, contributing to the Panic of 1857, a depression which spread across the globe and lasted, in the United States, until the Civil War. This passage has never been published in full.

51 *PJ* 4: 441–2.
52 Humboldt, *Views,* pp. 160–1.
53 *PJ* 4: 319; 4:68–9.
54 *PJ* 4: 230–1; *Walden,* pp. 306–9.
55 Michel Serres, *The Natural Contract,* 1992; Ann Arbor: University of Michigan Press, 1995, pp. 34, 33.
56 *PJ* 5: 309.
57 Jean-Christophe Bailly, *The Animal Side,* New York: Fordham University Press, 2011, p. 28.

Chapter 3

1 Luce Irigaray and Michael Marder, *Through Vegetal Being: Two Philosophical Perspectives,* New York: Columbia University Press, 2016.
2 Henry David Thoreau, *Walden,* ed. Jeffrey S. Cramer, New Haven and London: Yale University Press, 2004, p. 126. All subsequent citations from this book will be followed in-text by the corresponding page number in parentheses.
3 This ethos remains quite strong in Thoreau, who goes so far as to project it onto plants: "The West of which I speak is but another name for the Wild; and what I have been preparing to say is, that in Wildness is the preservation of the World. Every tree sends its fibres forth in search of the Wild." Henry David Thoreau, *Wild Apples and Other Natural History Essays,* ed. William Rossi, Athens and London: The University of Georgia Press, 2002, p. 75.
4 Thoreau, *Wild Apples,* p. 86.
5 Ibid., p. 118.
6 Henry David Thoreau, *The Maine Woods,* New York and London: Penguin Books, 1988, p. 165.
7 Compare this to the following statement: "In this haphazard manner, Nature surely creates you a forest at last, though as if it were the last thing she were thinking of. By seemingly feeble and stealthy steps—by a geologic pace—she gets over the greatest distances and accomplishes her greatest results" (Henry D. Thoreau, *Faith in a Seed: The Dispersion of Seeds and Other Late Natural History Writings,* ed. Bradley P. Dean, Washington, DC and Covelo, CA: Island Press, 1993, p. 36).
8 Nonetheless, he had to hire helpers for ploughing (*Walden,* p. 53).
9 Thoreau does so in a few places in his texts, such as this passage arguing for a necessarily incomplete cultivation of the soil, as much as of a human being: "I would not have every man nor every part of a man cultivated, any more than I would have every acre of earth cultivated: part will be tillage, but the greater part will be meadow and forest, not only serving an immediate use, but preparing a mould against a distant future, by the annual decay of the vegetation which it supports" (Thoreau, *Wild Apples,* p. 85).
10 Thoreau, *Wild Apples,* p. 24.

Chapter 4

1   Among the most prominent examples of this "plant turn," we count Robin
    Wall Kimmerer's *Braiding Sweetgrass*, Michael Marder's *Plant-Thinking*,
    Eduardo Kohn's *How Forests Think*, Anna Tsing's *Mushroom at the End of
    the World*, Jeff Nealon's *Plant Theory*, and Emanuele Coccia's *The Life of
    Plants*—all of which were published between 2013 and 2016.
2   Emanuele Coccia, *The Life of Plants: A Metaphysics of Mixture*, trans. Dylan
    J. Montanari, Cambridge: Polity Press, 2017, p. 5; Jeffrey Nealon, *Plant
    Theory: Biopower and Vegetable Life*, Stanford: Stanford University Press,
    2015, p. xv.
3   Thoreau's thoughts of plants and planting are disseminated throughout his
    entire work, but this short essay will focus primarily on his most explicitly
    political text, "Resistance to Civil Government," and on *Walden*'s "Bean-Field"
    chapter, which Thoreau composed around the same time.
4   Henry David Thoreau, *Walden, Civil Disobedience, and Other Writings*, ed.
    William Rossi, New York: W.W. Norton, 2008, p. 105. All references to these
    texts will henceforth be given directly in the text in parentheses.
5   Leo Marx, *The Machine in the Garden: Technology and the Pastoral Ideal in
    America*, Oxford: Oxford University Pres, 2000, p. 242.
6   Michel Foucault, *Security, Territory, Population: Lectures at the Collège de
    France, 1977–1978*, ed. Michel Senellart, trans. Graham Burchell, New York:
    Picador, 2007, p. 125.
7   Foucault, p. 134, qtd. in Daniel Nemser, *Infrastructures of Race:
    Concentration and Biopolitics in Colonial Mexico*, Austin, TX: University of
    Texas Press, 2017, p. 14.
8   Nemser, *Infrastructures of Race*, p. 14.
9   "[G]overnment is not related to the territory," Foucault notes, "but to a sort of
    complex of men and things. The things government must be concerned about
    […] are men in their relationships, bonds, and complex involvements with
    things like wealth, resources, means of subsistence, and, of course, the territory
    with its borders, qualities, climate, dryness, fertility, and so on" (Foucault,
    Security, Territory, Population, p. 134).
10 Coccia, *The Life of Plants*, p. 4.
11 Nealon, *Plant Theory*, p. 11.
12 Nealon explicitly declares that at the "ascendency of biopower," animals
    took plants' place (p. 118). Coccia is less consistent. In the introduction, he
    claims that philosophy has *always* overlooked plants, "more out of contempt
    than out of neglect" (p. 3), arguing that plants are consistently denied the
    ontological dignity (sometimes) granted to animals because of humans'
    narcissistic incapacity to empathize with beings they do not see themselves in.
    As a consequence of this "metaphysical snobbery," plants are little more than
    objects of mass consumption. He presents this anti-botanical sentiment as
    timeless *(no one has ever)*, but at the same time he hints that it is a byproduct
    of an old epistemic prejudice that was consolidated in the nineteenth century,
    which saw an unprecedented "policing effort … to force the disappearance of
    any trace belonging to *the natural* from the domain of knowledge" (p. 18).

13 Animals, Coccia asserts, can select their participation in the world: they can migrate, hide, or retreat in the face of danger. Plants, on the other hand, "have no selective relation to what surrounds them." Space is not up for negotiation: "Plant life is life as complete exposure, in absolute continuity and total communion with the environment" (p. 5). Nealon also notes this difference as he distinguishes between the concept of animal "world"—which, for him, is a "backdrop" for (and thus phantasmatically preexists) the emergence of individuated living beings—against the plant "territory," which "co-appears with individuation" (p. 86). I do not have the space to develop this point here, but I want to register a hesitation about this narrative: Nealon and Coccia, it seems to me, fail to genealogize the figure of "the animal" itself, which is a biopolitical concept that can only be conceived as fugitive, as disappearing, insofar as it is a being wholly dependent on its milieu and invested with a life over which it can claim no real ownership. Foucault shows this when he demonstrates the centrality of the concept of "conditions of existence" to the new field of biology, which conjugates every individual life in the *conditional*, making its flourishing contingent on certain internal organic functions or on a given environment.

14 Coccia, *The Life of Plants*, p. 37.

15 Ibid., p. 39. Coccia notes that the atmosphere comes from the leaf, the operator of photosynthesis; plants and the world are thus coextensive, irresistibly imbricated in one another. Immersion is not just a spatial determination but a metaphysical principle: "to be immersed is not reducible to finding oneself *in* something that surrounds and penetrates us. Immersion ... is first of all an *action* of mutual compenetration between subject and environment." The notion of immersion leads to a "formal identity between passivity and activity," the "radical identity of being and doing" (p. 37). This is where the difference with Thoreau starts showing: by postulating an absolute nonseparability of plant and atmosphere, a perfect material coincidence between the two, Coccia leaves no room for action: "organisms do not need to go beyond or outside themselves to reinvent the face of the world; they have no need to act ... : through the simple act of being they already fashion the cosmos" (p. 39). Later, he claims that to "recognize that the world is a space of immersion means ... that there are no real or stable frontiers" (p. 43). This is a profoundly ahistorical and depoliticizing account, in stark contrast with Thoreau's insistence on "fronting" the world (Jane Bennett, *Thoreau's Nature: Ethics, Politics, and the Wild*. Modernity and Political Thought, Newbury Park, CA: SAGE, 1994, p. 35).

16 Nealon, *Plant Theory*, pp. 103–6.

17 Wolfe, qtd. by Nealon, *Plant Theory*, p. 110.

18 Cary Wolfe, *Before the Law: Humans and Other Animals in a Biopolitical Frame*, Chicago: University of Chicago Press, 2013, p. 103.

19 According to Wolfe, "discrimination, selection, self-reference, and exclusion cannot be avoided." Nealon repeatedly returns to Wolfe's bonobo vs. sunflower example as evidence that plants are consistently spurned by animal studies scholars. Nealon retorts that if "we are, in fact, to rethink the question of life from the ground up, we can't go into the discussion having chosen what already counts as life and what doesn't—bonobos yes, sunflowers no"

(p. 110). Wolfe's point is not that sunflowers are not alive, of course, but that all forms of life are not equally in need of the same type of care and protection, or more precisely that we cannot and should not indiscriminately provide care and protection to all forms of life simply on account of their being alive. I return to this point in the last section of the essay.

20 Nealon, *Plant Theory*, p. 117. Nealon follows Deleuze and Guattari, who, in their analysis of early capitalism's capture of the land, use a germinal metaphor to designate the "undecidable [as] the germ and locus [*le germe et le lieu*] par excellence of revolutionary decisions" (Gilles Deleuze and Félix Guattari. *A Thousand Plateaus: Capitalism and Schizophrenia 2*, trans. Brian Massumi, Minneapolis: University of Minnesota Press, 2003, p. 473).

21 Foucault defines the population as "a multiplicity of individuals who are ... biologically bound to the materiality within which they live" (Foucault, *Security, Territory, Population*, p. 37).

22 The management of biological subjects is made possible by their inherent susceptibility to environmental influences. Kyla Schuler has shown how nineteenth-century biopower managed populations through their powers to be affected by and to respond to external stimuli, and how these "powers" were differentially distributed along racial and gender lines. "Racial and sexual difference were not assigned the role of immutable, static qualities of the individual body in the nineteenth century," Kyla Schuller explains. "Rather, race and sex functioned as biopolitical capacities of impressibility and relationality that rendered the body the gradual product of its habit and environment, differentially positioning the claims of individuals and races for belonging in the nation-state. The notion of impressibility developed in the nineteenth century in conjunction with the emergent framework of the population, an entity governed by the processes of contagion, probability, and risk" (Kyla Schuller, *The Biopolitics of Feeling: Race, Sex, and Science in the Nineteenth Century*, Durham: Duke University Press, 2017, pp. 5–6).

23 Foucault, *Security, Territory, Population*, p. 37.

24 This is especially true of Coccia. For all its praise of compenetration and universal mixture, Coccia's book is surprisingly binaristic in its strict opposition between the rightful metaphysics of plant life—which came first, and upon which animals depend for life—and the fraudulent, if dominant, metaphysics of animal life—illegitimate because derivative, unconsciously driven by the heterotrophic nature of the metaphysician (heterotrophy denotes the "uprooted" life of animals, which feed on complex organic substances; autotrophy, on the other hand, designates plants' ability to feed themselves by turning inorganic substances into nutrients). Coccia subordinates heterotrophy to the autotrophy, justifying this move both temporally (plants came first) and functionally (there cannot be animal life without plant life), but he treats it as a matter of ontological superiority: he relishes the fact that plants can live without us, but we cannot live without plants. In other words, he does not rethink the hierarchy he denounces so much as he inverts it.

25 Nealon, *Plant Theory*, p. 64.

26 Foucault, *Security, Territory, Population*, pp. 37–8.

27 On this, see Ingrid Diran, and Antoine Traisnel, "The Poetics of Geopower: Climate Change and the Politics of Representation," in *Climate Realism: The*

Aesthetics of Weather, Climate, and Atmosphere, eds. Lynne Badia, Marija Cetinić, and Jeff Diamanti, London: Routledge, 2020.

28 A few paragraphs later, Thoreau confesses to having tasted his beans, but he still asserts himself a follower of Pythagoras, who forbade his disciples to eat beans—possibly because of their undesirable effects on the eater, possibly because they were a higher form of vegetable in which human souls could migrate after death, but more likely, as Plutarch suggests, as a warning against the temptation to take part in public life (beans were used as voting ballots) Plutarch, *Moralia, vol. I: The Education of Children. How the Young Man Should Study Poetry. On Listening to Lectures. How to Tell a Flatterer from a Friend. How a Man May Become Aware of His Progress in Virtue*, trans. Frank Cole Babbitt, Cambridge, MA: Harvard University Press, 1927, p. 29. There might still be another explanation if we remember that the Pythagorean tradition modeled a prototype of pastoral power antithetical to the Platonic conception of politics. The Pythagoreans, Foucault notes, derive "*nomos*, the law, from *nomeus*, that is to say the shepherd. The shepherd is the lawmaker insofar as he distributes food, directs the flock, indicates the right direction, and says how the sheep must mate so as to have good offspring … in this Pythagorean type of literature, there is the idea that the magistrate is *not characterized by his power, strength, and decision-making ability* so much as by the fact that he is above all the *philanthrōpos* who loves those under his jurisdiction" (Foucault, *Security, Territory, Population*, p. 188, emphasis added).

29 Eric J. Sundquist, *Home as Found: Authority and Genealogy in Nineteenth-Century American Literature*, Baltimore: Johns Hopkins University Press, 2019, p. 66.

30 Stanley Cavell, "The Uncanniness of the Ordinary," The Tanner Lectures on Human Values, April 3 and 8, 1986. Lecture Library: The Tanner Lectures on Human Values, https://tannerlectures.utah.edu/_documents/a-to-z/c/cavell88.pdf, p. 112.

31 See, for instance, Scott Lauria Morgensen, "The Biopolitics of Settler Colonialism: Right Here, Right Now," *Settler Colonial Studies* 1, no. 1 (2011), pp. 52–76.

32 Thus Thoreau's manual labor makes him aware of the land itself as a record of violent history, which tends to elude Yankee farmers. "Antebellum agriculture seemingly erodes any trace of an Indian past," notes Ross Martin, whereas "Thoreau sees arrowheads erupting with each rake's blow, and so flying forth to volley thoughts upon farmers" (Ross Martin, "Fossil Thoughts: Thoreau, Arrowheads, and Radical Paleontology," *ESQ: A Journal of Nineteenth-Century American Literature and Culture* 65, no. 3 (2019), p. 439).

33 "Thoreau here renounces both the definitive knowledge of individual varieties and the systematic and exhaustive description of a universal order," writes William Stowe. Plants, in other words, are by no means unknowable or unnamable, but knowing and naming are *acts*, forms of participations that do not presume a nature passively awaiting discovery. Thoreau's is an "epistemology of contact," as Laura Dassow Walls explains, where knower and known are co-produced (Laura Dassow Walls, *Seeing New Worlds: Henry David Thoreau and Nineteenth-Century Natural Science*, Madison: University of Wisconsin Press, 1995, p. 143).

34 Tellingly, Thoreau uses the word "plant" eleven times as a substantive and twenty-two as a verb in *Walden*.

35 Michel Foucault, "The Subject and Power," *Critical Inquiry* 8, no. 4 (1982), p. 789. Foucault and Austin are both committed to rethinking what it means to "act" on another person, materially and discursively. When Austin attempts to parse illocutionary acts from perlocutionary acts, indeed, he admits that "the notion of an act is unclear." The concept of "perlocutionary act" enables him to view acts from the point of view of their consequences and without returning acts to the intention of the actor (J. L. Austin, *How to Do Things with Words*. ed. J. O. Urmson and Marina Sbisà, Cambridge, MA: Harvard University Press, 1975, p. 106).

36 Robin Wall Kimmerer, *Braiding Sweetgrass: Indigenous Wisdom, Scientific Knowledge, and the Teaching of Plants*, Minneapolis: Milkweed Editions, 2013, p. 127.

37 Henry David Thoreau, *Faith in a Seed: The Dispersion of Seeds and Other Late Natural History Writings*, Washington, D.C.: Island, 1993. I borrow the idea of "vegetable locomotion" from Julien Nègre, *L'Arpenteur vagabond. Cartes et cartographies dans l'oeuvre de Henry David Thoreau*, Lyon: ENS Éditions, 2019, p. 298.

38 Thoreau, *Faith in a Seed*, p. 80.

39 In the conference he gave for the Tanner Lectures on Human Value, Cavell notes that *Walden* "deals in endless repetition" in order to capture the oddness of the everyday (Cavell, Tanner Lectures, p. 105). Elsewhere, however, Cavell interprets the apparent "obviousness" of the bean-field chapter as a way to deride the century's tendency to turn nature into parables (Stanley Cavell, *Senses of Walden: An Expanded Edition*, Chicago: University of Chicago Press, 1972, p. 21). As Cavell sees it, Thoreau referred to writers like John Evelyn (whom Cavell presents as a moralist and a pseudo philosopher, p. 22), only mockingly. But there is little "moralizing" going on in Evelyn. On the contrary, Thoreau values him for his philosophy grounded in practice. The lesson he derives from reading Evelyn is that there is "no compost or lætation whatsoever comparable to this continual motion, repastination, and turning of the mould with the spade" (Evelyn, qtd. in *Walden*). Plants, Evelyn explains, "are nourished by things of like affinity with the constitution of the soil which produces them, and therefore it is of singular importance to be well read in the alphabet of Earths and composts" (John Evelyn, *Terra: A Philosophical Discourse of Earth, Relating to the Culture and Improvement of it for Vegetation, and the Propagation of Plants, &c. as it was presented to the Royal Society, April 29, 1675*, York: A. Ward, 1778, p. 49). Following Evelyn, we can see that hoeing (or repastinating) does not serve as a metaphor for writing, as Cavell suggests, so much as it is the tediousness of Thoreau's writing—and of *Walden*, which, Cavell concedes, "sometimes seems an enormously long and boring book" (Cavell, *Senses of Walden*, p. 20)—that best translates the monotony of tilling one's garden. Evelyn's *Philosophical Discourse of Earth* is primarily a compendium of the types of soil in which plants flourish, the kinds of dungs one can use as fertilizer (grass-fed cattle, sheep, swine, horse, pigeon), etc. Its repetitious structure is reminiscent of Thoreau's later work on the dispersion of seeds.

40 Historian Robert A. Gross argues that the bean-field chapter is a "hoax" that targets the agricultural reformers of the time, who campaigned for the most intensive use of the land (modeled on English agriculture, which worked with little space). "By contrast, Thoreau claimed to have done just the opposite. He started with exhausted, barren land, did nothing to improve it, obtained little from it, and announced himself quite content" Robert A Gross, "The Great Bean Field Hoax: Thoreau and the Agricultural Reformers." *The Virginia Quarterly Review: A National Journal of Literature and Discussion* 61, no. 3 (1985), accessed February 13, 2020, https://www.vqronline.org/essay/great-bean-field-hoax-thoreau-and-agricultural-reformers.

41 Bennet, p. 48. The bean-field chapter explicitly stages the metamorphosis of its author: "It was no longer beans that I hoed, nor I that hoed beans." For Cavell, the interest of the chapter lies in the continual re-birth of *Walden*'s paltry "hoer-hero," who battles weeds and woodchucks (Cavell, *Senses of Walden*, p. 22). Jane Bennett likewise reads this chapter as Thoreau's treatise on individuation, which "requires a certain orientation to human and nonhuman others." Both scholars note that the singularity of the Thoreauvian self—the kernel of Thoreau's politics—is paradoxically produced by habitual repetition. The self is not a given but the product of an endless process of self-making, of *deciding*. Bennett remarks that in order to "grow character," "one must cast the weeds aside in favor of those thoughts, ideas, images, and inclinations specific to the idiosyncratic experience that is one's own life" (p. 34.) But that which works at becoming a self is, by definition, not (yet) a self. On what ground, then, are these decisions to be made, since one does not yet have a life of "one's own"? This decision can only be made following laws that are in part extrinsic to the self: since one cannot posit that the self knows itself *before* it grows into being, one must imagine a self that is by nature "eccentric" (p. 32)—that exists at the boundary of the self and the world. Stranger still, the "wild" outside does not preexist the self but co-emerges with it in a perpetual confrontation between self and nonself. This confrontation is not innocent, hence the martial lexicon of the bean-field chapter: Thoreau "acknowledges injustice and falsity as elements within discriminations and valuations, but these elements neither exhaust these practices nor counsel him to abandon them" (p. 37). Thus, Thoreauvian politics for Bennett will be found in and founded on an ethos of *measure*: on the one hand, a form of reserve or "continence" toward wild instincts, and on the other, a caution not to "overcultivate" one's self for fear of exhausting one's wild nature.

42 Branka Arsić, *Bird Relics: Grief and Vitalism in Thoreau*, Cambridge, MA: Harvard University Press, 2016, p. 141.

43 Arsić shows that in Thoreau, life is not the opposite of death but a principle of mutability that runs through human, animal and vegetal bodies alike (as well as through seemingly inert substances). What separates different states of animacy are not degrees of liveness but of health. The pathological body is no "less alive" than the healthy one: "Never dead yet never healthy, life is made of two forces that never reconcile yet remain inseparable" (p. 243).

44 Esposito, qtd. in Arsić, *Bird Relics*, p. 142.

45 Ibid.

46 *Pace* Nealon, I would say that biopower posits life as absolutely unownable
    and fugitive. Insofar as it acts *indirectly* on bodies, biopower must recognize
    that organisms are not hermetic and self-same but eminently porous and
    susceptible to change. It is in light of this strange power *of* life (to vanish, to
    elude capture) that a less deleterious biopolitics *can* be envisioned.
47 Nealon, *Plant Theory*, pp. 118–19.
48 Arsić shows that the paradigm for Thoreau's vitalist ontology is the leaf, which,
    following Goethe, Thoreau "elevated into the pattern of all life" (p. 229). Insofar
    as it continues to live even after it is detached from the tree, the leaf instantiates
    a life in constant mutation: "the fragile protraction of life in decaying leaves
    becomes for Thoreau an emblem of the immortality of all vegetal life" (p. 232).
    "There is nothing inorganic," Thoreau exclaims in *Walden* in front of a heap
    of fallen leaves. In his diary for the first voyage on the Merrimack, Thoreau
    describes nature as "a vast manufactory of leaves.—the leaf is her constant cipher.
    It is grass in the field … it flutters on the oak,—it springs in the mould upon
    a jar—and in animal, vegetable, and mineral—in fluids and in crystals—plain
    or variegated—fresh or decayed, it acts a principal part in the economy of the
    universe" (from Thoreau's journal, qtd. in Robert Richardson, *Henry Thoreau: A
    Life of the Mind*, Berkeley: University of California Press, 1988, p. 157).
49 In the 1840s, Thoreau was already familiar with Asa Gray's *Natural System
    of Botany* and Edward Tuckerman's study of lichens, and he had already
    begun engaging plants in a more systematic fashion by the time *Walden* was
    published. However, when he hoed his beans at Walden Pond, he still lived by
    the motto "learn science & then forget it" (Dassow Walls, *Seeing New Worlds*,
    pp. 129–30).
50 Mather's words—excerpted from this sermon on the Salem Witch Trials, *The
    Wonders of the Invisible World* (1693)—reference Jeremiah's lamentation:
    "Yet I had planted thee a noble vine, wholly a right seed: how then art thou
    turned into the degenerate plant of a strange vine unto me?" (Jeremiah 2:21).
    On the role played by the jeremiad in Puritan communal life and the American
    body politic more broadly, see Sacvan Bercovitch, *The American Jeremiad*,
    Madison: University of Wisconsin Press, 1978. On plant hybridization, see
    Mather's 1717 "Curiosa Botanica," a letter to specimen collector and Royal
    Society fellow James Petiver, in which he describes experimenting with Indian
    corn of two different colors. His account is said to have influenced Linnaeus's
    binomial system of classification based on floral reproductive organs.
51 Sylvia Wynter, "Novel and History, Plot and Plantation," *Savacou* 5 (1971), p. 95.
52 Ibid.
53 Anna Lowenhaupt Tsing, *The Mushroom at the End of the World: On the
    Possibility of Life in Capitalist Ruins*, Princeton: Princeton University Press,
    2017, p. 39.
54 Evelyn recommends experimenting with "artificial compositions" of soil
    and "to modify the air around" plants in order to transplant exotic fruit
    like oranges, figs, pomegranates to colder climes, that is, to have them be
    "endenizoned amongst us, and grow every generation more reconcileable to
    our climate" (p. 50). "Endenizon" designates the process by which a foreigner
    adopts the laws of a new country. We also find the term in Locke's "Letter for
    Toleration," written around the same time as Evelyn's *Terra*.

55 Crèvecoeur, J. Hector St John de Crèvecoeur, *Letters from an American Farmer and Other Essays*, ed. Dennis D. Moore. Cambridge, MA: Belknap, 2013, p. 32. On the endurance of Crèvecoeur's botanical framework in nineteenth-century works, see Erin E Forbes, "Vegetative Politics from Crèvecoeur to Hawthorne," *J19: The Journal of Nineteenth-Century Americanists* 8, no. 1, 2020: 43–66.

56 Susan Scott Parrish explains that eighteenth-century European colonists were invested in the "subjection of matter," but they also believed that bodies were deeply susceptible to environmental influences: "Nature was thus not only understood as a potential stock of resources or a plot of property ... it was also breathed in, drunk, eaten, absorbed under the skin, and incorporated into one's faculties" (Susan Scott Parrish, *American Curiosity: Cultures of Natural History in the Colonial British Atlantic World*, University of North Carolina Press, 2006, p. 78). "Many colonial writers," Monique Allewaert observes of eighteenth-century American planters, "described how people, like plants, entered into vegetative states in the plantation zone" (Monique Allewaert, *Ariel's Ecology: Plantations, Personhood, and Colonialism in the American Tropics*, Minneapolis: University of Minnesota Press, 2013, p. 34). See also Greta LaFleur, *The Natural History of Sexuality in Early America*, Baltimore: Johns Hopkins University Press, 2020, esp. chapters one and four.

57 Nemser, *Infrastructures of Race*, pp. 133–4. The racist logic of what Nemser calls the "uneven distribution of vulnerability" perdured well into the nineteenth century and beyond, as Kyla Schuller shows in *The Biopolitics of Feeling*.

58 Michel Foucault, *The Order of Things*, qtd. in Nemser, p. 136.

59 For Nemser, the "fetishization of 'things themselves' and the erasure of context" in the classical age prompted "the rise of institutional collections like botanical gardens." But already the global circulation of plants was challenging this tidy taxonomic ideal: "imperial botany never entirely ignored external determinants—temperature, atmospheric pressure, humidity, latitude, and so on—in either theory or practice. On the contrary, these factors too were abstracted and quantified, converted into precise measurements alongside those of the plants to which they were linked" (p. 140).

60 Pastoral power, for Foucault, is a kind of "everyday government" that doesn't say its name: a natural, or naturalized, government, predicated on the idea that "each individual ... from the beginning to the end of his life, and in his every action, had to be governed and had to let himself be governed" (Michel Foucault, "What is Critique?" In *The Politics of Truth*, trans. Lisa Hochroth and Catherine Porter, ed. Slyvère Lotringer, New York: Semiotext(e), 2007, p. 43).

61 Foucault, *Birth of Biopolitics*, p. 53.

62 Michel Foucault, *On the Government of the Living: Lectures at the Collège de France, 1979–1980 and Oedipal Knowledge*, ed. Michel Senellart, trans. Graham Burchell, New York: Picador, 2012, p. 173.

63 Ibid., p. 14.

64 Henry David Thoreau, *Walden, Civil Disobedience, and Other Writings*, ed. William Rossi, New York: W.W. Norton, 2008, p. 224. A Few paragraphs below, Thoreau makes this explicit: "But, to speak practically and as a citizen, unlike those who call themselves no-government men, I ask for, not at once no government, but *at once* a better government."

65 On the question of resistance in Foucault, see Maurizio Lazzarato, "From Biopower to Biopolitics," *Pli* 13 (2002), pp. 1–10.

66 Thoreau first wrote "Civil Disobedience" as a lecture he delivered in Concord in 1848. The text was first published under the title "Resistance to Civil Government" in a collection of essays edited by Elizabeth Peabody in 1849. About the text's two titles—"Civil Disobedience" and "Resistance to Civil Government"—Michel Imbert notes that in the first the adjective "civil" is attached to disobedience, and in the second to government. This reversibility suggests that Thoreau is not simply opposed to government. Michel Imbert, "Le Seuil de résistance dans Resistance to Civil Government," in *Littérature et politique en Nouvelle-Angleterre*, ed. Thomas Constantinesco and Antoine Traisnel, Actes de la recherche à l'ENS, no. 7, 2011, p. 71.

67 In the plantation context, writes Wynter, history is "itself, fiction; a fiction written, dominated, controlled by forces external to itself. It is clear then, that it is only when the society, or elements of the society rise up in rebellion against its external authors and manipulators that our prolonged fiction becomes temporary fact," Wynter, "Plot and Plantation," p. 95).

68 On the "paradox of the shepherd" who "must keep his eye on all and on each," see Foucault, *Security, Territory, Population*, pp. 174–5.

69 Ibid., p. 125.

70 Ibid., pp. 126–7.

71 Ibid., p. 173.

72 Ibid., p. 36.

73 Kyle Powys Whyte, "Too Late for Indigenous Climate Justice: Ecological and Relational Tipping Point." Published in *WIREs Climate Change*, October 23, 2019 https://doi.org/10.1002/wcc.603.

74 Emerson, "Life of Henry David Thoreau," in *Walden*, p. 407.

75 On the political import of Thoreau's huckleberry-picking party, see Imbert, "Le Seuil de résistance," pp. 76–7.

Chapter 5

1 See François Bouteau, "Les plantes prennant-elles de decisions?" *Sciences et Avenir*, 868 (2019): 40.

2 Michael Marder, *Plant-Thinking: A Philosophy of Vegetal Life,* New York: Columbia University Press, 2013.

3 Anthony Trewavas, *Plant Behaviour and Intelligence,* Oxford: Oxford University Press, 2015.

4 Eduardo Kohn, *How Forests Think: Toward an Anthropology Beyond the Human,* Berkeley: University of California Press, 2013.

5 Stefano Mancuso and Alexandra Viola, *Brilliant Green: The Surprising History and Science of Plant Intelligence,* Washington, DC: Island Press, 2015, and Stefano Mancuso, *The Revolutionary Genius of Plants: A New Understanding of Plant Intelligence and Behavior,* New York: Atria, 2018.

6 Jeffrey T. Nealon, *Plant Theory: Biopower and Vegetable Life,* Stanford: Stanford University Press, 2016.

7   Monica Gagliano, John C. Ryan, and Patrícia Vieira, *The Language of Plants: Science, Philosophy, Literature,* Minneapolis: Minnesota University Press, 2017.
8   N. Katherine Hayles, *Unthought: The Power of the Cognitive Unconscious,* Chicago: University of Chicago Press, 2017.
9   Hayles, p. 20.
10 Ibid.
11 Ibid.
12 Ibid. Of key importance to Hayles's project is the "interpenetration" of biological and technical cognition. She uses plant cognition in order to refine her understanding of technical cognition as a process that "interprets information within contexts that connects it with meaning" (p. 22). But I am tempted to work in the other direction: namely, from the supposition that the investigation of artificial intelligences does not take attention away from forms of what could be called "natural" intelligence or biological cognition, but rather allows us to see them with new eyes. Already, investigations of networked systems of embodied knowledge and algorithmic understandings of natural phenomena have allowed fields like cognitive biology to offer important new perspectives on how we understand the epistemic complexities of all life forms, even plants and humble unicellular organisms (p. 16). As Hayles herself asserts, "a convenient site to explore the complex interactions that arise when [cognitive biology's] perspectives on cognition confront traditional views on intelligence is the world of plants" (pp. 16–17).
13 Charles Darwin, *The Power of Movement in Plants* [1880], ed. Francis Darwin, Cambridge, MA: Cambridge University Press, 2009, p. 572.
14 Ibid., p. 573.
15 Sharon Cameron, *Writing Nature: Henry David Thoreau's Journal,* Chicago: University of Chicago Press, 1989, pp. 66, 75.
16 Stanley Cavell, *In Quest of the Ordinary: Lines of Skepticism and Romanticism,* Chicago: University of Chicago Press, 1994, p. 69.
17 Henry David Thoreau, *Excursions, The Writings of Henry David Thoreau, vol. IX,* Boston and New York: Houghton, Mifflin and Co., 1893, p. 237.
18 Henry David Thoreau, *The Writings of Henry David Thoreau: Journals,* 14 vols, ed. Bradford Torrey, Boston: Houghton Mifflin, 1906, vol. 2, pp. 201–2. Hereafter abbreviated as *J,* followed by the volume and page number. References to the Princeton edition of Thoreau's journals will be given parenthetically in the text as *PJ,* followed by the volume and page number (Henry David Thoreau, *The Writings of Henry David Thoreau: Journal,* 8 vols. to date, editor-in-chief, Elizabeth Witherell, Princeton: Princeton University Press, 1991–2002). See Asa Gray, *Manual of the Botany of the Northern United States,* London: J. Chapman, 1848.
19 Henry David Thoreau, *Walden,* ed. J. Lyndon Shanley, Princeton: Princeton University Press, 2004, p. 138. All references to *Walden* are hereinafter cited parenthetically as *W.*
20 Laura Dassow Walls, "The Value of Mutual Intelligence," in *Thoreau at 200: Essays and Reassessments,* ed. Kristen Case and K. P. Van Anglen, Cambridge, MA: Cambridge University Press, 2016, pp. 185–6.

21 Henry David Thoreau, "Wild Apples," in *Excursions*, ed. Joseph J. Moldenhauer, Princeton: Princeton University Press, 2007, p. 203. References to *Excursions* are hereinafter cited parenthetically as *E*.
22 Thoreau's loon is a model of animal intelligence, or wild thinking, insofar as it confounds human thinking. Animal cognition in the nineteenth century was often described in terms of "cunning," that is, as a form of calculative thinking that outwits the human predictive thought. We could compare Thoreau's use of cunning to that of Emerson in *English Traits*, in which cunning is a supplementary form of intelligence: "Nature has endowed some animals with cunning, as a compensation for strength withheld" Ralph Waldo Emerson, *The Complete Works of Ralph Waldo Emerson*, vol. 7, ed. Edward Waldo Emerson, Cambridge, MA: Riverside Press, 1904, p. 120.
23 To borrow a phrase from Charles Shepherdson's *Lacan and the Limits of Language,* New York: Fordham University Press, 2008.
24 In the context of the swamp, he muses that "[b]oth a conscious and an unconscious life are good. Neither is good exclusively, for both have the same source. The wisely conscious life springs out of an unconscious suggestion" (*J* IX: 38).
25 Branka Arsić, *Bird Relics: Grief and Vitalism in Thoreau,* Cambridge, MA: Harvard University Press, 2016, pp. 223–4.
26 Ibid., p. 225.
27 Mutual intelligence works against the metaphysical biases of life and death, health and pathology that over-code the human perception of natural phenomena. Disease and decay (although the affected organism is given to disempowerment and destruction) are *per se* beyond good and evil, normal and pathological: what is a disease but the heterogeneous assemblage of bacteria or viral bodies, each with their own collective desire to persevere in their own beings? What is decay if not a generative process of life? To think non-anthropocentrically is to think diagrammatically about the shifting assemblages of agents and cognizers that constitute planetary life without imputing human values upon them. Thoreau invites us to this realization, even if he does not "liquidate" the human (as Sharon Cameron claims) but rather seeks to understand the existential intensity of what it is to be human as an often important actant in these assemblages.
28 In a comment published in the *New Scientist* on July 26, 2017, Anthony Trewavas asserts that "[p]lants, too, have their own low cunning": "We equate behaviour with visible movement and elevate nerve cells in reasonable numbers as the only means of learning, remembering and delivering intelligence. A simple definition of intelligence as behaviour that profits from experience during the life cycle fits immune systems perfectly. In the single-celled *Physarum* slime mould, intelligent behaviour arises from sophisticated and complex networks of tens of thousands of proteins and thousands of protein-modifying enzymes. Higher plants, Earth's dominant life form, continue to develop in the face of a variable and usually unpredictable environment. They learn and profit from experience by adjusting their characteristics. It is easy to demonstrate that plants remember former parts of their experience over many months and even years. That, too, is intelligent

behaviour" (*New Scientist*, https://www.newscientist.com/letter/mg23531360-900-1-editors-pick-plants-too-have-their-own-low-cunning/).

29 See, for example, Kristen Case, "Knowing as Neighboring: Approaching Thoreau's Kalendar," *J19: The Journal of Nineteenth-Century Americanists* 2, no. (2014): 107–29.

30 Mancuso, *The Revolutionary Genius of Plants*, pp. 13–5.

31 Henry David Thoreau, "Autumnal Tints," in *E*, p. 257.

32 See the epigraph above. Emerson writes in *Natural History of Intellect*: "The idea of vegetation is irresistible in considering mental activity. Man seems a higher plant. What happens here in mankind is matched by what happens out there in the history of grass and wheat. This curious resemblance repeats, in the mental function, the germination, growth, state of melioration, crossings, blight, parasites, and in short all the accidents of the plant. Under every leaf is the bud of a new leaf, and not less under every thought is a newer thought. The plant absorbs much nourishment from the ground in order to repair its own waste by exhalation, and keep itself good. Increase its food and it becomes fertile. The mind is first only receptive. Surcharge it with thoughts in which it delights and it becomes active. The moment a man begins not to be convinced, that moment he begins not to convince" Ralph Waldo Emerson, *The Complete Works of Ralph Waldo Emerson: Natural History of Intellect, and Other Papers*. vol. 10, ed. Edward Waldo Emerson, Cambridge, MA: Riverside Press, 1904, p. 24.

33 To reiterate Thomas Nagel's infamous formulation.

34 Kohn, *How Forests Think,* pp. 77–8.

35 Cf. Laurent Dubreuil, *The Intellective Space: Thinking beyond Cognition,* Minneapolis: Minnesota University Press, p. 2015.

36 Mancuso, *The Revolutionary Genius of Plants*, p. 77.

37 Ibid.

38 See Trewavas, *Plant Behaviour and Intelligence*, pp. 188–9, 269.

39 We might also understand Thoreau's agricultural ruminations as opening a georgic strain in his wild thinking. As Michael Ziser notes in his *Environmental Practice and Early American Literature*, Thoreau "[subordinates] his own aesthetic and scientific labors to the long tradition that unites the agricultural classic with the 'old farmer's pocket-book' and the '*Farmer's Almanack*.' What seemed to be a poetic fancy confined to a prior moment in American enviro-cultural history begins to seem instead like a forward-looking engagement with an ongoing story of agroecological interaction. Significantly, this is also the moment at which Thoreau begins his natural historical observations in earnest, beginning the detailed phenological records that would culminate in the last years of his life in the massive charts of natural phenomena. Although this ecocentric turn might be seen as a turn away from the pragmatic and materialistic researches of the agricultural tradition toward a purely scientific project, Thoreau's late natural history work in fact achieves its fullest sense only in the context of the georgic renaissance announced by Daniel Lee. As its name suggests, the phenological Kalendar is designed to aggregate observations over time to produce an anticipation of the coming environmental conditions. What

farmers looked for in their pocket-books and almanacs, Thoreau sought
in his notes and charts" (Michael Ziser, *Environmental Practice and Early
American Literature*, Cambridge, MA: Cambridge University Press, 2013,
pp. 175–6).

40   Oliver Sacks, *The River of Consciousness*, New York: Knopf, 2017,
     pp. 68–70.

41   Gilles Deleuze and Felix Guattari, *What Is Philosophy?* trans. Hugh
     Tomlinson and Graham Burchell, New York: Columbia University Press, 1994,
     pp. 212–13.

42   See Raymond Ruyer, *Neo-Finalism*, trans. Alyosha Edlebi, Minneapolis:
     Minnesota University Press, 2016. As Mark Hansen explains in his
     introduction to the text: "In contrast to the overwhelming tendency of
     Western philosophical texts to privilege the higher-order operations of
     human consciousness, Ruyer insists that primary pyschism or consciousness
     is fundamental, with secondary pyschism or consciousness being either a
     subordinate development from it or, in the most radical formulation, an
     appearance of this sole primary form" (p. xv).

43   Elizabeth Grosz, *The Incorporeal: Ontology, Ethics, and the Limits of
     Materialism*, New York: Columbia University Press, 2017, p. 216.

44   William James, *The Principles of Psychology*, vol. 1 [1890], New York: Dover,
     1950, p. 148.

45   Grosz, *The Incorporeal*, p. 217.

Chapter 6

1   For the production of *Dispersion*, see Bradley P. Dean's Chronology and
    Editor's Notes (*Faith in a Seed: The Dispersion of Seeds and Other Late
    Natural History Writings*, ed. Bradley P. Dean, Washington, DC: Island
    Press, 1993) as well as Laura Dassow Walls, *Henry David Thoreau: A Life*.
    University of Chicago Press, 2017, pp. 457–92. Thoreau's *Journal* was a record
    of Concord, which is likely one reason he didn't make entries during his
    travels West in 1861.

2   Sharon Cameron, *Writing Nature: Henry Thoreau's Journal*, Chicago:
    University of Chicago Press, 1989, p. 47.

3   Henry David Thoreau, *The Writings of Henry David Thoreau: Journals*,
    14 vols, ed. Bradford Torrey, Boston: Houghton Mifflin, 1906, VIII:
    1570–1. Hereafter abbreviated as *J*, followed by the volume and page
    number. A number of recent critics have also argued that the mounds
    of natural facts that Thoreau collected offer a meticulous phrenological
    record that allows a retrospective tracing of Holocene patterns turning
    to Anthropocene ones (Richard Primack, *Walden Warming: Climate
    Changes Comes to Thoreau's Woods*, University of Chicago Press, 2014;
    Sarah Dimick, *Climactic Arrhythmias: Global Warming, Literary Form,
    and Environmental Time*, 2016, University of Wisconsin-Madison, PhD
    dissertation). For these critics what Thoreau offers is empirical data that
    allows us to determine Holocene patterns and from this to diagnose our
    own moment.

4   *Dispersion* is not a primer for journal keeping but rather a short and
    condensed account of the mode of seeing and understanding forest shape he
    developed across the long period he wrote the *Journal*. In short, the primer
    would make it possible for readers to gain something of the forest vision
    Thoreau gained by journaling about "nature writing itself," but to gain it more
    quickly, simply, and portably.
5   On figuration as shape-making and breaking, see Amanda Goldstein, *Sweet
    Science: Romantic Materialism and the New Logics of Life*, Chicago: University
    of Chicago Press, 2017, especially chapter two, "Equivocal Generation." This
    article draws on Goldstein's pioneering work while also striving to chart a
    sharper distinction between the problems of figure and meaning.
6   Branka Arsić, *Bird Relics: Grief and Vitalism in Thoreau*, Cambridge, MA:
    Harvard University Press, 2016, p. 182. My thanks to Ingrid Diran for her
    help with this formulation and for her immensely generous and helpful
    feedback on this article.
7   In September of 1860, Thoreau delivered the lecture "The Succession of Forest
    Trees" that was published with the same title in the *New York Weekly Tribune*
    later that same month, culminating in an epistolary exchange between the
    Tribune's editor Horace Greeley and Thoreau. Thoreau spent the rest of the
    fall of 1860 expanding the "Succession" for *Dispersion*: in fact, it was while
    gathering material for the manuscript in an early December storm that he came
    down with the virus that activated the latent tuberculosis that ultimately killed
    him. He produced the first draft of *Dispersion* in the fall and early winter of
    1860 and then revised the manuscript in the fall of 1861 and again in 1862 when
    it was clear his illness was terminal. The manuscript remained unfinished on his
    death in May 1862, although the shorter "Succession" was soon republished in a
    posthumous volume of work edited by Thoreau's sister Sophia Thoreau and his
    friend Ellery Channing. For the production of *Dispersion* as well as the editorial
    processes posed in publishing it, see Richardson, "Introduction: Thoreau's Broken
    Task" as well as Dean, Editor's Notes, both in Thoreau, *Faith in Seed*, pp. 3–17;
    217–70. See also Walls, *Henry David Thoreau: A Life*, pp. 457–92.
8   Walls, *Henry David Thoreau: A Life*, pp, 458–99, 472–4.
9   Richard Feynman's provocation that "Trees come from the air" (*Fun to Imagine*
    BBC2 1983) offers a latter-day variation on Thoreau's account of astral forests.
10 Henry David Thoreau, *Dispersion of Seeds. Henry David Thoreau: Faith in
    a Seed: The Dispersion of Seeds and Other Late Natural History Writings*,
    edited by Bradley P. Dean, Island Press, 1993, p. 111. All references to
    Dispersion of Seeds will be to this edition and given parenthetically in the text.
11 See Laura Dassow Walls, *Seeing New Worlds: Henry David Thoreau and
    Nineteenth-century Natural Science*, Madison, WI: University of Wisconsin
    Press, 1995, pp. 179–211; for a proto-agro-ecological reading, see Gary Paul
    Nabhan's forward to *Faith in a Seed*; for a historical reading, see Robert D.
    Richardson's introduction to the same.
12 Joan Burbrick, *Thoreau's Alternative History: Changing Perspectives on
    Nature, Culture, and Language*, Philadelphia: University of Pennsylvania
    Press, 1987, p. 123.
13 See Randall Fuller, *The Book that Changed America*, New York City: Viking,
    2017. Primack, *Walden Warming*; Dimick, *Climactic Arrhythmias*. Joel
    Gladstone does read *Dispersion* as a manifestly literary experiment but one

focused on technologies of remediation that estrange human readers from nonhuman nature (Joel Gladstone, "Low-Tech Thoreau," *Criticism* 57, no. 3 (2015): 349–376).

14 My thanks to Ingrid Diran for pointing out to me that morphology is a common feature of language and plants.

15 Thoreau revised the drawings to accompany these arboreal texts between the *Journal* and the manuscript of *Dispersion*. In the *Journal*, he writes the names of each stand of trees; in the manuscript, he produces a crude iconic map of trees as they might look from above.

16 That Thoreau denotes these lines using the surveyor's term *rods* recalls that the aim of human geometry has often been the determination of property.

17 Wendy Wheeler, *Expecting the Earth*, London: Lawrence and Wishart, 2016, p. 4.

18 Ibid., 4–5.

19 As Ingrid Diran suggests, the grid shape of human property organizations suggests that the "cross of cross purposes might be literal" (email correspondence, June 16, 2020).

20 John Locke proposed figure or shape as a primary quality of phenomena, that is to say a quality that exists independently of any observation of the phenomena and color as a secondary quality, that is to say a relational quality that arises from the observer's relation to the phenomenon. Thoreau clearly understands color as a relational quality that emerges from the relation between a phenomenon, the medium through which it is perceived, and the observer. However, the shapes of things—of conical pines and circular oaks—emerge from a relation between phenomena. Shape, too, then results from relational processes and for this is not simply an intrinsic quality of phenomena. If the shapes of pine trees, fruit, and forests are always conical, this derives from a relation of wind and pines so frequently repeated that it gives rise to a formative principle. But that sometimes the shape of a pine, its fruit, or a forest departs from the ovoid, and that the pine in relation to oak turns from a cone to a circle, recalls that shape, too, emerges from relation across coproducing energetic and material phenomena.

21 Henry David Thoreau, *A Week on the Concord and Merrimack Rivers / Walden; Or, Life in the Woods / The Maine Woods / Cape Cod*, ed. Robert F. Sayre, New York: Library of America, 1985, p. 354.

22 In this sense, Thoreau's forest geometry puts together life and earth sciences in ways that unsettle biopolitical governmentality and that rhyme with what Elizabeth Povinelli calls *Geoontology* (Elizabeth Povinelli, *Geontologies*, Durham: Duke University Press, 2016).

23 Henry David Thoreau, *Collected Essays and Poems*, ed. Elizabeth Hall Witherell, Library of America, 2001, p. 388.

24 Ibid.

25 Thanks to Ingrid Diran for suggesting this formulation.

26 Thoreau, *Collected Essays and Poems*, p. 391.

27 My thanks to Ingrid Diran for this formulation.

28 *J* XIV: 346.

29 Ibid.

30 See Thoreau's early poem, "Rumors from an Aeolian Harp" (1842), which he also included in *A Week on the Concord and Merrimack Rivers*.

31 Sherman Paul, *The Shores of America*, Champaign: University of Illinois Press, 1958, p. 400.

32 Branka Arsić's discussion of the curious literalism of Thoreau's writing and figures and Amanda Goldstein's discussion of the materiality of figure are both key influences on my own interpretation here. Note that if the sort of reading I offer here comes close to what is often called the "new materialism," what I am describing is less focused on matter than it is on energy and energy transfer, a physical process that, while it might be thought in terms of matter, can also be theorized in terms of *force*, which was one of the key problems of nineteenth-century science and which might, I suspect, be the real fundament of so-called new materialists, who always want their matter moving and doing. Noting that it's (dissipating) force and power at work in this theory of figuration, and linking this focus on force to Engel's and Marx's work on the same, especially in the *Dialectics of Nature*, might go some way—albeit a way not traveled much here—toward thinking how such thought bears on the problems of power and politics. Elaborating this point would require emphasizing that force itself is not a substance or essence but the not-entirely-predictable expression of the relations particular to a milieu at a given place and moment in time. It's an expression of (natural) history.

33 Cameron, *Writing Nature*, p. 44.

34 By this account figuration, whether human or not, never achieves correspondence as a copy of one phenomenon in another but instead as a translation of one phenomenon in another in a way that produces a difference and disjunction between the first phenomenon and which reorients, secrets, and transmits its effects. If the play of earth, water, and wind makes a shape that is replayed by leaves, or if the passage of a wind produces a fledgling pine forest that in turn shapes how human beings walk, none of these shapes are foreordained or implied by the trajectory of the wind, of the forest that comes in its wake, or of the human beings walking through it. Nor are the wind, the forest, and the winding walk of human beings copies of the same pre-existing thing. The anterior phenomenon inflects a posterior one. For this reason, the shape taken by the second phenomenon is not entirely afterward the first one, nor is it parallel to it. Rather, the second phenomenon is an extension of the first phenomenon in a new material situation and for this reason it is not parallel to it but part of a metonymic chain, or better yet a metamorphic chain since this is not the carrying across of a name but a carrying across of a formative power.

35 Obviously any interpretation of a figure would move it from the presemiotic to the semiotic register, so it is possible—but not necessary—for any figure to become a trope that bears significance.

36 *J* XIII: 155.

37 The sound imitated could of course carry meaning for the animal that utters it even if the human who repeats it to designate this being might not have access to this animal's meaning. This sound could then also have a diverse range of meanings across different sorts of semiotic communities, some human and some not, and these meanings needn't intersect.

38 In fact, rather than presuming naïve correspondence, this Thoreauvian figuration presumes no signifier can possibly be equivalent to the concept it signifies. Such figure proliferates differences instead of annulling them. For a

sharply argued and reasoned analysis of how such a similar theory of figure augments difference, including temporal disjunctions, see Goldstein, *Sweet Science*, pp. 100–35, chapter "Sweet Semiosis."

39 *J* XII: 1588–9.
40 Thanks to Ingrid Diran for pushing me to more sharply articulate this final point and for contributing the wonderful "pinefy."
41 *J* XII: 1588–9.
42 Ibid.
43 Thoreau then goes on to compare human beings' coats to animals' coats, which suggests that the problem is not simply the relation of vegetable to human being but of vegetable to animal being (Thoreau, *Dispersion*, p. 97).
44 Thoreau, *Collected Essays and Poems*, pp. 367–8.
45 Ibid.
46 This turn of phrase and idea is indebted to Frédéric Neyrat's work in progress, which conjoins the terrestrial and the planetary by casting the earth as a wandering star. See Frédéric Neyrat, "Planetary Antigones: The Environmental Situation and the Wandering Condition." *Qui Parle*, 25, no. 1 (2016): 35–64.
47 Not before because previously these New England grounds were not forests but plains controlled by indigenous (probably Wôpanâak although Thoreau doesn't specify) controlled burns so that corn and berries could be grown (Thoreau, *Dispersion*, pp. 58, 156, 168).

Chapter 7

1 Louisa Kussin offers the most convincing account of what lead to Thoreau's invitation to speak at the 1860 agricultural fair; see Kussin, "The Concord Farmers Club and Thoreau's 'Succession of Forest Trees,'" *The Thoreau Society Bulletin*, 173 (1985): 1–3.
2 Henry Chandler Cowles, "The Ecological Relations of the Vegetation on the Sand Dunes of Lake Michigan," *Botanical Gazette* 27 no. 2 (1899): 95–117.
3 Levi Stockbridge, *Report from Eighth Annual Report of the Secretary of the Massachusetts Board of Agriculture,* Boston: White, 1861, pp. 276–8; facsimile rpt., Walter Hesford, "The 1860 Concord Cattle-Show: An Official Account," *Thoreau Society Bulletin*, 132 (1975): 6–7.
4 The Society's president in 1860 was George Boutwell, a former Governor of Massachusetts, whose remarks were included in *Transactions of the Middlesex Agricultural Society for the Year 1860*, cited in Hubert H. Hoeltje, "Thoreau as Lecturer," *New England Quarterly* 19 (1946): 492–3.
5 See Robert Thorson, *The Boatman: Henry David Thoreau's River Years*, Cambridge, MA: Harvard University Press, 2017 and *Walden's Shore: Henry David Thoreau and Nineteenth-Century Science,* Cambridge, MA: Harvard University Press, 2014; and Laura Dassow Walls, *Seeing New Worlds: Henry David Thoreau and Nineteenth-Century Natural Science,* Madison: University of Wisconsin Press, 1995.

6   See Alan D. Hodder, *Thoreau's Ecstatic Witness*, New Haven: Yale University Press, 2001; and Branka Arsić, *Bird Relics: Grief and Vitalism in Thoreau*, Cambridge, MA: Harvard University Press, 2016.

7   Walls, *Seeing New Worlds*, pp. 208–9.

8   Henry David Thoreau, *Excursions*, ed. Joseph J. Moldenhauer, Princeton: Princeton University Press, 2007, p. 136.

9   Scholarship on Thoreau's accounts of Native American cultures and peoples is diverse and often divergent; for early accounts of his interest in indigenous lifeways, see Robert F. Sayre, *Thoreau and the American Indians*, Princeton: Princeton University Press, 1997 and Phillip E. Gura, "Thoreau's Maine Woods Indians: More Representative Men," *American Literature* 49, no. 3 (1977): 366–84; for a revisionary consideration addressing a broader range of texts, see especially Joshua David Bellin, "In the Company of Savagists: Thoreau's Indian Books and Antebellum Ethnology," *The Concord Saunterer*, 16 (2008): 1–32, and "Red Walden: Thoreau and Native America," *Thoreau at Two Hundred: Essays and Reassessments*, New York: Cambridge University Press, 2016, pp. 75–87.

10 Thoreau, *Excursions*, p. 140.

11 Ibid.

12 See Emily Dickinson, "These are the days when birds come back," in *The Poems of Emily Dickinson*, Variorum Edition, ed. R. W. Franklin, Cambridge, MA: Belknap Press of Harvard University Press, 1998, p. 155.

13 In his correspondence with Greeley, who remained unconvinced about seeds, Thoreau continued to make his case for the germination of forest flora. Greeley then printed their exchange as a coda to "The Succession of Forest Trees" in the *New York Weekly Tribune* on February 2, 1861.

14 Thoreau, *Excursions*, p. 160.

15 Ibid.

16 The biblical reference is to John 3: 19.

17 See Antonio Blitz, *Fifty Years in the Magic Circle: Being an Account of the Author's Professional Life; His Wonderful Tricks and Feats; With Laughable Incidents, and Adventures as a Magician, Necromancer, and Ventriloquist*, Hartford: Belknap & Bliss, 1871.

18 Henry David Thoreau, *The Writings of Henry David Thoreau: Journals*, 14 vols, ed. Bradford Torrey, Boston: Houghton Mifflin, 1906, I: 3. Hereafter abbreviated as *J*, followed by the volume and page number. The journal entry is from October 24, 1837.

19 See Asa Gray and William Starling Sullivant, *A Manual of the Botany of the Northern United States: From New England to Wisconsin and South to Ohio and Pennsylvania Inclusive, (the Mosses and Liverworts by Wm. S. Sullivant,) Arranged According to the Natural System*, 1st ed., Boston: James Munroe, 1848.

20 *J* II: 202–3.

21 Thoreau, *J* II: 202–3. The journal entry is from May 20, 1851.

22 *J* II: 204–5.

23 Ibid.

24 *J* II: 391.

25 Ibid. The journal entry is from August 17, 1851.

26 Sharon Cameron, *Writing Nature* p. 34.
27 *J* VI: 426.
28 Ibid.
29 Ibid. The journal entry is from August 7, 1854.
30 *J* X: 127. The journal entry is from October 26, 1857.
31 *J* XI: 126–7. The journal entry is from August 26, 1858.
32 Ibid.
33 *J* XII: 347. The journal entry is from September 24, 1859.
34 *J* XIII: 94. The journal entry is from January 17, 1860.
35 *J* IX: 407. The journal entry is from June 5, 1857.
36 *J* X: 127.
37 *J* X: 40. The journal entry is from September 24, 1857.
38 *J* VIII: 335. The journal entry is from May 13, 1856.
39 *J* I: 140. The journal entry is from June 15, 1840.

Chapter 8

The J. Brian Key Fund of the Johns Hopkins University provided funds for the consultation of *The Dispersion of Seeds* manuscript located at the Berg Collection of English and American Literature of the New York Public Library. The William C. Archie Arts and Humanities Research Fund of Wake Forest University funded the consultation of relevant archival materials located at the Pierpont Morgan Library and at Harvard University's Houghton Library. For their responses to earlier versions of this essay, I am indebted to Maria A. Windell, Sharon Cameron, Theo Davis, Brigid Doherty, Michael Fried, Neil Hertz, Amanda Hockensmith, Claire Jarvis, Michael Klotz, Michael Moon, Lisa Siraganian, Irene Tucker, Priscilla Wald, and the anonymous reader and editors of *Criticism*.

1 For recent essays that disassociate Thoreau from this general problematic, see Deak Nabers, "Thoreau's Natural Constitution," *American Literary History* 19, no. 4 (2007): 824–48; and Theo Davis, "'Just apply a weight': Thoreau and the Aesthetics of Ornament," *ELH* 77, no. 3 (2010): 561–87. Both of these essays identify aspects of Thoerau's works that are invested in the alteration or modification of nature rather than in the apprehension or adequate representation of its intrinsic worth. Nabers argues that when approached through *The Reform Papers* it becomes clear that Thoreau "vigorously insists upon our need to interfuse the world of nature with the world of men" (p. 827). Davis argues that Thoreau's works feature an "account of form as the uncontrolled effect of human and natural forces, situations, and impacts" and thereby advances an aesthetics that "resists shaping nature…or making it symbolically meaningful [but] still entails intervention and alteration" (pp. 583, 580). Also see Theo Davis, *Ornamental Aesthetics: The Poetry of Attending in Thoreau, Dickinson, and Whitman*, Oxford: Oxford University Press, 2016, pp. 37–90.

2   Henry David Thoreau's *The Dispersion of Seeds* was left in manuscript at
     his death in 1862 and was first transcribed, compiled, edited, and published
     in 1993 by Bradley P. Dean. This essay refers to Dean's reading text of *The
     Dispersion of Seeds* as published in *Faith in a Seed: The Dispersion of Seeds
     and Other Late Natural History Writings,* ed. Bradley P. Dean, Washington,
     DC: Island Press, 1993; hereafter cited in the text as D. A facsimile of the
     manuscript, which is in the New York Public Library, was consulted while
     preparing this essay for publication.
3   The recent works of Anne-Lise François, Samuel Weber, and Giorgio
     Agamben represent influential versions of the poststructuralist commitment
     to conserving or maintaining potentiality (see Anne-Lise François, *Open
     Secrets: The Literature of Uncounted Experience,* Stanford: Stanford
     University Press, 2008; Giorgio Agamben, *Potentialities: Collected Essays in
     Philosophy,* Stanford: Stanford University Press, 2000; and Samuel Weber,
     Benjamin's -abilities, Cambridge, MA: Harvard University Press, 2010).
     On "possibility" in works by François and Agamben, see Pieter Vermeulen,
     "The Future of Possibility," review of Anne-Lise Francois's *Open Secrets:
     The Literature of Uncounted Experience, Postmodern Culture* 18, no. 2
     (2008).
4   Jay David Bolter and Richard Grusin, *Remediation: Understanding New
     Media,* Cambridge, MA: MIT Press, 1999, p. 65.
5   On Thoreau's relation to geologic "deep time," see Laura Dassow Walls, *Seeing
     New Worlds: Henry David Thoreau and Nineteenth-Century Natural Science,*
     Madison: University of Wisconsin Press, 1995, pp. 42–5. For other accounts
     of *deep time,* see Wai Chee Dimock, *Through Other Continents: American
     Literature across Deep Time,* Princeton: Princeton University Press, 2006;
     Dipesh Chakrabarty, "The Climate of History: Four Theses," *Critical Inquiry*
     35, no. 2 (2009): 197–222; and Mark McGurl, "The Posthuman Comedy,"
     Critical Inquiry 38, no. 3 (2012), p. 53.
6   See Jonathan Crary, *Techniques of the Observer: On Vision and Modernity
     in the Nineteenth Century,* October Books, Cambridge, MA: MIT Press,
     1990; and *Suspensions of Perception: Attention, Spectacle, and Modern
     Culture,* Cambridge, MA: MIT Press, 1999. See also Friedrich Kittler,
     Discourse Networks 1800/1900, Stanford: Stanford University Press, 1990;
     Gramophone, Film, Typewriter, Stanford: Stanford University Press, 1999; and
     Optical Media: Berlin Lectures 1999, London: Polity, 2010.
7   R[ichard] W. B. Lewis, *The American Adam: Innocence, Tragedy, and
     Tradition in the Nineteenth Century,* Chicago: University of Chicago Press,
     1955, pp. 21, 23. See Leo Marx, *The Machine in the Garden: Technology
     and the Pastoral Ideal in America,* Oxford: Oxford University Press, 1964,
     pp. 341–53. Among the essays and studies that take up Marx's reading of
     Thoreau, see especially Walter Benn Michaels, "*Walden*'s False Bottoms,"
     in *Glyph,* vol. 1, ed. Samuel Weber, Baltimore: Johns Hopkins University
     Press, 1977, pp. 132–49; Barbara Johnson, "A Hound, a Bay Horse, and a
     Turtle Dove: Obscurity in *Walden,*" in *A World of Difference,* Baltimore:
     Johns Hopkins University Press, 1987, pp. 49–56; William Cronon, "The
     Trouble with Wilderness," in *Uncommon Ground: Rethinking the Human*

Place in Nature, ed. William Cronon, New York: W. W. Norton, 1995, pp. 69–90; and Philip Fisher, *Still the New World: American Literature in a Culture of Creative Destruction,* Cambridge, MA: Harvard University Press, 1999. Although the bulk of post-1960s criticism is invested in Thoreau's commitments to the givenness of nature, other scholarship evaluates Thoreau's ability to transform nature into a site of self-recognition or otherwise make it available for human use. See Sherman Paul, *The Shores of America: Thoreau's Inward Exploration,* Urbana: University of Illinois Press, 1958; Perry Miller, *Consciousness in Concord: The Text of Thoreau's Hitherto "Lost Journal" (1840–1841),* Boston: Houghton Mifflin, 1958; and Frederick Garber, *Thoreau's Redemptive Imagination,* New York: New York University Press, 1977, and *Thoreau's Fable of Inscribing,* Princeton: Princeton University Press, 1991.

8   Sharon Cameron, *Writing Nature: Henry Thoreau's Journal,* Chicago: University of Chicago Press, 1985, pp. 89, 75.

9   Lawrence Buell, *The Environmental Imagination: Thoreau, Nature Writing, and the Formation of American Culture,* Cambridge: Harvard University Press, 1995, pp. 115, 143, 144; the discussion of Cameron is on, pp. 125–7, 473. Also see Stanley Cavell, *The Senses of Walden,* Chicago: University of Chicago Press, 1972; John Hildebidle, *A Naturalist's Liberty,* Cambridge, MA: Harvard University Press, 1983; and Lawrence Buell, *Writing for an Endangered World,* Cambridge, MA: Harvard University Press, 2001, and *The Future of Environmental Criticism,* Oxford: Oxford University Press, 2005.

10   Timothy Sweet, "Projecting Early American Writing," *American Literary History* 22, no. 2 (2010), p. 420. As Sweet explains, recanonized as "green," Thoreau emerges as a writer who is "devoted at once to seeking self-awareness and to extending empathy to nonhuman life" and whose writings therefore respond to "the environmental degradation wrought by technological development and economic growth" by initiating "a reevaluation of the natural world as having intrinsic worth" (pp. 419–20). Also see Richard J. Schneider, ed., *Thoreau's Sense of Place: Essays in American Environmental Writing,* foreword by Lawrence Buell, Iowa City: University of Iowa Press, 2002.

11   Ursula Heise and Meredith McGill are among those who critique this institutionalization. See Ursula K. Heise, *Sense of Place and Sense of Planet: The Environmental Imagination of the Global,* Oxford: Oxford University Press, 2008; and Meredith L. McGill, "Common Places: Poetry, Illocality, and Temporal Dislocation in Thoreau's *A Week on the Concord and Merrimack Rivers,*" *American Literary History* 19, no. 2 (2007): 357–74.

12   See Jacques Derrida, *The Animal That Therefore I Am,* ed. Marie-Louis Mallet, trans. David Wills, New York: Fordham University Press, 2008; Cary Wolfe, *Animal Rites: American Culture, the Discourse of Species, and Posthumanist Theory,* Chicago: University of Chicago Press, 2003; and David Wills, *Dorsality: Thinking Back through Technology and Politics,* Minneapolis: University of Minnesota Press, 2008.

13 W[illiam] J. T. Mitchell, "The Rights of Things," foreword to Wolfe, *Animal Rites*, p. xiii.

14 Ibid., xi.

15 Jane Bennett, *Vibrant Matter: A Political Ecology of Things,* Durham: Duke University Press, 2010, pp. xiii, ix, 116–17. Also see Mark Hansen, *Feed Forward: On the Future of Twenty-First Century Media,* Chicago: University of Chicago Press, 2015 and David Wills, *Inanimation: Theories of Inorganic Life,* Minneapolis: University of Minnesota Press, 2016.

16 Branka Arsić, *Bird Relics: Grief and Vitalism in Thoreau,* Cambridge, MA: Harvard University Press, 2016, pp. 163, 310.

17 As Dominic Pettman discusses, "automatic responder" is one of the ways that Derrida characterizes René Descartes's account of the animal. See Dominic Pettman, *Human Error: Species-Being and Media Machines,* Minneapolis: University of Minnesota Press, 2011, pp. 112–3; and Derrida, *The Animal,* pp. 85–7.

18 Gilles Deleuze, "Eight Years Later: 1980 Interview" (1980), in *Two Regimes of Madness: Texts and Interviews 1975–1995,* ed. David Lapoujade, trans. Ames Hodges and Mike Taormina, New York: Semiotext[e], 2007, p. 179. See also Gilles Deleuze and Félix Guattari, *A Thousand Plateaus: Capitalism and Schizophrenia,* trans. Brian Massumi, Minneapolis: University of Minnesota Press, 1987, pp. 323–37.

19 Deleuze and Guattari, *A Thousand Plateaus,* p. 328.

20 Giles Deleuze, *Expressionism in Philosophy: Spinoza,* New York: Zone Books, 1990, p. 67; cited in Bennett, *Vibrant Matter,* p. xi. Deleuze argues that Spinoza's "new logic" of "real distinction" as "formal distinction" (a logic in which "it is formal distinction that provides an absolutely coherent concept of the unity of substance and the plurality of attributes") is "profoundly Anticartesian" insofar as Descartes is strongly opposed to "conceiving a real distinction between things ... which isn't attended by a division of being" (pp. 65–7).

21 As noted in Robert D. Richardson's "Thoreau's Broken Task" (*D,* 3–17), the belief that forest trees and plants could be generated spontaneously was a "prevalent concept" in North America around 1860. For Thoreau, the lay sense that forest trees and plants can be generated spontaneously and, hence, were recently created in the places where they are currently found growing, is backed by the version of *special creationism* advanced by Louis Agassiz. Agassiz argues that individual species are immutable entities, that these species originated in separate acts of creation (according to a divine plan), and that the current geographical distribution of species is identical to that of earlier periods. Thoreau had articulated what Michael Burger calls his "dispersal-dependent theory of [forest] succession" as early as 1856; by 1860, Agassiz's account was being challenged in North America by supporters of Charles Darwin such as Asa Gray. In *The Dispersion of Seeds,* Thoreau cites Darwin's *The Origin of Species* (1859), and it is evident from the comments Thoreau made about Agassiz and Darwin in his *Journal* and extract books that what he mainly objected to about Agassiz's theory was its account of the geographical distribution of species (*D,* 25, 75, 102). Accordingly, Thoreau's documentation of both the modes

by which seeds are occasionally transported and the ways that seeds are suited for such modes of transport is legible as both a contribution to Darwin's theory and a challenge to Agassiz's. See Hunter Dupree, "The First Darwinian Debate in America: Gray versus Agassiz," *Daedalus* 8, no. 3 (1959): 560–9; Bradley P. Dean, "Henry D. Thoreau and Horace Greeley Exchange Letters on the 'Spontaneous Generation of Plants,'" *New England Quarterly* 66, no. 2 (1993): 630–8; Michael Burger, "Henry David Thoreau's Science in *The Dispersion of Seeds*," *Annals of Science* 53, no. 4 (1996): 381–97; Walls, *Seeing New Worlds;* Peter J. Bowler, "Geographical Distribution in the *Origin of Species*," in *The Cambridge Companion to the "Origin of Species*," ed. Michael Ruse, Cambridge: Cambridge University Press, 2009, pp. 153–73; Henry James Clark, *Mind in Nature, or the Origin of Life, and the Mode of Development of Animals,* New York: Appleton, 1865; and George B. Emerson, *Report on the Trees and Shrubs Growing Naturally in the Forests of Massachusetts,* 1846; repr., Boston: Little Brown, 1875. On ecology, geology, and evolution in *The Dispersion of Seeds,* see Juliana Chow, "Partial Readings: Thoreau's Studies as Natural History's Causalities," in *Anthropocene Reading: Literary History in Geologic Times,* ed. Tobias Menely and Jesse Oak Taylor, University Park: Penn State University Press, 2017, pp. 117–31. On evolution, race, and materialism in Thoreau, see Cristin Ellis, *Antebellum Posthuman: Race and Materiality in the Mid-Nineteenth Century,* New York: Fordham University Press, pp. 61–96.

22 Clark, *Mind in Nature*, p. 29.

23 Ibid., p. 314.

24 Buell, *Environmental Imagination,* p. 170.

25 Henry David Thoreau, *The Writings of Henry David Thoreau: Journal,* 8 vols. to date, editor-in-chief, Elizabeth Witherell, Princeton: Princeton University Press, 1991–2002, 4: 33. Hereafter abbreviated as *PJ*, followed by the volume and page number; and René Descartes, *Discourse on Method and Meditation on First Philosophy,* 1637; repr., London: Everyman, 2004, p. 43. For one such more recent critique, see Pettman, *Human Error.*

26 Perry Miller, *The New England Mind: The Seventeenth Century,* Cambridge, MA: Harvard University Press, 1954, p. 214.

27 Cameron, *Writing Nature,* pp. 11, 5, 47. On "selfless perception" in Thoreau also see Arsić, *Bird Relics,* pp. 29–113, 251–322.

28 Ibid., pp. 10, 47. As Cameron and Richard Grusin demonstrate, a number of Thoreau's works imply that writing in a particular mode will make their author natural and feature direct representations of such humanly produced natural texts and their consumption. By contrast, *The Dispersion of Seeds* focuses on the production of such texts and does so in order to render such a project's requirements, modes, and consequences (the focus of the current essay). See Cameron, *Writing Nature;* and Richard Grusin, "Thoreau, Extravagance, and the Economy of Nature," *American Literary History* 5, no. 1 (1993): 30–50.

29 Buell, *Environmental Imagination,* pp. 144, 155.

30 *PJ* 1: 243.

31 Alan Trachtenberg, "Photography: The Emergence of a Keyword," in
Photography in Nineteenth Century America, ed. Martha A. Sandweiss,
New York: Henry N. Abrams, 1991, p. 21.

32 Walter Benn Michaels, "Action and Accident: Photography and Writing,"
in *The Gold Standard and the Logic of Naturalism: American Literature
at the Turn of the Century,* Berkeley: University of California Press, 1987,
p. 218. On *automaticity* and *indexicality* in nineteenth- and twentieth-century
writing on photography, also see Walter Benn Michaels, "Photographs and
Fossils," in *Photography Theory,* ed. James Elkins, Art Seminar, vol. 2, New
York: Routledge, 2008, pp. 431–50; and Patrick Maynard, *The Engine of
Visualization: Thinking through Photography,* Ithaca: Cornell University
Press, 1997.

33 Irene Tucker, "Picturing Utilitarianism: John Stuart Mill and the Invention
of a Photographic Public," *Criticism* 50, no. 3 (2008): p. 412. For Tucker
it is important to note that, for Fox Talbot, photography's capacity to
produce unmediated perceptions is, itself, a product of human agency—that
is, on Tucker's account, it is crucial to recognize that Talbot identifies this
particular aspect of "the photographic" as the outcome of a series of directed
technological innovations.

34 Henry David Thoreau, "Walking" (1862), in *Excursions,* ed. Joseph J.
Moldenhauer, Princeton: Princeton University Press, 2007, pp. 217–18.

35 While Thoreau's conception of photography is largely consistent with what
Trachtenberg, Michaels, and others locate as the dominant conception
of photography in the nineteenth century, it is nevertheless the case that
there was not a singular, univocal conception of what photography was,
what its chief aspects were, or what it would mean to export or generalize
photographic features. Accordingly, various versions of "the photographic"
are instantiated by the various appearances of photography in works of
nineteenth-century American literature—as explicit elements of plot, as
formal organizing principals, as generalized logics, and so on. For example,
in two short notices on "The Daguerreotype" for *Alexander's Weekly
Messenger* (January 15 and May 6, 1840) Edgar Allen Poe reiterates a
claim often made about the daguerreotype—that one can infinitely magnify
any portion of a daguerreotype's surface so as to render with extreme
clarity normally imperceptible details of photographed objects' surfaces—
and amplifies it into a conception of "photography" as an apparatus for the
spatialization of objects that makes them available for superficial access.
In 1844's "The Purloined Letter," Poe then generalizes and formalizes
this conception of the photographic by presenting it as a technique for
accessing spaces through the continual resolution of selected aspects of
their exterior arrangements—a mode of accessing spaces that Poe terms
"detection" and juxtaposes to the investigative mode of accessing spaces by
taking them apart in order to gain access to their interiors. (For a different
account of Poe's relation to the photographic, see James Lastra, *Sound
Technology and the American Cinema*, New York: Columbia University
Press, 2000, pp. 1–5.) On the other hand, it is also not the case that the

capacity to produce desubjectivized recordings was exclusively associated
with photography. This is made particularly clear in studies such as Lisa
Gitelman's *Scripts, Grooves, and Writing Machines,* Stanford: Stanford
University Press, 1999 and Stephen Best's *The Fugitive's Properties,*
Chicago: University of Chicago Press, 2004—of note, in this regard, are
Gitelman's focus on the practices of "phonography" in America prior to
Edison's 1877 invention of the mechanical phonograph, and Best's account
of the intersections of sound-reproduction technologies and the discourses
of slavery.

36   *PJ* 1: 243.

37   The standard accounts of both the history of photography generally and in
     America note that in the early 1860s mobile photography (i.e., outside of
     a studio) was limited by the extreme bulkiness of photographic equipment,
     the awkwardness of operating the camera, and the labor intensiveness of
     the production of a photograph. These histories also note that while the
     aspiration to produce instantaneous photographs—and to thereby capture
     motion—was a feature of photography since its inception in 1839, it
     was not until the 1870s that photographers such as Eadward Muybridge
     and Etienne-Jules Marey were able to capture natural motions that were
     invisible to humans due to their rapidity. Thoreau's project, then, differs
     essentially from those of Marey and Muybridge in that while their aim
     was to capture motions that were invisible because of their instantaneity
     Thoreau's was calibrated to capture motions that were invisible due to their
     spatial extension and temporal duration. And, accordingly, while Marey
     and Muybridge required and engineered means of instantaneous capturing
     (of breaking down a rapid natural motion into smaller units that were then
     recombined), Thoreau's project involved long periods of capturing slow
     natural motions which were then compressed, condensed, averaged, and
     coordinated in order to compose humanly apprehensible representations
     of the dispersion of seeds. See William Welling, *Photography in America:
     1839–1900,* New York: Thomas Y. Crowell, 1978; Beaumont Newhall,
     The History of Photography: From 1839 to the Present, New York: The
     Museum of Modern Art, 1982; *Photography in Nineteenth Century
     America,* ed. Martha A Sandweiss; Marta Braun, *Picturing Time: The Work
     of Etienne-Jules Marey (1830–1904),* Chicago: University of Chicago Press,
     1992; Mary Ann Doane, *The Emergence of Cinematic Time Modernity,
     Contingency, the Archive,* Cambridge, MA: Harvard University Press, 2002;
     and Jimena Canales, *A Tenth of a Second: A History,* Chicago: University
     of Chicago Press, 2009. For alternative accounts of Thoreau's relationship
     to photography, see Sean Ross Meehan, "Pencil of Nature: Thoreau's
     Photographic Register," *Criticism* 48, no. 1 (2006): 7–38, and Arsić, *Bird
     Relics,* pp. 213–23.

38   For Crary, see *Techniques of the Observer* and *Suspensions of Perception;*
     and, for Kittler, see *Discourse Networks, Gramophone, Film, Typewriter,*
     and *Optical Media.* Crary's *Techniques of the Observer* and *Suspensions
     of Perception* offer an account of media-culture in which the nineteenth
     century is characterized by the emergence of a regime of "subjective vision"
     in which the basis of perception is grounded in the materiality of the

observer's body—an account of perception in the nineteenth century that Crary identifies as a generalization and extension of M. H. Abrams' *The Mirror and the Lamp: Romantic Theory and the Critical Tradition,* Oxford: University of Oxford Press, 1953—and in which this grounding constitutes the embodied subject as a "site of both knowledge and power" as described by Michel Foucault in *Discipline and Punish: The Birth of the Prison,* 1975; New York: Pantheon, 1978 and elsewhere. Accordingly, for Crary, insofar as photography works to imply a model of perception in which perceptions are "disembodied" and, hence, "incorporeal," the popularity of photography in the nineteenth century can be ascribed to the way in which it worked to obscure the institutionalization of "subjective vision" by phantasmaticly implying the availability of a superseded model of perception (that which Abrams identifies as Lockean) and the equally unavailable version of subjectivity that this model supports (that which Foucault identifies as the "free" or "classical" subject). Kittler's *Discourse Networks 1800/1900, Gramophone, Film, Typewriter* and *Optical Media* offers an account of media-culture in which the history of the nineteenth century is, essentially, a history of the becoming autonomous of technology in which the "media revolution" of the 1880s—the near-simultaneous invention of three storage devices: film, the gramophone, and the typewriter—installs "the discourse network of 1900" which obviates the conscious/unconscious distinction by eliminating the basis of intentional action, thereby rendering humans as the instruments of newly autonomous "technological media." In such an account, in the 1800s writing gets identified as a medium that is capable of storing perceptions (an identification that amounts to a standardization of what Abrams describes as the project of Romantic poetry), and this capacity is then understood as an instance of writing automatically registering effects sourced in the emergent technological media that will compose the discourse network of 1900.

39 The term *naturization* was suggested by Michael Fried in response to an earlier version of this essay.

Chapter 9

1 Henry David Thoreau, *Journal,* vol. 3: 1848–1851, ed. John C. Broderick, Robert Sattelmeyer, Mark R. Patterson, and William Rossi, Princeton: Princeton University Press, 1990, p. 211. Quotations from the Princeton editions of Thoreau's *Journal* (produced as part of the series, *The Writings of Henry David Thoreau,* ed. Elizabeth Hall Witherell et al.) will henceforth be cited internally as *PJ* followed by the volume and page number. However, since the Princeton editions of the *Journal* are currently only available through vol. 8 (ending with Thoreau's entry for September 3, 1854), for all entries after this date I will be citing from *The Journal of Henry David Thoreau,* 14 vols, ed. Bradford Torrey and Francis H. Allen, Boston: Houghton Mifflin, 1906, which will be cited internally as *J* followed by the volume and page number.

2   Walter Harding, "Thoreau's Sexuality," *Journal of Homosexuality* 21, no. 3 (1991): 24–5. See also Henry Abelove, *Deep Gossip,* Minneapolis: University of Minnesota Press, 2005.

3   Perry Miller, *Consciousness in Concord,* Boston: Houghton Mifflin, 1958; Michael Warner, "Walden's Erotic Economy," in *Comparative American Identities: Race, Sex, and Nationality in the Modern Text,* ed. Hortense J. Spillers, New York: Routledge, 1991. See also Michael Warner, "Thoreau's Bottom," *Raritan* 11, no. 3 (1992): 53–79.

4   Henry David Thoreau, *Walden,* ed. Lyndon Shanley, Princeton: Princeton University Press, 1971, p. 141 (Henceforth *W* in internal citations); Michael Warner, "Walden's Erotic Economy," p. 158.

5   Warner, "Walden's Erotic Economy," p. 157. As Warner elaborates elsewhere, while "Thoreau repeatedly expressed a longing for self-transcendence through the love of another man," in his mid-nineteenth-century moment, "the available language of sexuality allowed him neither to legitimate that longing nor even to describe it except as an abstract longing, disjunct from practice and from the body" (Warner, "Thoreau's Bottom," p. 63).

6   For further examples of Thoreau's tendency to eroticize his relation to nature, see Harding, "Thoreau's Sexuality," pp. 40–1. Although beyond the purview of this study, it is worth noting that a penchant for casting encounters with nature in emphatically erotic terms appears across a range of nineteenth-century authors. Thus, for instance, in Hawthorne's *The Marble Faun,* Donatello lays "himself at full length on the turf and presse[s] down his lips, kissing the violets and daisies, which [kiss] him back again, though shyly, in their maiden fashion" (Nathaniel Hawthorne, *The Marble Faun,* Harmondsworth: Penguin, 1990, p. 74). Or again, Goethe's Faust demands, "Where can I grasp you, infinite nature? You breasts, you sources of all life, where?" (J. W. V. Goethe, *Urfaust* ll, pp. 102–3, cited in Robert J. Richards, *The Romantic Conception of Life: Science and Philosophy in the Age of Goethe,* Chicago: University of Chicago Press, 2002, p. 327). For a fascinating study of vegetal poetics in nineteenth-century art, and particularly of the ways in which vegetality was invoked to encode queer sexualities in late nineteenth-century culture, see Alison Syme, *A Touch of Blossom: John Singer Sargent and the Queer Flora of Fin-de-Siècle Art,* University Park: Pennsylvania State University Press, 2010.

7   Harding, "Thoreau's Sexuality," pp. 40–1.

8   In suggesting that the hetero/homo binary was consolidated around 1900, I do not mean to discount Warner's valuable analysis, in "Thoreau's Bottom," of the ways in which a heteronormative logic of sexual difference informed discourses of sexuality well before its codification in late nineteenth sexology. Too, in referencing sexology's "consolidation" of sexual categories, I do not mean to suggest that those categories were coherent, a distinction Eve Sedgwick's now-classic account of the contradictory and syncretic nature of our sexual categories makes critical. See Sedgwick, *Epistemology of the Closet,* Berkeley: University of California Press, 1990.

9   David Halperin, *How to Do the History of Homosexuality,* Chicago: University of Chicago Press, 2002, pp. 9, 26.

10 For an exciting and thought-provoking recent discussion of how pre-sexological theories of sexuality might fruitfully help us to unsettle and reorganize the politics of sexuality today, see Greta LaFleur, *The Natural History of Sexuality in Early America,* Baltimore: Johns Hopkins University Press, 2018. The eighteenth-century environmental theory of biological and racial divergence, in relation to which LaFleur derives a conjugate eighteenth-century environmental theory of sexuality, is one important historical source for what I will describe here as Thoreau's sense of vegetal porosity to—his ability to be brought to "fruition" by—sensory stimulations in his environment.

11 Peter Coviello, *Tomorrow's Parties: Sex and the Untimely in Nineteenth-Century America,* New York: New York University Press, 2013, p. 32.

12 For a comprehensive history of the anthropocentrism of Western thinking about plant sexuality, see Lincoln Taiz and Lee Taiz, *Flora Unveiled: The Discovery and Denial of Sex in Plants,* Oxford: Oxford University Press, 2017.

13 See Elaine Miller, *The Vegetative Soul,* New York: State University of New York Press, 2002, pp. 56–7.

14 Quoted in Michael Marder, *The Philosopher's Plant,* New York: Columbia University Press, 2014, p. 12.

15 Ibid., p. 16.

16 On the fall and rise of the thesis of sexes in plants, see Taiz and Taiz, *Flora Unveiled.* For an eighteenth-century perspective on this history, see Charles Alston, "A Dissertation on the Sexes of Plants" (1754), in *Essays and Observations, Physical and Literary, read before a Society in Edinburgh,* ed. Medical Society of Edinburgh, 3, vols, I: Edinburgh: Hamilton and Balfour, 1754, pp. 205–83.

17 Carl Linnaeus, *Praeludia sponsaliorum plantarum* ["Prelude to the Betrothal of Plants"] (1729); reprinted Uppsala: Almqvist and Wiksell, 1908.

18 Properly speaking, hermaphroditic self-pollination is biologically distinct from asexual reproduction in plants. In conflating these two reproductive mechanisms here, I only mean to highlight the way in which, when viewed through the lens of human reproduction, self-pollination is asexual insofar as it allows the individual to reproduce without intercourse with another. For a fuller account of Linnaeus' treatment of hermaphroditism in plants, see Maja Bondestam, "When the Plant Kingdom Became Queer: On Hermaphrodites and the Linnaean Language of Nonnormative Sex," in *Illdisciplined Gender: Engaging Questions of Nature/Culture and Transgressive Encounters,* ed. Jacob Bull and Margaretha Fahlgren, Heidelberg: Springer International Publishing, 2016.

19 J. G. Siegesbeck, *Botanosophiae verioris brevis sciagraphicia* (1737) cited in Taiz and Taiz, *Flora Unveiled,* p. 387.

20 Charles Alston, "A Dissertation on the Sexes of Plants," p. 238; Richard Polwhele, "The Unsex'd Females: A Poem" (1798) cited in Sam George, "'Not Strictly Proper for a Female Pen': Eighteenth-Century Poetry and the Sexuality of Botany," *Comparative Critical Studies* 2, no. 2 (2005), 199.

21 See, for instance, Taiz and Taiz, *Flora Unveiled,* pp. 384–7.

22 See, for instance, Taiz and Taiz, *Flora Unveiled*, pp. 391–2, and George, "'Not Strictly Proper for a Female Pen.'"

23 Thoreau sent this essay, along with another entitled "Love," to his friend, Harrison Blake, on the news of Blake's engagement in September 1852. Together, these two essays constitute Thoreau's only writings to address themselves centrally and explicitly to the subject of human sexuality.

24 H. G. O. Blake to Thoreau, August 1852, collected in *Letters of a Spiritual Seeker,* ed. Bradley Dean, New York: W. W. Norton, 2005, p. 67.

25 Thoreau, "Chastity & Sensuality," in *Early Essays and Miscellanies,* ed. Joseph J. Moldenhauer and Edwin Moser, Princeton: Princeton University Press, 1975, p. 277 (henceforth *EEM* in internal citations).

26 See Miller, *The Vegetative Soul.* It is worth noting that a version of this distinction remains current today. As it is put in modern scientific terms: "[W]hile animals typically complete the construction of their final bauplan during the embryological phases of development, the formation of a plant embryo constitutes a mere fraction of the entirety of the continuously changing phenotype associated with ongoing organogenesis." William Friedman and Pamela Diggle, "Charles Darwin and the Origins of Plant Evolutionary Biology," *Plant Cell* 23, no. 3 (2011), 1194.

27 Goethe, "Morphologie" cited in Richards, *The Romantic Conception of Life*, p. 454.

28 Thoreau, "The Natural History of Massachusetts," in *Excursions,* ed. Joseph J. Moldenhauer, Princeton: Princeton University Press, 2007, p. 25.

29 See too Thoreau's *Journal* entry for September 7, 1851: "We all have our states of fullness and of emptiness, but we overflow at different points. One overflows through sensual outlets, another through his heart, another through his head, and another perchance only through the higher part of his head, or his poetic faculty. It depends on where each is tight and open. We can, perchance, then direct our nutriment to those organs we specially use" (*PJ* 4: 55).

30 For an important, if somewhat differently vectored reading of this crucial line, see Peter Coviello, "'The Wild Not Less Than the Good': Thoreau, Sex, Biopower," *GLQ: A Journal of Lesbian and Gay Studies* 23, no. 4 (2017): 509–32.

31 Theresa Kelley, *Clandestine Marriage: Botany and Romantic Culture,* Baltimore: Johns Hopkins University Press, 2012, p. 2.

32 Kelley, *Clandestine Marriage,* p. 6.

33 Miller, *The Vegetative Soul,* p. 59.

34 For an illuminating elaboration of Thoreau's anti-taxonomic thought, see Branka Arsić, *Bird Relics: Grief and Vitalism in Thoreau,* Cambridge, MA: Harvard University Press, 2016, pp. 172–5.

35 Warner, "Thoreau's Bottom," p. 67.

36 Warner, "Walden's Erotic Economy," pp. 172–3.

37 Coviello, *Tomorrow's Parties,* pp. 45, 43.

38 Ibid., p. 216 n22.

39 Ibid., p. 38.

40 Warner, "Walden's Erotic Economy," pp. 158–9.

41 Coviello, *Tomorrow's Parties,* p. 38.

42 Elizabeth Freeman, *Time Binds: Queer Temporalities, Queer Histories,* Durham: Duke University Press, 2010, p. 15.

43 For concise introductions to queer ecology, see, for instance, Catriona Sandilands and Bruce Erickson, "A Genealogy of Queer Ecologies," in *Queer Ecologies: Sex, Nature, Politics, Desire,* ed. Catriona Sandilands and Bruce Erickson, Bloomington: Indiana University Press, 2010, and Timothy Morton, "Queer Ecology" *PMLA* 125, no. 2 (2010): 273–82.

44 David Eng, Judith Halberstam, and José Esteban Muñoz, "What's Queer about Queer Studies Now?" *Social Text* 84–85, no. 3–4 (2005), 3.

45 Jordana Rosenberg, "The Molecularization of Sexuality: On Some Primitivisms of the Present," *Theory & Event* 17, no. 2 (2014).

46 Catriona Sandilands makes a version of this point in her comments at a roundtable discussion on queer ecology, see Gordon Brent Brochu-Ingram, Peter Hobbs and Catriona Sandilands, "Queer Ecologies Roundtable Discussion Part 4: Queer Ecologies at the Limits," *UnderCurrents* 19 (2015), pp. 60–1.

Chapter 10

1 Thoreau died on May 6, 1862. A month before his death his sister Sophia, who helped him revise the manuscripts for publication and who took dictation of his letters to the publishers, sent off the final version of "Wild Apples" along with Thoreau's last letter, dated April 2, 1862, to the *Atlantic Monthly* which published the essay in November. See Dean's editorial note on "Wild Apples," in Henry David Thoreau, *Wild* Fruits, ed. Bradley P. Dean, New York: W. W. Norton & Company, 2000, p. 312. All references to *Wild Fruits* are to this edition and will be given parenthetically in the text as WF, followed by a page number. References to "Wild Apples" are also from this edition, but will be designated as WA in order to distinguish them from other segments in *Wild Fruits*.

2 Robert Richardson, *Henry David Thoreau: A Life of the Mind,* Berkeley: University of California Press, 1986, p. 224.

3 Quoted in Laura Dassow Walls, *Henry David Thoreau: A Life,* Chicago: University of Chicago Press, 2017, p. 366. Interestingly, although "Walking" was written before "Wild Apples," the insights about wild fruits' running wild from cultivation that serve as the focal point of the latter piece inform in hindsight the former lecture which Thoreau understood to be the progenitor of all of his subsequent writing.

4 Henry David Thoreau, *Walden, Civil Disobedience, and Other Writings,* ed. William Rossi, New York: W. W. Norton, p. 261. All references to "Walking" are from this edition, rendered parenthetically in the text as W and followed by a page number.

5 Bradley P. Dean, *Faith in a Seed,* Washington, DC: Island Press, 1993, p. 79.

6 Henry David Thoreau, *The Writings of Henry David Thoreau: Journals,* 14 vols, ed. Bradford Torrey, Boston: Houghton Mifflin, 1906, III: 83–4. Hereafter abbreviated as *J*, followed by the volume and page number.

7   New genetic research has shown that "*M. sylvestris* has contributed so extensively to the apple's genome that the modern apple is actually more similar to the sour crabapple than to its Kazakhstani ancestor, *M. sieversii*." E. Coart et al., "Chloroplast Diversity in the Genus *Malus*: New Insights into the Relationship between the European Wild Apple (*Malus sylvestris*) and the Domesticated Apple (*Malus domestica*)," *Mol. Ecol* 15, no. 8 (2016): 2171–82. See also, *Boyce Thompson Institute*, "New Genomic Insights," https://www.sciencedaily.com/releases/2017/08/170815095041.htm. Accessed January 20, 2020.

8   See, for example, Lawrence Buell, *The Environmental Imagination: Thoreau, Nature Writing, and the Formulation of American Culture*, Cambridge, MA: Harvard University Press, 1995, p. 363; Robert Sattelmeyer, *Thoreau's Reading: A Study in Intellectual History with Bibliographical Catalogue*, Princeton: Princeton University Press, 1988, p. 89, Richardson, *Henry David Thoreau: A Life of the Mind*, pp. 383–4; David Robinson, *Natural Life: Thoreau's Worldly Transcendentalism*, Ithaca: Cornell University Press, 2004, p. 196; Laura Dassow Walls, *Henry David Thoreau: A Life*, p. 480; Cristin Ellis, *Antebellum Posthuman: Race and Materiality in the Mid-Nineteenth Century*, New York: Fordham University Press, 2018, p. 78.

9   The coincidence of Thoreau's botanical interests with his reading of Darwin's theory of evolution would better be viewed in the context of Thoreau's rejection of Agassiz's theory of special creation.

10   Bradley P. Dean, "Henry D. Thoreau and Horace Greeley Exchange Letter on the 'Spontaneous Generation of Plants,'" *The New England Quarterly* 66, no. 4 (1993), p. 631. See Also Michael Berger, "Henry David Thoreau's Science in *The Dispersion of Seeds*," *Annals of Science*, 53 (1996): 381–97.

11   Branka Arsić, *Bird Relics: Grief and Vitalism in Thoreau*, Cambridge, MA: Harvard University Press, 2016, p. 173. As Arsić explains, in striving "to understand each singularity that occupies the 'present' in the uniqueness of its phenomenality," Thoreau's explorations "privilege the singular as opposed to the categorical and taxonomical" (pp. 175, 172).

12   Ralph Waldo Emerson, "To the Public—Editors' Address," *Massachusetts Quarterly Review* 1 (1847), p. 3.

13   The gas was first integrated in 1772 but its widespread use didn't begin until 1862. In 1874 the anesthetic was philosophically popularized by Paul Benjamin Blood in "Anesthetic Revelation" (the pamphlet that influenced William James's understanding of conversion as a series of ecstatic transformations of the self in *The Varieties of Religious Experience*), which defined the gas's influence as a "primordial" "ecstatic" state and "the gist of philosophy."

14   Branka Arsić, "Thoreau's Vegetal Ontology: The Aerial, the Rootles, and the Analogous," in this volume, p. 5.

15   Richardson, *A Life of the Mind*, pp. 239–40.

16   Robinson, *Natural Life*, p. 197.

17   Ibid., p. 195.

18   Michael Marder, *Plant-Thinking: A Philosophy of Vegetal Life*, New York: Columbia University Press, 2013, p. 5.

19   Henry David Thoreau, *Walden, Civil Disobedience, and Other Writings*, p. 224.

20   Charles Dewey, *A History of the County of Berkshire, Massachusetts*, Pittsfield: Samuel W. Bush, 1829, p. 39.

21 Frank Davidson, "Melville, Thoreau, and 'The Apple-Tree Table,'" *American Literature* 25, no. 4 (1954), pp. 479–80. Davidson establishes convincing parallels between Thoreau's and Melville's respective adaptation of Dewey's story, details that the latter lacks: "Both mention the heat of an urn as a factor in the hatching of the insect. Both use a green tree in association with a resurrection. Both make of the table a festive board about which a family sits, and both have those gathered about it frightened as they hear the gnawing of the insects. ... For 'The Apple-Tree Table,' then, Melville, it would seem, really had more imaginative stimulus from *Walden* than from *The History of the County of Berkshire*" (Ibid., 483–4).

22 Barbara Johnson, *A World of Difference,* Baltimore: Johns Hopkins University Press, 1987, pp. 54–5.

23 Walls, *Henry David Thoreau: A Life,* p. 271.

24 John Cage, "Preface to *Lecture on the Weather*," in *Empty Words, Writings '73–'78,* Middleton: Wesleyan University Press, 1979, p. 5.

25 *Lecture on the Weather,* musical score, Cage's instructions for instrumentation. The score is held in the New York Public Library.

26 Cage, "Preface," pp. 4–5.

27 Paula Oliver Rau, Ph.D. dissertation "John Cage: Prints, Drawings, and Watercolors, 1978–1992," 2005, p. 44.

28 Cage's indebtedness to Thoreau was profound and is well-documented. *Empty Words* (1973), *Score without Parts (40 Drawings by Thoreau): Twelve Haiku* (1978), *17 Drawings by Thoreau* (1978), and *Déreau* (1982) are some of his most famous works in which Thoreau's writings figure not only as the artwork's material but as its method. For more on Cage and Thoreau, see Jannika Bock, *Concord in Massachusetts, Discord in the World: The Writings of Henry Thoreau and John Cage,* Berlin-New York: Peter Lang, Internationaler Verlag der Wissenschaften, 2008; Francine Amy Koslow, *Henry David Thoreau as a Source for Artistic Inspiration,* Amherst: University of Massachusetts Press, 1985; David Nicholls, *The Cambridge Companion to John Cage,* Cambridge: Cambridge University Press, 2002.

29 Cage, "Preface," p. 5.

Chapter 11

1 Ralph Waldo Emerson, "Thoreau," *The Atlantic,* August 1862.

2 For a comprehensive discussion of the politics of seed distribution in nineteenth-century America, see Courtney Fullilove, *The Profit of the Earth: The Global Seeds of American Agriculture,* Chicago: University of Chicago Press, 2017.

3 See Philip Pauly, *Fruits and Plains: The Horticultural Transformation of America,* Cambridge, MA: Harvard University Press, 2007.

4 William Flagg, *The Woods and By-Ways of New England,* Boston: J.R. Osgood, 1872, pp. 426–33, qtd. in Pauly, *Fruits and Plains.*

5 Fullilove, *The Profit of the Earth,* chapter four.

6 Nathaniel Hawthorne, *The Scarlet Letter,* New York: Penguin, 1962, pp. 12, 14.

7   Contemporary author Jhumpa Lahiri drew on this idea of unaccustomed earth as the title for her second collection of short stories, all of which deal with issues of transculturation among Bengali immigrants in the United States. See Lahiri, *Unaccustomed Earth*, New York: Vintage, 2008.

8   Henry David Thoreau, *Wild Fruits: Thoreau's Rediscovered Last Manuscript*, ed. Bradley Dean, New York: W. W. Norton, 2001, p. 5.

9   For more on Thoreau and property boundaries, including his work as a surveyor, see "Act One," in Daegin Miller's *This Radical Land: A Natural History of American Dissent*, Chicago: University of Chicago Press, 2018.

10 Laura Dassow Walls profoundly reoriented the conversation about Thoreau when she showed how he developed an investment in empiricism across his career that was not at odds with his holistic beliefs. See Laura Dassow Walls, *Seeing New Worlds: Henry David Thoreau and Nineteenth Century Natural Science*, Madison: University of Wisconsin Press, 1995. Building on this foundation, others have drawn out the various implications of this materialist approach. Cristin Ellis, for instance, has shown how such close study of the natural world formed the basis for Thoreau's moral convictions, including his anti-slavery stance. Racial science and abolitionist argument, she illustrates, both turned to biology and embodiment as the foundation for moral claims. See chapter two in Cristin Ellis, *Antebellum Posthuman: Race and Materiality in the Mid-Nineteenth Century*, New York: Fordham University Press, 2018. Kristen Case has revealed how Thoreau's empirical approach to the study of plants avoided the kind of systematic detachment promulgated by formal botany. His process of observation favored an intimacy and connection often thought to run counter to scientific study. See Kristen Case, "Knowing as Neighboring: Approaching Thoreau's Kalendar," *J19* 2, no. 1 (2014): 107–29. And Branka Arsić urges us to take Thoreau's words literally, showing how his philosophy of life offered a radical view of individuals as composed of ever-changing affinities between different forms, collapsing the stable hierarchies of life favored by many scientists at the time. See Branka Arsić, *Bird Relics: Grief and Vitalism in Thoreau*, Cambridge, MA: Harvard University Press, 2016.

11 Thoreau, *Wild Fruits*, p. 169. Of course, Thoreau draws extensively on book learning in *Wild Fruits*.

12 Ibid., p. 5.

13 Conevery Bolton Valencius, *The Health of the Country: How American Settlers Understood Their Health and Their Land*, New York: Basic Books, 2002. This is an idea that is not so different from the kind of transcorporeality that Stacy Alaimo describes in *Bodily Natures: Science, Environment, and the Material Self*, Bloomington: Indiana University Press, 2010. Contemporary environmental justice scholars and activists remind us of the very real ways in which environmental exposure to toxins shapes human health.

14 Henry David Thoreau, *The Writings of Henry David Thoreau: Journals*, 14 vols, ed. Bradford Torrey, Boston: Houghton Mifflin, 1906, vol. II, p. 214. Hereafter abbreviated as *J*, followed by the volume and page number.

15 Thoreau, *Wild Fruits*, p. 118.

16 This same passage appears near the end of Thoreau's 1860 address on "The Succession of Forest Trees" with some slight variations (including the spelling of "potiron").

17 Walls, "Believing in Nature: Wildness and Wilderness in Thoreauvian Science,"
    p. 15.
18 Wildness held a particularly important place in Thoreau's philosophical
    beliefs, given its relationship to "absolute freedom," and its provision of
    "nourishment and vigor" ("Walking").
19 Nelson argues that Thoreau saw wildness as a recuperative force present in
    even the most settled settings. See Barbara Nelson, "Rustling Thoreau's Cattle:
    Wildness and Domesticity in 'Walking,'" in *Thoreau's Sense of Place: Essays in
    American Environmental Writing,* ed. Richard Schneider, Iowa City: University
    of Iowa Press, 2000, p. 258.
20 William Scheick has argued that for Thoreau "nature is not a howling
    wilderness but a home. Man must leave his artificial house in order to enter
    this genuine home" (112). See Scheick, "The House of Nature in Thoreau's
    A Week," *ESQ* 20, no. 2 (1974): 111–16.
21 *J* IV: 158–9.
22 *J* IV: 159.
23 *J* XIV: 329.
24 "Nature in Motion," *Putnam's Monthly Magazine of American Literature,
    Science, and Art* 5, no. 25 (February 1855).
25 *J* I: 200.
26 *J* III: 343.
27 Michael Pollan, "Weeds Are Us," *The New York Times,* November 5, 1989.
28 Emerson, "Thoreau."
29 *J* II: 219.
30 James Finley, "A Free Soiler in His Own Broad Sense: Henry David Thoreau
    and the Free Soil Movement," in *Thoreau at Two Hundred,* ed. Kristen
    Case and K. P. Van Anglen, Cambridge: Cambridge University Press, 2016,
    p. 32. Lance Newman, "Environmentalist Thought and Action," in *The
    Oxford Handbook of Transcendentalism,* ed. Joel Myerson, Sandra Harbert
    Petrulionis, and Laura Dassow Wall, Oxford: Oxford University Press.
31 Henry David Thoreau, "The Succession of Forest Trees," reprinted in *"Wild
    Apples" and Other Natural History Essays*, ed. William Rossi, Athens:
    University of Georgia Press, 2002, p. 95.
32 *J* XIV: 331.
33 *Wild Fruits,* p. 169.
34 Ibid., p. 79.
35 Ibid., p. 80.
36 Ibid., p. 169.
37 Bellin, Joshua. "In the Company of Savagists: Thoreau's Indian Books and
    Antebellum Ethnology," in *Concord Saunterer* 16 (2008): 1–32. Richard
    Schneider also notes that Thoreau shared a sense with geographers like Guyot
    that "in the face of [European] technological ingenuity and persistence, the
    Indian ... must be doomed to extinction" (p. 57). See Schneider, "'Climate
    Does Thus React on Man': Wildness and Geographic Determinism in
    Thoreau's 'Walking,'" in *Thoreau's Sense of Place: Essays in American
    Environmental Writing,* ed. Richard Schneider, Iowa City: University of Iowa
    Press, 2000, pp. 44–60.

38   Richard B. Primack, *Walden Warming: Climate Change Comes to Thoreau's Woods,* Chicago: University of Chicago Press, 2014.

39   Thoreau's cabin by Walden Pond has led to scholarly discussions of the cabin as a domestic space. See, for example, Maura D'Amore's, "Thoreau's Unreal Estate: Playing House at Walden Pond," *The New England Quarterly* 82, no. 1 (2009): 56–79. D'Amore argues that Thoreau "invites his readers … to play house outside of town," a way of managing urban desire for rural experiences (p. 59).

40   Primack, *Walden Warming*, p. 2.

Chapter 12

1   Fanny Elizabeth Appleton, LONG 21597 (1836), Longfellow House-Washington's Headquarters National Historic Site.

2   Ralph Waldo Emerson, *Journals and Miscellaneous Notebooks*, vol. 4 (1832–1833), ed. William H. Gilman, Cambridge: Belknap Press of Harvard University Press, 1960, pp. 222–6.

3   Frederick Goddard Tuckerman, "Wild Flowers Gathered in Scotland and England during the Summer of 1851. Greenfield September 1, 1851," MS Am 1349, vol. 11, Houghton Library, Harvard University.

4   Appleton and Tuckerman's pilgrimages are not unlike the journey the seventeenth-century Japanese poet, and innovator of the haiku form, Matsuo Basho, took to the north of Japan, in search of locations where an earlier poet had composed.

5   Tuckerman, "Wild Flowers."

6   William Wordsworth, *Poems, in Two Volumes, and Other Poems, 1800–1807,* ed. Jared Curtis, Ithaca: Cornell University Press, 1983, p. 680.

7   Frederick Goddard Tuckerman, "Wild Flowers, Greenfield 1850," MS AM 1763. Houghton Library, Harvard University. For these poetic references, see Emily Dickinson, "Pink—Small—Punctual," in *The Poems of Emily Dickinson,* ed. Robert Franklin, Cambridge: Belknap Press of Harvard University Press, 1998, poem number 1356 (all subsequent citations of Dickinson's poems refer to this edition, and provide the poem, rather than, page number; John Greenleaf Whittier, "The Mayflowers," *The Poetical Works,* vol. 2, 1894, pp. 36–7); Ralph Waldo Emerson, "The Humble-Bee," in *Collected Poems and Translations,* New York: Library of America, 1994, pp. 31–3.

8   Henry Wadsworth Longfellow, "Family Papers, 1815–1972." LONG 27930 Box 58, folders 13, 20, 21, and LONG 1786–1787. Separated Materials. Longfellow House-Washington's Headquarters National Historic Site.

9   CA Conrad, *A Beautiful Marsupial Afternoon,* Seattle: Wave Books, 2012, pp. 1, 2, 4, 168–9.

10   For a small selection of examples, see Dickinson, "When I count the seeds," (F51) or "Nature—sometimes sears a Sapling" (F314).

11   Dickinson, "By my Window have I for scenery" (F797).

12   Dickinson, "Of Bronze - and Blaze" (F319).

13 Branka Arsic, *Bird Relics: Grief and Vitalism in Thoreau,* Cambridge: Harvard University Press, 2016, pp. 15–17.

14 On spring as a poem: Henry David Thoreau, *The Writings of Henry David Thoreau: Journal,* 8 vols. to date, editor-in-chief, Elizabeth Witherell, Princeton: Princeton University Press, 1991–2002, 8: 220–4. Hereafter abbreviated as *PJ,* followed by the volume and page number.

15 *PJ* 4: 28.

16 Henry David Thoreau, *A Week on the Concord and Merrimack Rivers,* Boston: J. Munroe, 1849, p. 362.

17 Ibid., pp. 362–3.

18 Herman Melville, *Pierre, or the Ambiguities,* Evanston: Northwestern University Press, 1971, p. 304.

19 *PJ* 4: 195.

20 *PJ* 4: 279.

21 Thoreau, *A Week,* p. 301.

22 Dickinson (F1491).

23 Walt Whitman, "A Backward Glance O'er Travel'd Roads," *Leaves of Grass* (1891–2).

24 William Wordsworth, "Preface of 1800," in *Wordsworth & Coleridge: Lyrical Ballads,* New York: Routledge, 1991, p. 291; Percy Bysshe Shelley, "A Defense of Poetry," in *Selected Poetry & Prose,* New York: W. W. Norton, 2002, p. 511; Thoreau, *A Week,* p. 91. For a recent treatment of Shelley's poetry in the general sense and its implications for contemporary poetry and public life, see Oren Izenberg, *Being Numerous: Poetry and the Ground of Social Life,* Princeton: Princeton University Press, 2011, pp. 17–22.

25 Thoreau, *A Week,* p. 342.

26 Henry David Thoreau, *Walden,* Princeton: Princeton University Press, 1971, p. 91.

27 Henry David Thoreau, "Natural History of Massachusetts," *The Dial: A Magazine for Literature, Philosophy, and Religion* 3, no. 1 (1842): 19–40.

28 *PJ* 1: 337–8.

29 Thoreau, *A Week,* pp. 91, 99, 316.

30 Samuel Taylor Coleridge, *Coleridge's Criticism of Shakespeare,* ed. R. A. Foakes, London: Athlone Press, 1989, p. 52; John Keats, *The Selected Letters of John Keats,* ed. Lionel Trilling, New York: Farrar, Straus, and Young, 1951, p. 113.

31 *PJ* 4: 28.

32 See Robert Sattlemeyer, *Thoreau's Reading: A Study in Intellectual History,* Princeton: Princeton University Press, 1988; William Carpenter, *Vegetable Physiology and Systematic Botany,* London: Henry G. Bohn, 1858, p. 16.

33 Harland Coultas, *What May Be Learned from a Tree,* New York: D. Appleton, 1860.

34 Willis, Charles G., Brad Ruhfel, Richard B. Prismack, Abraham J. Miller-Rushing, and Charles C. Davis, "Phylogenetic Patterns of Species Loss in Thoreau's Woods Are Driven by Climate Change" (2008). *PNAS* 10.1073 (October 27, 2008). Accessed December 15, 2014; Conrad, *A Beautiful Marsupial Afternoon,* p. 2.

35 *PJ* 4: 28.

36 Coultas, *What May be Learned from a Tree*, pp. 100–4, 13.
37 Thoreau, "Walking," in *Walden, the Maine Woods, and Collected Essays &
    Poems*, New York: Library of America, 1985, p. 770.
38 Thomas Wentworth Higginson, "Preface," in Emily Dickinson, *Poems of
    Emily Dickinson*. First series, ed. Mabel Loomis Todd and Thomas Wentworth
    Higginson, Boston: Roberts Brothers, 1890, p. 10.
39 *PJ* 3: 43.
40 *PJ* 3: 224–7.
41 Herman Melville, "[June] 1851 letter to Nathaniel Hawthorne," in *The
    Writings of Herman Melville, vol. 14: Correspondence,* ed. Lynn Horth,
    Evanston and Chicago: Northwestern University Press and The Newberry
    Library, 1993, p. 193.
42 *PJ* 5: 112.
43 *PJ* 3: 331.
44 Thoreau, "Walking," 770.
45 Thoreau, *A Week*, p. 266.
46 Ibid., p. 404.
47 Conrad, *A Beautiful Marsupial Afternoon*, p. 1, qtd. Alice Notley, p. 163.
48 Brian Teare, "En Plein Aire Poetics," *Poetry Foundation*, January 21, 2019.
    Web. Accessed October 30, 2019.
49 Henry David Thoreau, *Indian Notebooks* (1847–61) MA 596–606. MS.
    Morgan Library. *A Week* is also full of references to indigenous culture and
    records. See my essay "Apple Trees in the Archive" for further coverage of
    these sections of that book.
50 Conrad, *A Beautiful Marsupial Afternoon*, pp. 172, 167.
51 Brian Teare, *Doomstead Days,* New York: Nightboat Books, 2019, pp. 28,
    56, 68.
52 Brian Teare, "Tall Flatsedge Notebook," in *Companion Grasses,* Richmond:
    Omnidawn, 2013, pp. 37–44, 81.
53 Teare, "Quaking Grass," pp. 31, 30.
54 *PJ* 3: 113.
55 Ibid., pp. 113–14.
56 Teare, *Companion Grasses,* pp. 102–9.
57 Teare, *Doomstead Days,* pp. 15–17.
58 Conrad, *A Beautiful Marsupial Afternoon*, p. 2.
59 Frederic Jameson, *The Political Unconscious: Narrative as a Socially Symbolic
    Act*, Ithaca: Cornell University Press, 1981, p. 35.

BIBLIOGRAPHY

Abelove, Henry. *Deep Gossip*. Minneapolis: University of Minnesota Press, 2005.

Albanese, Catherine L. *Reconsidering Nature Religion*. Harrisburg, PA: Trinity Press, 2002.

Allewaert, Monique. *Ariel's Ecology: Plantations, Personhood, and Colonialism in the American Tropics*. Minneapolis: University of Minnesota Press, 2013.

Alston, Charles. "A Dissertation on the Sexes of Plants" In *Essays and Observations, Physical and Literary, Read before a Society in Edinburgh*, Vol. 1. Edited by Medical Society of Edinburgh. Edinburgh: Hamilton and Balfour, 1754.

Arsić, Branka. "Letting Be: Thoreau and Cavell on Thinking after the *Bhagavat Gita*." *Belgrade Journal for Media and Communications* 7 (2015): 13–42.

Arsić, Branka. "Thoreau's Vegetal Ontology: The Aerial, the Rootless, and the Analogous," in *Dispersion: Thoreau and Vegetal Thought*. Edited by Branka Arsić, 1–20. New York: Bloomsbury Press, 2021.

Arsić, Branka. *Bird Relics: Grief and Vitalism in Thoreau*. Cambridge, MA: Harvard University Press, 2016.

Austin, J. L. *How to Do Things with Words*. Edited by J. O. Urmson and Marina Sbisà. 2nd ed. Cambridge, MA: Harvard University Press, 1975.

Beer, Gillian. *Darwin's Plots: Evolutionary Narrative in Darwin, George Eliot and Nineteenth-Century Fiction*. Cambridge: Cambridge University Press, 2000.

Benn Michaels, Walter. "Action and Accident: Photography and Writing." In *The Gold Standard and the Logic of Naturalism: American Literature at the Turn of the Century*. Berkeley: University of California Press, 1987.

Bennett, Jane. *Thoreau's Nature: Ethics, Politics, and the Wild*. Newbury Park: SAGE, 1994.

Bennett, Jane. *Thoreau's Nature: Ethics, Politics, and the Wild*. Lanham, MD: Rowman and Littlefield, 2000.

Bennett, Jane. *Vibrant Matter: A Political Ecology of Things*. Durham: Duke University Press, 2010.

Bercovitch, Sacvan. *The American Jeremiad*. Madison: University of Wisconsin Press, 1978.

Berger, Michael. "Henry David Thoreau's Science in *The Dispersion of Seeds*." *Annals of Science* 53 (1996): 381–97.

Blitz, Antonio. *Fifty Years In the Magic Circle: Being an Account of the Author's Professional Life; His Wonderful Tricks And Feats; With Laughable Incidents, And Adventures As a Magician, Necromancer, And Ventriloquist*. Hartford: Belknap & Bliss, 1871.

Bolter, David Jay and Richard Grusin, *Remediation: Understanding New Media*. Cambridge, MA: MIT Press, 1999.

Bondestam, Maja. "When the Plant Kingdom Became Queer: On Hermaphrodites and the Linnaean Language of Nonnormative Sex." In *Illdisciplined Gender: Engaging Questions of Nature/Culture and Transgressive Encounters*, edited by Jacob Bull and Margaretha Fahlgren. Heidelberg: Springer International Publishing, 2016.

Bonneuil, Christophe, and Jean-Baptiste Fressoz. *The Shock of the Anthropocene: The Earth, History and Us*. Translated by David Fernbach. London: Verso, 2017.

Boyce Thompson Institute, "New Genomic Insights." https://www.sciencedaily.com/releases/2017/08/170815095041.htm

Buell, Lawrence. *The Environmental Imagination: Thoreau, Nature Writing, and the Formation of American Culture*. Cambridge, MA: Harvard University Press, 1995.

Burbrick, Joan. *Thoreau's Alternative History: Changing Perspectives on Nature, Culture, and Language*. Philadelphia: University of Pennsylvania Press, 1987.

Cage, John. *Empty Words, Writings '73–'78*. Middleton CT: Wesleyan University Press, 1979.

Cameron, Sharon. *Writing Nature: Henry Thoreau's Journal*. Chicago: University of Chicago Press, 1989.

Case, Kristen. "Knowing as Neighboring: Approaching Thoreau's Kalendar." *J19: The Journal of Nineteenth-Century Americanists* 2, no. 1 (2014): 107–29.

Case, Kristen and K. P. Van Angle, eds. *Thoreau at 200: Essays and Reassessments*. Cambridge: Cambridge University Press, 2016.

Cavell, Stanley. *In Quest of the Ordinary: Lines of Skepticism and Romanticism*. Chicago: University of Chicago Press, 1994.

Cavell, Stanley. "The Uncanniness of the Ordinary." The Tanner Lectures on Human Values. https://tannerlectures.utah.edu/_documents/a-to-z/c/cavell88.pdf

Cavell, Stanley. *Senses of Walden: An Expanded Edition*. Chicago: University of Chicago Press, 1972.

Channing, William Ellery. *Thoreau: Poet-Naturalist*. Boston: Roberts Brothers, 1873.

Clark, Henry James. *Mind in Nature, or the Origin of Life, and the Mode of Development of Animals*. New York: Appleton, 1865.

Coart, E. *et al.* "Chloroplast Diversity in the Genus *Malus*: New Insights into the Relationship Between the European Wild Apple (*Malus sylvestris*) and the Domesticated Apple (*Malus domestica*)." *Mol. Ecol.* 15, no. 8 (2016): 2171–82.

Coccia, Emanuele. *The Life of Plants: A Metaphysics of Mixture*. Cambridge: Polity, 2019.

Coleridge, Samuel Taylor. *Coleridge's Criticism of Shakespeare*, ed. RA Foakes. London: Athlone Press, 1989.

Conrad, CA. *A Beautiful Marsupial Afternoon*. Seattle: Wave Books, 2012.

Coviello, Peter. *Tomorrow's Parties: Sex and the Untimely in Nineteenth-Century America*. New York: New York University Press, 2013.

Coviello, Peter. "'The Wild Not Less than the Good': Thoreau, Sex, Biopower." *GLQ: A Journal of Lesbian and Gay Studies* 23, no. 4 (2017): 509–32.

Cowles, Henry Chandler. "The Ecological Relations of the Vegetation on the Sand Dunes of Lake Michigan." *Botanical Gazette* 27, no. 2 (1899): 95–117.

Crèvecoeur, J. Hector St John de. *Letters from an American Farmer and Other Essays*. Edited by Dennis D. Moore. Cambridge: Belknap, 2013.

D'Amore, Maura. "Thoreau's Unreal Estate: Playing House at Walden Pond." *The New England Quarterly* 82, no. 1 (2009): 56–79.

Darwin, Charles. *The Power of Movement in Plants* [1880]. Edited by Francis Darwin. Cambridge: Cambridge University Press, 2009.

Daston, Lorraine. *Against Nature*. Cambridge: MIT Press, 2019.

Darwin, Charles. *The Origin of the Species* (1849). *From So Simple a Beginning: Darwin's Four Great Books*. Edited by Edward O. Wilson. New York: W. W. Norton, 2005.

Davidson, Frank. "Melville, Thoreau, and 'The Apple-Tree Table.'" *American Literature* 25, no. 4 (1954): 479–88.

Davis, Theo. "'Just apply a weight': Thoreau and the Aesthetics of Ornament." *ELH* 77, no. 3 (2010): 561–87.

Deacon, Terrence. *Incomplete Nature: How Mind Emerged from Matter*. New York City: W. W. Norton & Company, 2013.

Dean, Bradley P. "Henry D. Thoreau and Horace Greeley Exchange Letter on the 'Spontaneous Generation of Plants.'" *The New England Quarterly* 66, no. 4 (1993): 630–8.

Dean, Bradley P., ed. *Letters of a Spiritual Seeker*. New York: W. W. Norton and Company, 2005.

Debaise, Didier. *Nature as Event: The Lure of the Possible*. Durham: Duke University Press, 2017.

Deleuze, Gilles. "Eight Years Later: 1980 Interview" (1980). In *Two Regimes of Madness: Texts and Interviews 1975–1995*. Translated by Ames Hodges and Mike Taormina. Edited by David Lapoujade. New York: Semiotext[e], 2007.

Deleuze Gilles and Félix Guattari. *A Thousand Plateaus: Capitalism and Schizophrenia*. Translated by Brian Massumi. Minneapolis: University of Minnesota Press, 1987; 2003.

Derrida, Jacques. *The Animal That Therefore I Am*. Translated by David Wills. New York: Fordham University Press, 2008.

Descartes, René. *Discourse on Method* In *The Philosophical Writings of Descartes*. Cambridge, MA: Cambridge University Press, 1985.

Descartes, René. *Discourse on Method and Meditation on First Philosophy*. London: Everyman, 2004.

Descola, Philippe. *Beyond Nature and Culture*. Translated by Janet Lloyd. Chicago: University of Chicago Press, 2013.

Dewey, Charles. *A History of the County of Berkshire, Massachusetts*. Pittsfield: Samuel W. Bush, 1829.

Dickinson, Emily. *The Poems of Emily Dickinson*. Edited by R. W. Franklin. Cambridge, MA: Belknap Press of Harvard University Press, 1998.

Diederichsen, Dietrich. "Animation, Dereification, and the New Charm of the Inanimate." *e-flux journal,* no. 36 (2011).

Dimick, Sarah. *Climactic Arrhythmia's: Global Warming, Literary Form, and Environmental Time.* 2016. University of Wisconsin-Madison, Ph.D. dissertation.

Diran, Ingrid, and Antoine Traisnel. "The Poetics of Geopower: Climate Change and the Politics of Representation." In *Climate Realism: The Aesthetics of Weather and Atmosphere in the Anthropocene.* Edited by Lynne Badia, Marija Cetinić, and Jeff Diamanti, New York: Routledge, 2020.

Doyle, Richard. *Darwin's Pharmacy: Sex, Plants, and the Evolution of the Noosphere.* Seattle: University of Washington Press, 2011.

Dubreuil, Lauren. *The Intellective Space: Thinking Beyond Cognition.* Minneapolis: Minnesota University Press, 2015.

Ellis, Cristin. *Antebellum Posthuman: Race and Materiality in the Mid-Nineteenth.* New York: Fordham University Press, 2018.

Emerson, Ralph Waldo. "Thoreau." *The Atlantic,* August 1862.

Emerson, Ralph Waldo. "To the Public – Editors' Address." *Massachusetts Quarterly Review,* no. 1 (1847): 3.

Emerson, Ralph Waldo. *The Complete Works of Ralph Waldo Emerson.* Edited by Edward Waldo Emerson. Cambridge, MA: Riverside Press, 1904.

Emerson, Ralph Waldo. *Journals and Miscellaneous Notebooks.* Cambridge, MA: Belknap Press of Harvard University Press, 1960.

Emerson, Ralph Waldo. *Collected Poems and Translations.* New York: Library of America, 1994.

Emerson, Ralph Waldo. *Essays and Poems.* New York: Library of America, 1996.

Eng, David, Judith Halberstam, and José Esteban Muñoz. "What's Queer about Queer Studies Now?" *Social Text* 84–5, nos. 3–4 (2005): 1–17.

Evelyn, John. *Terra: A Philosophical Discourse of Earth, Relating to the Culture and Improvement of It for Vegetation, and the Propagation of Plants, &c. as It Was Presented to the Royal Society,* April 29. 1675. York: A. Ward, 1778.

Feynman, Richard. "What Is Science," In *The Pleasure of Finding Things Out: The Best Short Works of Richard P. Feynman.* Edited by Jeffrey Robbins. New York: Basic Books, 2005.

Finley, James. "A Free Soiler in His Own Broad Sense: Henry David Thoreau and the Free Soil Movement." In *Thoreau at Two Hundred.* Edited by Kristen Case and K.P. Van Anglen. Cambridge: Cambridge University Press, 2016.

Finley, James, ed. *Henry David Thoreau in Context.* Cambridge: Cambridge University Press, 2017.

Foucault, Michel. "The Subject and Power." *Critical Inquiry* 8, no 4 (Summer 1982): 777–95.

Foster, David R. *Thoreau's Country: Journey through a Transformed Landscape.* Cambridge, MA: Harvard University Press, 1999.

Foucault, Michel. *Security, Territory, Population: Lectures at the Collège de France, 1977–1978.* Translated by Graham Burchell. Edited by Michel Senellart. New York: Picador, 2007.

Foucault, Michel. *On the Government of the Living: Lectures at the Collège de France, 1979–1980 and Oedipal Knowledge.* Translated by Graham Burchell. Edited by Michel Senellart. New York: Picador, 2012.

Foucault, Michel. "What is Critique?" In *The Politics of Truth*. Translated by Lisa Hochroth and Catherine Porter. Edited by Slyvère Lotringer. New York: Semiotext(e), 2007.

Forbes, Erin E. "Vegetative Politics from Crèvecoeur to Hawthorne." *J19: The Journal of Nineteenth-Century Americanists* 8, no. 1 (Spring 2020): 43–66.

Freeman, Elizabeth. *Time Binds: Queer Temporalities, Queer Histories*. Durham: Duke University Press, 2010.

Friedman, William, and Pamela Diggle. "Charles Darwin and the Origins of Plant Evolutionary Biology." *Plant Cell* 23, no. 4 (2011): 1194–207.

Fuller, Randall. *The Book That Changed America*. New York: Viking, 2017.

Fullilove, Courtney. *The Profit of the Earth: The Global Seeds of American Agriculture*. Chicago: University of Chicago Press, 2017.

Gagliano, Monica, John C. Ryan, and Patrícia Vieira. *The Language of Plants: Science, Philosophy, Literature*. Minneapolis: Minnesota University Press, 2017.

George, Sam. "'Not Strictly Proper for a Female Pen': Eighteenth-Century Poetry and the Sexuality of Botany." *Comparative Critical Studies* 2, no. 2 (2005): 191–210.

Gladstone, Joel. "Low-Tech Thoreau." *Criticism* 57, no. 3 (2015): 349–76.

Goethe, Johann Wolfgang von. *The Metamorphosis of Plants* (1790). Translated by Douglas Miller. Cambridge, MA: MIT Press, 2009.

Goldstein, Amanda. *Sweet Science: Romantic Materialism and the New Logics of Life*. Chicago: University of Chicago Press, 2016.

Gray, Asa. *Manual of the Botany of the Northern United States*. London: J. Chapman, 1848.

Gross, Robert A. "The Great Bean Field Hoax: Thoreau and the Agricultural Reformers." *The Virginia Quarterly Review: A National Journal of Literature and Discussion* 61, no. 3 (Summer 1985). https://www.vqronline.org/essay/great-bean-field-hoax-thoreau-and-agricultural-reformers.

Grosz, Elizabeth. *The Incorporeal: Ontology, Ethics, and the Limits of Materialism*, New York: Columbia University Press, 2017,

Halperin, David. *How to Do the History of Homosexuality*. Chicago: University of Chicago Press, 2002.

Harding, Walter. "Thoreau's Sexuality." *Journal of Homosexuality* 21, no. 3 (1991): 23–45.

Hawthorne, Nathaniel. *The Scarlet Letter*. New York: Penguin, 1962.

Hayles, N. Katherine. *Unthought: The Power of the Cognitive Unconscious*. Chicago: University of Chicago Press, 2017.

Hesford, Walter. "The 1860 Concord Cattle-Show: An Official Account." *Thoreau Society Bulletin*, no. 132 (1975): 6–7.

Hesse, Mary B. Hesse. *Models and Analogies in Science*. Notre Dame: University of Notre Dame Press, 1966.

Higginson, Thomas Wentworth. "Preface" in *Poems of Emily Dickinson*. Edited by Mabel Loomis Todd and Thomas Wentworth Higginson. Boston: Roberts Brothers, 1890.

Hodder, Alan D. *Thoreau's Ecstatic Witness*. New Haven: Yale University Press, 2001.

Hoeltje, Hubert H. "Thoreau as Lecturer." *New England Quarterly* 19 (1946): 492–3.

Hoffmeyer, Jesper. "The Semiotics of Nature: Code Duality." In *Essential Readings in Biosemiotics*. Edited by Donald Favareau. New York: Springer, 2010, 583–628.

Humboldt, Alexander von. *Cosmos*. New York: Harper & Brothers, 1859.

Humboldt, Alexander von. *Views of Nature*. Translated by Mark M. Person. Chicago: University of Chicago Press, 2014.

Imbert, Michel. "Le Seuil de résistance dans Resistance to Civil Government." In *Littérature et politique en Nouvelle-Angleterre*. Edited by Thomas Constantinesco, and Antoine Traisnel, *Actes de la recherche à l'ENS*, no. 7. Paris: *Actes de la recherche à l'ENS* (2011).

Irigaray, Luce and Michael Marder, *Through Vegetal Being: Two Philosophical Perspectives*. New York: Columbia University Press, 2016.

James, William. *The Principles of Psychology*. New York: Dover, 1950.

Johnson, Barbara. *A World of Difference*. Baltimore: Johns Hopkins University Press, 1987.

Johnson, Rochelle. "'This Enchantment Is No Delusion': Henry David Thoreau, the New Materialisms, and Ineffable Materiality." *ISLE: Interdisciplinary Studies in Literature and Environment* 21, no. 3 (2014): 606–35.

Jonas, Hans. *The Phenomenon of Life: Toward a Philosophical Biology*. Evanston: Illinois University Press, 2001.

Kelley, Theresa. *Clandestine Marriage: Botany and Romantic Culture*. Baltimore: Johns Hopkins University Press, 2012.

Kimmerer, Robin Wall. *Braiding Sweetgrass: Indigenous Wisdom, Scientific Knowledge, and the Teaching of Plants*. Minneapolis: Milkweed Editions, 2013.

Kittredge, George Lyman. "Cotton Mather's Scientific Communications to the Royal Society." *American Antiquarian Society* (April 1916): 18–57.

Kohn, Eduardo. *How Forests Think: Toward an Anthropology beyond the Human*. Berkeley: University of California Press, 2013.

Kussin, Louisa. "The Concord Farmers Club and Thoreau's 'Succession of Forest Trees.'" *The Thoreau Society Bulletin*, no. 173 (1985): 1–3.

LaFleur, Greta. *The Natural History of Sexuality in Early America*. Baltimore: Johns Hopkins University Press, 2018.

LaFleur, Greta. *The Natural History of Sexuality in Early America*. Baltimore: Johns Hopkins University, 2020.

Latour, Bruno. *Down to Earth: Politics in the New Climatic Regime*. Cambridge, MA: Polity, 2018.

Lazzarato, Maurizio. "From Biopower to Biopolitics." *Pli* 13 (2002): 99–113.

Lewis, R.W.B. *The American Adam: Innocence, Tragedy, and Tradition in the Nineteenth Century*. Chicago: University of Chicago Press, 1955.

Liebig, Justus. *Animal Chemistry* (1842). New York: Johnson Reprint Corp, 1964.

Linnaeus, Carl. *Praeludia sponsaliorum plantarum* (1729). Reprinted Uppsala: Almqvist and Wiksell, 1908.

Locke, John. "A Letter Concerning Toleration." In *A Letter Concerning Toleration and Other Writings*. Edited by Mark Goldie. Indianapolis: Liberty Fund, 2010, 1–68.

Longfellow, Henry Wadsworth. "Family Papers, 1815–1972." LONG 1786–1787, 27930.

Mancuso, Stefano. *The Revolutionary Genius of Plants: A New Understanding of Plant Intelligence and Behavior*. New York: Atria, 2018.

Mancuso, Stefano and Alexandra Viola. *Brilliant Green: The Surprising History and Science of Plant Intelligence*. Washington, DC: Island Press, 2015.

Marder, Michael. *Plant-Thinking: A Philosophy of Vegetal Life.* New York: Columbia University, 2013.

Marder, Michael. *The Philosopher's Plant.* New York: Columbia University Press, 2014.

Martin, Ross. "Fossil Thoughts: Thoreau, Arrowheads, and Radical Paleontology." *ESQ: A Journal of Nineteenth-Century American Literature and Culture* 65, no. 3 (2019): 424–68.

Marx, Leo. *The Machine in the Garden: Technology and the Pastoral Ideal in America.* New York: Oxford University Press, 1964.

Meehan, Sean Ross. "Ecology and Imagination: Emerson, Thoreau, and the Nature of Metonymy." *Criticism* 55, no. 2 (2013): 299–329.

Melville, Herman. *Pierre, or the Ambiguities.* Evanston Northwestern University Press, 1971.

Miller, Elaine. *The Vegetative Soul.* New York: State University of New York Press, 2002.

Miller, Perry. *The New England Mind: The Seventeenth Century.* Cambridge, MA: Harvard University Press, 1954.

Miller, Perry. *Consciousness in Concord.* Boston: Houghton Mifflin, 1958.

Moller, Mary Elkins. *Thoreau and the Human Community.* Boston: University of Massachusetts Press, 1980.

Morgensen, Scott Lauria. "The Biopolitics of Settler Colonialism: Right Here, Right Now." *Settler Colonial Studies* 1, no. 1 (2011): 52–76.

Morton, Timothy. "Queer Ecology." *PMLA* 125, no. 2 (2010): 273–82.

"Nature in Motion." *Putnam's Monthly Magazine of American Literature, Science, and Art* 5, no. 25 (1855).

Nealon, Jeffrey. *Plant Theory: Biopower and Plant Life.* Stanford: Stanford University Press, 2015.

Nègre, Julien. *L'Arpenteur vagabond. Cartes et cartographies dans l'oeuvre de Henry David Thoreau.* Lyon: ENS Éditions, 2019.

Nelson, Barbara. "Rustling Thoreau's Cattle: Wildness and Domesticity in 'Walking'." In *Thoreau's Sense of Place: Essays in American Environmental Writing.* Edited by Richard Schneider. Iowa City: University of Iowa Press, 2000.

Nemser, Daniel. *Infrastructures of Race: Concentration and Biopolitics in Colonial Mexico.* Austin: University of Texas Press, 2017.

Neyrat, Frédéric. "Planetary Antigones: The Environmental Situation and the Wandering Condition." *Qui Parle* 25, no. 1 (2016): 35–64.

Nixon, Rob. *Slow Violence and the Environmentalism of the Poor.* Cambridge, MA: Harvard University Press, 2013.

Page, H.A. *Thoreau: His Life and Aims.* Boston: James R. Osgood & Co., 1877.

Parrish, Susan Scott. *American Curiosity: Cultures of Natural History in the Colonial British Atlantic World.* Chapel Hill: University of North Carolina Press, 2006.

Paul, Sherman. *The Shores of America.* Champaign: University of Illinois Press, 1958.

Pettman, Dominic. *Human Error: Species-Being and Media Machines.* Minneapolis: University of Minnesota Press, 2011.

Povinelli, Elizabeth. *Geontologies.* Durham: Duke University Press, 2016.

Primack, Richard. *Walden Warming: Climate Changes Comes to Thoreau's Woods.* Chicago: University of Chicago Press, 2014.

Rau, Paula Pliver. "John Cage: Prints, Drawings, and Watercolors, 1978-1992." Ph.D. dissertation. diss., Virginia Commonwealth University, 2005.

Richards, Robert J. *The Romantic Conception of Life: Science and Philosophy in the Age of Goethe*. Chicago: University of Chicago Press, 2002.

Richardson, Robert. *Henry David Thoreau: A Life of the Mind*. Berkeley: University of California Press, 1986; 1988.

Rigby, Kate. "Art, Nature, and the Poesy of Plants in the Goethezeit: A Biosemiotic Perspective." *Goethe Yearbook* 22, no. 1 (2015): 23–44.

Robinson, David. *Natural Life: Thoreau's Worldly Transcendentalism*. Ithaca: Cornell University Press, 2004.

Ross, Linda Mayer. *The Justice of Mercy*. Ann Arbor: University of Michigan Press, 2010.

Ruyer, Raymond. *Neo-Finalism*. Translated by Alyosha Edlebi. Minneapolis: Minnesota University Press, 2016.

Rosenberg, Jordana. "The Molecularization of Sexuality: On Some Primitivisms of the Present." *Theory & Event* 17, no. 2 (2014). muse.jhu.edu/article/546470.

Sacks, Oliver. *The River of Consciousness*. New York: Knopf, 2017.

Sandilands, Catriona, and Bruce Erickson. "A Genealogy of Queer Ecologies." In *Queer Ecologies: Sex, Nature, Politics, Desire*. Edited by Catriona Sandilands and Bruce Erickson. Bloomington: Indiana University Press, 2010.

Sandilands, Catriona, Gordon Brent Brochu-Ingram, and Peter Hobbs. "Queer Ecologies Roundtable Discussion Part 4: Queer Ecologies at the Limits." *UnderCurrents* 19 (2015): 60–1.

Sattelmeyer, Robert. *Thoreau's Reading: A Study in Intellectual History with Bibliographical Catalogue*. Princeton: Princeton University Press, 1988.

Scheick, William J. "The House of Nature in Thoreau's *A Week*." *ESQ* 20, no. 2 (1974): 111–16.

Schuller, Kyla. *The Biopolitics of Feeling: Race, Sex, and Science in the Nineteenth Century*. Durham: Duke University Press, 2017.

Sedgwick, Eve. *Epistemology of the Closet*. Berkeley: University of California Press, 1990.

Serres, Michel. *The Natural Contract*. Ann Arbor: University of Michigan Press, 1995.

Shamir, Milette. "Manliest Relations." In *Boys Don't Cry?: Rethinking Narrative of Masculinity and Emotion in the U.S.* Edited by Milette Shamir and Jennifer Travis. New York: Columbia University Press, 2002.

Shepherdson, Charles. *Lacan and the Limits of Language*. Fordham, NY: Fordham University Press, 2008.

Skrbina, David. *Panpsychism in the West*. Cambridge, MA: MIT Press, 2005.

Steigerwald, Joan. *Experimenting at the Boundaries of Life: Organic Vitality in Germany around 1800*. Pittsburgh: University of Pittsburgh Press, 2019.

Stockbridge, Levi. *Report from Eighth Annual Report of the Secretary of the Massachusetts Board of Agriculture*. Boston: William White, 1861.

Stowe, William. "Linnaean Poetics: Emerson, Cooper, Thoreau, and the Names of Plants." *Interdisciplinary Studies in Literature and Environment* 17, no. 3 (2010): 567–83.

Sundquist, Eric J. *Home as Found: Authority and Genealogy in Nineteenth-Century American Literature*. Baltimore: Johns Hopkins University Press, 2019.

Syme, Alison. *A Touch of Blossom: John Singer Sargent and the Queer Flora of Fin-de-Siècle Art*. University Park: Pennsylvania State University Press, 2010.

Taiz, Lincoln, and Lee Taiz. *Flora Unveiled: The Discovery and Denial of Sex in Plants*. Oxford: Oxford University Press, 2017.

Teare, Brian. "En Plein Aire Poetics." *Poetry Foundation*, January 21, 2019.

The American Heritage Dictionary. Boston: Houghton Mifflin, 1992.

Thoreau, Henry David. *A Week on the Concord and Merrimack Rivers*, ed. C.F. Novde. Princeton: Princeton University Press, 1980.

Thoreau, Henry David. *A Week on the Concord and Merrimack Rivers/Walden; or, Life in the Woods/The Maine Woods/Cape Cod*. ed. Robert F. Sayre, New York: Library of America, 1985.

Thoreau, Henry David. "Chastity & Sensuality." In *Early Essays and Miscellanies*, edited by Joseph J. Moldenhauer, and Edwin Moser. Princeton: Princeton University Press, 1975.

Thoreau, Henry David. *Collected Essays and Poems*. Edited by Elizabeth Hall Witherhell. New York: Library of America, 2001.

Thoreau, Henry David. *Excursions*. Edited by Joseph J. Moldenhauer. Princeton: Princeton University Press, 2007.

Thoreau, Henry David. *Faith in a Seed: The Dispersion of Seeds and Other Late Natural History Writings*. Edited by Bradley P. Dean, Washington, DC: Island Press,1993.

Thoreau, Henry David. *Indian Notebooks*. (1847–1861) MA 596-606. MS. Morgan Library.

Thoreau, Henry David. *The Journal of Henry D. Thoreau*. Edited by Bradford Torrey and Francis H. Allen. New York: Dover, 1962.

Thoreau, Henry David. *The Journal of Henry David Thoreau*. Edited by Bradford Torrey. 14 vols. Boston: Houghton Mifflin, 1906.

Thoreau, Henry David. *Letters of a Spiritual Seeker*. Edited by Dean P. Bradley, New York: W. W. Norton, 2005.

Thoreau, Henry David. *The Maine Woods*. New York and London: Penguin Books, 1988.

Thoreau, Henry David. *The Maine Woods*. Princeton: Princeton University Press, 1971.

Thoreau, Henry David. "The Natural History of Massachusetts." In *Excursions*. Edited by Joseph J. Moldenhauer. Princeton: Princeton University Press, 2007.

Thoreau, Henry David. *The Writings of Henry David Thoreau*. Edited by Franklin Sanborn. Boston: Houghton Mifflin, 1906.

Thoreau, Henry David. *The Writings of Henry David Thoreau: Journal*. Editor-in-chief Elizabeth Witherell. 8 vols. Princeton: Princeton University Press, 1991–2002.

Thoreau, Henry David. *Thoreau's Wild Flowers* Edited by Geoff Wisner. New Haven: Yale University Press, 2016.

Thoreau, Henry David. *Walden*. Edited by J. Lyndon Shanley. Princeton: Princeton University Press, 1971.

Thoreau, Henry David. *Walden*. Edited by Jeffrey S. Cramer. New Haven and
   London: Yale University Press, 2004.
Thoreau, Henry David. *Walden*. Princeton: Princeton University Press, 1971.
Thoreau, Henry David. *Walden and Civil Disobedience*. Edited by Owen Thomas.
   New York: W. W. Norton, 1966.
Thoreau, Henry David. *Wild Apples and Other Natural History Essays*. Edited by
   William Rossi. Athens and London: The University of Georgia Press, 2002.
Thorson, Robert. *Walden's Shore: Henry David Thoreau and Nineteenth-Century
   Science*. Cambridge, MA: Harvard University Press, 2014.
Thorson, Robert. *The Boatman: Henry David Thoreau's River Years*. Cambridge,
   MA: Harvard University Press, 2017.
Trachtenberg, Alan. "Photography: The Emergence of a Keyword." In *Photography
   in Nineteenth Century America* Edited by Martha A. Sandweiss. New York:
   Henry N. Abrams, 1991.
Trewavas, Anthony. *Plant Behaviour and Intelligence*. Oxford: Oxford University
   Press, 2015.
Tsing, Anna Lowenhaupt. *The Mushroom at the End of the World: On the Possibility
   of Life in Capitalist Ruins*. Princeton: Princeton University Press, 2017.
Tucker, Irene. "Picturing Utilitarianism: John Stuart Mill and the Invention of a
   Photographic Public." *Criticism* 50, no. 3 (2008): 411–46.
Tuckerman, Frederick Goddard. "Wild Flowers, Greenfield 1850." MS AM 1763.
   Houghton Library, Harvard University.
Tuckerman, Frederick Goddard. "Wild Flowers Gathered in Scotland and England
   during the summer of 1851. Greenfield September 1, 1851." MS Am 1349, vol.
   11, Houghton Library, Harvard University.
Walls, Laura Dassow. "Believing in Nature: Wilderness and Wildness in
   Thoreauvian Science." In *Thoreau's Sense of Place: Essays in American
   Environmental Writing* Edited by Richard J. Schneider. Ames: University of
   Iowa Press, 2000.
Walls, Laura Dassow. *Henry David Thoreau: A Life*. Chicago: University of
   Chicago Press, 2017.
Walls, Laura Dassow. *Material Faith: Thoreau on Science*. Boston: Houghton
   Mifflin, 1999.
Walls, Laura Dassow. *Seeing New Worlds: Henry David Thoreau and
   Nineteenth-Century Natural Science*. Madison: University of Wisconsin Press,
   1995.
Warner, Michael. "Thoreau's Bottom." *Raritan* 11, no. 3 (1992): 53–79.
Warner, Michael. "Walden's Erotic Economy." In *Comparative American Identities:
   Race, Sex, and Nationality in the Modern Text*. Edited by Hortense J. Spillers.
   New York: Routledge, 1991.
Wheeler, Wendy. *Expecting the Earth*. London: Lawrence and Wishart, 2016.
Whyte, Kyle Powys. "Too Late for Indigenous Climate Justice: Ecological and
   Relational Tipping Point." *WIREs Climate Change*, October 23, 2019. https://
   doi.org/10.1002/wcc.603
Williams, Raymond. *Keywords: A Vocabulary of Culture and Society*. New York:
   Oxford University Press, 1983.

Willis, Charles G., Brad Ruhfel, Richard B. Prismack, Abraham J. Miller-Rushing, and Charles C. Davis. "Phylogenetic patterns of species loss in Thoreau's woods are driven by climate change." *PNAS* 10.1073 (Oct. 27, 2008).

Wordsworth, William. *Poems, in Two* Volumes, *and Other Poems, 1800–1807*. Edited by Jared Curtis. Ithaca: Cornell University Press, 1983.

Wolfe, Cary. *Before the Law: Humans and Other Animals in a Biopolitical Frame.* Chicago: University of Chicago Press, 2013.

Wynter, Sylvia. "Novel and History, Plot and Plantation." *Savacou* 5 (1971): 95–102.

Ziser, Michael. *Environmental Practice and Early American Literature.* Cambridge, MA: Cambridge University Press, 2013.

INDEX

Abelove, Henry 165
aesthetics 112, 116, 120, 145, 162, 264 n.1
affirmative reading 222
Agassiz, Louis 11, 44, 47, 96, 267 n.21, 276 n.9
agency 14, 18, 19, 27, 30, 39, 42, 49, 50, 53, 88, 95, 99–100, 139, 144–6, 148, 149, 150, 155–6, 163, 164, 184, 190, 240 n. 55, 269 n.33
agriculture 99–100, 101, 129, 249 n. 32, 251 n.40
  Jacksonian 76–8, 80
Albanese, Katherine 39
animal, animals 7–8, 45, 50–1, 55–6, 66, 71, 72–4, 87, 93, 94, 96–7, 146, 149–51, 154–8, 167, 170, 174, 193, 210, 233, 241 n.64, 246 n12, 247 n.13, 248 n.24, 261 n.37, 262 n. 43
  animality 74, 145
  as auxiliaries for planting 77, 84
  intelligence 256 n.22
  pollinators 190, 211, 212
  sensuality 178
  sexuality 176, 177, 178
  studies 71–4, 146, 247 n. 19
Anthropocene 39–40, 108, 201, 258 n.3
apple 23, 31–2, 53, 62–3, 88, 96, 98, 100–1, 177, 189–203, 213, 276 n.7
Appleton, Fanny Elizabeth 217–8
Aristotle 63, 170
Arsić, Branka 28, 78, 82, 92, 105, 106, 129, 143, 146, 194, 207, 222,

238 n.23, 239 n.42, 251 n.43, 252 n.48, 261 n.32, 273 n. 11, 278 n.10
asceticism See chastity
asexual reproduction 172, 175
  hermaphroditism 171–2
  in Linnaean botany 170–2, 173–4
  metamorphosis 167, 169, 176, 182–3, 186–7
  nonbinary gender (see hermaphroditism)
  non-heteronormativity of 169, 170, 171–2
  Platonic theory of 170
  pornography 172
  and queer theory 169, 186–7
  resistance to identity 169, 181, 182–3, 187
  Romantic theory of 167, 176, 183
  sexual inversion 170–1, 173–4
astral 124–6, 220
atmosphere 24–7, 31–2, 46–7, 48, 50, 56, 62, 115–16, 126, 136, 151, 227, 247 n.15
Austin, J. L. 76, 250 n.35
auto-heteronomy 59, 60, 62, 64–7

Bailly, Jean-Christophe 57
Beer, Gillian 11, 15
Bennett, Jane 38, 78, 146, 147, 237 n.9, 242 n.4, 247 n.15, 251 n.41, 267 n.15, 267 n.20
bifurcation 49, 52, 56 See also dualism
biopolitics 70, 73, 74, 78–9, 84, 145, 252 n.46
biosemiosis 18, 106, 111, 112, 120, 124

Bolter, Jay David, and Richard Grusin
    144
Buell, Lawrence 143, 145, 154, 155,
    162
Burbrick, Joan 108

Cage, John 201–3, 274 n. 25,
    277 n.28
Cameron, Sharon 87, 105, 106, 118,
    119, 136, 143, 145, 162, 256
    n.27, 268 n.28
Case, Kristen 244 n. 35
Cavell, Stanley 75, 87–8, 250 n.39,
    251 n.41
celibacy See chastity
chastity 165–6, 169, 173–80, 185
Coccia, Emanuele 69, 71–4, 246 n.12,
    247 n.13, 247 n. 15, 248 n.24
colonial implantation 71, 75, 80, 84
color/chromography 107, 111, 116,
    125, 126
Conrad, C. A. 220, 227, 229–30, 234
correspondence 14, 119, 134, 200, 261
    n.38
Coviello, Peter 169, 184–6
Cowles, Henry Chandler 129
Crary, Jonathan 144, 164, 270–1 n.38
critical zone 42, 243 n.17
cunning 91, 92, 94, 256 n.22
Cuvier, Georges 11, 81, 236 n.20

Darwin, Charles 19, 41, 42, 44–5, 47,
    87, 89, 97, 98, 107, 108, 116,
    129, 191, 192, 198, 209, 228,
    243 n. 17, 267 n.21, 276 n.9
Daston, Lorraine 42, 49
Dean, Bradley P. 148, 160
Deleuze, Gilles 33, 267 n.20
    and Felix Guattari 72, 102–3, 146,
    147, 248 n.20
Descartes, René 38, 49, 52, 146, 156
Descola, Philippe 13, 40
Dickinson, Emily 131, 220–1, 224,
    227
dualism 38, 42, 49, 50, 54, 195 See
    also postdualism

earth 3–7, 12–13, 24, 26, 29, 30, 33,
    46, 48, 55, 57, 63–7, 76–7,
    88, 89–91, 93–4, 98, 99–102,
    107–8, 114, 116–18, 124, 125,
    130, 135, 147, 149, 155, 157,
    160, 168, 181, 194, 195, 207,
    210, 211, 221, 227, 231, 235 n.
    4, 235 n.5, 237 n.16, 238 n.26.
    238 n. 28, 238 n. 31, 250 n.39,
    261 n.34
Earth 37, 39, 40, 41, 45, 48, 50, 56,
    57, 202, 212, 221, 262 n.46, 278
    n.7
ecoerotics 168, 181–4, 185–6
ecology 42, 45, 47, 49–50, 51, 53, 85,
    86, 88, 90, 95, 96, 97, 101, 122,
    126, 141, 186
    queer 186–7, 275 n.43, 275 n.46
Emerson, Ralph Waldo 1, 9, 15, 17, 38,
    41–2, 43, 44, 46, 47–8, 49, 84,
    88, 94, 193–4, 205–7, 211, 214,
    217–9, 240 n.55, 240 n.59, 256
    n.22, 257 n.32
energy 41, 106, 116, 117–18, 119, 125,
    126, 178, 202, 261 n.32
equipment 147, 148, 164
Esposito, Roberto 73, 78–9, 82
Evelyn, John 80, 249, 250, 251
ethics 16, 17, 19, 30, 70, 71, 92, 93, 106,
    107, 123, 124, 126, 145, 200
ethology 90

figure/figuration 105, 106, 107, 108,
    111–12, 113–15, 116–17, 118,
    119, 120, 122, 124, 259 n.5
forest 32, 48, 53, 54, 55, 88, 95,
    97–100, 101, 106, 107–9, 111,
    113, 115, 117, 123, 125, 126,
    128–9, 131–5, 139, 141, 147,
    148, 153, 154, 159, 160, 162,
    179, 191, 213, 226, 233, 237 n.
    11, 245 n. 7, 245 n. 9, 260 n.22,
    267–268 n.21
geometry 106, 111, 116, 124, 125,
    260 n.22
thinking 94–8

Foucault, Michel 70, 73, 74, 76, 78,
    81–3, 246 n.9, 247 n.13, 248
    n.21, 250 n.35, 253 n.60, 271
    n.38
Freeman, Elizabeth 186
fruit 2–4, 8, 22, 26, 31, 56, 63, 66, 81,
    83, 90, 96, 97, 100, 101, 113,
    136, 137, 150, 154, 167, 174,
    176, 182–3, 184, 189, 190–2,
    194, 196, 198, 207, 208, 210,
    213, 225–8, 275 n.3
fruition 134, 167, 168, 174–6, 177–8,
    181–2, 184

Goethe, Johan Wolfgang von 11, 114,
    176, 183, 226, 252 n.48
Goldstein, Amanda J. 259 n.5, 261
    n.32, 262 n.38
Gray, Asa 2–4, 44–5, 46, 54, 88, 97, 135,
    228, 235 n.2, 235 n.4, 252 n.49,
    255 n.18, 263 n.19, 267 n.21
Grosz, Elizabeth 103

Halperin, David 168–9
Harding, Walter 165, 168
Hayles, N. Katherine 86–7, 98, 101
Hegel, Georg Wilhelm Frierdrich 7–10,
    13, 15, 29
Hesse, Mary B. 11, 14. 236 n18
Hodder, Alan 129
Hölderlin, Friedrich 176
holism
    empirical 39
    rational 242 n. 7
homosexuality 165–6, 168–9
Humboldt, Alexander 41, 42, 44, 45,
    46, 49, 50, 54–5, 81, 228, 243
    n.16, 244 n.38

indigeneity 19, 130, 205, 212, 213
influence 14, 16, 21–6, 31, 32, 35
instinct 91, 92, 95, 97, 99, 101, 130,
    151, 167, 170, 176–80, 186, 251
    n.41
intelligence 88–94, 101
Irigaray, Luce 59

Jackson, Charles T. 44
James, William 103, 276 n.13
Johnson, Barbara 200
Johnson, Samuel 226
Jonas, Hans 40

Kelley, Theresa 183
Kimmerer, Robin Wall 76, 249
Kittler, Friedrich 144, 164, 265 n.6
Kohn, Eduardo 86, 98

Latour, Bruno 17, 40, 146
Lewis, R. W. B. 145
Liebig, Justus von 50, 244 n. 40
Light 2–4, 12, 24–5, 47, 87–102,
    107, 108, 111, 115–17, 124–6,
    132–5, 140, 163, 203, 227–8,
    230
Linnaeus, Carl 170–2, 173–5, 182–3
Locke, John 52, 252 n.54
Longfellow, Henry Wadsworth
    218–20
Lyell, Charles 97

Mancuso, Stefano 86, 93, 98–9
Marder, Michael 17, 86, 170, 197
Marx, Karl 66, 261 n.32
Marx, Leo 70, 145, 154, 246 n.5, 263
    n.7, 240 n.50
materialism 20, 29, 30, 37–8, 39, 40,
    42, 278 n.10
    vs. idealism 87
    materialist vitalism 129, 146
    new 30, 38
materiality 38, 39, 49, 51, 53, 102,
    103, 137, 155, 160, 162, 270
    n.38
    of language 55–6
    of consciousness 102–3
matter 2, 5, 8, 29, 38, 39, 42, 43, 50,
    51, 66, 90, 101, 103, 126, 146,
    160, 226–7
maturation See theory of
    development
meaning 14, 18, 39, 67, 106, 111, 112,
    118, 120–4, 203, 211

Melville, Herman 41, 199, 222, 228, 277 n.21
metamorphosis 9, 50, 67, 87, 90, 114, 118, 167, 169, 176, 177, 181, 182, 186, 187 *See also* theory of development
metaphor 91, 115–16, 117, 119, 123, 124, 138, 171–5, 177, 179, 206
Michaels, Walter Benn 163, 269 n.32
milieu 3, 6, 73–4, 78, 83, 112–15, 118, 123, 125
Miller, Elaine 176, 183
Miller, Perry 165–6
Milton, John 218, 228
Mitchell, W. J. T. 145–6
Monod, Jacques 96
morphology 11, 108, 129, 135, 170, 171, 172, 176 *See also* figure/figuration

Nealon, Jeffrey 71–4, 79, 86, 246, 247, 251
Nemser, Daniel 70, 81, 253 n.57, 253 n. 59
natural history 16, 38, 44, 52, 106, 199, 219, 225, 233
naturalism 40, 128
naturalization 145–7, 154–64, 212, 213
nature
    deanimation of 38, 40, 43
    local 42, 43, 45, 48, 49
    nature as wild 49
    recording function of 144–7, 159–64
    religion 39
    specific 42, 43, 45, 49
    as universal natural law 42–3
nod, nodding 15, 23, 25–7, 29
nonhuman 21, 22, 28–9, 31, 35, 39, 41, 49, 61, 82, 85, 88, 90, 91, 98, 100–1, 103, 112, 118–19, 121–2, 124, 130, 143, 145–6, 186–7, 198
not-reading 157–60

ontology 1, 9, 11, 15, 16, 17–20, 41, 66, 76, 79, 182–3, 186–7, 200

paradigm shift (Thomas Kuhn) 39, 41, 242 n. 13
Peirce, Charles Sanders 98
personification 121
phenology 93, 101
philanthropy 62–64, 249 n.28
photography 144, 231, 163–4, 269 n.32, 269 n.33, 269–70 n.35, 270 n.37, 271 n.38
photography 266–7, 267–8
plant
    cosmopolitanism of 210–11
    intelligence 18, 86–8, 92, 94, 95, 99–102
    memory 93–5
    Neoplatonic 43
    Plato 5, 170–1, 172, 173, 175, 176, 178, 194, 233, 249 n.28
    Platonic 5, 173, 178, 249 n.28
    Platonism 5
    sensation 85–7, 101–3
    theory 69, 71–4, 84
    thinking 17, 20, 45, 47, 54, 61, 66, 86, 244 n.48, 246 n.1, 254 n.2, 276 n.18
Pliny 100
poetry 20, 56, 106, 173, 218, 220, 222–34
    in the common sense 221–2, 224–5, 229
politics 16, 17, 19, 41, 70, 71, 73, 78, 79, 83, 84, 193, 215, 225
    garden 70, 78–9, 84
    identity 169, 187
    of planting 70, 76, 79–80
Pollan, Michael 86, 211
postdualism 40, 49, 50, 54
posthuman, posthumanism 38, 71, 50–1, 143, 145–6
power 22, 24, 25, 70, 118, 125–6, 139, 149, 187, 199, 203
    enchantment-power 30
    figural 117

pastoral 70, 73, 76, 82–4, 248, 252
pasture 70, 82–4
  of place 42
  tropological 121
Powers, Richard 98
Primack, Richard 214–15
psychedelia 30–2

queer 53, 166, 168, 184–7, 220, 244
    n. 48

remediation 144–5, 147, 260 n.13
reproductive, reproductivity 66,
    93, 116, 167, 169, 171, 172,
    175, 177, 181, 182, 184, 186,
    190, 19
resistance 14, 71, 74, 82–4, 184–5,
    187, 200
rhetoric 14, 30, 75, 128–33, 140, 171,
    200
rhizome 4, 6, 7, 10, 72
rhizosphere 98–9
Romanticism, Romantic 30, 34, 43,
    121, 167, 173, 176, 183, 217,
    224–6
root 2–9, 22, 31, 38, 47, 48, 52, 60,
    66, 71, 78, 87–9, 98, 135, 140,
    149, 170, 194, 207, 210, 211,
    213, 226–7, 228, 229, 233, 235
    n.4, 235 n. 5
Rosenberg, Jordy 187
Ruyer, Raymond 103

Sacks, Oliver 102
Saint-Hilaire, Étienne Geoffroy 11
sand 33, 34, 55, 65, 75, 101, 102, 114,
    117, 134, 211, 220
  foliage 33, 55, 114
Sandilands, Catriona 275 n.46
Schuller, Kyla 248
seeds 53, 76–7, 79–80, 82, 88, 90,
    95–7, 99, 101, 107, 109,
    113–15, 117, 121, 123, 128–32,
    139, 144, 147–58, 179, 190,
    191, 206, 209, 210, 212, 220,
    226–8
self-cultivation See theory of
    development

Serres, Michel 37, 56
sexuality 19, 166, 168–87
spontaneous generation 77, 107,
    147–8
Steigerwald, Joan 49, 242 n. 4,
    244 n. 38
sundial 48
Sweet, Timothy 145
symbiosis 49, 56, 86, 92, 95, 99, 101
sympathy 23, 26, 27–30, 46, 59–67,
    90, 237 n.5, 238 n. 28, 239 n.38,
    239 n.41

taste 88, 100–1, 131, 180, 192, 201,
    203, 208
taxonomy 42, 81, 169, 171, 181–3,
    187, 197
Teare, Brian 228–34
technology 18, 20, 74, 144, 145,
    151–4, 162–4, 206
terrennial 37, 40–1, 57
terrestrial 17, 38, 39, 40, 65, 107–8,
    125, 148, 157
textuality 159–62
theory
  of development 165, 167, 169,
    174–84, 186
  vegetal 2
  vegetal reproductivity (see fruition)
  of vegetal sexuality 167–9, 173–6,
    177–80, 181–4, 186–7
Thoreau, Henry David
  "Autumnal Tints" 18, 48, 87, 88,
    108, 111–12, 115–16, 125–6
  Cape Cod 32
  "Chastity & Sensuality" 173–7
  "Civil Disobedience" 81, 82, 200,
    201
  Dispersion of Seeds 18, 77, 88, 105,
    143–64, 212
  "Higher Laws" 166, 177–80, 184
  Journal 1, 2, 9, 11, 24, 25, 30, 31,
    32, 46, 47, 54, 55, 56, 87–94,
    97–9, 105, 106, 117–22, 128,
    132, 133, 134–41, 145, 157,
    160–2, 162–4, 166, 167, 181–4,
    193–6, 197, 199, 201–2, 208,
    210, 212, 222, 223, 225, 227–8

Kalendar 87, 94, 189, 214, 234
"Ktaadn" 155
"Natural History of Massachusetts"
    15, 224
"Resistance to Civil Government"
    82–4
"Succession of Forest Trees" 18, 87,
    88, 95–6, 127–33, 141, 212
Walden 18, 22, 27, 33, 37, 41, 43,
    45–6, 47, 50, 52, 55–6, 59–60,
    62–7, 69, 71, 74–9, 82–4, 87, 90,
    99, 101–2, 114, 116, 119, 145,
    155, 162, 166, 177, 199, 200,
    201, 214, 224
"Walking" 90, 163, 189–90, 195,
    200, 201, 227–8, 230
A Week on the Concord and
    Merrimack Rivers 44, 222–4,
    225–6, 229–30
"Wild Apples" 18, 19, 48, 55, 87,
    88, 90, 91, 100, 101, 189–203,
    209
Wild Fruits 18, 88, 189, 208, 212–3
Thorson, Robert 129
Trachtenberg, Alan 163, 269 n.35
transtemporality 220, 222, 228–9
Trewavas, Anthony 86, 95, 99
tropology 120, 121–2, 124
Tucker, Irent 163
Tuckerman, Frederick Goddard
    217–18

vegetal
    becoming-vegetal 184
    intelligence 94–5, 101
    life 3, 6, 7, 10, 15, 59, 69, 89, 101,
        102, 177, 194, 219

theory 2, 183
thought 16, 135–9
vegetally 17, 22, 31, 173, 175–8,
    182, 183, 186
Viola, Alessandra 86
violence 71, 73, 76, 79, 82–3
vitalism 30, 38, 78, 102–3, 112, 120,
    127, 129, 140, 146

Warner, Michael 165–6, 184–6
Walls, Laura Dassow 15, 17, 39, 43,
    52, 90, 106, 108, 129, 200, 207,
    209, 249, 251, 278 n.10
Wheeler, Wendy 111
White, Gilbert 44
Whitman, Walt 21–3, 26, 34, 224
wild
    home 209–10, 213
    plants 207, 208, 209
    thinking 90–1, 97, 100, 101, 103
    the Wild 22, 190, 202
wilderness 54, 90, 152, 154, 201,
    209–10
wildness 22, 90, 91, 178–9, 190, 195,
    196, 200–1, 205, 207, 209, 210
Williams, Raymond 37–8
Wills, David 145
wind 18, 26–8, 53, 55–7, 77, 88, 89,
    95–7, 101, 107, 108, 111, 115,
    116, 117, 118, 124, 125, 128,
    131, 135–6, 146, 149–50, 152,
    181, 190, 192, 210, 212, 227
Wolfe, Cary 72–3, 145, 247 n.19
Wordsworth, William 218–19
Wynter, Sylvia 80, 254 n.67

Zandt, Antonio (Signor Blitz) van 132

Milton Keynes UK
Ingram Content Group UK Ltd.
UKHW020327020924
447705UK00008B/143